The Irish Novel
A Critical History

Twayne's Critical History of the Novel

Herbert Sussman, Series Editor
Northeastern University

The Irish Novel
A Critical History

JAMES M. CAHALAN
Indiana University of Pennsylvania

Twayne Publishers
A Division of G. K. Hall & Co. • *Boston*

The Irish Novel: A Critical History

James M. Cahalan

Copyright 1988 by G. K. Hall & Co.
All rights reserved.
Published by Twayne Publishers
A Division of G. K. Hall & Co.
70 Lincoln Street
Boston, Massachusetts 02111

Copyediting supervised by Barbara Sutton.
Book production by John Amburg.

Typeset in 11 pt. Malibu
by Williams Press, Inc. Albany, New York.

Printed on permanent/durable acid-free paper
and bound in the United States of America.

Library of Congress Cataloging-in-Publication Data

Cahalan, James M.
  The Irish novel: a critical history / James M. Cahalan.

  p.   cm. — (Twayne's critical history of the novel)
  Bibliography: p.
  Includes index.
  ISBN 0-8057-7850-0
  1. English fiction—Irish authors—History and criticism.
2. Ireland in literature.   3. Northern Ireland in literature.
I. Title. II. Series.
PR8797.C34   1988
823'.009'89162—dc19   88-7229
                                                                CIP

To Lea Masiello

Contents

Acknowledgments

I want to thank several colleagues and friends who each read part of this work and made many helpful suggestions: Denis Cotter, Wayne E. Hall, Klaus Lubbers, Philip O'Leary, and Hugh B. Staples. My general editor at Twayne, Herbert Sussman, gave me copious help on every portion of this book. Declan Kiberd read my entire manuscript and sent me several stimulating suggestions. My friend Maja Chaszar translated Klaus Lubbers's book in German for me—a huge task she kindly undertook, cheerfully pursued, and tirelessly completed. My research assistant, Rimas Galenas, contributed a great deal of careful and insightful work, both tedious and critical, without which my work would have progressed much more slowly.

A number of my other graduate students at Indiana University of Pennsylvania—Jay Pomponio, Mara Rainwater, Bill Yahner, Charles Marr, Phoebe Wiley, Marilyn Durfee, Steve Hazenstab, Sandra Vrana—read parts of my manuscript and contributed to discussions in my doctoral seminars that constituted part of my thinking for this book. My mother and father, Lee and Bill Cahalan, read this work and made helpful suggestions. Máirín Nic Eoin kindly wrote to me about Eoghan Ó Tuairisc's novels. I received crucial assistance from librarians at the National Library of Ireland, Trinity College, Dublin, and especially from those at Indiana University of Pennsylvania—Mary Sampson, Carol Connell, David Kaufman, Richard Chamberlin, William Lafranchi, Larry Kroah, and others—who proved inexhaustible and provided help without which this book could not have been written. Nor could it have been completed without the financial assistance provided to me by Indiana University of Pennsylvania Faculty Research and Graduate School grants as well as library funds, and by a 1986 Summer Stipend from the National Endowment for the Humanities. Crucial assistance in the writing of this book came from these and other individuals—including Catherine Renwick and Sandra Vrana, who made it possible for me to meet my deadline with the index. Any remaining errors and shortcomings are my own.

Indiana, Pennsylvania
October 1988

Chronology

1798   Unsuccessful Irish rebellions in counties Wex-
       ford, Antrim, and Mayo.

1800   Act of Union between Great Britain and Ire-
       land. *Castle Rackrent* by Maria Edgeworth.

1803   Robert Emmet's rebellion and execution in
       Dublin. Gerald Griffin born.

1806   *The Wild Irish Girl* by Sydney Owenson.

1808   *The Wild Irish Boy* by Charles Maturin.

1809   *Ennui* by Edgeworth.

1812   *The Absentee* by Edgeworth.

1817   *Ormond* by Edgeworth.

1820   *Melmoth the Wanderer* by Maturin.

1825   *Crohoore of the Billhook* by Michael Banim.

1826   *The Boyne Water* and *The Nowlans* by John
       Banim.

1827   *The O'Briens and the O'Flahertys* by Owenson.

1829   Catholic Emancipation granted. *The Collegians*
       and *The Rivals* by Gerald Griffin.

1831   Anti-Protestant Tithe Wars begin. National
       schools instituted with English as the sole
       language of instruction.

1832   *Dublin Penny Journal* begins.

1833–1877   *Dublin University Magazine.*

1839   *Fardorougha the Miser* by William Carleton.

1842–1892   *The Nation.*

1841   *Charles O'Malley, the Irish Dragoon* by Charles
       Lever.

1842   *Handy Andy* by Samuel Lover.

1843   Daniel O'Connell's campaign for repeal of the
       Union fails.

1845   "Great Hunger" begins. *Valentine McClutchy*
       by Carleton. *The Cock and Anchor* by Sheridan
       Le Fanu.

1847   O'Connell's death. *The Black Prophet* by Carleton. *The Fortunes of Colonel Torlogh O'Brien* by Le Fanu.

1848   Abortive Young Ireland uprising. *The Emigrants of Ahadarra* by Carleton.

1856   *The Martins of Cro Martin* by Lever.

1858   Fenian movement founded.

1863   *The House by the Churchyard* by Le Fanu.

1867   Unsuccessful Fenian rising.

1872   *Lord Kilgobbin* by Lever.

1879   Michael Davitt's Land League founded. *Knocknagow* by Charles Kickham.

1882   James Joyce born.

1883   *Irisleabhar na Gaeilge (Gaelic Journal)* founded.

1886   Irish Home Rule Bill. *A Drama in Muslin* by George Moore. *Hurrish* by Emily Lawless.

1891   Death of Charles Stewart Parnell.

1892   *Grania* by Lawless.

1893   Douglas Hyde's Gaelic League founded.

1894   *The Real Charlotte* by Somerville and Ross.

1903   Wyndham Land Act. *The Squireen* by Shan Bullock. *Irish Life in Irish Fiction* by Horatio Sheafe Krans.

1904   *Séadna* by Peadar Ó Laoghaire.

1905   Sinn Féin founded. *The Lake* by George Moore.

1910   *Deoraíocht* (Exile) by Pádraic Ó Conaire.

1912   *The Charwoman's Daughter* and *The Crock of Gold* by James Stephens.

1913   Irish Volunteers formed. Dublin transport workers' lock-out and strike. *Father Ralph* by Gerald O'Donovan.

1916   Easter Rising in Dublin. *A Portrait of the Artist as a Young Man* by Joyce.

1918   *The Valley of the Squinting Windows* by Brinsley MacNamara.

1919   Anglo-Irish War begins. *The Wasted Island* by Eimar O'Duffy. *Ireland in Fiction* by Stephen J. Brown.

1921   Anglo-Irish Treaty establishes Northern Ireland.

1922   *Ulysses* by Joyce.

1922–1923   Irish Civil War.

1924   *The Black Soul* by Liam O'Flaherty. *Caisleáin Óir* (Castles of gold) by Séamas Ó Grianna.

1925   *The Informer* by O'Flaherty. *The Big House of Inver* by Edith Somerville.

1926   *Mr. Gilhooley* by O'Flaherty. *King Goshawk and the Birds* by O'Duffy.

1929   Censorship of Publications Act. *The Last September* by Elizabeth Bowen. *Adrigoole* by Peadar O'Donnell. *The Various Lives of Marcus Igoe* by MacNamara.

1932   *Skerrett* by O'Flaherty.

1933   *A Nest of Simple Folk* by Sean O'Faolain. *The Curse of the Wise Woman* by Lord Dunsany.

1937   Irish Free State Constitution. Douglas Hyde elected first president. *Famine* by O'Flaherty. *Peter Waring* by Forrest Reid.

1938   *Murphy* by Samuel Beckett.

1939   *Finnegans Wake* by Joyce. *At Swim-Two-Birds* by Flann O'Brien. *Call My Brother Back* by Michael McLaverty. *Men Withering* by Francis MacManus.

1939–1945   Ireland remains neutral during World War II.

1940–1954   *The Bell,* edited by O'Faolain to 1946 and O'Donnell to 1954.

1941   Death of Joyce. *The Land of Spices* by Kate O'Brien. *An Béal Bocht (The Poor Mouth)* by Flann O'Brien. *The Poor Mouth* was also published in English in the 1970s.

1946   *Land* by O'Flaherty. *The Unfortunate Fursey* by Mervyn Wall. *Land without Stars* by Benedict Kiely.

1948   Republic of Ireland declared. *Tarry Flynn* by Patrick Kavanagh.

1949   *Cré na Cille* (Churchyard clay) by Máirtín Ó Cadhain. *Redemption* by Francis Stuart.

1950   *Modern Irish Fiction—A Critique* by Benedict Kiely. *Molloy* by Beckett.

1951   *Malone meurt (Malone Dies)* by Beckett.

1952   *L'Innommable (The Unnamable)* by Beckett.

1953   *Watt* by Beckett.

1955   *The Lonely Passion of Judith Hearne* by Brian Moore.

1958   *The Feast of Lupercal* by Moore. *The Irish Novelists, 1800–1850* by Thomas Flanagan.

1959   *James Joyce* by Richard Ellmann.

1960   *The Country Girls* by Edna O'Brien.

1962   *The Silent People* by Walter Macken. *L'Attaque* by Eoghan Ó Tuairisc.

1963   *The Barracks* by John McGahern. *The Ferret Fancier* by Anthony C. West. *Thy Tears Might Cease* by Michael Farrell.

1965–1970   Economic advances in the Republic of Ireland.

1965   *The Emperor of Ice-Cream* by Moore. *The Dark* by McGahern. *The Waking of Willie Ryan* by John Broderick.

1966   *Langrishe, Go Down* by Aidan Higgins.

1967   Irish civil rights movement begun in Northern Ireland.

1968   *An Uain Bheo* (The moment of decision) by Diarmuid Ó Súilleabháin.

1969   British troops sent into Northern Ireland. *Strumpet City* by James Plunkett. *The Hungry Grass* by Richard Power. *Mrs. Eckdorf in O'Neill's Hotel* by William Trevor.

1971   *Black List, Section H* by Francis Stuart.

1972   *Catholics* by Moore. *Night* by O'Brien. *The Captains and the Kings* by Jennifer Johnston.

1973   Ireland enters the European Economic Community. *Birchwood* by John Banville.

1973   Economic recession throughout Ireland begins.

1974   *How Many Miles to Babylon?* by Johnston. *The Leavetaking* by McGahern. *Forces and Themes in Ulster Fiction* by John Wilson Foster.

1976   *Lig Sinn i gCathú (Lead Us Into Temptation)* by Brendán Ó hEithir.

1977   *Farewell Companions* by Plunkett.

1978   *Bogmail* by Patrick McGinley.

1979   *The Old Jest* by Johnston.

1980   *No Country for Young Men* by Julia O'Faolain. *Lamb* by Bernard MacLaverty. *The Past* by Neil Jordan. *The Leaves on Grey* by Desmond Hogan.

1983   *Cal* by MacLaverty.

1984   *The Railway Station Man* by Johnston. *Foggage* by McGinley. *The Summerhouse* by Val Mulkerns.

1985   Anglo-Irish Agreement. *The Killeen* by Mary Leland.

1986   *The Trick of the Ga Bolga* by McGinley.

1987   Charles Haughey replaces Garret Fitzgerald as Taoiseach (Prime Minister). *Fool's Sanctuary* by Johnston. *The Red Men* by McGinley.

Introduction

This book is the first comprehensive, one-volume history of the Irish novel ever published. This is intended not as a comment on my own critical ambition (or hubris), but on the peculiar treatment of my subject in the existing critical literature. As a distinct subject the Irish novel has had to overcome the tendencies of critics to ignore it entirely, to lump it together with the British novel, or to attend only to the works of its most celebrated practitioner, James Joyce. Ernest Baker absorbed the Irish novel into the English in his *History of the English Novel* (1924–39), just as Ireland itself had been annexed by Britain during centuries of tortured economic and political existence. Walter Allen continued this practice in his *The English Novel: A Short Critical History* (1954), and for decades it has been reflected in American courses on "The Modern British Novel" that include Joyce— who turned to Europe, not Britain, for his foreign literary inspiration. Subsuming "Anglo-Irish" writers within courses on English literature, when not ignoring them altogether, has been a form of cultural imperialism. As the Irish novelist and critic Anthony Cronin writes, "There is not much point in talking about Anglo-Irish literature. Whatever else these works are, they are not Anglo-anything, unless, that is, the work of Whitman or Hart Crane or Melville or Dos Passos or Scott Fitzgerald is Anglo-something" (1982, 11).

The American-dominated "James Joyce Industry" is a more subtle but even more pervasive form of cultural imperialism. As the greatest twentieth-century novelist in the English language, Joyce merits considerable critical attention and in fact actively encouraged it himself. Many scholars have made their names and their careers by writing about Joyce, with each Joycean breeding several others and perpetuating a tunnel vision that is often blind to other Irish novelists. Within Irish literary studies, one effect of the Joyce Industry has been to block attention to many other worthy Irish authors—and also to neglect, ironically enough, an adequate understanding of the place of Joyce's own novels within their most obvious context, the development of the Irish novel itself. Virtually every current critical approach—psychoanalytic, structuralist, poststructuralist, reader-response, feminist, Marxist, and others—has been applied to Joyce's novels, but many other Irish novelists, when not ignored entirely, have been subjected to an extremely limited range of critical methods, a point I shall take up in this book. Each one of the hundreds of dissertations, books, and articles on Joyce is one that does *not* examine the valuable work of Pádraic Ó Conaire, Kate O'Brien, Charles Lever, or dozens of other Irish novelists who might be named (and will be named in this book). Patrick Kavanagh wrote a memorable poem on the subject of "Who Killed James Joyce?" ("The weapon that was used / Was a Harvard thesis"), but at Joyce's wake we should mourn not Joyce but, more properly, the neglected remains of other Irish novelists.

I deliberately listed as my examples above a novelist in the Irish language (Ó Conaire), a woman (O'Brien), and a Protestant (Lever) because they represent groups that have often been victims of particular neglect. Writing about an earlier group of Gaelic writers, Daniel Corkery described their oppressed position in an Ireland increasingly dominated by the English and their language, in his book *The Hidden Ireland* (1925). Corkery's well-known phrase, "the hidden Ireland," has been borrowed much more recently by both Janet Madden-Simpson, to describe the treatment of women writers within an Irish critical tradition dominated by men (1984, 4), and Gerald Dawe and Edna Longley, who assert that "the 'Hidden Ireland' has now more claim to be Protestant than Gaelic" (1985, ii). Dawe and Longley emphasize that W. B. Yeats (who, ironically, was a Protestant) did much to encourage a critical code that celebrates southern Catholic writers as Irish at the expense of northern Protestant ones. Protestants represent a minority within Ireland, just as the Irish as a whole are outnumbered by the English in the British Isles. Yeats frankly admitted, "I generally dislike the people of Ulster, and want to keep them out" (quoted in Dawe and Longley, iv). W. J. McCormack agrees that "to an extent which is too infrequently recognized, critics of Anglo-Irish literature have derived their techniques from Yeats, and so have entered into a conspiracy with that formidable reviser of history" (1980, 266). Countering the older narrow nationalism and the discomfort of Irish Protestants, Irish members of the Field Day Theatre Company (1985)—Seamus Deane, Seamus Heaney, Brian Friel, Tom Paulin—advocate a more inclusive brand of Irishness, a new kind of nationalism.

With such powerful problems to be overcome, it is perhaps not quite so surprising that critics have examined the Irish novel only in bits and pieces. As Diane Tolomeo notes, "Few critics have attempted to deal with the development of Irish fiction" (1983, 268). In 1903 Horatio Sheafe Krans published the pioneering if necessarily limited book *Irish Life in Irish Fiction,* but for the most part his successors did not pursue the path he had cleared. In the most influential early twentieth-century study of Irish literature, *Ireland's Literary Renaissance* (1922), Ernest Boyd belittled Irish fiction in a single chapter subtitled "The Weak Point of the Revival." W. J. McCormack notes that the study of Irish literature at large "is still at what may be aptly called an infantile stage, obsessively concerned with certain prominent and important figures—Yeats, Joyce, Synge—but neglectful of the larger body of writing amongst which the masters must ultimately be placed" (1980, 266). A few valuable studies of the Irish novel during particular periods have appeared. Benedict Kiely's *Modern Irish Fiction—A Critique* (1950) is a short but useful examination of Irish fiction between 1920 and 1950. Thomas Flanagan's *The Irish Novelists, 1800–1850* (1958) was a pioneering book that oddly concluded that "the nineteenth-century novel established no tradition" and that Joyce "owed little to the work of his predecessors" (333). These claims, as we shall see, are far from the truth. Klaus Lubbers has published a very valuable book (1985a) in German, examining the development of the Irish novel up until 1900, and promises a second volume on the twentieth-century novel; an English translation of his work would be useful. Most recently of all, John Wilson Foster has authored *Fictions of the Irish Literary Revival: A Changeling Art* (1987), a large book that implicitly counters Ernest Boyd's dismissal of Irish fiction as "The Weak Point of the Revival." Several surveys of Irish literature as a whole (Fallis 1977; McHugh and Harmon 1982; Jeffares 1982; Deane 1986) provide useful overviews of the development of the Irish novel, but within limited contexts. My own first book examines the development of one subgenre, the Irish historical novel, over the course of its entire development (Cahalan 1983).

I intend for this volume to provide students and scholars with a starting point for more in-depth study, thereby stimulating both an appreciation of the Irish novel as a distinct subject and, I hope, further research and publication on some of the most neglected areas within the topic. Throughout this book I indicate the prevalent critical approaches to the Irish novel, continually linking assessments of the criticism to the story of the novel in Ireland, and suggesting (especially in my conclusion) some ideas for further research. For my purposes here, an "Irish novel" is any Irish author's novel that is set in Ireland. I seek to explain how the novels respond to the patterns of Irish history and are in fact a part of that history. In each chapter I briefly outline the relevant contours of Irish history; the beginning student should also consult one or more of the several valuable surveys of Irish history that are available (J. C. Beckett 1966; Lyons 1971; McCaffrey 1979; Moody and Martin 1984).

As indicated at several points throughout this book, in giving attention to a number of the better novelists I have been forced to neglect many minor talents. Yet, determined to avoid tunnel vision, I have cultivated a fairly broad view, examining in my seven chapters the works of more than eighty novelists—with my treatment of individual novelists varying in length from a paragraph to a full chapter—and briefly naming about thirty others while always seeking to provide a context for understanding rather than merely listing one author and title after another. My simple and necessary operative definition stated above means that I cannot examine here novels by Irish authors set abroad (Brian Moore's North American novels, for example) or novels by foreigners set in Ireland (such as Thomas Flanagan's *The Year of the French*). But I do include Joyce's *Finnegans Wake* and Beckett's novels, since they are set largely in Ireland inasmuch as they are "set" anywhere in particular (and inasmuch as they can be said to be "novels"). As we shall shortly see, one of the distinctive features of many Irish novels is that they are constantly interrogative of the genre as a whole, departing in many respects from various novelistic conventions.

True to my definition, I include in this book not only novels written and published in English but also novels in Irish. Irish is a Celtic language (best called "Irish" rather than "Gaelic" to distinguish it from Scottish Gaelic) as different from English as any other Indo-European language could be said to be, yet novels in Irish share many of the concerns and features of Irish novels in English, and are discussed here at the appropriate points in this history. A few novelists—most notably Flann O'Brien—published novels both in English and in Irish. It is well known that English as spoken and written in Ireland has been much influenced by Irish, especially in its vocabulary, verbal forms, and syntax (Ó Muirithe 1977; McCrum, Cran, and MacNeil 1986). When conversing with his English dean of studies, Stephen Dedalus in Joyce's *A Portrait of the Artist as a Young Man* becomes sharply aware of how "his language, so familiar and so foreign, will always be for me an acquired speech" (189). Irish English—the variety of English spoken in Ireland, also sometimes called "Hiberno-English" or "Anglo-Irish"— has created difficulties but also furthered artistic freedom for the Irish novelist, especially as we move from early nineteenth-century attempts to write dialogue to generally more sophisticated and often more imaginative uses of Irish English in our own century. I agree with Robert Welch (1985) that a continuity can be found in Irish literature, focusing on the rich interactions between Irish and English—while I cannot accept his notion of Gaelicism that would judge Yeats as more "Gaelic" than Breandán Ó hEithir (229). Alan Titley recalls Frank O'Connor's question about whether Irish literature in the two languages is a unified subject or "merely two unrelated subjects linked by a geographical accident" (1981, 116), and he concludes that "freagra simplí . . . atá ar cheist thosaigh Frank O'Connor. Dhá litríocht atá in Éirinn, litríocht na Gaeilge agus litríocht an Bhéarla . . . Sin uile"

(137) ["There's a simple answer to Frank O'Connor's question. There are two literatures in Ireland, the literature of Irish and the literature of English . . . That's everything"]. Between the romantic Gaelicism of Welch (writing in English) and the rigid literalness of Titley (writing in Irish) is a commonsense intermediate position: the knowledge that novels in English and novels in Irish are separated by language and the many social facts tied to it (such as the extremely small readership for Irish), yet are linked by common thematic concerns, materials, and influences (such as the oral storytelling tradition in both languages).

The Irish novel emerges as a distinct subject not only because of its unique setting, history, and use of language, but also because of a number of formal and subgeneric features that will be explored in the course of this study. One is the strong oral influence just mentioned. The book generally celebrated as the first truly Irish novel, Maria Edgeworth's *Castle Rackrent*, was written in (as Frank O'Connor put it about his own fiction) "the tone of a man's voice speaking" (1962, 29). The Irish novelist and critic Thomas Kilroy goes so far as to declare that "at the centre of Irish fiction is the anecdote" (1972, 301). This is not surprising in a country whose collected folklore is the most extensive, oldest, and richest in Europe. The strong influence of the pipe-smoking storyteller at the fireplace, the *seanchaí*, is linked to several distinctive formal (or perhaps I should say informal) and thematic features of the Irish novel: its loose, rambling approach to plot, with many Irish novels reading like a set of interwoven stories; its frequently stanceless and hardly ever "omniscient" narrators; and the preponderance of fantasy and attention to wild, bizarre details. All of these features can be found in, for example, *Ulysses*, the greatest Irish novel but one that is more frequently celebrated in criticism as the quintessentially high-modernist, European fiction.

Several distinctive subgenres within the Irish novel have been particularly popular and will merit exploration in the following chapters. Some of them are particular to Ireland: for example, the Big House novel, focusing on the decline of an aristocrat Irish family, and the realistic "peasant novel," at the other societal extreme, treating the difficult lives of the Irish poor in the countryside or small towns. Other subgenres represent strongly Irish varieties of more widespread forms: for example, the historical novel, using major events of Irish history as a backdrop for social fiction; the bildungsroman, examining the painful emergence of the youthful self in the face of a restrictive Irish society; the Gothic novel, merging otherworldly terror with the equally fearsome Irish folk tradition; and the fantasy or fabulist novel, inspired by sources as ancient as Celtic mythology and as modern as science fiction in creating new, highly entertaining imaginative worlds.

Few Irish novels have portrayed a stable way of life, and the fictional subgenres just listed could hardly be described as anchored in stability (in contrast to, for example, the novels of Jane Austen), because Irish society itself has been anything but stable. It may be that the conventional novel is a form for a made society, whereas the short story and unconventional novels that bear the strong stamp of the short story are forms for a society in the making. At an earlier stage in the development of American society, Nathaniel Hawthorne felt obliged to apply a different term— "romance"—to his novels. Similar was Henry James's remark that one cannot write a novel of manners about a society that has none. In England the rise of the novel has been frequently and correctly linked to the rise of the middle class, but in Ireland there was never much of a middle class until very recently—only since World War II and especially since the 1960s, one might properly say. It is therefore remarkable that the Irish novel "rose" at all, and not surprising that it frequently assumed quite different forms from those found in conventional English and American novels.

Discovering Voices: The Irish Novel before 1830

Traditional Critical Views of the Early Irish Novel

The traditional story of the birth of the Irish novel begins in the year 1800, when a young woman named Maria Edgeworth broke free from the pedantic, didactic influence of her learned, well-known father, Richard Lovell Edgeworth, to write and publish the first Irish novel, *Castle Rackrent*. This novel is told in the voice of Thady Quirk, a faithful, naive servant who appears to be unable to see through his degenerate landlord masters, the O'Shaughlins or "Rackrents." As with most good stories, there is a fair measure of truth to this one, and it has been told many times, in surveys of the "English" novel, of the romantic period, and of Irish or "Anglo-Irish" literature as well as in some studies of Edgeworth herself.

Yet along with a measure of truth comes an equal measure of critical fiction persistent enough to be called myth-making. For example, the book *was* published in 1800, but was written mostly several years earlier, between 1793 and 1796 (Butler 1972, 353–54). The date "1800," also the year of the Act of Union in which England annexed Ireland, offered a convenient, neat demarcation to literary historians who could say that "the Irish novel began in 1800." *Castle Rackrent* did establish Edgeworth's fame, but in 1800 she was thirty-two years old and already had at least four books to her name. Her father was not involved in her composition of *Castle Rackrent*, as he was with some of her other books, but he approved of it and very much enjoyed its success. Like Edgeworth's other novels, it was intended to educate as well as to entertain readers, even if its didacticism is less obvious or intrusive to the modern reader. "Faithful" Thady is an unusual narrator who does seem naive about his incompetent masters, yet he is also "faithful" in another sense: he recounts their failings in accurate detail, so we have no trouble seeing the Rackrents as the failures that they are. We also get the impression that Thady may see through them himself, even though he does not want to admit it. And at the end Thady's own son, the sly Jason, takes over their estate.

The story about *Castle Rackrent* also needs to be reexamined since in fact it was neither the first Irish novel, nor even appears to be a novel at all. (Some cultural or linguistic nationalists have also disputed the application of the adjective "Irish" to Edgeworth, but the introduction to this book should make clear that I do not agree with them.) It is true that a case for *Castle Rackrent* as the first *truly* Irish novel can be made, since it was apparently the first to adopt Ireland completely and thoroughly as both subject and setting, it was the first Big House novel, and in general it was the germ of so much that was to become central in the Irish novel—thematically, stylistically, and structurally. However, Irish authors published novels with Ireland at least partly providing subject and setting as early as the 1750s. Finally, although length has never adequately defined the novel as a genre, and it is true that the circuitous nature of Thady Quirk's tale makes it appear more novelistic than its length would indicate, it should be pointed out that *Castle Rackrent* (fifty-six pages long in one of its recent editions) is shorter than many of the individual "tales" published in collections of stories by Edgeworth's nineteenth-century contemporaries and a fraction of the length of most nineteenth-century novels, including her own *Ennui* (1809), *The Absentee* (1812), and *Ormond* (1817). *Castle Rackrent* is perhaps more accurately described as a novella or "tale."

If the story of this most celebrated and discussed of all nineteenth-century Irish novels—Is it a novel? Is it nine-teenth-century?—requires so much clarification, correction, and revision, one might wonder if we can even reasonably attempt to extend our story to the works of less celebrated novelists. In telling this new version of an old story there are many complexities to be faced, perhaps relished, and relatively little to go on. The literary historian and historical critic learns that the story of the Irish novel actually begins well before 1800, yet finds relatively few sources of facts and guidance for making informed judgments. The Marxist critic soon discovers that nearly every commentator on the early Irish novel, since long before Marx, has emphasized the sharp class differences among the novelists and the subjects of their novels, yet finds no body of concerted Marxist analysis of this phenomenon. The feminist immediately learns that the first major breakthroughs in the Irish novel were the fruits of the labors of two women, Maria Edgeworth and Sydney Owenson, yet finds very little feminist analysis of either writer; instead, feminist criticism on the Irish novel focuses much more often on the great male, James Joyce, and is largely a by-product of the traditionally male-domi-nated "Joyce Industry." Similarly, one can find many psy-choanalytic interpretations of Joyce's texts but hardly any of other Irish novels—even those that beg for it, such as Ed-geworth's *Ennui.* Poststructuralists and deconstructionists will discover in *Castle Rackrent* a fiction packed with ambiguity, ambivalence, and self-contradiction, but will not find (at least as of this writing) a single published deconstructionist or poststructuralist analysis of it; again, all the attention goes to Joyce. Perhaps only the critic whose prime interests are political or sociological will be stimulated by the existing critical literature surrounding the early Irish novel, as most of it emphasizes those themes—quite naturally so, since they were pervasive in early Irish fiction and remained strong in the works of later periods.

For any kind of critic there is an even earlier hurdle to be surmounted in approaching the early Irish novel: the "suspension of contempt or condescension," as Patrick Raf-roidi puts it. His admonition in 1973 still often applies today: "The current critical attitude towards nineteenth century Irish literature is, as we all know, one of condescension and even, at times, of downright contempt." Rafroidi cites as example a sentence from Donagh MacDonagh's introduction to the 1958 *Oxford Book of Irish Verse:* "The nineteenth century, parsimonious of genius in Ireland, relented towards its close and gave us William Butler Yeats" (quoted in Rafroidi 1973,

251). Nineteenth-century Irish novelists have traditionally been surveyed briefly and compared unfavorably to the great eighteenth- and nineteenth-century English novelists, and separated from the likes of Joyce, Beckett, and other twentieth-century Irish masters. Even Thomas Flanagan, a pioneer in the study of the early Irish novel, declared at the end of *The Irish Novelists, 1800–1850* that "the nineteenth-century Irish novel established no tradition," adding that "it matters not at all that there were Irish novelists before Joyce, for their work was entirely useless to him" (1958, 333–34). As we shall see, these assertions prove to be false. Joyce's use in *Finnegans Wake* of Sheridan Le Fanu's *The House by the Churchyard* (1863) is only the best-known example among a number of instances that I shall point to among Joyce's responses to the tradition of the Irish novel.

Treatment of the Irish novel before Flanagan's pivotal book in 1958 was sparse, scattered, and dominated by the nationalist ethos of Yeats, the extent of whose influence not only on subsequent Irish writers but on Irish literary criticism we have only begun to appreciate. In 1891 Yeats collected *Castle Rackrent* and other short fictions by a number of nineteenth-century Irish writers in a book entitled *Representative Irish Tales.* Contributing introductions to each author as well as to the whole collection, he gave highest marks to William Carleton in an assessment that has remained very influential, and he perpetuated that somewhat misleading story about how, "In 1800, Miss Edgeworth's imagination burst free from her didacticism and 'Castle Rackrent' was written and published" (34). Yeat's division of the writers into "gentry" and "peasantry" also proved very influential: "I notice very distinctly in all Irish literature two different accents—the accent of the gentry, and the less polished accent of the peasantry and those near them; a division roughly into the voice of those who lived lightly and gayly, and those who took man and his fortunes with much seriousness and even at times mournfully" (25). Yeats betrays here his romanticized view of the old feudal structure, composed of aristocracy and peasantry—with no room for the middle class—a bias that became even more evident in Yeats's later work. Thus the clearly middle-class John and Michael Banim and Gerald Griffin are lumped by Yeats among the peasantry as "those near them." He preferred the peasant Carleton even though he had to admit that the middle-class Griffin was probably "the most finished storyteller among Irish novelists" (31). Yet in his introduction to his 1889 collection of *Stories from Carleton,* Yeats judged Carleton to be the best Irish novelist "by right of the most Celtic eyes that ever gazed from under the brows of a story-teller" (quoted in Wolff 1980, 3). Yeats's influence was very evident in the first attempt at a comprehensive book on the nineteenth-century Irish novel, *Irish Life in Irish Fiction* (1903), by Horatio Sheafe Krans, who thanked Yeats in his preface (vi) and followed his split between "gentry" and "peasantry" in his chapter divisions. Yeats's nationalism was taken a step further in *Irish Literature and Drama in the English Language* (1936) by Stephen Gwynn, who rejected Edgeworth because she wasn't sufficiently "Irish."

Five decades after Columbia University Press published the first book on the Irish novel by Krans, they brought out Flanagan's Columbia dissertation, *The Irish Novelists, 1800–1850* (1958), which was also strongly nationalist and again celebrated Carleton's works in particular, but was much more thorough than Yeats and his followers had been. In a good line for book jackets, Yeats had declared about Ireland's stories that "they are Ireland talking to herself" (1891, 25). Yet Flanagan stressed that early Irish novelists wrote mostly for *English* publishers and for *English* as well as Anglo-Irish readers, exploring the ramifications of that fact and the importance of the perilous world of Irish politics in the works of Edgeworth, Owenson, the Banims, Griffin, and Carleton.

Flanagan's book has remained very influential and is often cited, but at the same time his work has been updated and corrected in several crucial respects during recent years. Important biographies of Edgeworth (Butler 1972) and Griffin (Cronin 1978) as well as critical studies on writers such as the Banims (Hawthorne 1975) have appeared. The late historian Robert Lee Wolff compiled an invaluable seventy-seven–title reprint series of nineteenth-century Irish fiction, published at the end of the 1970s, and in his introductory essays to these volumes added much new information and corrected Flanagan on a number of points. A book including chapters focused on the early Irish historical novel has appeared (Cahalan 1983), as well as a book on early nineteenth-century Irish writing in the context of European romanticism (Rafroidi 1972). Most recently and perhaps most importantly, the historical boundaries to the early Irish novel that were outlined by Flanagan—1800–1850, with birth in 1800 and death in 1850—have been opened up and extended both forwards and backwards. John Cronin's collection of essays on selected nineteenth-century Irish novels constantly asserts the continuity of the Irish novel and stresses themes introduced in the nineteenth century that are developed by Joyce and other twentieth-century Irish novelists—a link denied by Flanagan. "Tonally, thematically, linguistically, topographically, contemporary Irish fiction," Cronin insists, "constantly confesses its debt to the past" (1980, 18). Flanagan attacked the early–twentieth-century cultural nationalists Douglas Hyde and Daniel Corkery for ignoring nineteenth-century Irish writing in English; but Cronin points out in this respect that Flanagan neglects Thomas MacDonagh's *Literature in Ireland* (1916), in which earlier writers in English are viewed as hard-working writers who did their best to forge a new tradition (1980, 9). Most recent of all has been some pioneering work by two scholars, Ian Ross and Klaus Lubbers, staking out the earliest historical boundaries of the Irish novel in the late eighteenth century.[1]

Historical and Literary Backgrounds of the Early Irish Novel

Having prepared ourselves for the uneven, often murky terrain of this subject, let us, with the sincerity and desire for knowledge of Lemuel Gulliver, travel back to its beginnings. Where does the Irish novel begin? *With* Gulliver in Lilliput, in part. In *Gulliver's Travels* (1726) Swift did not create an Irish novel or found an Irish fictional tradition, but he did look ahead to other, later Irish satirists who wrote novels, such as Joyce, Eimar O'Duffy, and Beckett (Lubbers 1985a, 31; Mercier 1962). In its form of an imaginative travel fantasy written in the voice of a common person, Gulliver's narrative stands at the beginning of a tradition of Irish novels that includes Joyce's *Ulysses,* O'Duffy's *The Spacious Adventures of the Man in the Street,* and Flann O'Brien's *The Third Policeman.* Since the Irish-born Laurence Sterne's absurdist novel *Tristram Shandy* (1759–67) is also seen nowadays as foreshadowing the likes of Joyce's *Finnegans Wake* and O'Brien's *At Swim-Two-Birds,* we can see that it is possible to discover the features of a particular kind of Irish novel even among Irish writers who, although born in Ireland, did not choose to write novels about Ireland.

When searching for the origins of the Irish novel in the late eighteenth century, one really does feel like Gulliver standing among the huge Brobdingnagians. This is especially true when reading any of the surveys of the *English* novel concerning that century. For example, Walter Allen in *The English Novel* can speak majestically of the "Big Four" of Richardson, Fielding, Smollett, and Sterne (1954, 80), and Ian Watt in *The Rise of the Novel* has no trouble identifying the central theme of these writers as the forward-looking quest of their heroes whose "triumph in the big city has become the Holy Grail in the individual's secular pilgrimage" (1957, 204). The English novelists wrote for publishing houses that were increasing in number and prosperity and for readers whose sense of national and linguistic identity was strong, in a country whose middle class was well entrenched and expanding—a middle class that Watt and others rightly see as central to the growing prosperity of the English novel. In eighteenth-century Ireland there were far fewer publishers, no middle class to speak of, and no clear unified national or even linguistic identity.

Irish writers suffered under these deficiencies well into the nineteenth century because of a history in which England enforced Irish religious, political, and socioeconomic inferiority. After the defeat of Catholic King James by Protestant King William at the Battle of the Boyne in 1690, an anti-Catholic Penal Age was initiated that was not eased until the late eighteenth century and not ended until the Catholic Emancipation Act in 1828. By outlawing and penalizing Catholics, the Penal Code took an already existing, huge

Catholic underclass—mostly peasant farmers and laborers, many of whom were Irish speakers—and pushed that class ever more under. Anti-Catholic legal measures had virulent socioeconomic results: for example, a Catholic landlord could not follow primogeniture in his will; his land instead had to be divided equally among all of his sons, thus accelerating the extreme subdivision of holdings that afflicted an already overpopulated country. A "hidden Ireland" whose religion was illegal and whose culture was devastated suffered under the thumb of England and an elite Anglo-Irish upper class, with little or no room for any middle class.

With these eighteenth-century conditions in mind, it is not surprising that, as the historian J. C. Beckett stresses, "during that century no Irish novelist published a novel of Irish life" (1981, 102). While Beckett's assertion is not quite accurate, it is true that eighteenth-century novelists of Irish birth— often exiled, invariably writing for English publishers, and quite torn in their allegiances between Ireland and England— found it difficult to see themselves as writing specifically *Irish* novels, and their contemporaries as well as literary historians since then seldom identified them as Irish novelists. Even today W. J. McCormack, considering the Irish novel before *Castle Rackrent*, writes that "diligent though hardly arcane research will reveal scores of earlier novels. . . . Yet that material remains the stuff of a cultural archaeology" (1985, 97). The Irish novels of the late eighteenth century, though written by members of the Anglo-Irish upper class, represent as much a "hidden Ireland" as the Gaelic subculture celebrated by Daniel Corkery decades ago, long before the existence of any Irish novels predating *Castle Rackrent* was recognized.

Irish writers faced not only the overwhelming socioeconomic constraints of the dark Penal Age, but also the much older anti-Irish biases of English readers, biases that had long been perpetuated by English writers who were representative of the attitudes of their culture. Ever since Shakespeare's Macmorris had stumbled onto the stage in *Henry V*, muttering "What ish my nation?" an English "stage-Irish" tradition, in which Irishmen (like American blacks in minstrel shows) were presented as ignorant if often sly rogues and vagabonds, had kept Ireland at the level of stereotype. It seems perversely appropriate that the first novel with an Irish protagonist was entitled *The English Rogue* (1665, by Richard Head), and predictable that it played up the stage-Irish stereotype for obviously commercial reasons. The fictional hero invented by the Northern Irish, Carrickfergus-born Head (c. 1637–86) tells us that he was born in Ireland but is unwilling to consider himself Irish; he lives his life of crime in England except for a brief Irish foray when he shakes his creditors by running to Dublin, which is referred to as *"Divlin, quasi Divels Inn"* (Lubbers 1985a, 33 n. 1). This unlikely hero's night in Ireland sleeping among cows, pigs, and geese not only reflects stage-Irish stereotypes but also looks far ahead to the inflation of those stereotypes in Myles na gCopaleen/Flann O'Brien's novel *An Béal Bocht (The Poor Mouth)* (1941).

Since the twelfth century, English writings about Ireland had both reflected and influenced English attitudes, evolving all the way from reactionary prejudice to liberal sympathy. In the late twelfth century, Giraldus de Barris introduced the snobbish attitude of the "cultivated" Englishman looking at the Irish barbarians, an attitude that persisted for centuries. The seventeenth-century Edmund Spenser, Fynes Moryson, and John Davies were more informed but full of unabashed, arrogant pride concerning the English conquest of Ireland, described by Davies as *"a Perfect Conquest."* In his pamphlet, whose calm title, *Short Survey of Ireland,* contrasts with its intemperate, racist content, Barnabe Rych added that the Irish were in his view "more unciuill, more vncleanly, more barbarous and more brutish in their customs and demeanures, than in any other part of the world that is knowne" (quoted in Lubbers 1985a, 19–23). These attitudes were reversed in later books by William Petty and Arthur Young, whose level-headed examinations of the oppressed economic condition of Ireland caused them to become pro-Irish partisans in spite of the anti-Catholic opinions they might have held. Particularly pivotal was Young's *A Tour of Ireland* (1780), which appeared at the time of the birth of the Irish "Protestant Nation" and was described by Maria Edgeworth at the end of *Castle Rackrent* as "the first faithful portrait" of Ireland

(92). Young, who spent a year administering Lord Kings-
borough's estate in County Cork, was aware of the earlier
and "very gross misrepresentations of the Irish nation" by
the English, but sought very deliberately to counteract them.
The form of his popular and successful book—a travel account, including a chapter on Irish customs—influenced early
Irish novels, which are so often narrated by travelers and
which always seek to present and explain Irish characters
and customs to English readers. Novelists such as Edgeworth
would follow Young in seeking to counter English prejudices
and stereotypes of the Irish, while ironically creating new
ones of their own.

Young addressed not only ignorant English readers but
also Irish Protestant ones, encouraging them to be good
landlords and leaders. A receptive Protestant Irish readership
grew during the eighteenth century, as did the phenomenon
of Protestant Irish nationalism, which increased steadily on
into the nineteenth and twentieth centuries. Echoing the
sentiments of William Molyneux in his *Case of Ireland's Being
Bound by Acts of Parliament in England, Stated* (1698), Jonathan
Swift attacked English policies in Ireland from the time of
his first Irish pamphlet, *The Story of the Injured Lady Written
by Herself in a Letter to Her Friend, with the Answer* (written
in 1707 though not published until 1746). In his famous
*Modest Proposal for Preventing the Children of Poor People in
Ireland from Being a Burden to Their Parents or Country, and
for Making Them Beneficial to the Public* (1729), his satiric
speaker slyly suggests that both hunger and overpopulation
in Ireland could be solved if poor babies were "offered in
sale to the persons of quality and fortune through the kingdom." This practice would be effective since "a child will
make two dishes at an entertainment for friends," and though
fairly expensive "therefore very proper for landlords, who,
as they have already devoured most of the parents, seem to
have the best title to the children" (2146). In its wildly apt
fantasy and humble, pleading voice, Swift's *Proposal* looks
ahead to some of the best Irish novels with irony at their
core, such as Eimar O'Duffy's Cuanduine trilogy and Flann
O'Brien / Myles na gCopaleen's *An Béal Bocht (The Poor
Mouth)*.

Swift was a conservative Anglican who deeply resented his isolation from the hubbub of London in the backwaters of Dublin. He maintained only a snobbish tolerance for Catholics, and he believed that the Irish language should be abolished. But he transformed himself into a Protestant Irish patriot and provided a powerful voice for the patriotism that developed in his wake—culminating in the Protestant "Patriot Parliament" of Henry Grattan and Henry Flood that enjoyed a significant measure of Irish self-government after 1782, and exploding in the 1798 rebellions in Counties Wexford, Antrim, and Mayo led by Wolfe Tone, Edward Fitzgerald, and other Protestant United Irishmen. Protestants fought together with Catholics for Irish liberty in 1798, and were joined by Frenchmen under General Humbert in Mayo, but these rebellions were brutally crushed by the English forces, and the Irish parliament was rescinded soon thereafter, with Ireland's political annexation by England made complete by the Act of Union of 1800.

Irish Novels before 1800

Somewhere in the shadows of these much remembered events appeared several little remembered novels by Protestant Irish writers. The first novel set predominantly in Ireland was William Chaigneau's (1709–81) *The History of Jack Connor* (1752). Ian Ross calls it "an early and very successful attempt by an Irish writer to create within a European tradition an authentically Irish novel" (1982, 270). Like many an Irish novel that came after it, *Jack Connor* was a bildungsroman, focused on a young man who grows up during the early eighteenth century in Ireland, runs off to London and Paris, and abandons his Irishness (becoming "John Conyers"). Jack Connor eventually discovers, as Ross stresses, that the stability he seeks "is to be found only in his native land" (1982, 277). There he is guided and educated in responsibility by Lord Truegood, whose name is more obviously allegorical than Edgeworth's Herbert Annaly in *Ormond* (1817) but who serves the same moral function. *Jack Connor* helped establish the basic posture of the Protestant Irish novel: the targeting of English readers and the consequent intermediary role of the author, the attempt to meet and counteract English biases about Ireland; condescension coupled with good will and a humorous brand of anti-Catholicism as well as a belief in the need for Irish Catholic conversion to Protestantism; and the exposure of the abuses of absentee landlordism (Lubbers 1985a, 33).

Thomas Amory's *The Life of John Buncle* (1756 and 1766), a more eccentric novel, tells the tale of an Irish Unitarian who leaves Ireland, goes to England, is repeatedly married and widowed, meets many diverse Irish friends, and ends up immersed in utopian fantasies. Buncle links his eccentricities to his Irishness, telling his English readers who think his story peculiar: "Let it only be considered, that I was . . . carried an infant into Ireland, where I learned the Irish language, and became intimately acquainted with its original inhabitants." Ross stresses that *John Buncle*, as "a novel founded on anecdote, one which exploits a rich and rewarding seam of fantasy . . . throws some light on the origins of Irish fiction" (1983, 72). Buncle establishes a speaking narrative voice engaged in the telling of a seemingly formless, long tale—a pattern that would become very familiar in the Irish novel. His recollections of his student days at Trinity College, Dublin and his subsequent wanderings look ahead to Charles Lever's *Charles O'Malley* (1841).

Both *John Buncle* and Henry Brooke's (1703–83) *The Fool of Quality* (1771) seemed peculiar enough in form that Ernest Baker, historian of the English novel, wrote in 1935 that they were grouped among novels because "there was no other category nondescript enough to receive them" (quoted in Lubbers 1985a, 35). Like *Jack Connor, The Fool of Quality* is a bildungsroman about a young Protestant, Harry Moreland, who is trained to be a good landlord by a moral guide, in this case Harry's Uncle Henry. Unlike Chaigneau's racy tale, however, Brooke's novel is an earnest moral lesson, an educational novel. Brooke had encouraged the increase of Irish-English trade in 1759 and urged the easing of the Penal Code in 1761, views that are reflected in his novel (Lubbers 1985a, 39). His views are close to Arthur Young's and look ahead to Edgeworth's.

Charles Johnstone (1719–c. 1800), a Limerick-born journalist, published a formless novel entitled *The History of John Juniper* (1781) that was patterned after Fielding's *Jonathan Wild*, parodied the bildungsroman, and perpetuated the image of the stage-Irishman. Its hero is obsessed by "the darling pleasure of doing mischief." Son of a London Irish prostitute named Whiskey Nan, he runs away at sixteen, becomes a petty thief, and squanders a fortune. However, Johnstone's Oriental fantasy, *History of Arsaces* (1774), clearly allegorizes, in the vein of Swift, English oppression of Ireland, as when an inhabitant of the colony oppressed by the larger kingdom asks, "Who will work, when he knows that the fruit of his labour will be ravished from him?"

The Triumph of Prudence over Passion (1781) was published anonymously, perhaps because it is so different from other novels of the period and contains revolutionary opinions. Its author presents the advantages of being an unmarried female, and advocates the right of a woman to political freedom of speech. Lubbers describes it as the first national novel of Ireland because of its decidedly pro-Irish stance, stressing that it is no coincidence that the heroine's first letter to her friend Eliza Fitzgerald describes "our Volunteers" marching outside her window, and adding that this novel's main figures are referred to as "staunch patriots," London is seen as an evil city, and the shadiest figure is an Englishwoman (1985a, 41–43). The feminist motif in this early Irish novel should be noted (Ross 1980). The causes of Woman and of Ireland are linked here as they had been in Swift's first Irish pamphlet, *The Story of the Injured Lady Written by Herself in a Letter to Her Friend.*

Maria Edgeworth

These early novels established no tradition recognizable either during their period or for a long time since. However, they helped to pave the way among both readers and writers for novels that would openly announce themselves as Irish and attract attention to themselves as such. Published by Joseph Johnson in London in 1800 with the full title of *Castle Rackrent, an Hibernian Tale: Taken from Facts, and from the*

Manners of the Irish Squires, before the Year 1782, Maria
Edgeworth's first Irish tale definitely called attention to itself
as Irish. Even so, *Castle Rackrent* and Edgeworth's subsequent
Irish novels were considered by their earliest reviewers more
often as moral tales than as Irish ones; only in the 1820s,
when other Irish novelists were writing, was Edgeworth often
described as an Irish novelist, as for example in *Atheneum*
in 1828 when she was grouped with Sydney Owenson and
John Banim as one of "the three great describers of the lower
orders of Irishmen" (quoted in Lubbers 1985a, 68). Yet King
George III claimed that after finishing *Castle Rackrent* for the
first time, "I rubbed my hands and said what what—I know
something now of my Irish subjects" (quoted in Butler 1972,
359). The Irish-born critic John Wilson Croker feared the
effects of Edgeworth's writing on the masses, cautioning in
the *Quarterly Review* that "a strict literary police" would need
to be vigilant (quoted in Lubbers 1985a, 66).

As literary historian John Cronin notes, "in the presence
of all that historical significance, it is a positive relief to
remind oneself that it all began with a young girl imitating
one of her father's workmen," which is true except that at
age twenty-five Edgeworth (1768–1849) was no "young girl"
when she began writing the book in 1793. Cronin rightly
adds that "what has scarcely ever been remarked is that it
is also an amazingly funny book, which always works effectively to undercut pretension and to enlarge the novel's
moral force" (1980, 25, 35), a point which might just as well
have been made about Joyce's *Ulysses* and much of the
criticism about it. Indeed, *Castle Rackrent* introduces several
of the most distinctive features of the Irish novel that would
be evident in many books by many writers (and that would
find their deepest expression in *Ulysses*): Edgeworth's colloquial narrative voice (an innovation without which a *Huc-
kleberry Finn* as well as a *Ulysses* or many another Irish novel
would have been unimaginable) along with what the novelist
and critic Anthony Cronin has described as its "curious
stancelessness" and "absence of plot." He hypothesizes that
some Irish novelists "may have been simply incapable of
constructing an ordinary machinery of dramatic causation. It

may be that some of them, like Joyce, were uninterested in doing so" (1982, 25, 26).

Why do Irish novels tend to have strong narrators and weak plots? Perhaps partly because of the power and longevity of the oral storytelling tradition in Ireland, as well as the virtual absence of a middle class in Ireland as both subject and audience. These two crucial features of Irish society led the Irish novel in its form far away from English novels. Irish novelists did not write carefully plotted novels that drew on the relationships between and among the upper, middle, and lower classes, and aimed at a largely middle-class readership in their own country. Instead they more often introduced a storyteller as narrator who could only lament what was in class terms as well as in other terms a "broken world," as Sean O'Faolain called it, for whichever readers would "listen," and in the early nineteenth century those readers tended to be much more frequently English than Irish.

That is exactly what Thady Quirk, humble servant and the narrator of *Castle Rackrent*, does: he laments the lost, pseudo-feudal world in which reputedly faithful stewards like himself supposedly lived happily ever after on the estates of their good-hearted if incompetent landlords. Anthony Cronin points out that there had been many fairly obtuse narrators in previous novels in English, such as Defoe's *Moll Flanders*, but "what was new was Thady's perfectly modulated, colloquial manner" (1982, 23). Edgeworth modelled Thady's voice on that of John Langan, a steward on the Edgeworth family estate in County Longford, and reported that with that model nearby, Thady's tale flowed easily from her pen. As sources for the degenerate "Rackrent" (or abusive, overcharging) landlords, she had only to turn to any of the many incompetent Anglo-Irish landlords surrounding her, locating the image of the final, fatal Rackrent, Sir Condy, "in the last of her dissipated forebears, Protestant Frank, who died deep in debt and a fugitive from his estate" (Butler 1972, 354). Many of the book's first readers must have expected from the book's title some sort of romantic, Gothic tale complete with shadowy castles, secret identities, and blood and gore. Instead they got a pointedly realistic tale written in colloquial language that is not at all difficult for us now, after nearly two centuries of dialect stories of various kinds, but at the time was revolutionary and confusing enough to readers that Edgeworth added asterisked footnotes (for example, a long, fanciful reference to the ancient heritage of Thady's "great-coat"):

My real name is Thady Quirk, though in the family I have always been known by no other than 'Honest Thady', afterward, in the time of Sir Murtagh, deceased, I remember to hear them calling me 'Old Thady', and now I've come to 'Poor Thady'; for I wear a long great-coat* winter and summer, which is very handy, as I never put my arms into the sleeves; they are as good as new, though come Hollandtide next I've had it these seven years; it holds on by a single button round my neck, cloak fashion. (1)

Thady recounts how, in succession, Sir Patrick, Sir Murtagh, and Sir Kit ruined themselves with parties, drinking, lawsuits, politics, poor marriages, and long absences. After narrating the epic debauches of these earlier Rackrents, Thady begs the reader to "here let me pause for breath in my story" (54), before going on to tell, in part 2, how Sir Condy completed the family's process of self-destruction, losing the estate to Thady's scheming son Jason and also losing the affections of the equally opportunistic Judy M'Quirk.

It is understandable that so many commentators have declared *Castle Rackrent* to be the first Irish novel, for while we have seen that this assertion is not strictly accurate, Thady's tale begins so much that would become central in the Irish novel—even beyond its colloquial narrator and apparent formlessness and "stancelessness." It is the first "Big House" novel set on an Ascendancy estate, the first Irish family chronicle, and the first fictional book to make Irish history and politics central to its story and theme. Because of its Irish setting, it has also been called the first "regional novel" perhaps more than anything else. Yet this is true only within the context of the *English* novel and mostly because of Edgeworth's well-known influence on Sir Walter Scott, who "felt that something might be attempted for my own country, of the same kind with that which Miss

Edgeworth so fortunately achieved for Ireland," and went on to write his famous and popular historical novels about Scotland that in turn continually influenced nineteenth-century Irish novelists (Cahalan 1983, 2). The only novel by Edgeworth that focuses on a particularly specified region *within* Ireland is *Ormond* (1817), and the Irish regional novel begins before that with the works of Sydney Owenson.

Edgeworth was the first writer to establish a significant readership for Irish novels. After *Castle Rackrent* and up until Scott published *Waverley* in 1814, Edgeworth was "easily the most celebrated and successful of practising . . . novelists," with publishers paying her up to £2,000 for a single work while Jane Austen was offered a conditional £450 for *Emma* (Butler 1972, 1). In 1831 an *Edinburgh Review* writer noted about the Irish: "We had seen them alone in English crowds— solitary foreigners, brought over to amuse us with their peculiarities, but we had never been carried to Ireland, and made familiar with them by their own hearths, till for the first time, they were shown to us by Miss Edgeworth" (Harden 1984, 125). Edgeworth's knowledge that she was writing for English readers and her awareness about the earlier books aimed at presenting Ireland to those readers are both clear from beginning until end of *Castle Rackrent.* She follows the well-worn eighteenth-century conceit of the author as "ed-itor" of Thady's tale, adding footnotes and a glossary that place herself in an intermediary role between Irish, colloquial Thady and her fairly befuddled, standard-English–speaking readers, and also at a distance from her own caste and hence beyond the accusation that she was befouling her own nest. In her very first footnote (regarding the "great-coat"), which extends across the bottom of the book's first two pages (foreshadowing the comic use of footnotes in *Finnegans Wake* as well as in Flann O'Brien's *The Third Policeman*), Edgeworth cites at length "Spenser, in his 'View of the State of Ireland' " (36–37). Her last page refers to "Mr Young's picture of Ireland" as "the first faithful portrait of its inhabitants" as well as a list of stage-Irish characteristics that had "been brought upon the stage or delineated in novels" (92). She thus cites both the best and some of the worst English portraits of Ireland, framing her bold new canvas with her

readers' already existing mental pictures of Ireland, and presenting Thady's tale to them "as a specimen of manners and
character which is perhaps unknown in England" (92).

In Edgeworth criticism "two subjects tend to dominate
critical discussion: Edgeworth's historical importance as the
originator of the regional novel and the overriding and at
times overbearing moralistic and didactic strain of all her
writings" (Kilroy 1976, 29). Even more recently Kilroy adds
that "little close criticism of her works has yet appeared"
except for an article about the revisions of her English novel
Belinda (1983, 15). Following Thomas Flanagan's lead, most
analyses of *Castle Rackrent* have continued to be historical
in focus—so much so that Anthony Mortimer felt he had
to begin a recent, useful article entitled " 'Castle Rackrent'
and Its Historical Contexts," self-consciously:

Contemporary criticism has reached a stage where the kind of
exercise indicated by the title of this essay cannot be undertaken
with the old blithe confidence that its justification is self-evident.
Persuasive voices have been raised to warn us that history does
not provide access to some ultimate non-linguistic context that we
can use to control the significance of a literary text. So be it; but
the consequences of this salutary recognition need not be so
radically disturbing as is sometimes supposed. History does not
lose its value for the student of literature because its claim to
absolute authority has been undermined or because we recognize
history as an assembly of texts. (1984, 107)

At the same time that many recent American Joyceans are
inspired by the point of view of the European poststructuralists, Mortimer in Switzerland reasserts the importance of
history, as does Klaus Lubbers in Germany, who reminds us
that books do not fall from the sky but are rooted in human
society. Lubbers advocates a sociohistorical view of literature
that takes into account, especially in the case of Ireland, the
writer's background and milieu, intended readers, and the
reactions of the contemporary critics (1985a, 9).

The second chief preoccupation in Edgeworth criticism, her
didactic preoccupation with the need for enlightened agrarian
reform, is always discussed in terms of the influence of the

strong utilitarian, educational philosophy of her father, Richard Lovell Edgeworth. The notion that Edgeworth wrote her novels according to the specifications of her father has been encouraged by his undeniably strong influence on her work. Her own statement that her father wrote part of the description of King Corney's death in *Ormond* while dying himself, as well as evidence advanced fairly recently by Patrick Murray that her father also contributed some other passages (1971), has perpetuated the view that Maria was not an independent writer. Even her insistence, with her father's confirmation, that she wrote *Castle Rackrent* totally on her own has not been enough to overcome the condescending view that, in terms of her overall literary career, Daddy made her do it. *Castle Rackrent* is then seen as a brief escape from the father's later consistently overwhelming influence. In this view it does not seem to matter that *Castle Rackrent* argues the same thesis that her other Irish books do (although it is more deliciously implicit in *Castle Rackrent*): that Irish landlords needed to shape up or they would lose their estates.[2]

It is surprising that feminist critics to date have given Edgeworth relatively little attention. Essays with such an emphasis have recently been published by Colin and Jo Atkinson (1984) and Eiléan Ní Chuilleanáin (1985), but they focus on Edgeworth's English novel *Belinda* rather than on her Irish novels. Edgeworth is included in two books on *English* female novelists that are assessed hostilely by James Kilroy: "Linking of Edgeworth's novels with those of other women writers has not served their reputations well" (1976, 30). As far back as 1904, Kilroy notes, the later Irish novelist Emily Lawless had contributed a volume on Edgeworth to the "English Men of Letters series, and as if to underline her defiance of that series title, Lawless insists that previous English critics" failed to emphasize "how truly Irish her best works are" (1976, 26)—with Kilroy himself missing the irony of Edgeworth's inclusion in a *"Men* of Letters" series. Edgeworth learned a hard-headed pragmatism from her father, so many male critics decided that she was "unfeminine." She herself attacked feminine stereotypes: in *Castle Rackrent* she lambasted not only the male Rackrents, who were drunkards and fools, but their equally asinine wives, who locked themselves in their rooms or ran off quickly back to England, unable to face the realities of managing an Irish estate as Maria Edgeworth herself had been able to do. As Elizabeth Harden notes, "If she did not campaign publicly for women's rights, she quietly challenged women all along in her fiction to accept their rights to self-realization," adding that in contrast to Jane Austen's heroines, Edgeworth's are "less interested in catching husbands than in seeking knowledge, integrity, and self-fulfillment" (1984, 121–22).

An author ought to be allowed not only to succeed on her own merits, but to fail on her own too. Edgeworth's three Irish novels after *Castle Rackrent* are flawed by plots whose didacticism is too obvious, whose romance elements are too predictable, and whose characters are mostly too thin—making these novels fairly overt allegories. Traditional male critics blamed these qualities on Edgeworth's father and his influence rather than on the author's own artistic choices, mistakes, or lack of imagination. Probably none of them would place similar blame on Wordsworth for any of Coleridge's poetic shortcomings or deny Coleridge his own achievements, even though their literary collaboration was much closer, at the time *Castle Rackrent* appeared, than that of the Edgeworths.

The most recurrent issue in criticism on *Castle Rackrent* in recent years concerns the status of Thady Quirk as narrator: is he a naive dupe, a duplicitous trickster, or neither? Thomas Flanagan and many other earlier commentators on the novel assumed that Thady's essential quality is naiveté and that he fails to understand fully the story he is telling. During the 1960s James Newcomer attacked this view: "Faithful Thady indeed! . . . It is not difficult to remain in service to the family whose possessions are flowing from their pockets into his own" (1966, 176). He claimed that the "disingenuous" Thady, despite his assertions to the contrary, could only stand to gain from his son Jason's purchase of Sir Condy's lands. Duane Edwards advocated a middle course between Newcomer's view of Thady and the traditional one, arguing that Thady is not always shrewd and is not treated well by Jason. He concluded that Thady "is a sentimental, generally unreflective old man whose love of money causes him to ally himself with Jason, who for some unexplained reason abandons him" (1972, 125–26). Yet most critics have missed the point of a crucial aspect of Thady's story: the overriding hatred on the part of the peasantry for a "middleman" such as Jason. When the tenant farmers hear that Jason is buying Sir Condy's estate, even Thady admits that "the people one and all gathered in great anger against my son Jason, and terror at the notion of his coming to be landlord over them, and they cried: 'No Jason! no Jason! Sir Condy! Sir Condy! Sir Condy Rackrent for ever!'" (55). True to Irish social history and folklore, they detest the scheming, ruthless Irish middleman even more than the incompetent landlord. It has been argued that the "Rackrents," who as O'Shaughlins were probably Catholics, would have had to convert or "conform" to Protestantism in order to legally maintain their role as landlords in the eighteenth century—yet it has been little noted that "Attorney Jason" almost surely would have also had to conform in order to gain the power that he does. Catholic Thady cannot bring himself to comment on this course of action, which was detestable in Ireland and might very well have alienated Jason from Thady, and Jason lurks as a shadowy figure only at the borders of Thady's tale. In the Irish consciousness a middleman like Jason would have been capable of any conceivable deed, including turning his back on his father.

While every commentator on Edgeworth tries to make sense of the quirky Thady, articles focused on his particular status have petered out in recent years, suggesting that critics have run out of hypotheses about him. It is surprising, nonetheless, that his marvellously ambivalent narrative has not attracted a single deconstructionist critique as of this writing. It is equally remarkable, especially in light of all of the attention given to Edgeworth's father, that no psychoanalytic analysis of Edgeworth's work has appeared. Yet the plot of Edgeworth's second novel, *Ennui* (1809), ought to be very inviting to the Freudian. *Ennui* has received less critical attention than any of Edgeworth's novels, because its essentially simple, allegorical plot is not found to be appealing. The Earl of Glenthorn suffers from "an utter abhorrence and an incapacity of voluntary exertion," and concerning Ireland, the country of his birth, he has been influenced by his father, who "had a dislike to that country, and I grew up in his prejudices" (2, 4). Glenthorn can thus serve as a fitting lens for Edgeworth's English readers, who observe him traveling to Ireland and learning his proper responsibilities as an enlightened Edgeworthian landlord. The plot hinges on a secret that has to be discovered—that Glenthorn was switched at birth by his true mother, Ellinor, with Christy O'Donoghue, the true Lord Glenthorn, when it appeared that Christy would die, so that her own son could inherit the estate. When Glenthorn learns this secret, he turns over his estate to Christy and goes off to study law, thus learning self-reliance. But Christy has to contend with his wife's avarice, which almost ruins the estate, and decides that he prefers his blacksmith's forge. Glenthorn then resumes charge of the estate, having now prepared himself for his responsibilities, and marries purity, beauty, and money in Cecilia Delamere.

It is true that this plot is a transparent one, a moral lesson in how to overcome ennui, but that is part of what makes it interesting—along with Edgeworth's attempt at an *aristocrat* first-person narrator, following the peasant Thady. Glenthorn has two moral guides: Ellinor and the noble land-agent McLeod, who has not only managed the estate in model fashion but has founded an ecumenical school; he is the type of Edgeworthian role-model who can also be easily found in *The Absentee* and *Ormond*. If MacLeod and Ellinor are Glenthorn's guardian angels, Glenthorn's rich *first* wife is a morality Vice figure: she leaves him for the *bad* land agent, Crawley, and runs off to (significantly) England, where Crawley is eventually convicted of embezzlement. Edgeworth's novels are full of such decadent wives, studies in what Edgeworth herself did not wish to become. Of Freudian interest is Glenthorn's intense relationship with Ellinor, whom he perceives as an earth-mother, a Mother Ireland, even before he learns that she is (of course) his true mother. Maria Edgeworth's mother died in her youth, and her father went through a total of four wives, giving Maria close attention only after they settled in Edgeworthstown in 1782, when she was fourteen. It is apparent that Maria preferred to live at Edgeworthstown rather than abroad—so much so that she turned down a marriage proposal from a Scandinavian whom she loved—not for nationalist reasons but because of her attachment to her father and because she felt that the earth of Edgeworthstown was the only place where she was ever properly nurtured. It appears that much of this feeling is projected onto Glenthorn's attachment to the earth-mother Ellinor, who nursed him in infancy. At the same time, Edgeworth felt that to be practical she had to make a man her protagonist in this novel and her other Irish novels about how to become a good landlord.

The plot of *The Absentee* (1812) is very similar: Lord Colambre leaves behind decadent amusements in London and visits the family estate in Ireland anonymously. There he observes both the Good Land Agent, Burke, who like McLeod also runs a progressive school, and the Bad Land Agent, Garraghty, and declares unambiguously: "What I have just seen is the picture . . . of that to which an Irish estate and Irish tenantry may be degraded in the absence of those whose duty and interest it is to reside in Ireland to uphold justice by example and authority; but who, neglecting this duty, commit power to bad hands and bad hearts—abandon their tenantry to oppression, and their property to ruin" (202). Needless to say, he subsequently not only becomes a good landlord himself, but even convinces his absentee parents to return home to their estate. The latter part of *The Absentee* is devoted to Colambre's eventually successful quest for Grace Nugent. Such relationships are the least interesting parts of Edgeworth's romances in which Landlord Knight Slays Evil Agents and Wins Lady Love. The novel ends with the stated moral, "It's the growing fashion not to be an absentee" (333). Lubbers argues that the overwhelmingly positive English and American reviews of Edgeworth's didactic novels, in which she was championed as a kind of doctor of moral medicine, helped encourage her didactic streak. Even the often nasty John Wilson Croker acclaimed her as "our great moral teacher" (quoted in Lubbers 1985a, 67).

As if to compensate for the heavy didacticism of *The Absentee,* Edgeworth asked her father for a preface to what

turned out to be her last Irish novel, *Ormond* (1817), in which
he claimed that she had taken pains to hide its moral. The
moral was not hard to find, however, in this long tale of
how Harry Ormond learns a passion for the land from Corney
O'Shane and a progressive knowledge about how to manage
an estate from Sir Herbert Annaly (an Englishman clearly
modelled on Edgeworth's father), marrying Sir Herbert's
daughter Florence at the end, and moving onto the dead
"King Corney" 's estate. Like Edgeworth's other heroes, Ormond spends time in England (and in Paris) but can find
his true identity only in Ireland. This time, however, it is a
specifically identified *part* of Ireland, near Lough Rea in the
midlands. This use of setting reverses the English novel's
frequent focus on the big city as the place of fulfillment, as
in Fielding's *Tom Jones* (which Ormond reads and tries to
emulate), as Ormond learns lessons in the big city but can
be happy only in his own regional, rural place (Howard
1979, 334). We also find in *Ormond,* in contrast to her previous
Irish novels, less attention to Irish socioeconomics per se as
subject and more detailed focus on her hero's personal maturation. This is reflected in the contrast between the titles
The Absentee and *Ormond.*

Edgeworth felt unable or unwilling to write about Ireland
in her novels after her father's death in 1817 and after the
rise of Daniel O'Connell, causing her to feel that "it is
impossible to draw Ireland as she now is in the book of
fiction—realities are too strong, party passions too violent,
to bear to see, or care to look at their faces in a looking
glass. The people would only break the glass and curse the
fool who held the mirror up to nature" (quoted in Lubbers
1985a, 63). Edgeworth and Thady Quirk echo throughout
the Irish novel at least as far as the beginning of Joyce's
Ulysses (1922), when Stephen Dedalus peers into a mirror
and mutters, "It is a symbol of Irish art. The cracked lookingglass of a servant" (6).

Changing Times: The Career of Sydney Owenson

The growth of the Irish novel during the first three decades
of the nineteenth century was due not only to the pioneering

example of Maria Edgeworth, but even more to a vastly changed political climate. The crushing of the 1798 rebellions and the imposition of the Act of Union served only to increase Irish nationalism. The population of the country grew rapidly during this period, paving the way for a mass movement, which was provided by Daniel O'Connell. O'Connell was Ireland's George Washington, or in Irish terms "The Liberator" or "Counsellor," concerning whom there are more stories and anecdotes in the vast archives of the Irish Folklore Commission than any other figure in Irish history, even Cromwell (Cahalan 1983, 34–36). He became the great champion of the Catholic Emancipation movement to abolish the anti-Catholic penal code, toward this end organizing massive, nonviolent rallies, some of which attracted more than a hundred thousand people. Writers, journalists, and politicians rallied around the cause, and Catholic Emancipation was approved by Parliament in 1829—although by increasing the voting franchise from forty shillings to ten pounds, the act kept the poor people of Ireland disenfranchised, while class differences became even more marked.

Irish newspapers and journals increased in number during this period, and often tended to divide along political and religious lines. The pro-O'Connell *Dublin Morning Register*, for example, had its bitter anti-Catholic counterpart in the *Dublin Morning Star;* the *Irish Protestant*, in the *Irish Catholic;* the *Union Magazine*, in the *Anti-Union Weekly Magazine* (Lubbers 1985a, 49). Partly due to improved social conditions and increased interest in Ireland, a number of Irish novelists began to write and to find publishers. The long catalogue of Irish novels in Stephen Brown's seminal list of *Ireland in Fiction* (1919), if reorganized decade by decade, gets longer and longer as the nineteenth century proceeds (Cahalan 1983, 86). Many Irish fiction writers wrote part-time: for example, John Gamble (c. 1770–1831) was a doctor, John Bernhard Trotter (1775–1818) a lawyer, Robert Torrens (1780–1864) an economist, Michael James Whitty (1795–1868) a journalist. Their commitment to writing as a career as well as to the novel as a form was hazy: most of these lesser-known writers published collections of "tales," while a "tale" such as Eyre Evans Crowe's (1799–1868) "The Northerns of '98" in his collection *Yesterday in Ireland* (1829) was considerable enough to be called a novel (Lubbers 1985a, 111, 115). Crowe was one of several lesser-known authors of historical novels, which became more and more popular after the example of Sydney Owenson and of course Walter Scott—a group that included during this period James McHenry, W. H. Maxwell, Matthew Archdeacon, and, more significantly, John and Michael Banim (Cahalan 1983, 45). The rest of this chapter is devoted to the novelists who, after Edgeworth, made the biggest impact before 1830: Sydney Owenson, Charles Maturin, John and Michael Banim, and Gerald Griffin.

The second writer to achieve fame as an Irish novelist was Sydney Owenson (1776?–1859), who much to her own gratification became "Lady Morgan" when she married Sir Charles Morgan in 1812. Owenson affords in her life and works a most stimulating comparison and contrast with the first pivotal figure, Edgeworth. Like Edgeworth, Owenson aimed to put Ireland in a positive light for readers who were mostly English, stressing the oppression of the peasantry and the need for landlords to take care of their estates in Ireland. But Owenson was, on the one hand, as mediocre in her fiction-writing as Edgeworth was innovative, and on the other hand, as colorful in her life as Edgeworth was dull. Like Edgeworth, she lost her mother early in life and was raised by her father; but *her* father, Robert Owenson (born MacOwen), was literally a stage Irishman whose acting and producing career was shaky. Edgeworth, in fact, after reading Owenson's novel *Florence Macarthy,* which she detested, wrote in a letter, "God forbid, as my dear father said, I should ever be such a thing as that. It was for want of such a father she has come to this" (quoted in Wolff 1979a, v). Against her father's wishes, young Sydney worked as a governess in order to establish her independence. Meanwhile she wrote her first two novels, *St. Clair* (1803) and *The Novice of St. Dominick* (1805), two forgettable books in which she attempted to mythologize a past more exciting than her own humble upbringing. Her third novel, *The Wild Irish Girl* (1806) made her name as it went through seven editions in two years; by 1807 Sydney was playing the role of Glorvina, her cape-wearing, harp-bearing heroine, in salons and the popular press. She went on to add both her title by marriage and several more successful Irish novels: *O'Donnell, a National Tale* (1814), *Florence Macarthy, an Irish Tale* (1818), and *The O'Briens and the O'Flahertys, a National Tale* (1827), her only novel with any complexity or quality to it. She supported Catholic Emancipation and other causes of liberty, declaring herself a "national" novelist in the subtitles of her novels. In the roles of "Lady Morgan" and "the wild Irish girl," Owenson adopted a posture as thoroughly romantic as Edgeworth's was hard-headed and rationalistic. And "as much as any single force did Lady Morgan's novels make liberal opinion in England receptive to Irish claims," wrote Flanagan (1958, 137). She was both Protestant and Catholic by parentage and had misgivings about Daniel O'Connell's demagoguery, but opened her house to the Catholic Emancipation movement. " 'Tis there you'll find O'Connell spoutin' / And Lady Morgan making tay," boasted a Dublin street ballad of the time. She was praised by O'Connell: "To Irish female talents and patriotism we owe much. Need I say that I allude to Lady Morgan? Her name is received with enthusiasm by the people of the country where her writings create and perpetuate among the youth of both sexes a patriotic ardour" (quoted in Lubbers 1985a, 85).

Because of this Romantic, patriotic image, "criticism on Lady Morgan," as James Kilroy notes, "tends to repeat the familiar" (1983, 19). Both before and after Flanagan's book—beginning, in fact, with her first reviewers—critics generally disparaged her writing but emphasized her historical importance as a popular nationalist writer. In this context Colin and Jo Atkinson's feminist article (1980) on her life and work is a breath of fresh air. They take as their point of departure the claim of Owenson's biographer Lionel Stevenson that she was "the first successful professional woman author—the first to ride to social, intellectual and financial prestige entirely through her business-like exploitation of her literary talent" (1936, Preface, n.p.). The Atkinsons link as parallel developments the increase in the respectability of the novel as a literary form during the eighteenth century and the rise of women writers as well as feminism during the same period. They see Owenson as a pivotal figure "in the development from the 'exceptional,' like Aphra Behn [1640?–1689], to the

'ordinary' professional writer, like [Anglo-Irish] Julia Kavanagh [1824–1877]" (1980, 61). Writing a few years after Mary
Wollstonecraft's *Vindication of the Rights of Women* (1792)
and at the height of the popularity of Madame de Stael,
who published *Corinne* in 1807, Owenson was delighted to
be occasionally referred to as 'the Irish Corinne' " (Atkinson
and Atkinson, 1980, 69). Yet this was a time when as gifted
an essayist as Charles Lamb could say of a woman writer
that "if she belonged to me I would lock her up and feed
her on bread and water till she left off writing poetry"
(quoted in Atkinson and Atkinson 1980, 62). It is therefore
not surprising that John Wilson Croker repeatedly attacked
Owenson in articles whose tone is described by the level-
headed Klaus Lubbers as pathological (1985a, 88). When an
older Owenson, who was often derided as "Momma Morgan," analyzed the oppressed role of women in history in
Woman and Her Master (1840), male reviewers attacked her
book and even her looks, one of them "likening her to an
ugly and venomous toad" (Atkinson and Atkinson 1980, 89).

   But Owenson fought back. She responded to Croker by
caricaturizing him in *O'Donnel* as "Dexter, a despicable Irish
Protestant toady of the rich" (Wolff 1979b, xii), and as the
equally evil Con Crawley in *Florence Macarthy.* Upon her
death in 1859, an *Athenaeum* columnist commented, "Her
books were battles. . . . She wrote . . . in an age when to
be a woman was to be without defence, and to be a[n Irish]
patriot was to be a criminal" (Atkinson and Atkinson 1980,
73). She clearly saw her writing career as not only a way
to champion the causes of Ireland, Woman, and Liberty, but
a means of lifting herself out of poverty and demeaning
dependence into prosperity and fame, inspired in particular
by the example of Fanny Burney. Between 1800 and 1840
she produced some seventy volumes, including nine novels,
and unlike Edgeworth, whose father chose her publishers,
Owenson did her own negotiating. She wrote: "I am sick of
the jargon about the idleness of genius. All the greatest
geniuses have worked hard at everything—energetic, persevering, and laborious" (Atkinson and Atkinson 1980, 72).

   Owenson's life is much more interesting than her novels.
Significantly, in light of the success of Arthur Young's *Tour*

of Ireland, The Wild Irish Girl (1806) was commissioned as a travel book about Ireland by her London publisher Richard Phillips, who was disappointed when she delivered a novel instead (Lubbers 1985a, 31). He must have changed his mind when he observed the book's sales. Readers devoured Owenson's account of how Mortimer, the profligate Ascendancy hero, falls in love with "the wild Irish girl," Glorvina, and her wild, romantic country. The bare bones of Owenson's plot is borrowed from Edgeworth, and her perspective is like that of Arthur Young and the other travel writers for English readers. But her romantic setting—Owenson, like Yeats, believed that Sligo was the most mystical Irish county—and her florid writing, compared to Edgeworth's balanced, eighteenth-century prose, are like night to day. One example from one of Mortimer's many letters home will suffice:

Glorvina made no reply; but turned full on me her "eyes of dewy light." Mine almost sunk beneath the melting ardour of their soul-bearing glance.
Oh! child of Nature! child of genius and of passion! why was I withheld from throwing myself at thy feet; from offering thee the homage of that soul thou hast awakened; from covering thy hands with my kisses, and bathing them with tears of such delicious emotion, as thou only has power to inspire? (2:40)

Like Mortimer, Owenson's readers fell in love not only with Glorvina but also with the new version of Ireland she embodied—a shadowy, Celtic, and above all romantic place. Hers was a new and persistent kind of vision to be embodied in the Irish novel. Like Edgeworth, Owenson also appended footnotes. Her message is encapsulated in the epigraph from *Uberti's Travels through Ireland in the 14th Century* that is positioned on her title page: "this race of men, though savage they may seem, / The country, too, with many a mountain rough, / Yet are they sweet to him who tries and tastes them." Her romantic tale was very popular on the Continent—in Germany, for example, more so than the novels of either Edgeworth or Maturin, because "in the shadow of Ossian it was the minstrel boys and the wild Irish girls who carried the day" (O'Neill 1980, 47).

O'Donnel (1814) was planned as a historical novel about the Elizabethan hero Red Hugh O'Donnell, but Owenson found herself overwhelmed by the historical details of his story. So instead she wrote a romantic story about how one of his modern-day descendants—the first *Catholic* gentleman hero in an Irish novel—falls in love with a brilliant governess employed by a landlord with liberal Edgeworthian principles whose name, Glentworth, sounds suspiciously like that of the protagonist of Edgeworth's *Ennui*. Richard Lovell Edgeworth had written to Owenson congratulating her on *The Wild Irish Girl*, but it was her next novel, *Florence Macarthy* (1818), that Maria Edgeworth detested, even though (or perhaps because) it ended with the Edgeworthian sentence, "Ireland can best be served in Ireland."

By the time of her last Irish novel, *The O'Briens and the O'Flahertys* (1827), Owenson had become more ambivalent about her role in Daniel O'Connell's Ireland, and this novel is thus more pessimistic and somewhat more complex than the earlier romances. Its plot leans exhaustively on concealed identities. At the end her hero, Murrogh O'Brien, marries Beavoin O'Flaherty, the mysterious, beautiful ex-nun who has repeatedly saved Murrogh from various catastrophes in the course of the book. Beavoin tried to reform the Catholic institution of which she was a part, but then abandoned it; Owenson was sympathetic to the plight of Catholics in the Ireland of her time, but negative about Catholicism itself.

Her novels are in large part a series of romanticized self-projections, from Glorvina to Beavoin and including her most transparent heroine of all, the victimized novelist Florence Macarthy. Owenson's contribution to the development of the early Irish novel comes neither in characterization nor in plot, but in her role as an unabashed nationalist novelist who proved that a profit could be made singing Ireland's praises, and in her celebration, even if not very clear or consistent, of Ireland's romantic past, her focus on Irish history as fitting subject for fiction. This direction was followed by Owenson's most immediate successors, Maturin and the Banims.

Charles Maturin

Charles Maturin (1780–1824) is almost always assessed in criticism as a Gothic, romantic novelist, especially since his reputation has hinged mostly on his Gothic masterpiece, *Melmoth the Wanderer* (Kilroy 1976, 36–37). This focus is useful and understandable, for Maturin's life has a rather Byronic quality to it. He was a Trinity College graduate and an ordained Protestant minister whose eccentricities seem to have been somewhat akin to those of his bizarre protagonists. It is surprising that no biography of this curious author has been published. As in the case of his fellow Irish Gothicist Sheridan Le Fanu, Maturin was descended from French Huguenots and seemed always somehow an outsider in the political and cultural life of the Dublin in which he lived. However, from early in his career he wrote as a decidedly Irish novelist, and was befriended and encouraged by the great celebrator of "regional" fiction, Walter Scott.

After a first novel in the Gothic tradition of Ann Radcliffe, *Fatal Revenge* (1807), Maturin published two novels clearly inspired by Edgeworth and Owenson, *The Wild Irish Boy* (1808) and *The Milesian Chief* (1812). Published two years after Owenson's *The Wild Irish Girl* and at the height of her popularity, Maturin's first Irish novel was obviously meant to capitalize on her success. In it Lady Montrevor appears at a ball actually dressed as Glorvina, the Wild Irish Girl. His debts to Edgeworth are just as clear; like Edgeworth, Maturin includes footnotes about rural Irish life and dialect, and one of them refers directly to Edgeworth's *The Absentee* (20). His plot is straight out of Edgeworth and Owenson: an ostensibly English hero, Ormsby Bethel, makes his way to Ireland, where he marries an Irishwoman and falls in love with the country, resolving to become a spokesman in England for the Irish cause. Like their novels, *The Wild Irish Boy* "purports to give some account of a country little known" (Maturin 1808, 1:x). Before sending his hero to Ireland, however, Maturin establishes a broader Romantic context for his quest by describing Ormsby in the Lake Country reading

Ossian. His love plot contains the extra twist that Ormsby really loves the mother of the woman he marries but has to learn to love the daughter instead, a conceit that recurs in Maturin's third Irish novel, *Women; or, Pour et Contre: A Tale* (1818). Maturin's interest in women characters is evident in the latter novel as well as in *The Milesian Chief*, in which Maturin sends a *heroine* rather than a hero to the wilds of Connaught to abandon her English fiancé and fall in love with the grandson of an Irish chieftain. *Women* is unusual both because it is set in Dublin, with a protagonist who is a Trinity College undergraduate like Maturin himself, and since it maintains a focus on female characters so strong that Robert Lee Wolff declared the book "more important surely as an effort to study feminine psychology than as a novel of Ireland" (*Nineteenth Century Fiction*, 15).

These novels are no better artistically than Owenson's potboilers, but they show Maturin's interest in Irish realistic writing, which is also evident in *Melmoth the Wanderer*, despite the almost exclusively Gothic emphasis of the criticism on this novel. English reviewers ignored his early novels and treated *Melmoth* harshly (Lubbers 1985a, 123), but in translation it was very popular in France. *Melmoth the Wanderer* begins and ends in Ireland, establishing a cultural and autobiographical frame that is far from trivial. That *Melmoth* fits into an Irish tradition becomes clear when one considers it in light of other Irish novels. For example, it introduces as protagonist a Dublin student, as do Griffin's *The Collegians*, Charles Lever's *Charles O'Malley*, Joyce's *A Portrait of the Artist as a Young Man*, and Flann O'Brien's *At Swim-Two-Birds*. *Melmoth* begins and ends with an Irish Big House frame. Maturin adds some crafty peasants working as stewards on the Melmoth family estate who, like Owenson's peasant character M'Rory in *O'Donnel*, were probably modelled on Edgeworth's Thady Quirk, but also based on Maturin's own observations of rural peasant life during his year serving as a vicar in Loughrea. The novel begins realistically in Ireland and is then jolted into different, fantastic realms much as that other grim Dublin minister, Swift, transported Gulliver from England to the nether regions—and as happens in Eimar O'Duffy's *The Spacious Adventures of the Man in the Street* and O'Brien's *The Third Policeman.* As with Joyce and Beckett, the theme of exile is of central interest to Maturin. Moreover, most of the novel is a series of meandering, diverse "tales" unified more by theme than by storyline—a method central to what makes an Irish novel *Irish*, all the way from *Castle Rackrent* to *Ulysses* and beyond.

In this case, the unifying theme is the common Irish one of subjugation—how the individual is oppressed and how the spirit of love is ruined by rigid institutions, many of them religious. *Melmoth* is not the simplistic anti-Catholic tract that many another Protestant Gothic novel was. Maturin uses Inquisition scenes for their terrifying effects, but he also includes "The Tale of Guzman," in which a friendly priest rescues a fortune from the Church for a Protestant family. At least one critic regarded Maturin's last novel, *The Albigenses* (1824), although it was set in France, as a "plea for tolerance" in favor of Catholic Emancipation (Bostrom 1963, 162).

The basic conceit of Maturin's story seems bizarre but is in fact no more unusual than those found in later innovative Irish novels. From his own dying, miserly uncle, the nineteenth-century student John Melmoth inherits an obsession with his seventeenth-century ancestor and namesake, the Wanderer, who is said to be still alive. The younger Melmoth then listens to the tales told about the Wanderer just as we do. At the end of the novel the Wanderer himself appears at the farmhouse where his descendant is being told the tales about him, and dies, his corpse tossed into the sea by devils. As strange and Gothic as it is, *Melmoth* was founded on a didactic impulse as much as any of Edgeworth's novels were: Maturin's belief, expressed in one of his sermons as well as in his preface to the novel, that a man aware of his true value would not sell his soul to the devil for all the world's goods. He admitted that his earlier novels were too far beyond "the reach of life, or the tone and compass of ordinary feeling," emphasizing that "if I possess any talent, it is that of darkening the gloomy, and of deepening the sad; of painting life in extremes, and presenting those struggles of passions when the soul trembles on the verge of the unlawful and unhallowed" (Kramer 1973, 52). Maturin was

certainly not the last Irish novelist to focus on the darker
passions or to weave novels full of fantastic tales.

John and Michael Banim

John (1798–1842) and Michael Banim (1796–1874) were
the first Irish novelists who were thoroughly middle-class
and Catholic in background and sensibility—characteristics
that applied also to Joyce and many other of the best Irish
novelists later on, but were unheard of in an Irish novelist
when the Banims came on the scene in the early 1820s with
the pen-name "the O'Hara Brothers." They were also the
first completely regional Irish novelists in the true sense,
focusing in as much detail and as faithfully as they could
on their home district around Kilkenny. They wrote about
Irish peasants as much as did any of their Irish contemporaries, but their Catholic piety and the middle-class tenor of
their desire for respectability are evident and separate them
from Edgeworth, Owenson, and Maturin. They represent a
historical link between two writers who have tended to
overshadow them—between, as Mark Hawthorne puts it,
Edgeworth, "the Ascendancy lady who brought a little of
Ireland into the English novel," and William Carleton, of
peasant birth, an "Ulsterman who tried to write of Ireland
as he had known it for an audience that the Banims in part
helped to create" (1975, 6). With his pseudo-feudal preference
for the extremes of society (the aristocrats and peasants) and
his distaste for the middle class, Yeats of course preferred
Edgeworth and especially Carleton to the likes of the Banims,
and this predilection has recurred throughout criticism on
the nineteenth-century Irish novel; again, the tastes of Yeats
and of Scott, who praised Edgeworth, are more influential
in criticism down to our own day than one might expect.
Yet the Banims at their best wrote novels that are as good
as those by Edgeworth and Carleton, both of whom were
better at the shorter forms. The Banims were capable of
lapsing into a maudlin sentimentality that often flaws their
work, as was Carleton, but in their best books they captured
in powerful ways a life that had never been seen in fiction
before. All of the criticism on the Banims has to date been

historical and sociological in emphasis; this is understandable in light of the fact that such were the brothers' chief preoccupations.

John's more romantic life—one including a hopeless love for a young Protestant woman who died, followed by years of exile in London and his own premature death back home in Kilkenny from a spinal disease—predictably appealed much more to Yeats (1891, 93–97) than that of the more pedestrian Michael, who remained in Kilkenny as a shopkeeper and then postmaster, outliving his brother by thirty-two years. Neither brother's life has ever received the detailed, scholarly attention deserved; a close account of John's struggle to establish himself as a writer in London, where he wrote for the *Literary Register*, would be invaluable, especially since he was the first of myriad Irish Catholic novelists to seek out success in one of the big foreign capitals, abandoning exile whereas the likes of Joyce and Brian Moore would later thrive in it. Yeats's romanticized emphasis on John and neglect of Michael was followed by others, including Thomas Flanagan. John may have had the more artistic consciousness of the two, but Michael's pragmatic perspective included a greater knowledge of the folkways of the Kilkenny area, which both brothers drew on extensively in their novels.[3]

The Banims' work divides into three categories: an attempt to join realism to "otherworldliness," a focus on "life in the cabin," and an exploration of Irish history (Hawthorne 1980, 91–92). Often these categories overlap, as in *The Boyne Water*, a historical novel that employs Gothicism in the mode of Scott. Earnestly seeking to communicate these new materials to an English readership, the Banims often employ the familiar strategies of Edgeworth and Owenson—the English visitor as protagonist, the footnotes. Yet their novels are full of Irish-English dialogue to an extent that no earlier Irish novel is, and they add many Gaelic phrases and "translations from the Irish," much more so than even in *Castle Rackrent*. Furthermore, while *The Boyne Water* does employ the outsider-as-protagonist conceit, many of the Banims' novels are set completely within Ireland and deal entirely with native Irish characters. They were influenced by the increasing attention given to Irish folklore during the early nineteenth century, as for example in the collections of Thomas Crofton Croker.

The first three-volume set from "the O'Hara Brothers" in 1825 contained three relatively short novels: *Crohoore of the Bill-Hook, The Fetches,* and *John Doe.* The three categories outlined by Hawthorne are thus introduced from the beginning, for *Crohoore* focuses on "life in the cabin," *The Fetches* on Irish "otherworldliness," and *John Doe,* while not strictly a historical novel, does explore rural Irish political violence; it is one of their political novels that can be grouped with the historical ones. John's first novel, *The Fetches,* begins with a reference to an Anglo-Irish historian, "Stanihurst," much as Edgeworth might have done, and then proceeds to focus on an Ascendancy student at Kilkenny College, Harry Tresham, whose life is eventually destroyed in pursuing the Irish belief in "fetches" (doppelgänger ghosts) and moves from rationalism to madness, and is thus in both respects suspiciously similar to Maturin's Melmoth. The two brothers collaborated on *John Doe,* which introduces the subject of faction-fighting and rural, political guerrilla violence that Carleton later took up. In the mold of Edgeworth, two English officers stationed in Clonmel observe Irish affairs, with the English reader constantly kept in mind by the Banims. Since the Banims were ardent believers in the nonviolent political approach of Daniel O'Connell, they discredited the anonymous rebel "John Doe," whose involvement in political violence is revealed at the end to be an excuse for personal revenge.

The best of these first three novels and one of the better Irish novels of the nineteenth century is Michael's *Crohoore of the Bill-Hook,* recently described as "the most important fictional account of rural violence in nineteenth-century Ireland" by Mary Helen Thuente, who concludes that the worst violence is committed not by the peasantry but by the military and the gentry (1985, 138). Michael forthrightly asserted his realism in the midst of the novel, insisting that "this is no fancy-sketch" but rather "carefully copied from the life and the facts" (1:111). Michael's attention to realistic detail was encouraged by John, who wrote to him about the character collecting from Catholics the legally enforced dues supporting the Protestant Church of Ireland: "You tell me you intend to cut off the proctor's ears: slice them close to his head by all means; do not leave a shred; no honest man will say that he does not deserve the cropping" (quoted in Wolff 1979a, viii). The novel concerns the misunderstood peasant Crohoore, who has been adopted by the noble farming family, the Doolings, is accused of the murder of the father and mother, but at the end is both absolved of the crime and revealed to be their true son. Descriptions of Crohoore early in the novel sound like nineteenth-century anti-Irish cartoon caricatures, with "his nose, of the Milesian mould, long, broad-backed and hooked" and "his lips, that without much effort never closed on those disagreeable teeth . . . large, fleshy, and bloodless." Banim adds, "These features, all large to disproportion, conveyed, along with the unpleas-antness deformity inspires, the expression of a bold and decided character, and something else besides, which was maligning or mystery, according to the observation or mood of a curious observer" (1817–18). It seems clear that Banim intended to take the old anti-Irish stereotype of the sub-human, violent Irishman and explode it. As Crohoore asserts at the end of the novel, "All my life I was a poor friendless crature, the thing to be jeered at, an' throd upon, an' abused by every body" (2:91). He speaks forcefully in front of the courtroom at the end in a scene that exemplifies almost perfectly Flanagan's thesis that the early Irish novel "can be termed a kind of advocacy before the bar of English public opinion" (1958, 38).

In 1826 John Banim published his two best novels, *The Nowlans* and *The Boyne Water. The Nowlans* was inspired by a letter from Michael describing his visit to the rain-swept cabin of a rural Irish family who were concerned about the ill health of their son, an ex-priest or, in Irish terms, a "spoiled" priest. John positioned his brother's letter, some-what revised, at the beginning of the novel, lending to his tale an air of actuality, and then wove his most interesting if somewhat uneven story around it, narrating how the family and the son arrived at the sad state described in the letter. His theme is a bold one, the story quite new to Irish fiction: the conflicting demands of the spirit and the flesh in John Nowlan, a pious young man who becomes a priest. Having

resisted the charms of a young peasant woman, actually his
cousin, who tries to seduce him, John then commits the
ultimate "sin" by going off to live with a cultured Protestant
woman, Letty Adams, who shares his poverty in Dublin,
eventually dying in childbirth in a hovel. In its despairing
near-naturalism, in its gritty Dublin scenes, and in its focus
on the struggles of such a Catholic Irishman—a *priest*, no
less—*The Nowlans* is an entirely new kind of Irish novel and
a long way from the Ascendancy novels of Edgeworth. The
novel is flawed by an unfortunate, lengthy subplot about
Letty's evil brother—reflecting Banim's self-confessed greater
interest in character than plot—but John Nowlan and his
story look ahead, as John Cronin points out, to Joyce's
Stephen Dedalus, who experienced similar struggles peculiar
to a middle-class Irish Catholic male (1980, 51). *The Nowlans*
is the first of a long strand of Irish novels about priests or
would-be priests that would include not only Joyce's *Portrait*
but also George Moore's *The Lake*, Gerald O'Donovan's *Father
Ralph*, Richard Power's *The Hungry Grass*, and many others.
This novel "exhibits a pre-Victorian, Regency frankness in
sexual matters, describing John Nowlan's embraces with his
cousin Maggy, who later becomes proprietress of a bawdy-
house in Dublin, far more graphically than was usual in
1826" (Wolff 1979a, xix). Edgeworth called this novel "a
work of great genius," and Yeats admired the first half of
it (Cronin 1980, 57).

Closely modelled on Scott and based on careful historical
research on the Jacobite-Williamite War (1689–91), *The Boyne
Water* (1826) remains the best Irish historical novel of the
nineteenth century. Like Irish novelists before him and like
Scott in *Waverley*, Banim positioned initially touristy outsiders
as protagonists: Protestant brother and sister Robert and
Esther Evelyn, who wander into the glens of Antrim in the
north of Ireland. There they survive a Gothic tornado, fall
in love with Catholic Eva and Edmund O'Donnell from whom
they get separated by the war, learn to be tolerant of Ireland
and Catholicism, and emerge as emblems of how war ruins
love as well as examples of how Protestants can learn to
understand and love Irish Catholics. Written at the height
of the popularity of John Banim's hero Daniel O'Connell,

The Boyne Water was intended as a tract in favor of Catholic Emancipation, even more clearly than Owenson's *The O'Briens and the O'Flahertys*, Maturin's *The Albigenses*, or any of the other Irish and English novels provoked by that movement (Bostrom 1963). More than a tract, though, *The Boyne Water* was an exciting historical novel combining interesting fictionalized history, strong characterizations, Gothic settings, and lively dialogue. John's sequels—*The Last Baron of Crana* (1828c) and *The Conformists* (1828b), both focused on the eighteenth-century Penal Age—are weaker partly because Banim meekly revised them in the wake of the passage of the Catholic Emancipation Act in 1828, which he thought had solved the Catholic crisis, apologetically expressing the hope that his new volumes would not offend the English reader. In contrast, *The Boyne Water*, a stronger, longer, and more symmetrical novel, had ended with the insistence that the 1691 Treaty of Limerick, which had expressed conciliatory intentions toward Irish Catholics, had not yet been kept in 1826 (564). Michael Banim's *The Croppy* (1830) completed their historical saga with a tale of the 1798 rebellion in Wexford, which was critically praised, though not up to the level of *The Boyne Water* or Michael's own *Crohoore*.[4] Closely related to them is John's *The Anglo-Irish of the Nineteenth Century* (1828a), an anonymously published political novel that was so different from the Banims' other books that it was thought to have been written by Charles Morgan, Sydney Owenson's husband. Perhaps partly written as Banim's response to Edgeworth's and Owenson's novels that sent Protestant aristocrats to fall in love and learn responsibility in Ireland, *The Anglo-Irish of the Nineteenth Century* is much more pessimistic than *The Boyne Water* about achieving true Irish-English rapprochement; his protagonist Gerald Blount listens to many of the nasty Catholic Emancipation debates that Banim himself heard in both London and Ireland.

In the contemporary reviews of the Banims' novels, the Irish journals, especially the *Nation*, could not separate art from patriotism (Lubbers 1985a, 97, 110). To some extent this has remained true among the few assessments of the Banims' novels that exist—they are usually recognized as important historical pioneers in the Irish novel but short-changed critically. Yet *Crohoore of the Bill-Hook, The Nowlans,* and *The Boyne Water* are important novels that deserve more serious critical attention than they have received. Far inferior, unfortunately, are the Banims' novels after 1830, affected by their ambivalent reactions to the more diffuse directions of Irish politics after the great cause of Emancipation was left behind, and cut short by John's rapid physical deterioration and early death. John wrote to Michael, "We have given, perhaps, too much of the dark side of the Irish character; let us for the present treat of the amiable. Enough of it is around us" (Michael Banim 1842, iii). To modern tastes John had just scratched the surface of that "dark side" in *The Nowlans* and should have dug deeper. Instead he abandoned Ireland altogether in *The Smuggler* (1831), set in England, while Michael published the forgettable *The Ghost-Hunter and His Family* (1833), *The Mayor of Windgap* (1835), and *The Town of the Cascades* (1864). Almost as if to compensate for John's examination of the spoiled priest in *The Nowlans,* the two brothers collaborated on *Father Connell,* a sentimental portrait of the Banims' boyhood parish priest, published in 1842, the year of John's death.

Gerald Griffin

In 1823 John Banim had befriended Gerald Griffin (1803–40) in London, where the younger writer was also seeking to establish himself, and while the reclusive Griffin was seemingly incapable of fully accepting Banim's help, he too was a middle-class Catholic, and he admired Banim's writing and his determination to expose the life of the small farmers to English readers. His career was as contorted and perhaps even more tragic than Banim's, but before his short life was over he published in 1829, three years after Banim's own *annus mirabilis* of 1826, the best and most popular full-length Irish novel up until that date, *The Collegians,* and two other worthy ones, *The Rivals* and *Tracy's Ambition.* Like Banim, Griffin began as a journalist in London; made his name with Irish tales, novels (including historical novels), and songs (such as the well-known "Aileen Aroon"); maintained a hopeless love for a Protestant woman (married, in this case); permitted his Catholic moralism to eventually overwhelm his work; and died young—after two years of retreat into service as a Christian Brother in Cork. Griffin abandoned the English-visitor protagonist of his predecessors and departed from the Banims' focus on explicating public politics, turning instead to private concerns on purely Irish turf. While earlier Irish novels were "about Ireland," the importance of *The Collegians* is that in it Griffin for the first time simply "had written an Irish novel," as Flanagan put it (1958, 230). Griffin's life and work have fortunately received the close attention usually missing on nineteenth-century Irish novelists, in John Cronin's interesting biographical study and critical articles. In one of his articles (1969a) and in fact in all of his writings on Griffin, Cronin traces parallels between Griffin's work and Joyce's. In truth, Griffin's closest notable successor is more so the neglected but excellent novelist Kate O'Brien, who focused, a century after Griffin, on the moral dilemmas of middle-class, Catholic characters from their common native county of Limerick, just as Griffin did. In any event, these critical points—Griffin's departures from the Banims and his other predecessors as well as his introduction of some of the chief themes of later Irish novelists, such as a focus on the repressed lives of middle-class and poor Irish characters—emphasize just how pivotal a figure Griffin is.

The Collegians, published when Griffin was just twenty-six, was his great achievement and suggests what Griffin might have gone on to do had he not been hampered by the difficulties faced by an Irish writer of his era as well as by the pathetic peculiarities of his own life and personality. He never saw his parents again after they emigrated to Pennsylvania when he was seventeen, and the only family he became close to was that of Lydia Fisher, the married Quaker woman for whom he experienced a frustrated love. The extreme shyness and conservative Catholic piety that always colored his life made him decide to retreat from literature and the wider world into the Christian Brothers (the religious order most detested by Joyce) a year and a half before he died of typhus fever. To note a point of connection missed by Cronin, it is as if the fate willed on

Joyce by Flann O'Brien in his novel *The Dalkey Archive* had already been enacted in Griffin's life: O'Brien's protagonist encounters a Joyce who denies authorship of that "dirty" book *Ulysses* and confesses that he has instead been living in seclusion and writing pamphlets for the Catholic Truth Society. It was no joke for Griffin, though; he could find no other way to resolve his sad life. He tossed unpublished writings into the fire, not in order to reshape a *Stephen Hero* into a *Portrait,* going on to greatness, but as an act of surrender.

Yet *The Collegians* is as complete a social panorama of Irish life as was John Banim's *The Boyne Water* and stands as a better novel because its characters and plot are more compelling and its politics less overt. *The Collegians* is as didactic as anything by Banim or Edgeworth: Cardinal Gibbons, appropriately enough, summed up, in a preface to the 1898 edition of the novel, its moral as "the peace and happiness and content resulting from wisely contracted Christian marriage and conjugal fidelity, and likewise the dreadful evils that ill-assorted, clandestine marriages drag in their train" (x). Based on an actual case in County Clare in 1809, the novel focuses on Hardress Cregan, a member of the Ascendancy, who falls in love with the daughter of a ropemaker, Eily O'Connor, secretly marries her, but then permits his demented servant Danny Mann to "remove" her so that he can publicly marry the cultured, monied Anne Chute. The hero of the novel is Hardress's former Trinity College classmate and friend Kyrle Daly, Griffin's middle-class, Catholic image of perfection, who finally gets to marry his beloved Anne after Hardress is exiled and Danny executed following Eily's drowning. Rather than explicitly announced, Griffin's social values are implicit in his plot and characterizations: he condemns an Ascendancy that betrays the peasantry and champions a middle class that is seen as living in happy harmony with the peasantry. The novel is also populated by a number of compelling secondary characters, such as Hardress's grasping mother and Myles na Coppaleen, the noble Gaelic horseman and "perfect Ulysses" (87) who was subsequently transmogrified as both a major character in Dion Boucicault's even more popular play *The Colleen Bawn* (1860) and as the pseudonym of Brian O'Nolan (Flann O'Brien) in his brilliant satires in the *Irish Times,* but who remains a relatively minor character in Griffin's novel. The story opens with a comfortable, middle-class dinner scene at the Dalys' home comparable to the famous Christmas-dinner scene in Joyce's *Portrait* (Cronin 1980, 68).

The novel is better and more complex than even Griffin may have understood; he could never fathom why readers were as attracted as they have always been to Hardress, clearly intended by him as a villain, a confused and dishonest "half-sir," and less attracted to Kyrle, painted as Griffin's knight in shining armor. In his complex failure as a human being, Hardress is fascinating, while in his unambiguous success Kyrle is comparatively dull. Never having married, Griffin perhaps could not know the truth of the maxim that, at least in fiction, all happy marriages are the same while each unhappy one is unique—a syndrome advanced by at least one later Irish novelist, James Plunkett, as an explanation for why he downplayed a happy marriage in *his* novel (Cahalan 1978a, 88). While intended as a moral lesson, *The Collegians* developed into a compelling psychological novel that has caused Griffin to be compared, in one of the standard sources, to Dostoyevski (Cleeve 1967, 55). When Hardress's love for Eily is being ruined by his Ascendancy shame about her peasant status, he has a dream in which he hears Eily speaking in "that brogue" to his relatives and "on happening to look around upon her during dinner, he saw her in the act of pealing [*sic*] a potato with her fingers! This phantom haunted him for half the night" (197). He never orders Eily's death but "during his conversation with Danny Mann, the idea of Eily's death had flashed upon his mind, and for that instant it had been accompanied with a sensation of wilfull pleasure." After the deed Danny tells him, "De sign of death was on your face dat time, whatever way your words went" (296, 402). *The Collegians* recaptures the basic roles in the story of *Othello,* with Hardress as Othello, Danny as Iago, and Eily as Desdemona.

In Griffin's second-best novel, *Tracy's Ambition,* those roles are played by the land-agent Abel Tracy, his wife, Mary, and the evil Dalton, respectively—but with less complexity.

Dalton is "a fiend" (181) and Mary Dalton a thin character who is killed by revengeful peasants, at which point, Abel tells us, her lips "were chipped and dragged downward at the corners with a hideous look of pain and scorn" (191). The novel is made interesting by Abel Tracy, its narrator and protagonist, whose tragic flaw is the ambition that causes him to accept Dalton's advices, abuse his tenants, and allow himself to be ruined. In the nineteenth-century rural Irish social context, Abel Tracy is the hated "middleman," yet he is an interesting, sympathetic character. It is as if a later version of Edgeworth's Jason Quirk were allowed to tell *his* story. William Carleton would also write a novel about a middleman, *Valentine McClutchy* (1845b), but with his peasant consciousness, he made his book a biting satire, clear in his title, with no room for sympathy for the middleman. The middle-class Griffin, more sympathetic to the tortured class-consciousness of a middleman, framed his story as a tragedy—but then let Abel off the hook at the end, allowing him to get rid of his Iago and survive to "lead a peaceful life among a circle of merry friends," training to become a justice of the peace, with malevolent "ambition entirely set at rest" (287).

The *Othello*-like quality that is mostly a strength in these two novels illustrates Griffin's preference for "dramatic" writing, which instead becomes a weakness in his lesser novels. He was addicted to Shakespearean soliloquies, as in *The Rivals* when the local rebel hero Francis Riordan returns from exile to Ireland and delivers a ceremonial speech addressed to the hills and the earth around him. This novel includes some good chapters, especially chapter 8 with its comic Irish-English disquisitions in the rural hedgeschool on Virgil's *Aeneid*, containing "polysyllabic polymaths" that are "happy harbingers of such complex achievements in the Irish novel," Cronin goes so far as to say, "as the *Oxen of the Sun* episode in Joyce's *Ulysses*" (1978, xiii). But the novel as a whole is a romantic potboiler whose rebel hero is not a nationalist emblem as he would have been in a Banim novel, but a shadowy, chivalric, local hero who is not witnessed doing any violence and who, needless to say, wins his lady love over his evil "rival." Given Griffin's frustrated love for Lydia

Fisher, Riordan's romantic victory in this novel, like Kyrle Daly's in *The Collegians,* may well indicate powerful wishful thinking on the author's part.

Cronin might have added to his Joycean parallel the fact that Griffin, despite his quiet support for Daniel O'Connell, was in his writing surprisingly apolitical given the thoroughly political premises of Irish writing during his time. Even English readers must have noticed this. In Irish circles the nationalist *Citizen* typically expressed admiration after Griffin's death for his work, but lamented that "our departed brother" had not realized his true potential as a nationalist writer. Griffin wrote less about history and politics than did the Banims, perhaps partly because his home in the west of Ireland was more sheltered from violent events than was the Banims' Kilkenny (Lubbers 1985a, 150, 160, 155). Even in his almost obligatory historical novels, he was comfortable dealing only with remote, ancient Irish history, as in *The Invasion* (1832), or with an English rather than an Irish setting, as in *The Duke of Monmouth* (1836), a novel focused on the same period as and probably inspired by Banim's *The Boyne Water.* These are far inferior in quality and interest to *The Collegians. The Christian Physiologist* (1830), a pathetically didactic tale, prophesied the extent to which his Catholic piety would smother his writing.

In his best novel, though, Griffin provided for later Irish writers important proof that it was not necessary to write "about" Ireland and its history and politics in order to write a successful Irish novel, and that superior and popular results could be found by exploring local materials and private themes. Although they would never abandon the Irish obsession with history and politics, Irish novelists had thus considerably broadened their range since the beginning of the century.

2

Variations on Irish Themes, 1830–90

Historical and Critical Backgrounds

If Edgeworth, Griffin, and their compatriots had founded a distinct tradition for the Irish novel during the first three decades of the nineteenth century—otherwise a literary dark age in Ireland—this is not to suggest that any kind of golden age for the Irish novel was at hand. Far from golden, the middle and later years of the nineteenth century were in many ways the bleakest of all for the Irish novel. So they were too for Ireland, where a dark age was followed by a holocaust: the Great Famine or Hunger of 1845–51. With the passage of the Catholic Emancipation Act in 1829, it had appeared that a new era of Catholic liberty was beginning, and the publication of Griffin's immensely successful novel *The Collegians* the following year must have encouraged the notion not only that a Catholic could write a great work of fiction, but that Irish novelists were able to take on serious themes other than politics. But instead, both the conflict with England and the divisions within Irish society deepened, and in turn these problems were reflected by novelists whose political allegiances were complex and often contradictory and whose careers as novelists were difficult and uneven.

This period was marked by changes in the political climate and by an increase in Irish publishing and journalism. After helping Ireland win Emancipation, Daniel O'Connell, "the Liberator," began a campaign for a Repeal of the Union, an effort that proved to be a failure just as surely as the struggle for Emancipation had been a success. By the time of his death in 1847, O'Connell had become an object of ridicule for members of the Young Ireland movement, who saw themselves as stronger nationalists and turned to new nationalist movements in Europe for their models. Their leader,

Thomas Davis, was a Protestant intellectual who viewed O'Connell as a mere Catholic demagogue and, believing that literature and politics were equally commendable activities, founded the *Nation*, one of the two most popular and important Irish journals of the mid-nineteenth century. Its rival was the *Dublin University Magazine* (1833–77), which during its long life (for an Irish publication) published most of the leading Irish novelists of the period; indeed, two of them, Charles Lever and Sheridan Le Fanu, served as editors and Le Fanu as owner for several years. While the *Nation* was avowedly nationalist, the *Dublin University Magazine* established itself as an Irish forum yet was linked ideologically to English culture, if often critical of British political developments, and was strongly anti-Catholic in its editorial sentiments. Even though it saw itself as a "British" periodical, the *Dublin University Magazine* became unquestionably the most important periodical for Irish fiction writers and contributed more to the survival of the Irish novel than any other nineteenth-century publication.

The 1830s and 1840s saw an increase in Irish journalism in general. A number of short-lived Irish "penny journals" sought to reach the masses and help them overcome what was seen as their cultural isolation. The *Dublin Penny Journal* (1832–37), for example, published William Carleton and Samuel Lover among the novelists, and was read by both Protestants and Catholics. The penny journals reflected Irish politics and sectarianism. For example, the anti-Catholic, evangelical Caesar Otway, remembered mostly because he was Carleton's first publisher, expressed sentiments in the *Dublin Penny Journal* that provoked a *Catholic Penny Magazine* (1834–35) into existence—countered yet again and all too predictably by a *Protestant Penny Journal* (1834–36). Lover founded and illustrated the *Irish Penny Journal* (1840–41), its title suggesting the fact that Lover sought to hover a bit further above sectarian lines, publishing writers as different as Carleton and Anna Hall (Lubbers 1985a, 133).

The growth in Irish publishing and O'Connell's campaign to repeal the Union with England both encouraged Irish novelists in the early 1840s to explicate "the Irish problem" as their predecessors such as Edgeworth and the Banims had done. It is striking and more than coincidental that in 1845, for example, a majority of the important novelists considered in this chapter—Carleton, Lever, Hall, and Le Fanu—published novels that examined Irish conditions in a sympathetic light, even though none of the four can be considered a clear-cut nationalist; the latter three were thoroughly of the Protestant Ascendancy in sensibility as well as background, and Carleton, although born a Catholic peasant, converted to Protestantism and first made his name writing for Otway's strongly anti-Catholic *Christian Examiner*. Yet even writers such as these became Irish nationalists for a time in the early 1840s, basking in the glow of the *Nation* and the belief that Ireland was at last entering its long-awaited golden age.

Instead, the Famine arrived. During the decade after 1845 a million people died and another million were forced to emigrate. By the beginning of the twentieth century, the population of Ireland was only about half of what it had been in 1845, and even today Ireland remains very unusual among Western nations because its population is significantly lower now than it was in the early nineteenth century— about five million as opposed to about eight million. Technically, the Famine was not a "famine" at all, since after the beginning of the potato blight that caused it, other foods continued to be exported to England. The fact that the Great Hunger was not the result of a true famine but of a perverse economy that had Irish peasant farmers almost totally dependent on the ill-fated potato for their own food, while they harvested grains and sold dairy products to their Ascendancy and English masters, caused Irish nationalists to conclude that the English had caused, perhaps even willed, this greatest of all disasters in the long and calamitous history of Ireland. Matters may not have been that simple, but they looked that way to the survivors. As a peasant adage put it, "God sent the blight, but the English caused the Famine." Irish nationalism increased and strengthened slowly but surely between the years after the Great Hunger and the end of the century, becoming most evident in the Fenian or Irish Republican movement, the Land League, the Irish Home Rule movement, the Literary Revival, and later the Easter Rising of 1916. However, in the midst of and after the Great

Hunger as well as the extremely short-lived, ill-starred Young Ireland rebellion of 1848 (which was really more of a rhetorical gesture than anything else), Irish novelists generally expressed disillusionment.

In light of the disastrous historical and cultural conditions of the time, the most surprising fact is that novelists such as Lever and Lover retained a sense of humor—and the critics, especially the Irish nationalist critics, have never forgiven them for it. It is as if the Irish novel, after the persistent stridency and moralizing of Edgeworth, Owenson, the Banims, and Griffin, was ready for some comic relief. Carleton was capable of great comic scenes in his short fiction, while in his novels he felt constrained to be mostly "serious," perhaps partly because of the example of his predecessors. Yet he did attempt a satire in *Valentine McClutchy* (1845). Carleton appreciated the bizarre aspects of Irish life, as did the otherwise very different Le Fanu. In recent years Carleton has received a fair amount of critical attention, and W. J. McCormack (1980) published an excellent study of Le Fanu. Yet other novelists of the period have met with critical neglect and even scorn. Lover, Lever, Hall, Charles Kickham, and Emily Lawless for the most part have been belittled or ignored. Lover and Lever have been the objects of particular derision in the past not only because they have been viewed as stage-Irish humorists, but because it has been found amusing to link their last names, "Lover and Lever," in consonance and a proverbial pun.

When in search of any variety of critical approaches to Irish novelists of this period, the story is equally pathetic. Irish novelists of the early nineteenth century were also confined almost entirely within historical and sociological contexts, but at least they had their Thomas Flanagan, championing the tradition encapsulated in his title, *The Irish Novelists, 1800–1850.* The same Flanagan denied the continuance of that tradition, and he and others could cite Carleton writing in 1863, "Banim and Griffin are gone, and I will soon follow them . . . After that will come a lull, an obscurity of perhaps half a century" (quoted in Wolff 1980, 127). W. J. McCormack echoes Carleton, writing about the era of Le Fanu that "the apparent solidity of the novel tradition in Ireland is largely

an illusion generated in the minds of recent historians. . . .
It is difficult to point to a period when more than two or
three novelists of any ability were at work simultaneously."
He concludes that these novelists "are better regarded as
. . . 'a scattering of incoherent lives' " (1980, 250). Frank
O'Connor, an Irish writer who tried his hand at the novel,
asserted in *The Mirror in the Roadway: A Study of the Modern
Novel* that the nineteenth-century novel is "incomparably
the greatest of modern art forms . . . greater perhaps than
any other popular literary form since the Greek theatre," but
he was not referring to his own country's novels. O'Connor
enumerated "that great roll of names"—but did not include
any Irish names on it, expressing the conviction that, while
"the novel spread to America, Spain, and Italy, it is mainly
the product of England, France, and Russia" (1956, 3, 6).
Irish novelists of the mid- and late-nineteenth century have
had no book-length study devoted to them as a group, and
even when not suffering neglect or derision have attracted
no variety of critical attention. When James Kilroy points out
that "most of the criticism on William Carleton centers on
the mimetic aspect of his work" (1983, 13), he might just
as well be talking about all of the Irish novelists of this
period, for they have all been judged (and mostly judged as
wanting) according to how they portray Irish society. New
critical approaches to their work have not been forthcoming.
Yet these writers, as uneven as their novels written during
this difficult period are, do continue the development of the
Irish novel and make some new departures of their own
that, like those of their predecessors, can be linked to the
much better known and more kindly treated works of later
periods. Moreover, in individual works such as Carleton's
Fardorougha, the Miser (1839), Le Fanu's *The House by the
Churchyard* (1863), and Lawless's *Grania* (1892), novels worthy of consideration on their own merits were created.

William Carleton

William Carleton (1794–1869), the earliest and according
to most commentators the most important novelist of this
period, wrote some of the very best and also some of the

very worst fiction of his time. Both as an author and as a man Carleton was one of the most extreme and irregular personalities of his or any other period. Born into a large Gaelic peasant family in County Tyrone with a name anglicized from Ó Cearbhalláin or O'Carolan, a scholastically promising young man with large ambitions in spite of few natural advantages, Carleton at first intended to be a priest but became a "spoiled priest" after a brief visit to Maynooth Seminary. Then, with a copy of Le Sage's picaresque *Gil Blas* in his pocket—or at least so the story goes—Carleton wandered the countryside and eventually made his way to Dublin, where he converted to Protestantism and forged a new identity as a schoolmaster and contributor to Caesar Otway's *Christian Examiner.* When Otway advised Carleton to expose the follies of Irish Catholicism by writing as precisely as he could about the County Tyrone world he had left behind, he could not have known the dimensions or the future direction of the talent he was unleashing. Carleton's sketches for Otway soon grew into his *Traits and Stories of the Irish Peasantry* (1830, 1833). These stories impressed readers and critics much more as powerful portraits of Irish peasant life, more accurate in dialogue and detail than any previous Irish fiction, than as the anti-Catholic tracts they were originally supposed to be (an aspect that Carleton subsequently muted in revision and apologized for). Carleton discovered in the short story a form natural to him, since he had been bred within the native Irish oral storytelling tradition in Tyrone, and he did his best writing in the shorter form, crafting stories that are among the best in Irish literature, such as "Wildgoose Lodge" and "Going to Maynooth."

According to his own introduction to *Fardorougha, the Miser,* first published serially in the *Dublin University Magazine* in 1837–38, Carleton turned to the novel to prove that his memory was capable of more than only "a *short* story or so" (quoted in Lubbers 1985a, 169). *Fardorougha* (*fear dorcha* or "dark man" in Irish) is an effective novel because it incorporates vivid dialogue and strong characterizations in a story well focused on the protagonist's conflict between his destructive greed and his love for his son Connor. Like Griffin's *The Collegians, Fardorougha, the Miser* is a realistic

account in a rural setting of a character ruined by pride—
eschewing the frame of the "English visitor to Ireland" and
disquisitions on Irish politics in favor of a thoroughly Irish
story that says more about the lust for money, land, and
reputation than did the earlier textbook novels. Both novels
also contrast fatally flawed male protagonists with noble,
flawless women embodying authorial ideals of perfection—
Eily O'Connor in *The Collegians* and in the later novel both
Connor's future bride Una O'Brien and Fardorougha's wife,
significantly named Honor. Honor prophesies to Fardorougha,
"I wouldn't be surprised if the Almighty would punish your
guilty heart, by making the child he gave you, a curse,
instead of a blessin' " (27). The perfect woman, the voice of
conscience, became a well-worn character type throughout
later nineteenth-century Irish fiction.

Fardorougha is a "usurer" (105–06) and miser who nonetheless gains our sympathy, because Carleton treats his fatal
flaw more like a disease or mental illness than a willful evil;
he dies in madness at the end. One has to wonder if Carleton
presents Fardorougha's guilt over his unfaithfulness to his
own people so sympathetically and effectively partly because
he understood and in fact shared that kind of guilt. He
himself had abandoned his home, his religion, his culture
in order to achieve success and fame in Dublin. Chameleon-
like, Carleton shifted loyalties more than once out of ex-
pediency as much as a revision of his opinions—writing first
for the extremist Otway, then for the more moderate but
still Ascendancy *Dublin University Magazine*, then for the
strongly nationalist *Nation* in the mid-1840s, and eventually
for almost anyone who would pay him during his later years.
His was "the richest talent in nineteenth-century Ireland and
the most prodigally wasted" (Flanagan 1958, 255). Carleton
was often unscrupulous, as early as 1826 offering to demonstrate to English leaders a connection between terrorism
and the Catholic Emancipation movement. In 1843 he bitterly
attacked the editor of the *Dublin University Magazine*, Charles
Lever, as soon as he himself had jumped ship to the *Nation*,
and in the same year he offered only rather backhanded
praise even when he contributed an obituary on John Banim
to the *Nation* that was actually part of his campaign to have

Banim's government pension transferred to himself. That effort failed, and Carleton spent his last years wasting his talents in relative poverty. He never achieved his desire for the level of success of a Dickens, Thackeray, or Lever, and "all one has to do is compare the splendid forty-volume edition of Lever with the three-volume edition of Carleton's novels and tales which was crudely illustrated and printed in double columns on newsprint, published by Collier in 1882, to learn something about the sociology of literary taste and the publishing industry in [the] nineteenth century" (Cronin 1980, 8). Even at the height of his success, Carleton never earned more than £750 in a single year from his writing, and his books were often pirated by publishers (Morrison 1965, 224). Try as he might, he never fully lifted himself above the poverty in which he had begun. Later in his career even more than in his earlier years, Carleton must have appreciated Fardorougha's lust for money, his guilt, and his failure.

Carleton's novels made quite an impact but steadily declined in quality. After *Fardorougha*, *Valentine McClutchy* (1845b), *The Black Prophet* (1847), and *The Emigrants of Ahadarra* (1848a) are in that order his more interesting novels, while after the Great Hunger the artistic quality of his novels was no better than the depressed socioeconomic state of Ireland at the time. Written under the encouragement of Thomas Davis and the *Nation, Valentine McClutchy* is a bitter satire of the rural Irish economic way of life in which grasping middlemen oppressed poor laborers in the name of absentee landlords. Its tenor is suggested by the "humours" names assigned to its several villains: "McClutchy" or "Val the Vulture," the land agent or middleman in the tradition of Jason Quirk; Darby O'Drive, McClutchy's enforcer; Solomon McSlime, an attorney who mixes evangelism and a corrupt administration of the law; and the Reverend Phineas Lucre, a prosperous preacher, a kind of earlier-day Jerry Falwell. On the one hand, by adopting the mode of satire Carleton achieves a grim brand of humor and makes it clear that his is a polemical rather than a complex fiction: the demonic McClutchy is so evil that he evicts his own mother! On the other hand, his satire is more blatant and less artful than that of Swift.

The Black Prophet has been praised by many as Carleton's best novel, an estimation that clearly has more to do with sociology than art. Here was the case of a peasant novelist capturing vividly the suffering of the Great Hunger that was at its height in 1847 and "dedicating" his tale to the English prime minister, Lord John Russell. What more powerful polemical situation in Irish fiction could one ask for? Thomas Davis set the tone for future commentators by writing in 1845, "William Carleton is a peasant's son" (quoted in Flanagan 1958, 263). That apparently said all that needed to be said. Yeats and many others took up the very persistent celebration of Carleton as heroic peasant novelist. In the opening editorial of the *Carleton Newsletter* in 1970, Eileen Sullivan wrote that her publication would "not attempt to judge his literary output according to twentieth century diction and modern rules for story telling. Quite simply, we are striving for a meaningful dialogue about the voluminous output of an Irish peasant's son" (quoted in Kilroy 1976, 34).

But recognizing a "voluminous output" is not enough, not only in making critical judgments but also in seeking to understand the development of the Irish novel. Sullivan does emphasize elsewhere that it is unfortunate that "Carleton's works are too little known for the critic who uses structural analysis and the study of imagery; but both his short stories and novels can withstand this type of criticism. Moreover, his works can easily stand the probings of the mythic critic" (1970, 85). However, as in the case of the other novelists of this period, such varied approaches have not been applied to Carleton. Many have praised Carleton's novels, but one can empathize with Anthony Cronin's query in the *Irish Times* in 1974: "Does anyone read or re-read Carleton's novels nowadays, barring perhaps Mr. Benedict Kiely [who published a study of Carleton, *Poor Scholar*, in 1948] and a few students and academics?" (quoted in James O'Brien 1974, 6). This question is especially worth echoing after the sociologically interesting but aesthetically painful experience of reading *The Black Prophet*. It is true that it contains some marvellous dialogue as well as some gripping descriptions of famine based on the suffering Carleton had witnessed in his youth. No other nineteenth-century Irish writer wrote peasant dialogue better than Carleton, yet his awkward standard-English main narrative jars against the dialogue; Frank O'-Connor complained that for Carleton "there are not as many languages as there are people. There are only two languages—correct English and peasant English" (1967, 148). There are few better scenes in nineteenth-century Irish fiction than the one in which the prophesy-man and protagonist Donnel Dhu (or Black Donnel) foresees "famine-famine-famine! Doesn't the rottin' crops, the unhealthy air, and the green damp foretell it?" (1847, 20). It is significant that those who praise *The Black Prophet* usually point to scenes such as this rather than to the plot of the novel, which, as John Cronin in the fullest assessment of the novel admits, does not merely fail to support the book's theme but "positively undermines it . . . Carleton's boring twenty-year-old murder never acquires . . . sustaining significance" (1980, 92). The English prime minister and many of Carleton's other early readers must have been fairly confused: his preface promises political relevance but instead he delivers, as in the more focused *Fardorougha, the Miser* and *Valentine McClutchy*, the story of how a spotless heroine and noble young man achieve eventual happiness despite the worst efforts of a dark villain, Donnel Dhu in this case. From time to time Carleton remembers his political purpose and launches into lengthy digressions about absenteeism, bad English laws, and the like. But his Gothic tale and his political premise never fit together; the book lacks coherence.

As if aware of this failure, Carleton began his next novel, *The Emigrants of Ahadarra* (1848a), with the promise, "The work is not . . . a political one, nor encumbered with anything like a superabundance of mere political reflections. . . . I have not presumed to dictate to the legislator, nor to make suggestions to the mere politician" (v). He does not fully deliver on this promise, though. Telling the story of how the salutary McMahon family is pushed toward emigration, Carleton cannot help but "inquire into some of the causes that have occasioned it." He adds, "Let not our readers apprehend, however, that we are about to turn our fictitious narrative into a dissertation on political economy" (86)—and then proceeds to do just that for a few pages. As always, he makes use of a villain, the trickster Hycy Burke—who is forced to leave the country at the end in place of the McMahons. At the most painful point in Irish history, Carleton deserves credit for turning his attention to tales of starvation and emigration, themes later explored much more effectively in Liam O'Flaherty's *Famine*. Yet the disjointed *Black Prophet* and *Emigrants of Ahadarra* both fail as novels because of their lack of coherence in attempting to merge political polemic with the fictional plot and characters.

Carleton was a great storyteller but one leaves his novels, at least all of his later ones, with the feeling that for him the novel was a foreign form that he never fully understood or felt comfortable with. It is true that he did open up for the Irish novel materials that later, more fortunate writers would take up; for this reason Yeats and John Eglinton, looking for a prose model during the Literary Revival, inaccurately championed him as the first great Irish novelist. Perhaps most significantly of all for the future development of the Irish novel, Carleton wrote mostly for Irish publishers, and was proud of that fact, scorning those he saw as foreigners, such as Anna Hall, who had never been one of the peasants as he had. Writing for Irish publishers, he achieved fame but not fortune.[1]

Carleton's later career is best glossed in merciful brevity. After winning a small English pension and becoming disenchanted with the Young Irelanders who staged an abortive rebellion in 1848, he felt obliged to publish *The Tithe Proctor* (1848b), in which he went on the offensive against Irish nationalists and sought to expose Catholic militants who had attacked collectors of the Protestant tax in the 1830s. Throughout his career Carleton assailed those whom he saw as agrarian terrorists, as in his great story "Wildgoose Lodge," but in *The Tithe Proctor* he unfairly linked Daniel O'Connell to the perpetrators of violence. During the 1850s and 1860s Carleton's novels included ill-advised attempts at Edgeworthian Big House novels, such as *The Squanders of Castle Squander* (1852) and *The Black Baronet* (1857); at Gothicism, as in *The Evil Eye* (1860); and at historical fiction as an excuse for popular, lightweight romance, as in *Willy Reilly and His Dear Colleen Bawn* (1855) and *Redmond, Count O'Hanlon, the Irish Rapparee* (1862) (Cahalan 1983, 81–84). The poor young scholar among the hedgeschools became in the end a poor old novelist in the dingy post-Famine world of Dublin. Carleton's short stories are so good and he shows enough bright flashes of talent in his earlier novels that one can only wonder what he might have amounted to if he had been lucky enough to write under more favorable circumstances. He died of cancer of the tongue in 1869.

Anna Fielding Hall

The other writer to devote herself to fiction about the Irish peasantry during this period, Anna Fielding Hall (1800–81), had received Carleton's scorn because she was not a peasant herself—far from it. Having spent her youth in County Wexford, Hall went to London and in 1824 married Samuel Carter Hall, an influential editor who was responsible for the publication of many of her tales of Ireland. Like Lever and in contrast to Carleton, her books were comfortable commercial successes, were "charmingly illustrated by admired Victorian artists, were approved by reviewers, and went into edition after edition" (Baker 1936, 6:31). Her work invited comparison with Carleton's, especially since it began to appear in 1829, the same year that Carleton first went into print, and since like his it focused on the Irish peasantry. Hall explained that she sought in her stories to make the Irish peasantry "more justly appreciated, more rightly estimated, and more respected in England," while her strongly moralistic streak led her to be critical of what she saw as occasional laziness, intemperance, and recklessness among the peasantry (Sloan 1984, 18–19). Carleton angrily wrote, "Did she ever live with the people as I did? Did she ever dance and fight with them as I did? Did she ever get drunk with them as I did?" (Buckley 1974, 93). Carleton's dismissal of Hall as non-Irish was taken up by others, and her books were popular in England but not in Ireland (Lubbers 1985a, 138). Most critics have either echoed Carleton's sentiments

or ignored Hall's works altogether. James Newcomer, however, stresses that Hall shared with Edgeworth and Owenson
"an honest concern for the welfare of Ireland," insisting that
"it is critical, jingoist bosh that would deny them true insight
into Irish character and thinking," and claiming that her
novel *The Whiteboy* is relevant to an understanding of the
Northern Ireland crisis today (1983, 113, 114, 118–19). One
has to agree that Hall was interested in countering anti-Irish
sectarianism in both England and Ireland. Her perspective
on native Irish culture may have been somewhat distant, but
her point of view was progressive; when not engaged in
writing her books, she was involved in philanthropic work
and proselytizing for women's rights.

The Whiteboy (1845) appeared in that year when seemingly
almost every Irish novelist was out to publish a nationalist,
pro-Irish novel, at the height of the popularity of Young
Ireland and, sadly, on the eve of the Great Hunger. Hall
was no exception, showing that she no longer shied away
from the national cause in favor of regionalism as she had
in her Wexford tales, the two volumes of *Sketches of Irish
Character*. In this novel she sends her hero, Edward Spencer,
to Ireland on a steamship to look after his estate in County
Cork. On board he is given a quick course in Irish politics
and culture by two veterans of the country, Lady Mary
O'Brien, who emphasizes that there are really two separate
cultures in Ireland, and Dean Graves, who cautions him that
"all knowledge of Ireland, acquired by hearsay, leads to
dreams" (1:26). It is interesting to hypothesize that Hall may
have selected her hero's name as a somewhat ironic echo
of that famous imperialist chronicler of Ireland, Edmund
Spenser, and certainly her positioning of him on board a
steamship is a fitting metaphorical extension of the old
Edgeworthian visitor-to-Ireland perspective.

Hall's story of this idealistic landlord is in many ways
Edgeworthian. *The Whiteboy* has been compared to Edgeworth's *Ennui*, with the difference that Hall's hero is from
the outset eager to get to Ireland and reform the situation;
he doesn't need to be converted, having already devoured
books about Ireland in order to prepare himself for his
journey. Furthermore, it is significant that his trip is sped

along by steamship; Hall suggests that such modern innovations will help shorten the gap between England and
Ireland, alleviate absenteeism, and generally help the English
and Irish to understand each other better. Finally, Hall up-
dates Edgeworth by examining an Irish rebel, the Whiteboy
Lawrence Macarthy, which Edgeworth feared to do. Like
John Banim in *John Doe* and Carleton in *Rody the Rover* (also
published in 1845), Hall portrays her rebel as vengeful and
lacking any true national consciousness. Examining Macarthy
through Spencer's eyes, Hall does not agree with the rebel,
but seeks to understand him. Macarthy is a contrast to his
kind-hearted half-sister Ellen Macdonnel, who has an education that Macarthy lacks and predictably falls in love with
Spencer and marries him at the end. Hall thereby meta-
phorically joins a male, English John Bull to female Ireland
just as Edgeworth, Owenson, and the Banims had done in
earlier novels.

Hall assures her readers at the end that "the people are
now politically as well as morally exalted—their onward
strides are becoming rapid as firm, firm as rapid; and though
for a time they may be disturbed and distressed, though
blood may even be spilt—yet, in the end, Ireland will become
prosperous" (2:301). Concerning her hero, H. R. Krans commented that "the task of taming the savage Whiteboy, and
reforming the character, manners, and customs of the wild
Irish peasant, he performs with a celerity and a measure of
success more often obtained in didactic novels than in the
real world" (1903, 119). Coming as it did on the eve of the
Great Hunger, Hall's optimistic prediction was pathetically
inaccurate.

Samuel Lover

Along with the pointedly polemical Carleton and the mod-
erately didactic Hall, there emerged two novelists who, like
Hall, were attacked by the nationalists as non-Irish, Ascendancy writers but who cultivated a sense of humor that
Hall lacked: Samuel Lover (1797–1868) and Charles Lever
(1806–72). These two writers shared similar backgrounds,
humorous attitudes, considerable popularity, and almost a

surname. Yet as much as "Lover and Lever" have been identified as a pair, they were quite different kinds of writers whose writings reflect quite different achievements. They emerged on the literary scene at around the same time. Both writers responded to the English demand for stage-Irish humor, but Lever is much the better writer, and his many novels reflect a process of development lacking in Lover's works.

A sense of the attitudes of English readers is crucial to an understanding of Lover's novels, for more than any other Irish novelist he sought to meet the English demand for stage-Irish characters. When in 1831 the *Edinburgh Review* evaluated the Irish novel from Edgeworth to Griffin, asserting that English readers had become more informed about the Irish than they had been at the beginning of the century, this claim was true of only a small minority, for much ignorance remained. Worse, a backlash in attitude occurred during the 1830s and 1840s, most clearly reflected in the cartoon caricatures of the Irish in the English magazine *Punch,* where drawings of playful "Paddy" were replaced by those of dagger-bearing, simian monsters (Lubbers 1985a, 184–85). Undoubtedly this nastier treatment of the Irish in British periodicals reflected English fears, conscious or unconscious, about Catholic Emancipation, the Repeal movement, Young Ireland, rural rebels, and in general the growth of Irish nationalism. When in his novels Lover offered comic relief to these fears and gratified English attitudes about the Irish, he quickly became very popular in England but unpopular with the Irish nationalist press. Even though the picture of Ireland in Lover's books was a long way from Yeats's view, the influential Yeats was surprisingly tolerant of Lover— asserting that Lover "had a good deal more poetry in him than Lever" while his was "the glamour of distance"— perhaps because Lover's Dublin Ascendancy background, interest in painting and folklore, and feudal view of Ireland were so similar to his own. Yeats admitted that "his books are put together in a haphazard kind of way—without beginning, middle, or end" (1891, 304).

A positive if insubstantial portrait of Ireland, *Rory O'More* (1837) began as a ballad and was then rewritten as a novel and ultimately a play. Lover subtitled the novel *A National Romance* and in it sought to demonstrate to English readers that any Irish excesses during the 1798 rebellion were the fault of a few fanatics and that many idealists were involved in the nationalist movement. Like Yeats, Lover found his heroes in the aristocracy and in the peasantry: in Horace de Lacy, who comes to Ireland as a scout for the famous rebel leader Wolfe Tone and falls in love with Rory's sister Mary, overcoming his class prejudice against her rather than being ruined by it like Griffin's Hardress Cregan; and Rory, who travels to France with de Lacy during the rebellion and then leaves for America at the end with his new wife Kathleen Regan and with Horace and Mary. The escapist tenor of this novel, even though its purported subject was the bloodiest rebellion in modern Irish history, is obvious in its geography: Lover avoids the rebellion altogether by removing his heroes to France, since he felt that the rebellion was "too fearful . . . for mortal pen to be trusted with" (quoted in Sloan 1982, 34). Living in London since 1835, he chose to send them into exile at the end to reflect his own attitude that there was nothing left to be done in Ireland.

As a witty, clever survivor, Rory O'More is not really a true stage-Irishman at all. As a "national romance" this novel does not fit the mode created by Lover in his other Irish novel, by far his most famous, *Handy Andy* (1842), which fixed the very popular, very negative reputation that has been attached to its author ever since then. Always receiving the most attention is the character of Andy, which Yeats claimed "created the stage Irishman" (quoted in Lubbers 1985a, 179) but really only perpetuated this very old type. This is made clear from the opening sentence: "Andy Rooney was a fellow who had the most singularly ingenious knack of doing everything the wrong way" (3). This episodic novel is full of ludicrous exchanges, one example of which will suffice:

Andy presented himself at the counter, and said, "I want a letther, sir, if you plaze."
"And who do you want it for?" said the postmaster, in a tone which Andy considered an aggression upon the sacredness of

private life: so Andy thought the coolest contempt he could throw upon the prying impertinence of the postmaster was to repeat his question.

"I want a letther, sir, if you plaze?"

"And who do you want it for?" repeated the postmaster.

"What's that to you?" said Andy.

The postmaster, laughing at his simplicity, told him he could not tell what letter to give him unless he told him the direction.

"The directions I got was to get a letther here,—that's the directions."

"Who gave you those directions?"

"The masther."

"And who's your master?"

"What consarn is that a' yours?"

"Why, you stupid rascal! if you don't tell me his name, how can I give you a letter?"

"You could give it if you liked; but you're fond of axin' impidint questions, bekaze you think I'm simple."

"Go along out o' this! Your master must be as great a goose as yourself, to send such a messenger."

"Bad luck to your impidince!" said Andy; "is it Squire Egan you dar to say goose to?" (10)

In spite of his idiocy Andy becomes a hero, finally getting married, becoming an aristocrat, and sitting down to dinner with the gentleman-poet Edward O'Connor, who like Horace de Lacy in *Rory O'More* serves as a type of romanticized nobility. *Handy Andy* is also full of the worst exploits of degenerate landlords, especially O'Grady of "Nick or Nothing Hall," but most commentators remember only stage-Irish Andy, not the Ascendancy characters lampooned much more harshly by Lover. Like Andy, Lover's peasant characters in general are bathed in a nostalgic innocence born of the fact that Lover's acquaintance with peasants was limited to boyhood summer vacations.

Even more suggestive about the form of the Irish novel than any of this novel's characters is the structure of *Handy Andy*—or rather its lack of structure. *Handy Andy* first began to appear in the *Bentley Miscellany*, edited by Charles Dickens, and was then expanded, as Lover explains to his "kind reader" in his opening notice: "Much revision and the introduction of fresh matter has taken place, with a view to the development of story and character necessary to a *sustained* work; for the first paper of Handy Andy was written without any intention of continuation, and required the amendments and additions I have mentioned" (1842, n.p.). At the end he exclaims, "Kind reader! the shortening space we have prescribed to our volume, warns us we must draw our story to an end" (380). His parting "respectful adieu till next year" (380) reinforces the sense that Lover saw Andy's tale as capable of indefinite continuation. He conceived his "novel," in other words, as formless, as simply a collection of meandering tales. At one point he inserts as chapter 23 "The Marvellous Legend of Tom Connor's Cat," a six-page literary folktale that has nothing in particular to do with the book's main "plot." Just as the reactionary, anti-Irish attitudes on the part of English readers and publishers influenced what an author like Lover felt he could write about, Victorian serial publishing offered to Irish novelists such as Carleton, Lover, and Lever, who had very limited readerships in Ireland, encouragement to write thoroughly episodic tales, thereby reinforcing an already existing Irish predilection.

Charles Lever

The beginnings of Charles Lever's career as a novelist point even more clearly to this episodic, serial impulse. He sent his first sketches to the *Dublin University Magazine* in 1836 with a note that indicated that he had no intention of writing a novel: "I send you Article No. 1 of a series which will include scenes and stories at home and abroad,—some tragic, others (as in the present case) ludicrous. I have had an invitation from Colburn to furnish a two or three volume affair, but I am not in the vein for anything longer or more continuous than magazine work at present" (quoted in Lubbers 1985a, 196). Nonetheless, always game for an adventure and attracted by success, Lever was convinced by publishers—who were "wonderful fellows" altogether, he wrote—to expand his entertaining fictions, and he quickly learned that magazine-writing and novel-writing could proceed hand in glove. He wrote his first novel, *The Confessions of Harry*

Lorrequer (1839), serially for the *Dublin University Magazine* and was encouraged by its editors to lengthen its conclusion. The preface to his second, most popular novel, *Charles O'Malley, the Irish Dragoon* (1841), made no bones at all about his manner of writing: "The success of *Harry Lorrequer* was the reason for writing *Charles O'Malley.* . . . The ease with which I strung my stories together—and in reality the *Confessions of Harry Lorrequer* are little other than a note-book of absurd and laughable incidents—led me to believe that I could draw on this vein of composition without any limit whatever" (1:xi). He added that when asked to write such a novel, "I was ready to reply, *not one, but fifty.* Do not mistake me and suppose that any overweening confidence in my literary powers would have embolded me to make this reply; my whole strength lay in the fact that I could not recognize anything like literary effort in the matter. If the world would only condescend to read that which I wrote precisely as I was in the habit of talking, nothing could be easier than for me to occupy them" (1:xiii). Lever did not manage fifty novels, but nearly that many—his collected works run to thirty-seven volumes. In contrast to the always struggling Carleton, Lever's "accumulated earnings from his works were over fifty thousand pounds" (Buckley 1974, 131).

As we can see, Lever was refreshingly self-critical and unpretentious about his work—more so than many novelists of his era whose works were far inferior to his. This was not merely a disarming pose that Lever adopted publicly in his prefaces to his readers, but an attitude that he confessed privately to his fellow writers as well. He wrote to Maria Edgeworth in 1846, "I have no constructiveness in my head; the most I am capable of is the portraiture of certain characters with more or less of contrast of 'relief' between them. These once formed, I put them *en scène,* to die out in an early chapter when their vitality is weak—if stronger, to survive to the end of the volume" (quoted in Buckley 1974, 130). Lever rightly points here to the basis of his novels in character and anecdote more than in plot, as was also true of most Irish novelists writing in a country where the oral storytelling heritage was much stronger than that of the traditional novel. At the end of *Charles O'Malley* Lever apologized for his "blunders" and wryly added, "My publisher, excellent man, has a kind of pride about printing in Ireland, and he thinks the blunders, like the green cover of the volume, give the thing a national look" (2:496). No doubt Lever intended this as a typically self-deprecating remark, but we can also read it as pointing to the developing tradition within the Irish novel of deliberately breaking novelistic conventions and confounding traditional form. In this sense, the novels of Lever and many of his Irish contemporaries look ahead to *Ulysses* and other celebrated, deliberate "blunders" in the twentieth century.

Lever was very popular in England, where he was known as "Dr. Quicksilver," "Harry Rollicker," "the Lord of romantic misrule," and the friend of Dickens, Thackeray, and Trollope. Yet in Ireland he was condemned from the beginning of his career and has been either belittled or neglected ever since then, for the same reason that the English loved him: he made fun of Irishmen. The vitriolic Carleton led the attack, writing in the *Nation* in 1843 that Lever was a plagiarist, unpatriotic, and totally lacking in taste, offering "disgusting and debasing caricatures of Irish life and feeling, as the characteristics of our country." Carleton implied in 1836 that Lever had been guilty of plagiarism in his story "The Black Mask," but the story had actually been pirated by a literary agent. Although he had published considerably in the *Dublin University Magazine*, which ran *Fardorougha, the Miser* serially, Carleton did not contribute a single story to the magazine during Lever's editorship, between 1842 and 1845 (Meredith 1972, 11–12). Lever remained generous to Carleton in reviews and letters, and Carleton's attack on him in 1843 may have been one of several factors that influenced Lever to write more nationalist, serious novels after that date.

As in the cases of Hall, Le Fanu, and Carleton himself, 1845, the year of the Great Hunger, marked a transition in Lever's work, with the publication of *The O'Donoghue* and *St. Patrick's Eve*, both of which took English policies to task and presented more somber portraits of Ireland. The better of these was *St. Patrick's Eve*, describing the cholera epidemic in County Clare in 1832, which Lever had witnessed during his term of service as a doctor working in the poor districts.

Many of his later novels, particularly *The Martins of Cro Martin* (1856) and *Lord Kilgobbin* (1872), are as nationalistic as anything Carleton ever wrote, and even though he outlived Carleton by only three years, Lever continued to develop and prosper as a writer fully two decades past when Carleton had burnt himself out. He reacted in his novels to post-Famine Ireland while Carleton remained frozen in pre-Famine Ireland and romanticized a mythical past in his later, forgettable books. Lever's style is fluent and entertaining, while many of Carleton's novels are very hard going. Yet Yeats and most other influential Irish critics accepted and perpetuated the label with which Carleton had branded Lever in 1843, reading "no further than *Harry Lorrequer* and *Charles O'Malley*. They got hold of the wrong Lever" (Jeffares 1980, 104). Only very recently have scholars begun to revise this view of Lever, and still to date no critical book on this most prolific of all nineteenth-century Irish novelists has appeared. Lever's wild sense of humor seems out of place in a nineteenth-century literary Ireland where nationalist piety was a weightier force than art. Yet in his life and work he prefigures Joyce, Flann O'Brien, Samuel Beckett, and other twentieth-century Irish writers who, within a very different modernist and post-modernist ethos, have been celebrated for many of the same reasons for which Lever was condemned by Irish nationalists in the nineteenth century.

Even the social label attached to Lever was not quite accurate. He was derided as an Ascendancy writer, but more precisely he was, like Lover, from the Dublin upper-middle class, and after graduating from Trinity College he always earned his living, first as a doctor and then as a novelist. At the same time, his was not the moralism of the middle-class Griffin or the Banims or the upper-class Edgeworth, all of whose basic attitudes to life were really quite similar to each other and different from that of the racy Lever. Lever's life included adventures even wilder than anything contained in the romantic imagination of Sydney Owenson. After graduating from Trinity in 1827, for example, the story has it that Lever set off for Canada, was held captive by a native American tribe, was rescued by a squaw with whom he fell in love, walked the streets of Québec in moccasins and feathers, and returned to Dublin with a canoe that he often used in the Grand Canal. After his early success as a writer in Dublin, he spent the rest of his life after 1846 in voluntary exile on the Continent, living most of his later years in Trieste, where he was appointed British Consul by Lord Derby with the explanation, "Here are £600 a year to do nothing; and you, Lever, are the very man to do it" (quoted in Krans 1903, 64). As Anthony Cronin writes, "One hopes that James Joyce, who went into voluntary exile in the same city, may have made a pilgrimage or two to his grave. They had, strange to say, quite a lot in common: an unorthodox patriotism; a good deal of contempt for the plot-making process; and, above all, of course, a sense of humour" (1982, 60). Like Joyce, Lever continued while in exile to write about Ireland, his view of his native country mellowing and his portraits of Irish characters becoming more positive.

Among the few recent critical attempts to do justice to Lever's later, more serious novels, there continues a tendency to discount his earlier, light-hearted ones. In the midst of the pervasive didacticism of the nineteenth-century Irish novel, however, Lever's early books are a comic breath of fresh air. Unlike Lover, he focuses on his own class by selecting English-born students and soldiers as his comic protagonists, drawing his humor from the middle and upper classes rather than from a distantly perceived peasantry as in Lover. Thus, as in the later "Irish R.M." stories of Somerville and Ross, Lever's novels exemplify the Ascendancy laughing at itself instead of at the peasantry and, rather than perpetuating the stage-Irishman, they create instead a "stage Anglo-Irishman" (Anthony Cronin 1982, 51). His main characters, a gang of Rackrents out for a good time, are always slick talkers who embody Lever's brand of spontaneous wit. When Harry Lorrequer invents a scenario for his listeners, for example, his method is very much like that of his creator in writing his novels: "Not a sound was heard as I lifted the bumper to my lips; all were breathless in their wound-up anxiety to hear of their countryman who had been selected by Picton— for what, too, they knew not yet, and, indeed, at this instant I did not know myself, and nearly laughed outright, for the two of ours who had remained at the table had so well

employed their interval of ease as to become very pleasantly
drunk, and were listening to my confounded story with all
the gravity and seriousness in the world" (1:15). In first-
person narratives, Lever allows Lorrequer and Charles
O'Malley to hold forth, taking listener and reader wherever
wit and imagination lead. Lever was critically consigned to
the Ascendancy, but truly his narrative sense is not essentially
different from the oral storyteller usually found among the
peasantry. Like the *seanchaí* of Irish folklore, Lever has his
sources and inspirations—particularly stories of Irish military
and student life, most especially those of his friend W. H.
Maxwell, whose *Stories of Waterloo* (1829) and *Wild Sports of
the West* (1832) had been very popular (Lubbers 1985a, 198).

   Charles O'Malley (1841), which moves from Trinity College
to the Napoleonic Wars to the west of Ireland, contains
Lever's most hilarious scenes. The opening Trinity College
chapters look ahead to Flann O'Brien's *At Swim-Two-Birds*
and J. P. Donleavy's *The Ginger Man*. These chapters are
dominated by O'Malley's roommate Frank Webber, who tells
stories to his professor about the dean which he asks him
to repeat to no one "except to your most intimate friends"
(1:111); and by O'Malley's servant Mickey Free, who baits
the parsimonious provost on the college steps with a coin
tied to a string (1:132–33). The funniest scene in any nineteenth-century Irish novel, an episode of sheer absurdity as
well as a bizarre commentary on the power of Irish patriotism,
comes when Webber convinces a crowd in Grafton Street
that a fugitive Irish rebel is trapped beneath a sewer grating,
and having incited them to dig up the street in order to free
the rebel, nonchalantly makes his way back to the college
(1:114–16). Lever proves in memorable scenes such as these
that one could abandon, not only the direct presentation of
Irish history and politics, but also the persistent attempt to
show the "Irish character" in the best light, and still write
a good Irish novel. He thus moves a step beyond Griffin,
who in *The Collegians* had departed from overt politics and
history but not from the portraiture of a flawless Irish character, in Kyrle Daly. Charles O'Malley cares little either for
upright moral conduct in the conventional sense or for the
cause of Ireland.

The chief criticism of Lever that still remains is that he was too obliging of nineteenth-century publishers and readers and not nearly demanding enough of his own considerable talent. Had he combined his irreverence for conventional novelistic form with a more careful devotion to writing and rewriting, he would have been a more important novelist than he was. In short, he wrote too much without revising: "The very number and length of his works seems an affront to the Twentieth Century ideal of conciseness" (Buckley 1974, 129). A full account of his many later novels awaits the much needed critical book on Lever that has not yet appeared.

Here, only the barest outline of his later development can be indicated by pointing to the two novels that are the best of his later, patriotic period. *The Martins of Cro Martin* (1856) suggests that Lever had repented the days of *Charles O'Malley* and his own picaresque youth. Its heroine is Mary Martin, modelled on Lever's friend Maria Edgeworth; she insists on taking care of the peasants on her family estate even after her elders sell their properties. Both the protagonist and the form of this Big House novel are based on those of Edgeworth. Lever draws on his experiences with the Clare cholera victims in describing Mary's efforts in County Galway in the 1830s, and utilizes his knowledge of Trinity College life in a serious vein this time, narrating the rivalry between earnest Joe Nelligan and unscrupulous Jack Massingbred—a contrast that recalls Kyrle Daly and Hardress Cregan in *The Collegians* but that is more balanced. A number of experiences—the cholera epidemic, the criticisms by Carleton and others, the Great Hunger and the course of Irish politics afterwards, his own mellowing in exile—had influenced Lever to write more somber novels.

Having tried to prove in *The Martins of Cro Martin* and several other novels that he too could be a patriot, in his last novel, *Lord Kilgobbin* (1872), Lever increased his nationalistic emphasis and also attempted a carefully plotted novel, as if to prove that he could write one. Writing after his wife's death and during his own last year, Lever is as serious here as he was comic in the 1840s. Half-Irish and half-Greek, the orphaned Nina Kostalergi comes from the Continent to live with her relatives at the home of the kind-hearted

Mathew Kearney, who is regarded as the true "Lord Kilgobbin" by the peasants and whose son Richard wants to
rackrent the tenants in order to support his Trinity College
life-style. The beautiful Nina rejects the crafty politicians who
woo her, including the familiar trickster type Joe Atlee, in
favor of the good Fenian rebel Dan Donogan, running off
with him to America at the end. Politically, this novel shows
just how far Lever had moved from his Ascendancy stereotype, his opposition to British policies deepening enough
to allow himself to make a Fenian his hero; psychologically,
Nina is Lever's romantic projection, the Continental exile
returned to Ireland, loved by its people, won over to Irish
patriotism, and removed to an idyllic New World. Like Mary
Martin, Nina is presented not as a pale heroine but as a
forceful, self-sacrificing woman (with *dark* hair in this case).
Lever's attention to these two independent-minded female
protagonists deserves further study, as does every aspect of
the career of this much maligned, much misunderstood, very
neglected, and quite gifted novelist.

Sheridan Le Fanu

Lever dedicated his novel *Luttrell of Aran* (1865) to Sheridan
Le Fanu (1814–73), who was by then editor as well as
publisher of the *Dublin University Magazine*, which Lever
had edited earlier. Like Lever, Le Fanu had been born in
Dublin, graduated from Trinity College, and came to writing
and editing after planning another career (law, in Le Fanu's
case). Both writers were more popular in England than in
Ireland—for the English enjoyed Le Fanu's Gothic tales almost as much as they had guffawed over Lever's comic
novels. We can thus see many similarities between these two
writers. However, their personalities and therefore the tenor
of their writing were utterly different: while Lever remained
essentially good-hearted and optimistic, Le Fanu was shadowy and pessimistic. He had adopted this point of view
early in life, when his father, an Anglican minister, had
moved the family from cosmopolitan Dublin to backward
Abington, County Limerick, where they were met by the
hostility of the peasantry to their church at the height of

the "Tithe Wars," waged against the forced tax exacted from Catholics to support the Anglican Church in Ireland. Years later, Le Fanu's best Irish novel, *The House by the Churchyard* (1863), was nostalgically set in eighteenth-century Chapelizod, with Le Fanu's narrator grimly reminding his readers that all of the novel's characters are now dead and the pleasant old town much changed.

In his shifting, somewhat confused political allegiances, Le Fanu's career is similar to that of William Carleton, with Le Fanu never able to overcome an Ascendancy conservatism learned in youth and Carleton always a spoiled priest and angry peasant. Both wrote for reactionary as well as nationalist periodicals at one time or another, responding to the demands of a variety of publishers (Cahalan 1983, 69). Le Fanu went to Trinity College with the fear and hatred of the peasantry that he had learned in Abington very firmly ingrained in him, writing home that "I intend speaking on every occasion at the Historical Society, of course in a favourably conservative strain, and it is no small consolation to me to think that while I am abusing the *Pisantry* in Dublin city, my brother may be shooting them in the country" (quoted in McCormack 1980, 50). Yet at the same time his mother was a great admirer of the 1798 rebel Lord Edward Fitzgerald, proudly keeping with her Fitzgerald's dagger that she had acquired, and the young Le Fanu romanticized the cause of Irish nationalism—as long as it involved the nobility and was safely confined to the past. His first two novels, *The Cock and Anchor* (1845) and *The Fortunes of Colonel Torlogh O'Brien* (1847), celebrated the Irish nationalism of the period of the Battle of the Boyne and the early eighteenth century, in deliberate imitation of Sir Walter Scott and especially John Banim's *The Boyne Water*. In that pivotal year of 1845, Le Fanu joined a committee organized by Gavan Duffy, the Young Ireland politician, to raise money for Banim's widow— a committee that included both Carleton and Lever, linked only by mutual respect for Banim. Duffy encouraged him to write *Torlogh O'Brien*, published by James McGlashan at the height of Young Ireland's popularity. Le Fanu thus toyed with Irish nationalism, but his basic attitudes are betrayed in *Torlogh O'Brien*, wherein the upper-class Catholic hero has to defeat the evil lower-class Catholic villain in order to marry into the Protestant Ascendancy at the end. In both of his first two novels, Le Fanu tells the story of how a Catholic hero proves himself in order to earn a place via marriage in the Ascendancy, portrayed as the proper place of any true Irishman, therein mythically merging the old Gaelic aristocracy and the post-Cromwellian Protestant Ascendancy (Cahalan 1983, 71–77).

Also contained in *Torlogh O'Brien* are the beginnings of the Gothic strain in his writing that would grow and make Le Fanu's name later, an element introduced in grisly scenes foreign to previous Irish historical novels. The villain Miles Garret receives his "just deserts" at the end, plunging over a "ghastly" cliff, his "skull . . . shattered like a gourd" (342), his corpse found later by wandering children. Le Fanu— who became the master of the ghost story, the author of stories set in England, *In a Glass Darkly*, and the similarly English novels *Uncle Silas* and *Wylder's Hand*, and the rival of Wilkie Collins—has been examined critically almost entirely within the context of English Gothicism (Kilroy 1983, 17). Fortunately, however, for an understanding of his Irish context—and after all, Le Fanu did live his entire life in Ireland—he has also recently been the subject of the best critical book on any single nineteenth-century Irish author: W. J. McCormack's *Sheridan Le Fanu and Victorian Ireland* (1980). In this probing psychological as well as political and literary study of Le Fanu's career, McCormack shows that Le Fanu's shadowy Gothicism was the result of his defensive view of Irish history and politics as well as his own personal failure and pessimism. After the short-lived Young Ireland rebellion of 1848, whose "socialist" leader John Mitchel was condemned by Le Fanu in the pages of the *Dublin University Magazine*, he rejected Irish nationalism and reasserted his conservatism, seeking but then passing up a Tory nomination for Parliament in 1852 before retreating altogether from politics. After his wife's death in 1858, he turned increasingly to Gothicism both in his fiction and in his life, surfacing to walk the streets only late at night in Dublin, where he became known as the "invisible Prince" (McCormack 1980, 197). He was very similar in his reclusive life-style and outsider status to his fellow Irish Huguenot and Gothicist, Charles Maturin.

During the 1850s Le Fanu published only one book (*Ghost Stories and Tales of Mystery*, 1851), but in 1861 he bought the *Dublin University Magazine*, became its editor, and wrote and serialized nine novels, an average of one per year, until he sold the magazine in 1869—and "as the financial demands of his journal kept dictating one novel after the next during this decade, Le Fanu's writing became progressively weaker, the plots looser, the characters thinner—and even the language finally lapsed into cliche" (Hall 1986, 61). His reputation as an Irish novelist has to rest on the first of these novels, *The House by the Churchyard* (1863), which like *Finnegans Wake* is set in Chapelizod, portrays the River Liffey as a nymph "always changing yet still the same," and even suggests in chapter 24 that life is a dream (Moynahan 1984, 12). Not surprisingly, Joyce had Frank Budgen help him incorporate part of this novel in *Finnegans Wake* and even cited it directly as "de oud huis bij de kerkegaard" (quoted in Harrington 1979, 50).

More germane to the development of the Irish novel as a whole than the specific uses of *The House by the Churchyard* in *Finnegans Wake* that have been noted by Joyceans is the overall form (or formlessness) of this novel. The form of *The House by the Churchyard* is central to the Irish novel in both the generic and structural senses. As clearly in its title as in Edgeworth's *Castle Rackrent*, Lever's *The Martins of Cro Martin*, and Edith Somerville's *The Big House of Inver* (1925), *The House by the Churchyard* is a Big House novel. In it Le Fanu charges his setting with Gothicism and adds a psychological realm to the political one introduced by Edgeworth, thus extending the possibilities of the Big House novel, that most popular and enduring subgenre within the Irish novel except for the Irish historical novel. More familiar is the way in which *The House by the Churchyard* "seems thoroughly shapeless when measured by the narrative conventions of the usual 19th-century novel. The features of Le Fanu's tale, all of which lay claim to his interests, resist any hierarchical ordering and, thus, create a fictional technique that later drew Joyce's attention to this work" (Hall 1986, 57). As we have

already seen, Joyce might well have been drawn to many a
nineteenth-century Irish novel in this regard.

Like Lever, Le Fanu immediately introduces a storyteller
of the Ascendancy, Charles de Cresseron (the name of one
of his Huguenot ancestors), who emphasizes the oral nature
of his tale: "We are going to talk, if you please in the ensuing
chapters of what was going on in Chapelizod about a hundred
years ago" (1:1). His tale is as full of villainous murders and
even more baroque in its mystery than other Gothic novels,
including Le Fanu's own subsequent English ones; what
distinguishes it from the others is that here Le Fanu "is
interested in the influence which mystery and evil have upon
a community, rather than upon a few individuals," and that
"there are many more 'pieces' in terms of characters and
narrative threads to *The House by the Churchyard* than there
are to a Collins novel" or other English Gothic novels (Gates
1984, 68).

True to the Irish novel, Le Fanu interweaves many plots
and many characters in a collage of stories rather than one
single big story: the quest of the melancholy Mervyn to clear
his name, make a fortune, and satisfy romance; the mysterious disappearance and reappearance of Charles Nutter;
the guilt and eventual apprehension of the murderer Charles
Archer (alias Paul Dangerfield); and several other smaller but
equally vivid plots or subplots. It is noteworthy, incidentally,
that the villain Archer/Dangerfield is by occupation Lord
Castlemallard's English agent—a rent-collector and middleman as villain, faithful to this convention evident in many
Irish novels. Along with all of the plots and subplots come
numerous stories and anecdotes about the House, a Gothic
place that embodies an old, mysterious Chapelizod. "I hope
the reader will pardon me for loitering so long in the Tiled
House, but this sort of lore has always had a charm for me;
and people, you know, especially old people, will talk of
what most interests themselves, too often forgetting that
others may have had more than enough of it" (1:131).
Politically and psychologically, the House is an emblem of
the decadence and certain demise of the Ascendancy in
Ireland as well as of Le Fanu himself.

Like Joyce memorializing Dublin in *Ulysses,* Le Fanu was adamant about the specificity and authenticity of his Irish setting in *The House by the Churchyard:* "I don't apologize to my readers, English-born and bred, for assuming them to be acquainted with the chief features of the Phoenix Park, near Dublin. Irish scenery is now as accessible as Welsh. Let them study . . ." (1:155). Such an expectation did not promise popularity in 1863. *The House by the Churchyard* sold only a few hundred copies, attracting few readers in England and Ireland, and when Le Fanu's next London publisher, Richard Bentley, demanded from him a three-volume "story of an English subject and in modern times," Le Fanu was only too willing to oblige him with *Uncle Silas* (1864), his most popular novel, in which he expanded on an earlier Irish story he had written. This is an English mystery novel complete with a tighter plot and a female protagonist true to the conventions of the 1860s Victorian thriller. As Wayne Hall writes, it is "a sensationalist novel with elements of Irishness," whereas *The House by the Churchyard* is "an Irish novel with elements of sensationalism." Even *Uncle Silas* sold only 847 copies, and Le Fanu's "disappointing sales and reviews fed his inherently pessimistic view of the world" as well as his desperation to churn out an English bestseller (Hall 1986, 68–70). His subsequent English novels were disappointing from almost every point of view, as Le Fanu wrote poorly in desperate search of a profit during the same years in the 1860s when Carleton was doing likewise. Le Fanu would have been remembered in literary history only in passing as author of *Uncle Silas* had he not fashioned the ghost stories that proved to be so influential on Bram Stoker and other later Gothicists. Yet *The House by the Churchyard* remains in many ways his most interesting and elaborate work, and one can only wonder what he might have accomplished had there existed the market for further Irish works such as this, in which Le Fanu wrote about what he knew best instead of selling out to an English readership that he could not understand as well as Wilkie Collins. This pathetic period of Irish book publishing, with only three publishers on the scene in Dublin—William Curry, James McGlashan, and James Duffy—smothered or ruined such promising talents as Le Fanu and Carleton, who managed memorable work in spite of it all but who might have become much greater novelists had more favorable conditions existed.

Popular Late Nineteenth-Century Novels and Charles Kickham's *Knocknagow*

Carleton's prediction that after his death there would be "a lull, an obscurity of perhaps half a century" in the Irish novel seems fairly accurate when considering the Irish novel in the later decades of the nineteenth century. As late as 1922 Ernest Boyd, celebrating the achievements of Yeats and Synge and their compatriots in *Ireland's Literary Renaissance*, treated the novel and fiction in general as the "low point" of the Revival, complaining of "the absence of good prose fiction" (374). The years between the death of Lover (1868), Carleton (1869), Lever (1872), and Le Fanu (1873) and the arrival of Somerville and Ross and George Moore toward the end of the century are the thinnest ones of all in the history of the Irish novel, in terms of quality. Not that no novels were being published: to the contrary, Irish novels increased in number during these years, with a number of minor writers responding to the successful example of the likes of Griffin, Carleton, and Lever. It is simply that most of these novels are not very good. Three subgenres, often overlapping, that had proven their popularity and adaptability were particularly prominent: historical novels, Big House novels, and regional or local color novels. There appeared numerous historical novels by names such as James Murphy, M. McDonnell Bodkin, L. MacManus, D. P. Conyngham, Randal McDonnell, and L. L. O'Byrne (Cahalan 1983, 86). These fed and were fed by the increasing strength of Irish nationalism during the late nineteenth century. Also published with fair frequency were Big House novels, such as William Allingham's unusual novel in heroic couplets, *Laurence Bloomfield in Ireland: A Modern Poem* (1864); Annie Keary's sentimental *Castle Daly: The Story of an Irish House Thirty Years Ago* (1875); Margaret Brew's tearjerker *The Burtons of Dunroe* (1880); and Charlotte Riddell's *The Nun's Curse*

(1888). Like Lever in *Lord Kilgobbin,* a couple of Big House novelists adapted this usually conservative form to stories of Fenian rebels, although with less success than Lever: Riddell in *Maxwell Drewitt* (1865) and T. Mason Jones in *Old Trinity* (1867) (Lubbers 1985a, 232–34).

It is not surprising that Fenian novels became popular around this time, for while the Fenian or Irish Republican Brotherhood, founded in 1858, was not a mass movement, it enjoyed considerable support among rural Irishmen angered by the recent Great Hunger. There is a large body of Irish folklore about Irish peasants aiding and abetting the Fenians (Cahalan 1983, 38). The Fenian leaders, who staged yet another abortive rebellion in 1867, made the militant, "physical-force" approach to Irish nationalism much more popular and even respectable than it had been during the old days of the Whiteboys and other unorganized, underground rebels. The Fenians began a popular newspaper, the *Irish People,* edited by Charles Kickham and others including John O'Leary, Yeats's nationalist mentor during the 1890s. Moreover, Irish nationalism was broadened during the late nineteenth century by its interaction with social issues, specifically the land question. The movement for tenants' rights won a reforming Land Act from a sympathetic Gladstone in 1870, and in 1879 a group of Fenians led by Michael Davitt and including Kickham forged a "New Departure" that led to the organization of the Land League, coined a new word and new, nonviolent political and economic strategy in the campaign of withdrawal against the County Mayo land agent Captain Boycott in 1880, and eventually led to the enactment of a system allowing tenants to buy their own farms through the Wyndham Land Act of 1903. Meanwhile, Fenianism and the Land League merged with constitutional nationalism in the Irish Home Rule Party led by Charles Stewart Parnell, "the uncrowned king of Ireland."

It is therefore at first quite surprising that when the Fenian leaders Charles Kickham and William O'Brien published novels, they told not Fenian tales but rather stories of sentimentalized, regional, local life. As Robert Lee Wolff writes, "Nobody who did not already know that Kickham had all his life been an extreme nationalist could possibly guess it from reading *Knocknagow*" (1979c, 36). This reaction is a testament not only to the increasing popularity of Irish regional novels—including everything from May Laffan Hartley's urban, Dublin novel *Hogan, M.P.* (1876) to Emily Lawless's study of the remote, rock-strewn Burren area of County Clare, *Hurrish* (1886)—during this period when the now much larger, nostalgic Irish emigré markets in Britain and America were very significant factors, but also to Kickham's and O'Brien's own experiences and sensibilities. Political prisoners often emerge from lengthy incarcerations not as hot-headed polemicists but as thoughtful, even contemplative individuals. For example, the Fenian activists and Land League founder Michael Davitt served two separate prison terms, doing significant reading and writing that led him to move beyond the narrow world of Irish politics in favor of wider involvements, world travel, and authorship of books about Australia, the Boer War, and Russia as well as Ireland (Cahalan 1976). While in prison William O'Brien wrote his novel *When We Were Boys* (1890), a nostalgic account of youth that left aside Irish politics except for criticisms of the reactionary tendencies of the Catholic Church in Ireland, thus looking ahead to Gerald O'Donovan and to Joyce (Lubbers 1985a, 235). O'Brien was close enough to his fellow Fenian Kickham that he completed Kickham's last novel *For the Old Land* (1886) after Kickham's death in 1882 (Wolff 1979c, xi). Kickham had written his first novel, *Sally Cavanagh* (1869), a love story, while in prison. His second novel, *Knocknagow; or, The Homes of Tipperary* (1879), warrants brief attention here because it was by far the most popular Irish novel of the second half of the nineteenth century and has been continually reprinted in Ireland throughout the twentieth century.

The immense popularity of *Knocknagow* is inseparable from the nationalist veneration surrounding its author, for as Benedict Kiely has commented, Kickham was for years in Ireland "a national piety" (quoted in Cronin 1980, 103), and *Knocknagow* was as Malcolm Brown wrote "the most important literary work ever written by a leading Irish revolutionist" (quoted in Wolff 1979c, ix). Born near Mullinahone, County Tipperary, to a prosperous Catholic shopkeeper and farmer,

Kickham (1828–82) became deaf after a gunpowder accident at age thirteen, was involved as a young man in the 1848 rebellion that so alarmed Sheridan Le Fanu, was sentenced to fourteen years' penal servitude and served four years at Woking and Portland Prisons, emerging with his health ruined but also with his status as author and statesman firmly established. When asked what he had missed while in prison, Kickham replied: "Children and women and fires" (quoted in Cronin 1980, 102). His most famous novel has quite rightly been regarded by commentators as a historical, social phenomenon; it will not bear any other critical approach. It was so popular that even people who had never read it were able to repeat its sayings, such as "The world is only a blue rag . . . have yer squeeze of it." Irish historians mention it as often as do literary critics, with the revisionist historian F. S. L. Lyons stressing Kickham's fundamental conservatism, despite his rebel activities (quoted in Wolff 1979c, ix). Kickham always longed for the life he had known in youth in small-town Tipperary. As one of the characters in *Knocknagow* remarks, "Security is the only thing to give a man courage" (228).

Kickham follows well-worn convention in *Knocknagow* by introducing as narrative lens an upper-class visitor from England, Henry Lowe, who tries to figure out Irish Catholicism and Irish life in general. He is terrified by the boom of the "Knocknagow drum" and alternately perplexed or amused by Irish life in general, as are his many predecessors in earlier Irish novels as well as Haines at the beginning of Joyce's *Ulysses*. Kickham tells a long-winded, disparate story— or set of stories, true to the form of the Irish novel—adding a long list of characters and gradually abandoning Lowe as lens. In many ways *Knocknagow* recalls *The Collegians;* like Griffin's novel, Kickham's book celebrates provincial, middle-class life in the west of Ireland, and several of his characters might have been copied from Griffin, especially Mat the Thrasher, the strong peasant trickster, from Griffin's Myles na Gopaleen.

The Collegians and *Knocknagow* were the two most popular Irish novels of the nineteenth century, and like Griffin's novel, *Knocknagow* was later adapted as a play, by Seamus de Burca in 1945 (Wolff 1979c, xi). However, Kickham's novel was more sentimental than *The Collegians* and poorly written. Kickham did not have Griffin's ability to mix with his moralisms the tragedy discovered in Hardress Cregan. His novel also recalls Carleton's *The Emigrants of Ahadarra,* as Kickham blends with his account of the happy homes of Tipperary the indication that many of them had been ruined by landlordism or abandoned through emigration; at the end of his story we are told that the village of Knocknagow no longer exists. He never reconciles this terrible social destruction with his sentimental point of view, though. At the end of *Knocknagow,* his remaining characters sit happily and incongruously listening to a bit of flute music, surrounded by rural devastation. " 'It is very pleasant,' returned Mary. 'Thank God, there are happy homes in Tipperary still! But'—she added, sadly . . . 'but KNOCKNAGOW IS GONE!' " (628). Why was this book so popular? Because Kickham's readers admired him and shared his nostalgia for the old, pre-Famine days and his celebration of traditional, provincial Irish ways.

Emily Lawless

Another novel that had a tremendous impact on the nationalist scene was Emily Lawless's *Hurrish* (1886), the story of a family feud set amidst the Land League struggles in County Clare. In its focus on a big-hearted peasant who clears himself at the end in court of a murder charge, this novel recalls Michael Banim's *Crohoore of the Bill-Hook.* Its book blurb cites English reviewers who praised it as "a picture of the Irish peasant as he really is" (n.p.). The *New York Times* reviewer said that as a study of the causes of rural Irish violence no other work "today . . . will carry more weight or reach a larger circle," and as if to prove the veracity of this prediction, Gladstone praised the novel as he prepared his arguments for Home Rule, stating that Lawless had presented to her readers "not as an abstract proposition, but as a living reality, the estrangement of the people of Ireland from the law." Yet Irish nationalists were not hospitable to Lawless. The *Nation* accused her of grossly exaggerating the violence of peasants, on whom she looked down from "the pinnacle of her three-generation nobility," and called *Hurrish* "slanderous and lying from cover to cover." Even though Lawless had painted Hurrish O'Brien and his sister-in-law Ally as saintly, the nationalist reviewers attacked her more negative characterizations of Hurrish's bloodthirsty mother and his foolish, bigoted neighbors the Bradys—thereby condemning the same kind of vivid, realistic portrayals in Lawless that they had earlier praised in Carleton. The difference was clearly that Lawless was born and bred in the Ascendancy rather than being a product of the peasantry like Carleton. Nationalists also did not like the fact that Lawless, like Anna Hall with her Edward Spencer, had developed a model landlord character, Pierce O'Brien, who is kind to his peasants and refuses to sign a warrant against Hurrish, and presented a negative view of the Land League. Ironically, the Ascendancy myth-maker Yeats reiterated the biased nationalist judgment of Lawless, grudgingly including two of her other books among his list of the "Best Irish Books" but cautioning that she was "in imperfect sympathy with the Celtic nature" (Brewer 1983, 121–23).

Rather, Lawless was in "imperfect sympathy" with *Yeats's* romanticized view of "the Celtic nature." Her novel *Grania* examines the peasantry more truthfully than anything Yeats ever wrote about peasants and is a close precursor to Synge's *Riders to the Sea* and other later, naturalistic treatments of the peasantry such as the stories and novels of Liam O'Flaherty. Yet Lawless, like Somerville and Ross, was kept an outsider to Yeats's literary revival movement; the romantic Yeats did not much like the pragmatic naturalism of these Ascendancy novelists, even though he admired Lady Gregory, whose background and (in several respects) worldview were similar to theirs.

Like Synge, Lawless found herself as an Irish writer after early, misdirected, foreign writings—the English novels *A Chelsea Householder* (1882) and *A Millionaire's Cousin* (1885). *Hurrish* is overly sentimental, betraying Lawless's fondness (like Kickham) for the novels of Charles Dickens, including "a deathbed scene Dickens would have coveted for his little Nell" (Brewer 1983, 123) in which the heroic Hurrish refuses to name the neighbor who has shot him. This novel's best feature is Lawless's detailed and imaginative attention to the rocky Burren region that is its setting—described as having "swallowed up" Hurrish's guilty, doomed enemy Maurice Brady as he walks off into exile at the end (330–31). Lawless maintained an almost professional, geological interest in the rock formations of the west of Ireland.

In her best novel, *Grania* (1893), set on Inis Meáin, the middle and most "primitive" of the three Aran Islands off Galway, Lawless powerfully synthesized this interest with the tragic, naturalistic story of a woman's attempt to establish her own identity. Protagonist and setting are fused: "This tall, red-petticoated, fiercely handsome girl was decidedly a very isolated and rather craggy and unapproachable sort of island" (64). Grania's tragedy is still common among the women of this small, barren, most persistently Irish-speaking spot in Ireland: she loves the island and wants to stay there but can do so only by subjecting herself to an arranged marriage to a thick-headed deadbeat, Murdough Blake, which would mean working herself into a premature old age. At the end she drowns while in search of a priest for her dying sister, finding "death on her own terms preferable to becoming his wife" (Brewer 1983, 125). Among nineteenth-century Irish novels, *Grania* is a rare proto-feminist gem, like an anonymous novel published two years earlier, *Priests and People: A No-Rent Romance* (1891), which in the midst of a negative account of the Land League agitation "also depicts, in the fate of the heroine, the almost inquisitorial pressure brought to bear on an individual about to break out of the circle of conformity enforced by the Church" (Lubbers 1986, 54). *Grania,* though, is a much more unified and better written novel than *Priests and People*. Its characterization of a trapped, desperate Irishwoman is a valuable antidote to all of the idealized heroines prominent in other nineteenth-century Irish novels.

Even if the plight of its protagonist were not so powerfully developed, *Grania* would remain significant in the history of the Irish novel because of its ethnographic and linguistic advances. Lawless presents a variety of effectively sketched Inis Meáin characters: "From the fully drawn Con O'Malley, Grania's hard-drinking father, to the nicely sketched gossips

Molly Muldoon and Peggy O'Dowd, these characters, with only a few exceptions, ring as true as Carleton's" (Brewer 1983, 125). Her approach to dialogue looks immediately and directly ahead to that of Douglas Hyde and John Synge: she shuns the old "brogue" approach that attempted to reflect Irish-English speech through unusual diction and aberrant spellings (as exemplified in the passage quoted above from Lover's *Handy Andy*), a failed strategy that Lawless stressed in her opening dedication "might surely be dispensed with," in favor of speech patterns faithful to the *syntax* of the Irish language. Published five years before Synge's first trip to Inis Meáin, *Grania* might very well have served as a model for his innovative plays, especially *Riders to the Sea* (1904), centered on a tragic heroine who laments in powerful Irish-English speeches the sons taken from her by the sea.

The two Lawless books grudgingly listed by Yeats were her historical novels, *With Essex in Ireland* (1890), originally published as an authentic sixteenth-century document but later publicly linked to Lawless; and *Maelcho* (1894), a romance set in the Elizabethan Ireland that she had earlier examined in her well regarded history entitled *The Story of Ireland*. Her historical novels intimate an almost deconstructionist reading of Irish history, since "what emerges is a decided view of Irish history which suggests that no one answer is adequate, that no side is the sole possessor of the right" (Brewer 1983, 126). Later Lawless stressed the Irishness of Maria Edgeworth in a 1904 biography of her predecessor, and wrote part of a novel about the 1798 rising in Mayo that was completed by Shan Bullock—*The Race of Castlebar* (1913). Like her fellow Ascendancy writers Hall, Lover, Lever, and in some ways Le Fanu, Lawless has been denied her place in Irish literary history according to a narrow nationalist critical code, but she fits squarely and significantly within the tradition of the Irish novel.

During the long, painful decades of the middle and later nineteenth century, Irish novels had included the optimistic lessons of Hall, the disparate polemics of Carleton, the stage-Irish escapism of Lover, the Anglo-Irish laughter as well as the reforming views of Lever, the baroque Gothicism of Le Fanu, the maudlin sentimentality of Kickham, the vivid naturalism of Lawless, and many features of numerous other, less notable novelists—all this during a period witnessing Ireland's darkest hours in the midst of England's glorious Victorian age. If these diverse tendencies indicate that no single "school" had been founded or dominant voice heard in the Irish novel, at the same time they are evidence of broader possibilities opening up. In the midst of all the strident guidebooks to Ireland for English readers that had been published at the beginning of the century, fictional options had seemed much narrower during those earlier years. After all the somber moralism of earlier nineteenth-century works, the comic relief offered by Lever or even Lover seemed in order. And after the more direct, almost textbook presentation of Irish politics seen in Edgeworth, Owenson, the Banims, and Hall, even a politician and rebel such as Kickham chose a more indirect approach. This period in the Irish novel may appear to be the bleakest and rockiest of all, but there are contained within it significant fictional lodestones as noticeable as the boldest promontories on Lawless's Aran Island.

3

Inventing Modern Forms, 1890–1920

A Historical Turning Point

The years of the Irish Literary Revival or Renaissance—most celebrated for its poetry and its plays, for Yeats, Synge, and Lady Gregory—also witnessed the first great flowerings of the Irish novel in its modernist forms. Aside from and in fact *previous* to the novels of Joyce, who also emerged during this period and will be treated separately in my next chapter, at least four novels were published that are masterpieces within the genre: Somerville and Ross's *The Real Charlotte* (1894), the best of all the Big House novels and the culmination of the nineteenth-century Irish novel; George Moore's *The Lake* (1905), the first fully modernist Irish novel, highly influential on Joyce; Pádraic Ó Conaire's *Deoraíocht* [Exile] (1910), the first great novel in the Irish language, arguably the first expressionistic novel in *any* language and one that looks ahead to the absurdists; and James Stephens's *The Crock of Gold* (1912b), the first great Irish fantasy novel and perhaps the best of that type.

This is indeed a period of numerous "firsts" and "greats" and "bests" in the Irish novel. Many other worthy Irish novels besides the four highlighted above were published during these years. Their similarities and links to the works of Joyce are clearer and more frequent than was the case with earlier Irish novels, even though Joyce did not deign for the most part to mention his peers or confess his debts to them. Lurking in the shadows of Joyce as well as the dramatists and poets of the Revival who have received so much attention are quite a number of good and even excellent novelists, who never organized themselves into an easily identifiable movement and who produced a greater diversity of works than their compatriots in the other genres. In this chapter about a dozen of these novelists will be examined. Also deserving of future critical attention are several other novelists whom I can only mention here, but who published popular novels during this period, and are briefly surveyed by Diane Tolomeo (1983)—including Henry de Vere Stacpoole, Louie Bennett, Erskine Childers, Annie M. P. Smithson, Conal O'Riordan, St. John Ervine, Geraldine Cummins, and Patrick MacGill. As a final example of the depth of this period, the best Irish historical novel of the era was written by none of the writers just mentioned, but by one William Buckley. Buckley's *Croppies Lie Down* (1903) abandoned the escapist romance formula with its happy ending, so pervasive among nineteenth-century Irish historical novels, in favor of a bleak, realistic story of the 1798 bloodbath in Wexford, thereby representing a significant turning point in the Irish historical novel (Cahalan 1983, 103–08).

What other novelistic riches may lie hidden?[1] Such discoveries contradict Ernest Boyd's somber assertion in *Ireland's Literary Renaissance* (1922), often since repeated, that "Anglo-Irish literature has been rich in poetry and drama, but the absence of good prose fiction is noticeable, when it is remembered that the romances of [Standish James] O'Grady were the starting point of the Revival" (374). Like many others, Boyd shows here that he was too much under the sway of Yeats, the pioneer of Irish poetry and drama whose blind spot was the novel. In search of a literary "father," Yeats praised O'Grady's books, which were interesting historical accounts but almost entirely deplorable fictional failures. In awe of the highly visible dramatists and poets organized by Yeats, Boyd failed to recognize the achievement of the novelists of the period; devoting only a single chapter to fiction writers, he betrayed his own blindness to the novel when he began his chapter by moaning, "Were it not for the essays of John Eglinton, the occasional prose pieces of A. E., and Yeats's two volumes of stories, one might say that the art of prose has been comparatively neglected" (374). Boyd's view could be dismissed as a meaningless, early critical mistake were it not so often repeated since then—as in a 1980 lecture by Thomas Flanagan in which he hyperbolized, even more extremely, that the Revival "was rich in poetry and drama, in essays and in critical theory, but it produced no novels."[2] In his generally excellent study of *The Irish Renaissance* (1977), Richard Fallis asserts that "the novel was not really a successful genre in Ireland during this period, particularly not the novel as we commonly understand it, a major narration dealing with real people in real situations" (156). Admirers of Somerville and Ross's *The Real Charlotte* or George Moore's *A Drama in Muslin* or *The Lake* might well take exception to Fallis's claim even within his stated terms; additionally, the limiting definition he suggests here does not leave room for the strong stream of fantasy that erupted in the Irish novel during the Revival, one of several features that distinguishes the Irish from the English or American novel.

If I return for a moment to my short list of four "greats" in chronological order—Somerville and Ross's *The Real Charlotte* (1894), George Moore's *The Lake* (1905), Pádraic Ó Conaire's *Deoraíocht* (1910), and James Stephens's *The Crock of Gold* (1912b)—several significant developments can be seen in miniature that suggest broader literary and historical changes during this era. The first novel was an essentially traditional, realistic work; the second, realistic but more experimental; the third, a nearly absurdist curiosity hanging on the barest of realistic threads; the fourth, a wild fantasy occasionally borrowing from Irish social realities for comic effects. Thus, before we ever get to Joyce, we can see in these novels by his compatriots the same kind of movement from realism and naturalism into experiment and fantasy that he pursued and that is also central (with dual, simultaneous traditions of realism and fantasy) in the Irish novel since then. Furthermore, Somerville and Ross and George Moore were Ascendancy ladies and gentleman; Ó Conaire and Stephens, proletarians. And if I list my literary historian's dozen of novelists in the more or less chronological order in which they will be examined in this chapter—Somerville and Ross, Shan Bullock, George Birmingham, O'Grady, Yeats, Moore, Gerald O'Donovan, Peadar Ó Laoghaire, Ó Conaire, Stephens, Daniel Corkery, and Seumas O'Kelly—we can see a shift from the Protestant Ascendancy to the Catholic middle class and the working class (with the cusp at Yeats and

Moore). None of this is squeaky clean—Moore was an upper-class Catholic, Stephens a proletarian Protestant—but it is clear that different kinds of novels were now being written by different kinds of novelists, and increasingly these writers tended to be middle-class or working-class Catholics. From the 1920s until the present day, middle-class Catholic novelists have outnumbered upper-class Protestant novelists, reversing the ratio seen in the nineteenth century. In other words, Ireland's novelists more and more came to reflect the constitution of the country's population as a whole.

This phenomenon was, of course, no coincidence. The Literary Revival was inextricably connected, as both cause and effect, to the history of the period, which was marked by a series of economic, political, and cultural revolutions. Historians and literary critics alike have long recognized this interrelationship, and several in-depth accounts of it are available (Howarth 1958; Thompson 1967; Fallis 1977; Costello 1977). However, the focus is generally on the poets and dramatists of the Revival, not on the novelists, except in John Wilson Foster's recent book (1987). Yet it is clear that these novelists were as inevitably and thoroughly bound up in the events of their age as were Synge and O'Casey. One cannot begin to understand the novels of Somerville and Ross or George Moore, for example, without knowing that a series of reforming Land Acts in the late nineteenth century led to the Wyndham Act of 1903, which encouraged an Ascendancy in decline to sell its lands on the best possible terms to the tenants. The Celtic Revival, marked by the foundation of Douglas Hyde's Gaelic League in 1893, which encouraged the study of Irish and celebrated Irish myth and folklore, has to be appreciated before the fiction of O'Grady or Stephens can be fathomed; without the Gaelic League, the novels in Irish by Ó Laoghaire and Ó Conaire would have been quite literally impossible. Turning to Stephens's novel *The Charwoman's Daughter*, it helps to know also that urban poverty in Dublin at the turn of the century was so bad that even a capitalist apologist, Arnold Wright in *Disturbed Dublin* (1914), admitted that conditions were worse than in Calcutta. The labor union leaders James Connolly and James Larkin were greeted by a receptive populace when they brought their considerable talents to Dublin and Belfast early in the century. The most celebrated event of all during these years, of course, was the Easter Rising of 1916, which had been fed by the Literary Revival; three of the seven signers of the Easter Proclamation were published poets. The Easter Rising was at first met with apathy on the part of most of the Irish people, but as fifteen of its leaders were summarily executed by the British, indifference was transformed into rage. Sinn Féin, the Irish independence movement, was born in the rubble of the Rising, and led to the Anglo-Irish War of 1919–21, the infamous Treaty of Partition of 1921, and the Civil War of 1922–23 between supporters of the Treaty, which split Ireland between the Unionist North and the Republican South, and its bitter opponents. All of these events, social and economic as well as political, are best examined in F. S. L. Lyons's *Ireland Since the Famine* (1971).

Overall, this was clearly as exciting and stimulating a time as the period of the Famine had been devastating and depressing. Irish novelists wrote with a much stronger sense of nationality in terms of their own values, their inspiration, and their readership. The old bowing and scraping to English readers largely evaporated, and the feeling grew that one could be unashamedly an *Irish* writer. At the same time, there also came to be seen a developing understanding among the novelists—encouraged especially by George Moore, writing in English, and Pádraic Ó Conaire, writing in Irish— that one could be both an Irish and a *European* novelist, inspired in particular by the great French and Russian novelists. Both tendencies, the turning inwards to Irishness and the reaching outwards to European novelists, led Irish novelists away from the slavish aping of Scott, Dickens, and the English novel in general that had severely limited the range and achievement of the nineteenth-century Irish novel.

Somerville and Ross

At first, Somerville and Ross appear to be novelists whose traditionalism contradicts the progressive developments that I have just sketched: they were Ascendancy writers who wrote Big House novels and began their careers by imitating the English romantic thriller. While they were traditionalists in some ways, however, they were progressives in others, and as a result their work is deceptively subtle. The cousins Somerville (Edith Somerville, 1858–1949) and "Ross" (Violet Martin, 1862–1915) were members of a Victorian Irish Ascendancy that expected to be in full control of their lands and their Big Houses, were used to a peasantry that remained in its "proper place," and maintained conservative ideas about sex and "good taste." Both cousins stood out in their families as independent-minded women, hunters, writers and artists, and advocates of women's suffrage; Somerville wore collars and ties, and as an author Martin adopted the appearance of a man's name. All these rather divergent characteristics are evident in their fiction. Especially since these two remarkable women formed the most successful literary partnership in modern Irish literature, it is surprising that no concentrated feminist study of their lives and writings has to date appeared, despite useful books by Hilary Robinson (1980) and Gifford Lewis (1985) and a chapter by Anthony Cronin (1982).

Only in recent years has the reputation of Somerville and Ross begun to recover from early critical neglect and scorn, the tenor of which was set again by Ernest Boyd, who devoted less than a paragraph in 1922 to their accumulated writings (and much more to lesser writers). Boyd offered only a backhanded compliment to *The Real Charlotte* as "a Balzacian study of Irish provincial types, drawn with a seriousness and an impartial sense of reality, which serve to heighten regret for the subsequent squandering of the authors' great talent upon the trivialities of a superficial realism" (386). Somerville and Ross remained outsiders, always displeasing someone: their comic *Irish R.M.* stories were condemned by nationalist critics like Boyd as throwbacks to the reputedly comic condescensions of Lover and Lever; English critics loved the same stories but cared less for their tragic, bleak novels; and the celebrated Literary Revival writers had little to do with them because they refused to join Yeats's movement. Violet Martin was actually a cousin of Lady Gregory, who wrote to her in 1901 inviting her to write a play, but she refused.

In 1922 Somerville was still of the opinion that "there is too much written about Ireland as a nation by the Dublin literary set when anarchy is prevailing in the country places. I am feeling rather sick of their brag and bunkum" (quoted in Lubbers 1985a, 228). As writers of masterfully accurate and effective rural Irish dialogue, Somerville and Ross were predecessors of Lady Gregory and Synge; the poet Patrick Kavanagh felt that they "had a better ear for Irish dialogue than anybody except James Joyce" (quoted in Cronin 1982, 82). Yet their point of view was much too realistic and pessimistic to allow them to entertain the apocalyptic myth-making of Yeats that came to dominate the Dublin literary movement.

Somerville and Ross were very popular with readers, however, who especially enjoyed their *R.M.* stories about "resident magistrate" Major Yeates and his comic difficulties in making any sense out of the native Irish population supposedly under his charge, stories which have been tremendously popular ever since their first appearance in 1899. Irish Literary Revivalists either ignored these stories altogether, or like Boyd scorned them as wasted, merely popular efforts or (worse yet) as anti-Irish Ascendancy tracts. They failed to notice that here, in the midst of the Ascendancy's fatal decline, was a case of the Ascendancy laughing at *itself* through Major Yeates, not at the more cunning peasantry. By having Flurry Knox always outsmart Yeates, Somerville and Ross reversed the positions of Lover's Handy Andy and his masters. To expose the follies of the Ascendancy and to entertain their readers, whether through comedy or tragedy, remained their dual aims.

They met in 1886 and formed an attachment that was to be the most important one in the life of each, with neither ever getting closer to a man than they were to each other, yet keeping their own relationship mental and spiritual rather than physical. When in 1919 Ethel Smith proposed to Somerville a sexual relationship, she declined, somewhat shocked (Lewis 1985, 205–06). They distrusted, in fact, the physical passions. The hardheaded Charlotte Mullen's fatal flaw in *The Real Charlotte* is her passion for Roddy Lambert; Somerville and Ross advise us, "A human soul, when it has broken away from its diviner part and is left to the anarchy of the lower passions, is a poor and humiliating spectacle, and it is unfortunate that in its animal want of self-control it is seldom without a ludicrous aspect" (267). In one way or another the "lower passions" also do in Dan Palliser in *An Enthusiast* (1921) and Shibby Pindy in *The Big House of Inver* (1925). Particular views of gender and of the life of the body and the life of the mind are central to all of the novels of Somerville and Ross, yet have never received sufficient critical attention, the focus having always been a sociopolitical one on their status as Ascendancy, Big House novelists—a status which is, in fact, inseparable from these other themes.

We speak of "Somerville and Ross," even though "Ross" died in 1915, because Somerville insisted that her writing continued to be a collaborative effort. They wrote their early works literally together, in a process so mutual as to make it virtually impossible to attribute particular words or sentences to one or the other. This was true from the time of their first novel, significantly entitled *An Irish Cousin* (1889), a Gothic romance much indebted to Le Fanu's English Gothic novel *Uncle Silas*. The best novel of the later period, *The Big House of Inver*, was in fact inspired by a letter written by Martin to Somerville in 1912.

Their apprenticeship was still incomplete in *Naboth's Vineyard* (1891), an attempt to capture Irish village life, about which they knew too little. In *The Real Charlotte* (1894), however, Somerville and Ross found a setting and theme truly their own: the Big House world of County Cork (though its opening chapter is set in a dingy area of Dublin, like John Banim's *The Nowlans* in its final chapters, parts of George Moore's *A Drama in Muslin*, and of course Joyce's novels). *The Real Charlotte* was the first Irish novel since Griffin's *The Collegians* to capture extensively and effectively a panorama of Irish society, including in this case a paralytic Ascendancy embodied in the Dysarts and also the oafish soldier, Hawkins; people trapped in the middle of a class conflict, especially Charlotte, who chats pleasantly with the Dysarts but is privately driven by a desire for money as well as marriage; and the peasants from whom Charlotte collects rents and with whom she can drive a hard bargain, even when they start speaking Irish in her presence. Charlotte is thus a descendant of Edgeworth's Jason Quirk, the middleman who effectively drove a wedge between the Ascendancy and the peasantry at considerable profit to himself.

The Real Charlotte is the first superior Irish novel (outside of Lever's somewhat more uneven *Lord Kilgobbin* and Lawless's *Grania*) with a female protagonist—or perhaps I should say protagonists, since there has been some debate about whether Charlotte Mullen or Francie Fitzgerald, of whom the authors were "fondest," is the protagonist. While it seems clear that Charlotte is the more central character, both are crucial to the story and the theme; they are "two of the most convincing and penetrating portraits of women in all literature" (Cronin 1982, 85). Both are partly victims of the men in the book: Christopher Dysart, truly the son of his apoplectic, invalid father; Roddy Lambert, the Dysart's land agent, a hopeless romantic liar with a serious problem about money; and Hawkins, the suitor with the golden tongue and papier-mâché heart. All three pursue beautiful young Francie, Charlotte's niece (although Charlotte prefers to describe her as a cousin) whom she has brought out from Dublin, although "pursue" may be too strong a word for Dysart. Somerville and Ross's portrait of the wealthy, paralyzed Dysarts reminds one of D. H. Lawrence's Lord Chatterley as symbol of a paralyzed and impotent social order, but here there is no heroic Mellors to rescue Lady Chatterley. Late in the novel when Christopher and Hawkins have both left Francie behind, she thinks, "They're all the same. . . . All they want is to spoon a girl for a bit, and if she lets them do it they get sick of her, and whatever she does they forget her the next minute" (249). Such a frank, colloquial critique of sexual relationships represents new language in an Irish novel. Hardress Cregan "spooned" Eily O'Connor in much the same fashion, but in *The Collegians* Griffin's narrative is limited to his middle-class, male perspective and decorative style. After marrying Roddy Lambert for the money and security he offers her, Francie is pitched from a horse and killed at the end of the novel.

Charlotte is tragic whereas Francie is pathetic. Based on a woman dead at the time of writing but well known to the authors, Charlotte has her strengths—her intelligence, her determination, her attempt to avoid the romantic illusions that overwhelm the novel's men. Somerville and Ross's Ascendancy relatives were none too fond of the novel in general, and especially of Charlotte. One of Somerville's brothers wrote to her angrily, "Such a combination of bodily and mental hideosity as Charlotte could never have existed outside of your and Martin's diseased imaginations" (quoted in Robinson 1980, 87–88). Lacking Francie's youthful beauty, Charlotte gains a more detached reader's sympathy with her persistent, quiet machinations to win Lambert, who doesn't deserve her. After he marries Francie instead, Charlotte turns mean, attempting to ruin him by demanding the money he owes her, but Francie's death cuts short her revenge. Admirably detailed in its depiction of Irish life yet powerfully focused almost like a classical tragedy on Charlotte's dilemma, *The Real Charlotte* is Somerville and Ross's best work and the greatest Irish novel of the nineteenth century.

The manner of Francie's death was strangely prophetic: in 1898 Martin was herself very badly injured in a fall from her horse while hunting, and was never in good health after that. Largely because of this accident, Somerville and Ross produced no other good novels before Martin's death in 1915. They published only, ironically enough, the hunting tales *The Silver Fox* (1898) and *Dan Russell the Fox* (1911) (along with *A Patrick's Day Hunt* [1902], *Slipper's ABC of Fox Hunting* [1903], and three volumes of *Irish R.M.* stories). By the time Somerville reasserted herself as a novelist during the decade following Martin's death, the effects of the Wyndham Land Act of 1903 had been seen, and she was able to chronicle the travails of an Ascendancy already dispossessed in three very interesting novels, *Mount Music* (1919), *An Enthusiast* (1921), and *The Big House of Inver* (1925). Having depicted in the Dysarts an Ascendancy family still nominally in control in the late nineteenth century, Somerville now recorded three other varieties of latter-day landlord foolishness in her final three Big House novels: a landlord who refuses to face the music and sell his lands, a dispossessed landlord and working farmer who falls prey to his own "enthusiasm," and an illegitimate daughter of illegitimate sons who nonetheless feels that hers is the only legitimate claim on the crumbling Big House of Inver. *Mount Music* and *An Enthusiast* are uneven novels, the first a narrow attack on an arrogant, outdated landlord, the second more interesting because in it Somerville records both her sympathy for the nationalist Irish movement and her lack of sympathy for the infant, would-be Irish state. Dan Palliser's fate in *An Enthusiast* suggests that Somerville felt it was impossible for an ex-landlord to survive in this brave new Irish world: at the end he rushes to the scene of an Irish rebel attack on the home of the woman he loves, intending to save her, and is shot dead by her husband, who fires from his window at the rebels.

The Big House of Inver is a more powerful novel—perhaps the best Big House novel—because once again it is focused on an unusual female protagonist (very different from her author) whose consciousness Somerville is nonetheless able to powerfully penetrate. As with Charlotte Mullen, the model was an actual woman, the keeper of an old castle whom Martin had described in a letter to Somerville in 1912 as "a strange mixture of distinction and commonness, like her breeding, and it was very sad to see her at the door of that great home. If we dared to write up that subject!" (quoted in Flanagan 1966, 75). The novel that resulted is as bleak as the *Irish R.M.* stories are lighthearted. With Lover and Lever in mind, Somerville had been proud that their first novel, *An Irish Cousin,* had been in her opinion the "first in the field of Irish country life which did not rollick." Now considering the later novels in light of the *R.M.* stories, Edith commented, "It gets sadder every day! I can't help it . . . I'm afraid the people who talk so much of our rollickingness will be rather sick. But *how* could a book about Ireland in 1920 rollick?" (quoted in Robinson 1980, 57 and 176). *The Big House of Inver* is much too weighty and somber to "rollick," but it certainly creaks a great deal in Gothic fashion. It was much influenced by the *Castle Rackrent* of Edgeworth, Somerville's one predecessor whom she unqualifiedly admired—not surprisingly, since they had so much in common.

Like *Castle Rackrent, The Big House of Inver* is a chronicle
novel that delves far back into the Prendeville family history
in order to learn how the protagonist has been reduced to
her present identity as "Shibby Pindy," a dispossessed peasant aristocrat, the "strange mixture of distinction and commonness" observed by Martin. Shibby is caught in the middle
of futility, like Edgeworth's Thady Quirk. Yet as a woman,
she is in character much more like Charlotte Mullen—determined, persistent, but doomed by society and her own
passions. She tries to live out the old Prendeville family
motto—"I take"—but she fails to do so. Her scheme to marry
her half-brother Kit to Peggy Weldon, who stands to inherit
the Big House, gets scrambled when Kit, committing one of
the traditional family sins, gets a peasant girl pregnant. Shibby
kills this unfortunate girl, but not before Peggy learns about
the affair and casts off Kit. At novel's end Shibby comes
upon the smoking shell of the burnt Big House, with Johny
Weldon, who picks up the pieces like crafty Jason Quirk,
wryly informing her that as an insurance agent he of course
had the house insured and thus stands to gain (whereas
Shibby is ruined by the event). This novel is the death knell
of the Ascendancy and of the Big House tradition so effectively examined by Somerville and Ross. Little could Edith
Somerville have imagined that the Big House *novel*, however,
would live on long after the death of the Big House itself,
providing one of the strongest strands among the Irish novels
of our own day.

    The death of Dan Palliser in the midst of a rebel raid at
the end of *An Enthusiast* was again sadly prophetic, for
Somerville's own brother, Admiral Boyle Somerville, was shot
dead on his doorstep by rebels in 1936. She wrote, "I will
not regard those dirty little sneaking assassins as representing
Ireland. Ireland is my country, not theirs" (quoted in Robinson
1980, 34). After *The Big House of Inver* she wrote only two
more novels, *French Leave* (1928) and *Sarah's Youth* (1938),
both novels of manners focused on the role of a young
woman within her family and society. Yet in *The Real Charlotte* and *The Big House of Inver*, Somerville and Ross had
achieved powerful portraits of Irish women, and thus represent a crucial link between nineteenth-century women writ-

ers such as Owenson and Lawless and later novelists such as Elizabeth Bowen, Kate O'Brien, and Jennifer Johnston.

Shan Bullock and George Birmingham

Two other Protestant novelists of the same period, minor authors but quite popular and very interesting, also devoted their best work to subtle critiques of the crumbling Ascendancy: Shan Bullock (1865–1935) and George Birmingham (1865–1950). This exactly contemporaneous pair were both from the opposite end of Ireland from Somerville and Ross, however, hailing from Fermanagh and Belfast respectively in the north. Both were closer to the middle class than to the Ascendancy, Bullock working all of his adult life as a civil servant in London, and "Birmingham," who was really Canon James Owen Hannay, in various Church of Ireland parishes in the south of Ireland and later England. The world of their novels, especially Bullock's, is summed up in the title of Bullock's novel *The Squireen*—a term describing a member of the small gentry, one that John Wilson Foster reminds us is "faintly contemptuous" (1974, 30)—and is very similar to the world of *The Real Charlotte* in its linking of money-grubbing and arranged marriages. Both Bullock and Birmingham adopt critical, satiric perspectives on the Northern Irish ruling class out of which they came. Although they held other jobs, both were very prolific writers, Bullock publishing more than twenty books and Birmingham more than eighty. Only a few of the best and most relevant novels of each can be mentioned here.

Bullock's two most interesting Irish novels, *The Squireen* (1903) and *The Loughsiders* (1924), focus on crafty, arrogant, and unscrupulous Protestant farmers who will do anything for money, including getting married. Writing from his detached and isolated position in London, Bullock seems to have been torn between admiration and scorn for the class of people he had left behind. On the one hand, his novels are spiced with sentences noting the neat prosperity of the northern Irish Protestant farmers in contrast to their less prosperous Catholic counterparts living on poorer land. As late as 1924 in *The Loughsiders,* he hearkened back to the old nineteenth-century direct address to English readers, telling them that "Irish homes are like that" (24). He added to his description of Richard Jebb's fishing the sentence, "You who go out for a day's sport on the Thames, suitably arrayed and laden with all kinds of expensive tackle, may well smile at this account" (16). This English-aimed novel and Somerville's *The Big House of Inver*, published in 1924 and 1925 respectively, show how persistent were the old nineteenth-century fictional modes in the Irish novel.

On the other hand, Bullock tells tales of farmers who make Jason Quirk look like a knight in shining armor. In *The Squireen* Martin Hynes ignores his true love in order to make a match with a farmer's daughter carrying a handsome dowry, Jane Fallon, who denounces the arrangement but can't stand up to her father's ultimatum: "That was plain speaking; what might Jane, a poor weak woman striving to do right, without friend or place of refuge, dare answer to it?" (102). Fate eventually rewards their loveless marriage with the degenerate Martin's death and Jane's abandonment of his farm and return to her father's. Having examined the course of an arranged marriage, Bullock subsequently posited to himself the question of what would happen if the woman refused the match, as does Rachel Nixon with Richard Jebb in *The Loughsiders*. He reminded the reader that "So Jane Fallon had done once on a time, you may remember, and so Rachel Nixon had told Richard she was ready to do rather than be haggled for like some beast in a fair" (177). Since writing *The Squireen* Bullock had completed *The Race of Castlebar* (1913), an unfinished novel by the late Emily Lawless, creator of the fictional Grania who resisted an arranged marriage at the price of her own death. Bullock appears to damn the farmer who tries to buy a wife like he would a cow—but in a satiric mode, in this case. Reminding us that Richard Jebb "lived in a country where in the long run only men counted" (210), Bullock describes in *The Loughsiders* the epic, perverse revenge of Jebb on Rachel for refusing to marry him. She later accepts the proposal of another farmer coached by Jebb, and he himself eventually marries Rachel's widowed *mother*, thereby obtaining their family farm in the end.

Birmingham adds to Bullock's social satire a biting political irony still very relevant today, focused on the paradox of Northern Protestants rebelliously insisting on their loyalty to Britain. Educated at Trinity College, Dublin and working for much of his life in southern parishes, Birmingham was more kindly disposed than Bullock to Irish Catholics, although he was generally wrongly dismissed by critics as either a superficial humorist or a bigot. Yet in *The Northern Iron* (1907) and *The Red Hand of Ulster* (1912), Birmingham reminds his readers that modern Protestant "loyalists" are descended from the Irish Volunteers, the stubborn radicals who began the 1798 rebellions. *The Red Hand of Ulster* turns on a bizarre scenario that seems only too real to the student of Northern Irish politics throughout this century: the loyalists are so opposed to Irish Home Rule that they demand British withdrawal and stage their own revolt in order to prevent Home Rule. As Tom Paulin comments about this novel, it "is a kind of documentary as well as being an amusing fantasy— and . . . it anticipates the documentary realism and satirical fantasy of much 1930s writing" (1984b, 120). Birmingham's novels, like those of Bullock and Somerville and Ross, provide subtle and entertaining critiques of an Ascendancy up against the ropes, extending the self-critical impulses contained in predecessors such as Edgeworth and Lever.

Standish O'Grady and W. B. Yeats

Born in the same year as Bullock and Birmingham, W. B. Yeats (1865–1939), the Moses of the Literary Revival, invented a version of Ascendancy that he saw as consistent with rather than opposed to Irishness, and he also nominated as "Father of the Irish Renaissance" (even though that title should be more properly ascribed to Yeats himself) a fellow Ascendancy idealist, Standish James O'Grady (1846–1928). Both Yeats and O'Grady were too devoted to a mythical view of history, however, to become successful novelists. Not that they didn't try: as Edward Hirsch reminds us, Yeats "had powerful early ambitions to be known as an Irish short story writer and novelist, and . . . worked continually at the craft of fiction during the fifteen year period between 1887 and 1902" (1983, 55); and O'Grady published a long list of prose works, including several novels, between the 1880s and the 1920s. O'Grady advanced an extended analysis of ancient and Elizabethan Irish history in order to celebrate older Irish aristocracies that he saw as powerful and noble. His reading of Irish history greatly appealed to Yeats, who added the eighteenth century as his own Ascendancy golden age to be celebrated in his later poetry and drama.

O'Grady and Yeats both chose to turn to the glorious past because the present reality of their Ascendancy class was grim and uninspiring. O'Grady first made his name as author of *The History of Ireland* (1878–81), which opened up the ancient era of Cúchulainn for Yeats and the other writers of the Literary Revival. As a journalist he went on to address himself to his own Ascendancy class, urging landlords in *The Crisis in Ireland* (1881) and *Toryism and the Tory Democracy* (1886) to take matters into their own hands, exercise their old responsibilities, and reform Irish agriculture and the system of landholding. When his pleas fell on deaf ears, O'Grady became a militant nationalist; the poet A. E. later said that O'Grady's books "contributed the first spark of ignition" to the Easter Rising, testifying to the rebel leader Pádraic Pearse's "love for the Cuculain whom O'Grady discovered or invented" (Marcus 1970a, 87).

As a writer O'Grady turned from history to fiction after finding the pages of a scholarly book by George Petrie still uncut in a library in Dublin, an experience about which his son later wrote that it "opened his eyes to the mistake he had made. The public were not attracted by a sober treatise. Fiction and romance were their intellectual delicacies. Accordingly . . . he rewrote the Celtic legends in the guise of a novel" (Marcus 1970a, 36). His trilogy *The Coming of Cuculain* (1894), *In the Gates of the North* (1901), and *The Triumph and Passing of Cuculain* (1920) is essentially an extended rewrite of his *History of Ireland* as romance, seeking to be more entertaining and more popular while at the same time perpetuating his own romanticized view of ancient Irish mythology. As Benedict Kiely has written, "O'Grady brought the heroes into Irish literature . . . heroes a little touched with the nineteenth century's and Standish O'Grady's ideas of what a hero should be" (1950, 59). O'Grady, unlike his cousin the Gaelic scholar Standish Hayes O'Grady, was entirely ignorant of the Irish language and had to depend on translations, which meant that Yeats's understanding of Cúchulainn as based on O'Grady was at best third-hand. O'Grady transformed earthy, often bawdy Irish saga into decorous, sexless Victorian romance. He also published several fictional accounts of the period of the Elizabethan Irish lords, Red Hugh O'Donnell and Hugh O'Neill, most notably *Ulrick the Ready* (1896) and *The Flight of the Eagle* (1897). However, he was unable to overcome his bookish devotion to history and his slavish imitation of Scott, writing fiction that was alternately ponderous and maudlin (Cahalan 1983, 88–102).

Nonetheless, Yeats, looking for a progenitor in the 1890s, proclaimed that O'Grady's *History* had "started us all" (quoted in Marcus 1970a, 76), causing Ernest Boyd (reiterating Yeats's view) to confer upon O'Grady the title of "Father of the Revival," even though O'Grady had no notion of organizing a literary movement. Yeats, of course, did have that notion and carried it through. Yet as John Frayne writes, "as impresario of the literary revival, he had less success in calling forth novelists than poets or playwrights" (1970, 366). He ranked O'Grady's books along with those of Carleton, Edgeworth, Griffin, and the Banims at the head of his lists of the "Best Irish Books," and his collection of *Representative Irish Tales* (1891) was very influential in forming a critical canon (such as it was) of nineteenth-century Irish fiction. "It must be said that as a critic of fiction, or as a writer of fiction," Leonard Orr argues, "Yeats is not of major significance" (1986, 152). However, his *influence*, as we have already seen, *was* major, and even his failed attempts to become a novelist are interesting and relevant.

Yeats insisted in one of his letters that his sole completed novel, *John Sherman* (1891), was "as much an Irish novel as anything by Banim or Griffin" (quoted in Marcus 1970b, 40). Its wooden opposites, the dreamer John Sherman and the intellectual John Howard, are generally cited by Yeatsians as early examples of the poet's idea of antithesis. Yet this novel, even though it fails because these characters are thin and unconvincing, recalls the novels of Edgeworth and Owenson at the same time that it prefigures those of George Moore and Joyce. Declaring that its theme was hatred of the London that John Sherman leaves behind, Yeats was determined that he not be seen as an English novelist using an Irish setting, and probably had this thought in mind when insisting that it was an Irish novel. His assertion was apt in other senses as well. When Sherman leaves the arid world of London to become a farmer, get married, and settle down in "Ballah" (Sligo thinly disguised), he is exerting the old Edgeworthian responsibility, also a prerogative in the novels of Owenson and Hall: the landed gentleman goes home to Ireland to take care of his land (even if Yeats's hero has only the foggiest notion of how to go about doing that). And as a study of the coming of age of an Irish dreamer, *John Sherman* looks immediately ahead to the more successful works of Moore and Joyce, *The Lake* and *A Portrait of the Artist as a Young Man*. Grappling with the problems of an Irish exile in England, it relates to the otherwise very different *Deoraíocht* by Ó Conaire.

Even more clearly prefiguring Moore and Joyce is *The Speckled Bird*, a novel that Yeats worked on between 1896 and 1902 but never finished. His 726 manuscript pages, however, have since been published. Again, this work is related thematically to his poetry and his short stories and also in perhaps less obvious but nevertheless significant ways to the development of the Irish novel, especially as it was about to blossom in Moore and Joyce. In it Michael Hearne experiences a spiritual awakening in the midst of complex dealings with his father, friends, and the murky London spiritualist world. Like Joyce's *Portrait*, *The Speckled Bird* includes a scene describing the protagonist's vision of a girl in the water as a prophecy, but Yeats, unable to integrate successfully such a vision into a realistic story line like Joyce would, at this point interrupted his manuscript (his indecision reflected by a missing page). Hirsch posits that "it may be that Yeats had so much trouble completing *The Speckled Bird* because his realistic narrative and his visionary poetics were essentially at odds with each other" (1983, 53). He adds: "Standing at the brink of modernism, Yeats's fictional works form a bridge between the difficulties of the epiphanic mode of the nineteenth century and the more fully integrated epiphanies that were yet to come" (66). The Stephen of Joyce's *Stephen Hero* often repeats Yeats's stories "The Tables of the Law" and "The Adoration of the Magi," choosing Robartes and Aherne as his spiritual guides. Concerning Joyce, Augustine Martin argues that "in the portrayal of the inner, artistic sensibility his debt to Yeats is greater than anyone has acknowledged, least of all Joyce himself" (1985b, 142). In fiction, Joyce succeeded where Yeats had failed to merge successfully artistic vision with social reality.

George Moore

The problems of Ascendancy at the turn of the century were met with realistic and satiric responses by Somerville and Ross, Bullock, and Birmingham; and with mythic and escapist visions by O'Grady and Yeats. The poses of George Moore (1852–1933) were more complex and sometimes inconsistent, as can be explained in part by his complicated and eclectic personality, starting with the fact that he was a *Catholic* landlord. Most Irish writers can be easily and clearly labeled as to class and religion, and as we have seen among Irish novelists up until Moore's time, the label usually reads either "Protestant Ascendancy" or (somewhat less frequently) "middle-class Catholic." Moore's anomalous position as a product of the Catholic gentry is further complicated by the fact that his family was originally Protestant but had married into a Spanish Catholic family for political and commercial advantage, and that Moore himself converted to Protestantism, like Carleton—but at the height of his fame, in 1903, rather than at the outset of his career. "Moore recognizes that the landlord system deserves to die," notes Seumas Deane, "but he cannot bear the thought that the peasantry will, in turn, take over. His ambivalence on this point is matched by that of Standish O'Grady and Yeats" (1986, 171)—and, one might add, by that of Somerville and Ross. Concerning the habits of his class, Moore himself wrote in *Parnell and His Island* (1887), "I am an Irish landlord, I have done this, and I shall continue to do this, for it is as

impossible for me as for the rest of my class to do otherwise;
but that doesn't prevent me from recognizing the fact that
it is a worn out system, no longer possible in the nineteenth
century, and one whose end is nigh." His ambivalence runs
deep in this book of essays, in which he could simultaneously
deplore the dirt and poverty of the peasants in condescending
fashion and then state that with the help of the Land League
"the scales fell from the eyes of the people, and the people
resolved to rid themselves of this plague" of landlordism
(quoted in Brown 1955, 19).

Then add the diversity of Moore's literary influences, most
of them championed by Moore and then rejected in their
turn: Pater, Zola, Huysmans, Balzac, Turgenev, Dujardin,
Dickens, Yeats, and Wagner, among others. The preponderance of Continentals in this list signals a new eclecticism
and a new European cosmopolitanism among Irish writers,
developments that were begun by Moore. In this sense, A.
Norman Jeffares is correct when he writes that "modern Irish
fiction can properly be said to begin with George Moore"
(1982, 202).

Moore's retreat from the discouraging realities of Irish
landlordism and his embrace of European, especially French,
modes of writing were linked phenomena. Like Violet Martin,
who always remembered her father's coffin being drawn
away past his lamenting tenants, Moore was marked by an
unforgettable memory: his astounded father's death from a
stroke in the midst of a rent boycott in 1870. Moore wrote,
"He died killed by his tenants, that is certain; he died of a
broken heart" (quoted in Hall 1980, 85). The young Moore
inherited his father's estate, and as soon as he achieved the
age of twenty-one he ran off to Paris, in 1873—more than
thirty years before Joyce began his own, very similar, much
more celebrated exile and began to immortalize his own
love/hate relationship with Ireland. Rather than follow a
single course, though, like Joyce—the Irish Homer in Europe
always memorializing Dublin—Moore followed several courses
and adopted a series of roles: the Parisian aesthete (1873–80),
the English novelist in London (1880–1901), the Irish Renaissance man in Dublin (1901–11), and the senior man of
letters removed again to London (1911–33). Each of these

geographical moves had its clear immediate motivation—attainment of the age of majority and independent wealth (1873); a rent boycott and the need to generate income (1880); an invitation to leave the sterile world of London and come to Dublin to help lead the Irish theater beside Yeats and his own cousin Edward Martyn (1901); and weariness with Dublin along with the impending publication of the first volume of his controversial memoir about the Literary Revival, *Hail and Farewell* (1911). And each of the geographical moves marked a series of stylistic shifts and artistic conversions that were in turn more numerous and more subtle than the geographical ones.

Between the publication in 1932 (on Moore's eightieth birthday) of a letter in the *Times* of London signed by many of "the principal writers and artists of the day" that praised Moore as "a master of English letters" (Cave 1978, 11), and the recent recognition by Jeffares and others that "modern Irish fiction can properly be said to begin with George Moore," lies not only a confusion about whether Moore was an English or an Irish writer, but also a gap of several decades during which his critical reputation was in decline. His status had shrunk to that of a minor English Victorian by the time literary historians fully remembered that Moore was undeniably an Irishman—with even his lengthy exiles in France and England and his immersion in the literature of Europe looking quite Irish, in the light of Joyce, Beckett, and others—and began to recognize just how pivotal were his contributions to the development of Irish fiction. The view of Moore as a French aesthete or an English novelist is quite understandable since Moore adopted for quite a while both of these poses, among others. He felt the likes of Zola and Balzac to be much more exciting than the Irish literary models available to him, and after his first move to London he made his name with thoroughly English novels, delighting in calling his most famous novel *Esther Waters* (1894) "the most English of all novels" (quoted in Hall 1980, 84). Its success and the success of *A Mummer's Wife* (1885), *Vain Fortune* (1891), and other novels, cemented Moore's reputation as a great "English" realistic and naturalistic novelist; even his titles have the look of having been selected to sound as English and

Victorian as possible. Yet like Le Fanu's *Uncle Silas,* which
Elizabeth Bowen declared to be an Irish novel disguised in
an English setting, it has been argued that *Esther Waters* is
really an Irish novel as well (Hall 1982). Here we shall limit
ourselves to two very important novels that are Irish in
setting as well as substance: *A Drama in Muslin* (1886) and
The Lake (1905).[3]

A Drama in Muslin is a surprising novel, so much so that
it appears that it may well have surprised Moore himself.
Telling the tale of the sordid expeditions of young, rural Irish
Ascendancy women led by their scheming mothers to the
Dublin "marriage market" centered on the Shelbourne Hotel
in Dublin, Moore painted small-minded, grim Dublin scenes—
nearly thirty years before "A Mother," "The Boarding House,"
and the other stories of Joyce's *Dubliners* (1914). In this
respect perhaps only the Dublin chapters of John Banim's
The Nowlans preceded Moore in their use of a depressing
Dublin setting; Moore's Dublin chapters and those of Somerville and Ross's *The Real Charlotte* a few years later
prefigure the full-blown exposés of Joyce. Moreover, Moore
was led to portray the story of a woman's eventual liberation
through his focus on Alice Barton, the sole escapee from the
prison of rigid roles staked out for women of her social caste.
This may have surprised Moore as much as anyone else, for
he did not subscribe to feminist or particularly pro-female
views. His characterizations of Alice Barton's scheming mother,
shallow sister, and foolish friends show that Moore entertained anything but unmitigated admiration for Ascendancy
women. Yet he came to identify with his protagonist and
must have felt compelled to find a way for her to escape
the closed confines of her social world. Alice does so by
marrying not a wealthy fop but a hard-working doctor who
is rejected by her mother, and leaving Ireland for London
with her husband to write and to raise a family, after having
been encouraged in this independent, artistic direction by a
Dublin writer resembling Moore himself.

Moore looked back on *A Drama in Muslin* as "the turning
point in his career" (Becker 1986, 149). He went on to make
a woman the protagonist of his most celebrated novel, *Esther
Waters,* and another was installed as the moral guide of

Father Gogarty in *The Lake,* thus becoming the first of two excellent Irish male novelists with his surname to write so sympathetically about women. The other is one of the best known contemporary Irish novelists, Brian Moore, while Edna O'Brien has also focused on women who escape Ireland for new lives in London. Interestingly, Moore's novels, like Somerville and Ross's, are full of strong women and weak men; Alice Barton's father is a dreamer much like Christopher Dysart and his father in *The Real Charlotte.*

A Drama in Muslin also led Moore away from the Zolaesque naturalism in which it was begun, as Moore moved from the narrow confines of Alice Barton's Ascendancy world to her liberation. He states his moral, a far from naturalistic one, late in the novel: "The ideal life should lie . . . in making the ends of nature the ends also of what we call our conscience" (288). Scenes in the novel that might have served naturalistic purposes become instead implied protests against unjust social conditions. For example, when hungry peasants stare in through the windows of the Big House at the foolish, opulent "Spinsters' Ball" underway inside, Alice Barton wants to do something about their poverty, and Moore suggests a link between the degradation of the peasants outside and that of the unmarried women inside. The parallel between peasants and women as economic objects is made even clearer when Mr. Barton haggles with his peasants over their rents at the same time that Mrs. Barton refuses a proposal for Olive Barton's hand on financial grounds.

A Drama in Muslin is part satire and naturalistic exposé, part bildungsroman recounting how Alice Barton achieves her freedom. As the latter, this novel, like *The Lake,* very directly foreshadows *A Portrait of the Artist as a Young Man.* Like Joyce's Stephen Dedalus, Alice is a Catholic who becomes an agnostic and a would-be writer and exile who must fly by the nets of family, religion, and nationality as well as the additional barriers linked to her gender. Alice is more of a nurturer than Stephen: she helps her unfortunate, pregnant friend May Gould. And as Alexander Gonzalez notes, "if her ambitions are not as lofty as Stephen's, then neither is she as arrogant as he" (1984, 161).

For many years Moore's and Joyce's mutual dislike and apparent neglect of each other concealed Moore's significant influence on Joyce, but more recently scholars have come to recognize this very definite link. Joyce, the middle-class Dubliner, didn't care for the Ascendancy Moore, attacking him with a couplet in his early broadside poem "Gas from a Burner": "Written by Moore, a genuine gent / That lives on his property's ten per cent." In return Moore referred to Joyce as a nobody, a "nothing," a "beggar," and said of *Ulysses*, "That's not art, it's like trying to copy the London Directory" (quoted in Ellmann 1982, 529). Moore named the protagonist of his most celebrated Irish novel, *The Lake*, after Joyce's infamous friend Oliver Gogarty, and when Gogarty's mother complained, Moore replied, "Madame, supply me with two such joyous dactyls and I will gladly change the name (quoted in Solomon 1973, 218–19). Joyce did just that, renaming his friend "Buck Mulligan" in *Ulysses*, and having Mulligan make derisive comments about Moore's French affectations and love of "French letters." Mulligan's comic plunge at the Forty-Foot in the first chapter of *Ulysses* may very well be a parody of Moore's hero's liberating swim at the end of *The Lake*, especially since Joyce indicated in a letter that he found Moore's description of the priest's buttocks quite laughable. The two novelists never met until 1929, and Moore said that he never read *Ulysses* before that year—six years after Yeats similarly indicated, in a letter to Olivia Shakespear, that if Joyce came to see him "I shall have to use the utmost ingenuity to hide the fact that I have never finished *Ulysses* (quoted in Orr 1986, 156). By 1929 Joyce's reputation had grown at a much quicker pace than Moore's, and he could afford to be a bit more gracious. When Moore died in 1933, Joyce asked Harriet Shaw Weaver to send a wreath to his funeral carrying the inscription "To George Moore from James Joyce," and "then filled his letters of the next two months with bitter references to the failure of the newspapers to mention his gift. It was as if in the end he felt the need to acknowledge publicly a debt that he had long owed, but could only then admit" (McCarthy 1983, 114). The Joyce who wrote in *Ulysses*, "A.E.I.O.U.," more readily expressing his gratitude to the benevolent poet who had assisted him and so many other young Irish writers, had been much more threatened by a rival Irish modernist novelist—and Moore in turn was overwhelmed by Joyce.

Turning to Moore's *The Lake* (1905), the Joycean student of *A Portrait of the Artist as a Young Man* (1916) will surely be immersed in a sense of déjà vu, even more than with *A Drama in Muslin*. It is the most direct and immediate precursor to the *Portrait* just as Moore's story collection *An Untilled Field* (1903) seems to be in many ways a rural introduction to Joyce's urban *Dubliners* (1914). Significantly, *The Lake*, although it developed into an epistolary and at the same time impressionistic novel, was originally planned as one of the stories for *The Untilled Field* (much as *Ulysses* began as an aborted *Dubliners* story). Again, the link between even the most sophisticated Irish novels and the storytelling tradition is evident. Moore, in fact, often regretted that he chose not to publish *The Lake* together with *An Untilled Field*, perhaps partly because the novel is so close thematically to the stories. It is framed as a series of letters between Father Gogarty and Rose Leicester (renamed as Nora Glynn in Moore's 1921 revision of the novel), a young unmarried schoolteacher whom Gogarty denounced from the pulpit during her pregnancy. Rose's letters cause Gogarty to reexamine and repent his harsh action, and ultimately to abandon his parish in favor of a life of liberty such as the one Rose has found in England. He fakes a drowning and swims across a lake in order to escape anonymously to New York, where "his mind would widen and deepen sufficiently to enable him to write something worth writing, something that might win her admiration" (260). Like Stephen Dedalus, Gogarty's final goal is nothing less than the "full possession of his soul" (262); the novel ends with his declaration that "My quest is life" (268) and with his meditations as he undertakes his exile.

The Lake and Joyce's *Portrait* share several other features, including well developed water and flower imagery and an inner, psychological narrative focus. Moore set himself the challenge that the chief conflict between Gogarty and Rose has already occurred before the beginning of the novel, and they never meet in its course. He dedicated his novel to the

French novelist Edward Dujardin; Joyce also expressed his debt to Dujardin, but the *Portrait* is much more extensively and directly indebted to Moore, who nearly perfected a method of writing "interior monologue" that Dujardin had merely sketched. *The Lake* is a marvellous read, an unprecedented work in the development of the Irish novel: a sharply focused, symbolist novel as much concerned with the process of writing itself as with the transformation of the protagonist. At the same time, *The Lake* looks back to a novel as old as Banim's *The Nowlans,* similarly dealing with the crisis of faith of an Irish priest, and in its story line and theme it is even more closely related to another novel of the period, Gerald O'Donovan's *Father Ralph.* Moore abandoned Ireland and the writing of avowedly Irish novels in 1911, but he had already made his indelible impression on the development of Irish fiction before that date, playing a major role in truly bringing the novel into the twentieth century.

Gerald O'Donovan

Literary historians have linked the inspiration for *The Lake* to the career of the "spoiled" priest Gerald O'Donovan—and also to that of Father Thomas Connellan, who did in fact escape the priesthood by faking a drowning in 1887 (John Cronin 1971). O'Donovan attracts our attention briefly here because he wrote an interesting, influential novel of his own; among the numerous Irish novels about priests, *Father Ralph* (1913) is unique because it was written by a priest. O'Donovan (1871–1942) had become a liberal, socially active cleric in Loughrea, publishing articles on progressive themes, becoming active in the Gaelic League, and supporting Yeats's dramatic movement. He left the priesthood in 1904 after his disagreements with his new, archconservative bishop reached a crisis stage. At that point O'Donovan went to Dublin and then on to London carrying a letter of introduction to publishers from Moore, who had become his friend. Moore began *The Lake* inspired in part by O'Donovan's break from the Church. The fact that at this time O'Donovan began signing himself "Gerald rather than "Jeremiah," his given name, ironically calls to mind that his career is the reverse of Gerald

Griffin's: O'Donovan left the priesthood and Ireland and established himself in London as a novelist examining the mores of his religion and his country.

Father Ralph is a highly autobiographical work. It invites interesting comparison not only with *The Lake* but also with the *Portrait*. Added to the private turmoil of a priest are many more complex, social causes for the crisis beyond a single ex-parishioner as in *The Lake*. The problems of O'Donovan's only partly fictional priest, Ralph O'Brien, begin in his earliest youth with his manipulative mother, who is determined that he become a priest and obsessive and unswerving in her devotion to the Church. O'Donovan thoroughly explodes the aura surrounding Maynooth, the famous seminary that had rejected William Carleton with such infamous results, by portraying Ralph's classmates as possessing no loftier moral qualities than hangers-on at a racetrack. He extensively recounts the bishop's merciless suppression of the parish club that Father Ralph idealistically begins, followed by his own mother's rejection of him. When asked upon deciding to leave the priesthood whether he hasn't lost his religion, he replies, "I am only trying to find it" (469). So pointed an exposé of a hypocritical Irish Church was unheard of before *Father Ralph*. Father Stephen Brown, the collector of Irish fiction, abandoned his detachment as a critic and betrayed his status as a member of the Catholic establishment by condemning *Father Ralph* as "seen with jaundiced eyes. It may fairly be said that there is scarcely a page of this book that does not appeal in one form or another to non-Catholic prejudice" (1919, 238). If so, Father Brown could not deny that this novel was written out of intimate and extensive Catholic experience. Predictably, Father Brown was no fonder of O'Donovan's next novel, *Waiting* (1914), which dealt with the obstacles to the marriage of a young Catholic and Protestant couple resulting from a papal decree.

Reading the ending of *Father Ralph*, published two years before the appearance of the *Portrait*, one expects that Joyce read this novel as well as *The Lake*. Alone, Father Ralph undertakes his exile: "He stood on the deck of the Holyhead mail boat, his eyes fixed on the receding Irish coast . . . Life was larger than his vision of it, and where he had read failure in life marked advance. . . . And then?" (493–94). As a novelist O'Donovan never lived up to the promise of *Father Ralph*. However, he inspired Moore with his courageous break from the Church and probably Joyce with his fictional account of it.

The Novel in Irish: Peadar Ó Laoghaire and Pádraic Ó Conaire

O'Donovan explored even more fully the crisis of faith captured by Moore. Another of Moore's ambitions during this period was to render Irish experience in the Irish language itself. This aim was carried out by other writers, including two novelists, one of whom was another though more conventional priest, Peadar Ó Laoghaire (1839–1920), and the other like Moore an inspired exile, Pádraic Ó Conaire (1883–1928), albeit of much humbler origins than Moore. At the height of his Literary Revival enthusiasm, Moore wrote his volume of stories *The Untilled Field* partly for translation into Irish, even though he did not know the language himself. In a process calling to mind Beckett's later and quite different immersion in French, Moore's story "The Wedding Gown" was translated into Irish by Tadhg Ó Donnchadha and then back into English by T. W. Rolleston, with Moore delighted to find it "much improved after [its] bath in Irish." *The Untilled Field* was published in Irish, but *An tÚr-Ghort* sold only about a hundred copies, and Moore's ambition to see the volume displayed in the Gaelic League window was never realized (Kiberd 1982, 21).

Even to *publish* the volume in Irish would have been unimaginable twenty years earlier, for writing and publishing in Irish had virtually died during the nineteenth century, reflecting the general decline of the language. A sympathetic French scholar wrote in 1880, "Irish literature would seem to be dead, at least in the old language, and will not revive again in spite of the efforts of the Society [for the Preservation of the Irish Language]," an organization that had been formed in 1876 to try to counteract the decline of the language (MacEoin 1969, 57). Few would have disagreed with this opinion in 1880. A venerable, vibrant literary tradition in Old, Middle, and early Modern Irish could be traced, ranging from the *Táin Bó Cuailnge* [The cattle raid of Cooley], an epic battle poem rivalling the *Iliad*, to the satiric poets of the eighteenth century, but by the nineteenth century writing in Irish appeared virtually extinct, and prose was the weakest genre of all. Some eighteenth- and nineteenth-century Gaelic romances resembled picaresque romances, but the lack of any widespread system of printing presses prevented the next step into the novel form, as Cathal Ó Háinle points out in his chapter on "An tÚrscéal nár Tháinig" (The nonarrival of the novel) (1978, 87–98). The Great Hunger was by far the single greatest killer of the language, because its victims tended to be Irish speakers; before that catastrophe about half of Ireland's people still spoke Irish, but by the end of the nineteenth century perhaps only about 15 percent of the population was Irish-speaking, and virtually none of them could read or write the language. Spoken Irish persisted in three fragmented and quite different dialects—Munster, Connacht, and Donegal Irish—and no standard written form of the language existed. Thus, the prospective writer of Irish faced three overwhelming obstacles: the lack of any clearly fixed language to write in, the absence of a tradition or a community of writers, and the fact that even if the writer somehow did manage to write, there would be no publishers to disseminate the writing and no reading public to read it. More subjectively, Irish had understandably come to be associated with failure, and to Irish-speaking peasants the wisest course of action for their children usually seemed to be to leave impoverished Irish-speaking areas and stop speaking the language as quickly as possible. In National Schools during the nineteenth century, English was used almost exclusively, and in some cases parents were encouraged to cut a notch in a stick tied by a string around their child's neck whenever an Irish word was spoken at home—thus alerting the teacher that it was time for corporal punishment to be inflicted in order to encourage the child to speak only English.

The grim decline of the Irish language has never been adequately overcome; today, the percentage of active native Irish speakers is only about 3 to 5 percent. However, the language began to receive much better treatment in the late nineteenth century, experiencing a celebrated revival that is still going on; writing and publishing in Irish are much more common today than at the turn of the century. Ironically, it all started in Brooklyn. As the great novelist Máirtín Ó Cadhain noted, "one can say that modern Irish writing began with the founding of the monthly *An Gaodhal* in Brooklyn . . . by a West of Ireland emigrant, Micheál Ó Lócháin, in 1881" (1971, 139). Two years later the *Gaelic Journal* or *Irisleabhar na Gaeilge* was begun in Dublin, and in 1893 Douglas Hyde and others founded the Gaelic League. Hyde was tremendously influential upon all of the writers of the Literary Revival in both languages with his collections of Irish poetry and folklore. These were often translated into a new, much more faithful form of Irish English, which Synge adopted and immortalized and which helped shape the syntax and diction of many writers, eradicating the old stage-Irish English full of "begorrah" and "top of the mornin' " and other words and phrases that Irish people never utter except in self-conscious jest.

Peadar Ó Laoghaire (or Peter O'Leary) joined the language movement late in life with a very didactic aim: he wanted to popularize the spoken Munster Irish of his native County Cork, and he wanted to do this in writings suitable for young people as dictated by his typical priestly moral code. Pádraig Ó Duinnín's *Cormac Ó Conaill* (1901) was technically the first novel in Irish ever published in book form (Ó Háinle 1978, 198), but Ó Laoghaire began serializing *Séadna* (1904) in the *Gaelic Journal* in 1894 to great acclaim. *Séadna* is an extended version of an international folktale following the Faust theme—the story of a shoemaker who sells his soul to the devil before eventually regaining it, as told beside the fireplace by a young girl to her even younger listeners. It was natural that Ó Laoghaire, like several nineteenth-century Irish novelists in English (and like Joyce with *Ulysses*), would serialize his episodic tale. It is obvious that this first significant novel in Irish is even more directly linked to the Irish storytelling tradition, whose influence on the early Irish novel in English I have already noted. Throughout the twentieth century the short story in Irish has been a much stronger

genre than the novel. Even the greatest novel in Irish, Máirtín Ó Cadhain's *Cré na Cille* (Churchyard clay) (1949) consists
of an epic series of separate oral narratives. The native Irish
storytelling tradition may have exerted itself even on the
gender of novelists—always male, with women making a
name for themselves in twentieth-century writing in Irish
only in poetry—as in the folk tradition the revered *seanchaí*
or storyteller was usually a man.

   With the authoritative air of a priest, Ó Laoghaire unambiguously announced his aim in his preface: "The language
of the story of *Séadna* has been framed specially for the
purpose of giving learners an opportunity and a means of
becoming acquainted with . . . Irish syntax. That is why the
story consists almost entirely of dialogue" (1898, iv). "The
reader can rest assured that while reading the story he is
reading *the actual speech of living Irish people who knew no
English*" (i). *Séadna* achieved a popularity unprecedented for
a work of fiction in Irish at the time. Recent critical estimations
of it are mixed: some complain that the work lacks the
narrative depth and development of character that we expect
from a novel (MacEoin 1969 and Ó Cadhain 1971), while
others defend it as a successful "folk-novel" (Breatnach 1969;
Ó Tuama 1976). *Séadna* is as much a children's book as
anything else, but an evaluation of it even on that basis is
confused by the fact that it originally appeared in an adult
journal. Those who defend it as a "folk-novel" ignore the
fact that it lacks the earthy, often ribald qualities of authentic
folk narratives; aiming himself at youthful readers for didactic
ends, Ó Laoghaire imposes on his folk sources his narrow,
puritanical worldview much as Standish O'Grady did. As a
novel *Séadna* is a failure because of its lack of development
of character and plot, although it is notable as a first attempt
and true to the tradition in which oral narrative is seen as
a natural source. Ó Laoghaire's campaign to impose Munster
Irish as the standard printed form did not quite succeed, but
at least he helped prod along efforts to arrive at a conventional orthography. Ó Laoghaire did not develop as a novelist;
Niamh (1907), his only other novel, attracted little attention.

   With his obsession with *caint na ndaoine*, the speech of
the people, Ó Laoghaire had no interest in anything that

was not Irish in the most thoroughgoing, chauvinistic sense. His type provided one model for the satiric explosion of the True Gael in Myles na gCopaleen's *An Béal Bocht (The Poor Mouth)* (1941), where we are presented with a speech in which literally nearly every other word is "Gaelach" or "Gaelic" or another form of these words. A much better writer than Ó Laoghaire, Pádraic Ó Conaire turned like George Moore to the great European fiction writers for his models. In this respect Ó Conaire followed the lead of Pádraic Pearse, who is best remembered as the leader of the Easter Rising of 1916 but who first made his name at the turn of the century as a short story writer in Irish and editor of the Gaelic League newspaper *An Claidheamh Soluis* (The sword of light). In a 1906 article that was undoubtedly read by Ó Conaire, Pearse wrote, "Will the ancients suffice as exemplars? Frankly, we are afraid not. We must get into touch also with our contemporaries—in France, in Russia, in Norway, in Finland, in Bohemia, in Hungary, wherever, in short, vital literature is being produced on the face of the globe . . . Irish literature, if it is to live and grow, must get into contact on the one hand with its own past and on the other with the mind of contemporary Europe" (quoted in Ó Háinle 1978, 201).

Pearse's call was taken up by Ó Conaire, a Galwayman who had a native command of Irish that Pearse lacked and was a better writer. Ó Conaire especially admired the great Russian novelists, writing in 1908 that they had searched in the depths for true humanity and "shouted out: This is the human being; this is man; this is the truth" (quoted in Ó Háinle 1984, 67). Like George Moore, Ó Conaire also took up Zola as an early literary hero. As a cosmopolitan, artful writer, Ó Conaire's influence on subsequent prose writers in Irish was at least as pivotal as Moore's was on Irish writers in English. He had none of Moore's inherited wealth, though, to help him pursue his European bent. Ó Conaire established the typical pattern of the serious writer of Irish in this century—the native speaker who emerges from an Irish-speaking area of the West and makes his career in Dublin or London. Ironically, Ó Conaire first established his name as a writer while working in the British civil service in London, winning a prize in 1904 with his short story "Páidín Mháire," before returning to Ireland in 1914 and eking out a living of sorts as a writer for a few years, until his death in 1928. Like all other writers of fiction in Irish, Ó Conaire published mostly short stories. He did, however, also write one remarkable short novel, *Deoraíocht* (Exile) (1910), which captures in unusual fashion the experience of being an Irish speaker in London, *"Cathair an Dorchadais"* (The city of darkness). It is the most innovative, forward-looking Irish novel in either language during this period before the arrival of Joyce as a novelist, rivalled in this respect perhaps only by James Stephens's *The Charwoman's Daughter* (1912a), which bears some similarities to it. Yet ignorance of the language prevented knowledge of this fascinating work by the more celebrated writers of the Literary Revival and has also prevented mention of it in most surveys of the period. It is a picaresque tale told by one Micil (although he neglects to name himself for quite a while), who lost an arm and a leg in an accident and was presented with a few pieces of gold in compensation. In London he is loved and mothered by The Big Redheaded Woman and exploited by Alf Trott (The Little Yellow Man), who signs him on as a freak for a circus sideshow and takes him to Galway, where he is temporarily married to the Fat Woman before he returns to London.

Gach ar tharla dom ó d'fhágas an baile le beagán airgid a shaothrú leis an mbean uasal seo a bhí i mo láthair anois a phósadh, bhí sé os comhair mo shúl. An timpiste a d'fhág i mo bhacach agus i m'uafás mé; an saol náireach a bhí agam leis an bhFear Buí; an cleamhnas a rinne seisean dom i dtosach; an easpa agus an tocras agus an gátar a bhí orm, agus mé ag fanacht le mo chuid airgid; an chaoi ar fhóir an Bhean Rua orm; teach lóistín An Chasúir agus a raibh de ghadaithe agus de rifínigh ann; an chaoi a mb'éigean dom suí chun boird le dríodar na cathrach ann; an chaoi a mbíodh an Bhean Ramhar ar mo thóir; chonaiceas an méid sin agus tuilleadh ag teacht agus ag imeacht ina bpictiúir shoiléire os mo chomhair. (119)

[Everything that happened to me, since I left home with my little bit of money to my current life with this lady I married, was in my sight. The accident that left me a cripple and a horror; the

shameful life with the Yellow Man; the match he made for me
at first; the need and hunger and difficulty I had, while waiting
for a bit of money; the way the Red Woman helped me; the
Hammer Pub and the thieves and riffraff there; the way I had to
sit down to a table with the scum there; the way the Fat Woman
pursued me; I saw all this coming and going in a clear picture in
my head.][4]

As in Flann O'Brien's *The Third Policeman,* only at the end
of the book do we learn that the protagonist has already
died—while lying in a park in London, in this case. Critical
explanations of the peculiar qualities of this book have only
recently been forthcoming. Ó Conaire has always been admired by a small, discriminating, devoted group of readers.
Recently the centenary of his birth attracted three appreciative
critical volumes (de Bhaldraithe 1982; Denvir 1983; and Ó
Broin 1984). Tomás Ó Broin emphasizes that *Deoraíocht* was
the first and perhaps the only truly expressionistic novel in
any language (1979). Like the plays of Brecht and Beckett,
Ó Conaire's novel emphasizes the loss of its protagonist's
identity and the reduction of other characters to just one or
two qualities—the greedy Little Yellow Man, the lustful Big
Redheaded Woman, and so on. These characters are closer
to the "grotesques" of the American southern writers Flan-
nery O'Connor or Carson McCullers than to anything else
in Irish fiction. Declan Kiberd adds a reading of the novel
as socialist in vision, arguing that it portrays the futility of
life under the capitalist system embodied in the exploitative
Little Yellow Man, and adding that the protagonist who is
treated like a freak is "merely a man with a deeper than
average apprehension of normality," like Joyce's Leopold
Bloom (1983, 47). Also like Bloom as well as the men in
George Moore and Somerville and Ross, Micil is an apparently
weak man dominated by strong women. *Deoraíocht* is the
kind of novel that can bear a variety of interpretations, and
it stands in a suggestive relationship to the other novels of
the period—particularly those of Moore, Stephens, and
Joyce—as well as to those of later innovators such as Flann
O'Brien/Myles na gCopaleen, Beckett, and others. Ó Conaire
was unable to repeat the feat. *Brian Óg,* published serially

in 1922 and 1923 and in book form in 1926, is a lightweight historical romance. *Deoraíocht* and its author have still not received their due, especially among mainstream critical works in English.

James Stephens

James Stephens (1880?–1950) was also an experimental novelist attracted to the Irish language, attending Gaelic League classes in Dublin, and although he chose to write in his native language, Stephens's English dialogue is in many respects influenced by Irish. For many years this diminutive man was a victim of the image he himself helped to create in *The Crock of Gold* (1912b)—that of the comic leprechaun. While always a popular author among readers, only in recent years has he been taken seriously by scholars, with critical books on his work appearing only within the last few years (Martin 1977; McFate 1979). Yet Stephens was the only Irish novelist of this period both accepted within the mainstream of the Literary Revival and at the same time befriended by the usually standoffish Joyce. A. E. told the youthful Frank O'Connor, "Stephens is a genius" (quoted in O'Connor 1967, 213), and in 1914 Yeats gave a speech reported in the newspapers in which he said, in a prophecy that may have backfired, "When the other day I read *The Demi-Gods* of Mr. James Stephens, I felt that he alone . . . could take care of the future of Irish literature" (quoted in Finneran 1975). Stephens's friendship with Joyce did not begin until 1927, and was initiated largely as a result of Joyce's love of co-incidence: Stephens claimed that he came into the world on 2 February 1882, the same day as Joyce, although in fact he may have been born on a different day in 1880; they shared a first name and each had one son and one daughter born to a woman he had not married. Joyce fancied the idea that they could sign any collaborative work "JJ & S" (also the trademark of John Jameson and Sons, his favorite brand of whiskey). Joyce was apparently serious in suggesting that Stephens could complete his *Work in Progress*—which of course became *Finnegans Wake* but about which he was discouraged in 1927—if he himself was unable to finish it (Finneran 1974).

More than trivial coincidences qualified Stephens for the job, for no other Irish novelist outside of Joyce had achieved more in the realms of fantasy and mythology. Stephens was also the only other novelist of the period to write a great Dublin novel—*The Charwoman's Daughter* (1912a). He had burst magnificently onto the scene in 1912, the year when both of his best novels were published. His background and his apprenticeship, served as a clerk-typist in Dublin law offices between 1896 and 1912, were humbler than Joyce's. As Stephens wrote, "The Dublin I was born to was poor and Protestant and athletic. While very young, I extended my range and entered a Dublin that was poor and Catholic and Gaelic—a very underworld. Then as a young writer, I further extended to a Dublin that was poor, and artistic, and political. Then I made a Dublin for myself, my Dublin" (quoted in Fallis 1977, 153). His early mentors were Arthur Griffith and A. E.; Griffith provided a forum for his first writings, political articles in Griffith's nationalist newspaper *Sinn Féin*, and A. E. showed him how a more eclectic life of the imagination could be added to his nationalism. Stephens's novels often rework in allegorical, fabulous terms the political points made in his *Sinn Féin* articles (Finneran 1975). For example, the Policeman in *The Charwoman's Daughter* is a representative of British rule in Ireland and becomes a villain partly as a result, yet the imaginative framework of this novel allows Stephens to explore these relationships in all of their subtlety rather than present simplistic political propaganda (Achilles 1981).

No writer whose chief artistic inspiration was William Blake could remain merely an anti-British polemicist. The central theme of all of Stephens's books is the movement beyond Blakean Innocence and Experience to some higher, unifying vision, and *The Crock of Gold* in particular celebrates the "Divine Imagination" and often directly borrows Blake's terminology and reacts to his ideas. To say that Stephens had essentially only one story to tell is to take nothing away from the richness of his early books, yet at the same time it is one explanation of the fact that he wrote little of note during the last twenty-five years of his life. The recurrent plot and characters as well as the patterns of fairy tale and fable in his novels readily attract a structuralist analysis such as that applied by Augustine Martin, who points out that Stephens's novels have "a symmetry which would satisfy Vladimir Propp's most classic formulations" about the structure of the fairy tale (1977, 1). In his first novel, *The Charwoman's Daughter*, a young girl sensually comes of age, falls under the power of an imposing, distant male (the Policeman), finds a truer and closer love (a young boarder, clerk, poet, and nationalist resembling Stephens himself), and approaches a higher consciousness by the end of the book. This basic plot, merging bildungsroman and fairy tale, recurs in *The Crock of Gold* (1912b), *The Demi-Gods* (1914), and *Deirdre* (1923). Martin points out that "the adolescent heroine, poised on the brink of womanhood, reappears as Caitilin, as Mary McCann in *The Demi-Gods*, and as Deirdre in his retelling of that mythic story; the Charwoman with her eloquence, ferocity, and possessiveness returns as the Thin Woman and Lavarcham; the Policeman is given a heroic reincarnation as Conchubar and the young clerk as Naoise" (1985b, 153). One might add that the Policeman corresponds also to the foreign god Pan, Caitilin's first lover in *The Crock of Gold*, and the boarder to the Irish god Aengus Og, who supplants the foreign usurper Pan as Caitilin's lover. Aengus Og replaces Pan because Stephens felt that he could best find the Divine Imagination within the vibrant Old Irish tradition. His subsequent novels *The Demi-Gods* and *Deirdre* took their inspiration from and dealt entirely with mythic Irish materials.

As in the career of Joyce as well as in the development of the Irish novel at large early in this century, Stephens's novels show an evolution out of realism into full-blown fantasy and myth. Introducing the simultaneous interests in realism and fantasy that would be very evident in the Irish novel as a whole during subsequent decades, Stephens injected a fairy-tale strand into his ostensibly realistic first novel, and then filled his fantastic fables with the earthiest realistic details of character, dialogue, setting, and plot. By naming his charwoman's daughter "Mary Makebelieve," Stephens

immediately announces that his first novel is no simple
realistic tale. One of the greatest strengths of *The Charwoman's
Daughter*, which is in many ways Stephens's best novel, is
the contrast that it develops between the grim, seedy reality
of Mary's life in the Dublin slums, and the rich, bright,
beautiful quality of the world as seen through her imaginative
eyes. By and large Stephens's Dublin is as generous, open,
and sunlit as the world of Joyce's *Dubliners* is mean, closed,
and dirty. The light of the beautiful epiphany that Stephen
experiences only when observing the young girl on Dollymont
Strand at the end of book 4 of the *Portrait* shines most of
the way through *The Charwoman's Daughter*. Stephens wrote
even more persistently about young women than did George
Moore. His is the generosity, though, of fable. Even when
Mary's policeman changes from a knight in shining armor
into a dragon who wants to devour her once he learns that
she is a mere charwoman's daughter, she is saved by the
young boarder and by Uncle Patrick, whose will bestows
money on the Makebelieves. The ending of this novel, which
like so many other Irish novels was originally serialized, is
open, leaving us with the words "Thus far the story of Mary
Makebelieve" (128).

A number of critics have refused to evaluate *The Crock of
Gold* as a novel, insisting that it is instead a fable, a fairy
tale, an allegory, or even a Menippean satire. It does of
course borrow from all of these genres, and it does not follow
many of the conventions of the novel. Neither, though, does
Castle Rackrent, Ulysses, At Swim-Two-Birds, or many another
Irish novel. Rather than toss out unconventional Irish novels
that do not conform to a definition conceived through analyses of eighteenth- and nineteenth-century English novels,
it seems more sensible to change the definition in order to
accurately describe the modern Irish novel, and the first
requirement that has to go is the realistic one. In *The Crock
of Gold* Stephens does not merely bend the realistic premise
as does Ó Conaire in *Deoraíocht:* he breaks it. Leprachauns
and gods mingle freely with peasants. The peasants are as
important as the gods; they show that Stephens is interested
not merely in an otherworld, but in our world. He wants to
take our world and deify it, make it divine. It matters that

it is Caitilin, the daughter of Meehawl MacMurrachu—as humble and realistic a peasant as anybody else in Irish literature—who goes off to live with and make love to gods. Meehawl's worries about this course of action are recorded in Irish-English dialogue as flavorful as anything in Synge: "Maybe the girl [is] lying dead in the butt of a ditch with her eyes wide open, and she staring broadly at the moon in the night time and the sun in the day until the crows would be finding her out" (48). This sort of talk is interspersed with the heady, highly amusing ruminations of the Irish Philosopher: "A proverb will run where a writ will not, and the follies of our forefathers are of greater importance to us than is the well-being of our posterity" (18–19). The overly intellectual Philosopher needs the divine liberation offered by the gods as much as beautiful young Caitilin does. At the end of the book Aengus Og and Caitilin head down to Dublin to free the Philosopher from jail and "the Intellect of Man . . . from the hands of the doctors and lawyers, from the sly priests, from the professors whose mouths are gorged with sawdust, and the merchants who sell blades of grass" (228).

It was Stephens's feat to combine Blakean vision with some of the funniest passages in Irish fiction. Yet he was at least as earnest as Yeats was in his apocalyptic visions, for he saw that Ireland needed liberation from its own narrow-mindedness and puritanism at least as much as from the political and economic oppression of England. The ironically named Irish Free State of the 1930s, which banned the best Irish books, would bear out Stephens's worst fears about Irish self-oppression. By then he was living in London, having left his position as registrar of the National Gallery of Ireland in 1925, and was thereafter best known as a lecturer and BBC broadcaster. During the period of the Literary Revival and the Easter Rising, it had seemed as if anything was possible in Ireland, but by the 1930s it was clear that Ireland had not heeded and would not heed Stephens's apocalyptic message. Frank O'Connor wrote that "Stephens, when his genius deserted him, was no talent" (1967, 213). One suspects that Stephens felt deserted or ignored by his Irish readership, who viewed *The Crock of Gold* as a mere leprachaun's lark rather than a prophetic book, and so he left Ireland. His artistic decline after his departure appears directly linked to his distance from an Ireland that had gotten worse instead of better.

Daniel Corkery and Seumas O'Kelly

Daniel Corkery (1878–1964) and Seumas O'Kelly (c. 1875–1918) are transitional figures who look ahead to the period of the Free State, minor novelists who do not quite succeed in illuminating the shadowy Ireland on their horizon but important influences on the next generation, especially in the case of Corkery. Like William Carleton, Frank O'Connor, and several other Irish fiction writers, Corkery and O'Kelly were better short-story craftsmen than novelists. Corkery was the chief early mentor of the master storywriters Sean O'Faolain and Frank O'Connor, and O'Kelly's "The Weaver's Grave" is a long story, almost a novella, that was acclaimed as a masterpiece and admired by Joyce. Published in 1917, the year after the *Portrait* appeared, Corkery's *The Threshold of Quiet* and O'Kelly's *The Lady of Deerpark* permit comparison and contrast to Joyce and other novelists of the period.

Like Stephens, Corkery had a fanatical interest in the Irish language and the native Irish tradition, and at the same time, like George Moore and Pádraic Ó Conaire, he was inspired by the great nineteenth-century European fiction writers, especially the Russians. He encouraged his fellow Corkmen O'Faolain and O'Connor to make their work thoroughly Irish yet model it on Turgenev, Gorky, and Maupassant. Like Joyce with Dublin, Corkery set about in *The Threshold of Quiet* to capture the lives of "quiet desperation" he had observed in Cork. The similarity stops pretty much there, though, for Corkery's solution is not the "silence, exile, and cunning" advocated by Joyce but rather acceptance, resignation, and Catholic piety. At the end of the novel Lily Bresnan enters a convent, and Martin Cloyne, who loves her and learns of her decision by letter, reacts by thinking that "the dark, bare, sodden hills he had been looking on that day . . . were filled with a light—a clear light that would shine for ever. Fearing a certain cold sense of loneliness—no more than that it seemed—that appeared to be drawing near, to be going to creep over him, he went upstairs" (310). For the next generation of writers Corkery held out acceptance whereas Joyce celebrated exile from Ireland. Corkery's considerable influence was exerted much more through his short stories and his study of eighteenth-century Gaelic literature, *The Hidden Ireland* (1925).

The Big House setting of Seumas O'Kelly's *The Lady of Deerpark* is a thin frame for a melodramatic, forgettable plot rather than the powerful, personal emblem that it was for Somerville and Ross. It indicates both the prevalence of the Big House tradition and the fact that a non-Ascendancy writer such as O'Kelly could not successfully enter it; he is far better writing about the gritty peasants of "The Weaver's Grave." It is interesting, though, that O'Kelly experiments a bit with interior monologue in *The Lady of Deerpark,* and his narrator Paul Jennings—like Jason Quirk, a land agent and middleman, but unlike Thady Quirk, a narrator capable of referring to the Greeks and Turgenev—has a Joycean notion of epiphany: "There are moments in the lives of men that are as flashlights, tense moments when innate things are revealed to us" (228). Alexander Gonzalez notes that in attempting an interior monologue passage, O'Kelly, like Joyce (and before him, George Moore), may have been influenced by Dujardin, and adds that "Joyce's shadow is clearly evident here, for not a single published account of Irish literary history acknowledges the fact that more than one Irishman experimented with the technique during these years" (1986, 93).

Before ever getting to Joyce, then, we have seen that the most celebrated strands in his work were already extensively evident in the Irish novel even before Joyce's first novel appeared—a new focus on Dublin (in *The Charwoman's Daughter*), yet with eclectic European inspiration (in Moore, Ó Conaire, and others) combined with an increasingly innovative approach and attention to the theme of exile (in *The Lake* and *Deoraíocht*), as well as the use of mythology (in Stephens). All of these developments underscore perhaps the most important shift in the modernist Irish novel that sets it apart from most of its nineteenth-century predecessors—Irish novelists no longer looked to the English novel for their chief inspiration. Henceforth their books would be brewed in their own eclectic, idiomatic way—different enough that many doubted whether some of these books were "novels" at all—drawing on a variety of influences brought together in a kind of Irish fictional stew. Irish novelists could now address themselves to Irish readers. No more bowing and scraping to Scott or attempts to recreate Dickens on Irish turf would be forthcoming. In fact, later novelists from around the world would soon be turning more often to Joyce, Beckett, and other Irish novelists as their models. Later Irish novelists took their cues not only from Joyce but also from the likes of Moore, Stephens, and, if they wrote in Irish, Ó Conaire. At the turn of the century it was as if the Irish novel had achieved its own epiphany, moving out of the shadows into the bright blaze of a very different era.

4

James Joyce and Joycean Scholarship: A Historical View

James Joyce, Irish Novelist

James Joyce (1882–1941), despite his attacks on the "rabblement" of the Irish Literary Revival, and even though he has been examined more often in other contexts—modernist, European, Homeric, philosophical, psychological—was in many ways the most thoroughly *Irish* novelist of this or perhaps any other period. This may be partly a function of the *thorough* bent of Joyce in general: not only thoroughly Irish, Joyce tended to become most thoroughly *everything* that he set out to be. He published only three novels—if *Finnegans Wake* can with any accuracy be called a novel—but in each of them rewrote the history of the novel, Irish and otherwise. Joyce's thoroughness, his fastidious and highly witty attention to details of all kinds, may in turn have been a function of his Irishness. His love of details reflects not merely the influence of his Jesuit education, which has been so much stressed, but also his status within an Irish literary tradition that always delighted in a highly ornamental style and that was characterized perhaps more by proliferation of details than by any structural unities, ever since the age of the Old Irish epic the *Táin Bó Cuailgne* (The cattle raid of Cooley) and the sacred ninth-century ornamental manuscript *The Book of Kells*. In *The Irish Comic Tradition* (1962), Vivian Mercier found Joyce's later work in particular to be very similar in spirit and tone to many of the satires and parodies of the Gaelic tradition.

Joyce revolutionized the Irish novel and the world novel, yet at the same time his novels very much grew out of and reacted to the tradition of the Irish novel. It is a peculiar phenomenon that this feature of his work has received relatively little critical attention. Largely because of Joyce's early attacks on the Irish Literary Revival, his voluntary exile to the Continent, and the tendency to identify Joyce himself with Stephen Dedalus (especially his anti-Irish aphorisms in *A Portrait of the Artist as a Young Man*), Joyceans have largely neglected the most obvious literary context of his novels—the tradition of the Irish novel as a whole. To his credit Ernest Boyd saw this trend developing as early as 1922: "The effort now being made to cut [Joyce] off from the stream of which he is a tributary is singularly futile. The logical outcome of this doctrinaire zeal of the coterie is to leave this profoundly Irish genius in the possession of a prematurely cosmopolitan reputation, the unkind fate which has always overtaken writers isolated from the conditions of which they are a part, and presented to the world without any perspective. . . . The fact is, no Irish writer is more Irish than Joyce" (404, 405).

Joyce himself liked to encourage this neglect in favor of attention to his literary relationships with Homer, Dante, Vico, Ibsen, and the other great Europeans, pretending that he knew nothing of the Irish language and keeping relatively quiet about Sheridan Le Fanu, George Moore, and the other Irish novelists whom he clearly read and was influenced by. In relation to the earlier Irish novel, Joyce's career exemplifies Harold Bloom's notion of the "anxiety of influence." Joyce shows an unconscious or conscious desire to "kill" or reject his Irish predecessors at the same time that his novels constantly confess his debt to them by revealing many features that are shared with other Irish novels. As I have pointed out in my previous chapter, many of the celebrated innovations in Joyce's novels were actually introduced by such immediate predecessors and contemporaries as Moore, Stephens, and Ó Conaire. The young Joyce shunned Moore, but he was much influenced by him. Even though Joyce ran off to the Continent during the same time that Moore embraced the Irish Literary Revival and joined the Abbey Theatre, Joyce was more truly Irish than Moore could ever be. Whereas writing about Ireland was just another of Moore's phases, Joyce remained in the words of Richard Fallis "the supreme insider of the urban Irish experience; three decades and more of exile in Paris, Zurich, and Trieste could not change that. Writing in a café in Zurich years away from home, he knew Dublin and Dubliners more fully than any resident of the Hibernian metropolis who never ventured farther afield than Chapelizod or Dalkey" (1977, 141). In fact, like many a nostalgic Irish exile, Joyce sought to become even more Irish in his later work than he had been earlier. That Joyce never wrote about anything but Ireland, always focusing on his native city of Dublin, is a truism in Joyce studies. However, the implications of that attachment in respect to the tradition of the Irish novel have remained vague.

As the "Joyce Industry" has burgeoned, more scholarly examinations of Joyce have been published and are now being published than all studies of all other Irish novelists combined. My chief interest is in the historical development of the Irish novel, and in these pages I intend to place Joyce's work in this context not only because it is my concern as well as my charge in this volume, but also because it has been, oddly enough, relatively neglected. At the same time, the popular schools of current literary theory—psychoanalytic, poststructuralist, reader-response, feminist, political—have much to contribute to our reading of Joyce, and in eclectic fashion, my own understanding has been influenced by them. In fact, as I suggest in my introduction and occasionally in the other chapters of this book, these current critical approaches could be applied to many *other* Irish novelists, including those whose works and careers seem to invite a particular approach even more than Joyce does. The student of Joyce needs to understand his place within the tradition of the Irish novel as a whole as well as something about currently prevalent approaches to his work and, in turn, the place of these approaches within the history of Joyce criticism since the 1920s. In the following pages a historical reading of Joyce's work as a novelist—kept brief in the knowledge that numerous other, fuller introductions are available to the student, and with a special focus here on the context of the Irish novel at large—will be followed by a concise overview of the history of Joyce criticism with

particular attention to the alternate readings provided in
recent years by psychoanalytic, structuralist, poststructuralist,
reader-response, feminist, Marxist, and Irish-nationalist
Joyceans.[1]

Joyce's Life and *A Portrait of the Artist as a Young Man*

James Joyce came to his novels with an Irishman's typical
love/hate relationship with his country. The young Joyce
aimed to study medicine for a while, and he very nearly
became a professional singer instead of a novelist. An anecdote about his rendition of a Thomas Moore ballad at a
recital says much about his irreverent attitude toward the
Irish Literary Revival as well as his delight in punning and
playing with language in order to turn it toward his own
ends. The story has it that, beforehand, Joyce told his cellist
friend that he would dare to insert an obscenity that no one
else would catch, as it would be lost in the fluid flow of the
song. Arriving at Moore's line about personified Romantic
Ireland, "Lovers are round her, sighing," Joyce winked at
the cellist and sang instead, "Lovers around *her arse sighing*"
(Plunkett 1972, 40). This is the same Joyce who, at the age
of twenty, told the then thirty-seven-year-old Yeats that he
was too old, and the same Joyce who had Stephen Dedalus
pronounce in *A Portrait of the Artist as a Young Man* that
"Ireland is the old sow that eats her farrow" (203). Yet it
was also Joyce who became in many ways more Irish than
the Irish Literary Revivalists themselves, in *Ulysses* and *Finnegans Wake*, two books that are full of Irish talk, ancient
Irish epic material, reactions to and uses of other Irish novelists, and a thoroughly Irish comic spirit. The young Joyce's
attacks and those of Stephen Dedalus are in many ways
those of the inveterately grumbling Dubliner. As the later
lifelong Dublin novelist James Plunkett comments, the typical
Dubliner views the world as a matter of " 'everything for
the worst in the worst of all possible worlds.' Even when
he says that to himself, he knows it's not true. But he gets
a certain impish enjoyment out of telling himself so" (quoted

in Cahalan 1986, 9). Even Stephen Dedalus, who is in some ways a caricature more negative than Joyce himself, feels himself to be incurably Irish whenever he encounters an Englishman or Anglo-Irishman, such as the Dean of Studies in *Portrait* and Haines and Deasy in *Ulysses.*

Born in Rathmines and educated by the Jesuits at Clongowes Wood and Belvedere preparatory schools as well as at the Royal University (now University College, Dublin), Joyce certainly resembled the fictional Stephen Dedalus, yet, equally clearly, he was more popular and upbeat. Whatever the connotations of the nickname may have been, it is worth remarking that the youthful Joyce was often called "Sunny Jim" within his family and was apparently quite well liked at Clongowes. It is true that he viewed his father's financial decline and his mother's Catholic piety as impediments to his success as he grew older. Stephen's bouts with his peers and with Catholicism certainly have their basis in fact, but his brother Stanislaus and others felt that Joyce overly dramatized these matters for the purposes of fiction. An older James Joyce would describe himself to a friend as "a man of small virtue, inclined to extravagance and alcoholism. Don't make a hero out of me. I'm only a simple middle-class man." Yet his life is a deeply fascinating one, and Richard Ellmann's biography (1982) is as good a read as many a fine novel. His identification in both his life and his work with the middle class was probably crucial to his success as a novelist; after more than a century of rural Irish novelists of usually either Ascendancy or peasant background, the middle-class, urban Joyce was very much in line with the broader tradition of the novel that he revolutionized.

Each of Joyce's earliest writings has a special significance. At age nine he is said to have written a poem entitled *"Et Tu,* Healy" attacking the opponents of the hero of his father and himself, Charles Stewart Parnell; he maintained a lifelong, quiet identification with his native land in spite of the conviction that Ireland too often frustrated its own best interests with narrow-minded chauvinism. In adolescence he wrote about Ulysses when assigned an essay on "My Favourite Hero"; we know well what became of that interest. His first significant publication was an essay at age eighteen on "Ibsen's New Drama" in the *Fortnightly Review;* when Ibsen sent him a note of thanks, the awestruck Joyce resolved to learn Norwegian and other languages and transform himself into an Irish European. It is well known that his essay "The Day of the Rabblement" (1901) attacked the Irish dramatic movement of Yeats and Lady Gregory, but it is seldom noted that it was published together with a feminist pamphlet written by his friend Francis Sheehy-Skeffington (the model for McCann in *Portrait*). More possessed of political ideals than the Stephen of book 5 of *Portrait,* the young Joyce of the turn of the century can be seen as a part of a new generation of critical young Irish writers and thinkers. On 16 June 1904, Joyce fell in love with Nora Barnacle. Philosophically opposed to the institution of marriage, and unable to live openly with Nora in Dublin, Joyce left for the Continent in September 1904, making permanent and successful the journey that had proven an abortive failure when he tried it twice on his own in 1902 and 1903. He spent the rest of his life in Trieste, Zurich, and Paris, returning to Ireland only briefly. He eventually married Nora Barnacle on 4 July 1931, but only to guarantee her legal inheritance. His move to Paris also marked the beginnings of his eventually successful career as a writer. Joyce was a perfectionist, refusing to delete or rewrite the most scathing stories of *Dubliners* (1914) in order to palliate publishers—one of whose printers destroyed the galleys at the press, convinced that they were obscene—even though the publication of the volume was thereby delayed for nearly a decade. The first version of *A Portrait of the Artist as a Young Man,* entitled *Stephen Hero,* was a very promising realistic novel, but Joyce tossed the manuscript onto the fire (although fortunately a goodly portion of it survived).

Dissatisfied and determined to try all over again for something better, Joyce rewrote *Stephen Hero* under the encouragement and discipline of serial publication in Ezra Pound's little magazine, the *Egoist.* It is well worth noting that Joyce first published each of his three novels serially, like many a nineteenth-century novelist; chapters of *Ulysses* appeared in the *Little Review* and segments of *Finnegans Wake,* always known before its book publication as "Work in Progress," in the little magazine *transition.* This serial publication may very well have contributed to Joyce's sense of a novel as an accretion of distinct stories, with each major part or episode distinguished by its own different style and mode. By the same token, *Dubliners* reads more like a novel than most story collections; in it Joyce sought to overlap and develop characterization, style, and theme as the volume moved from one story to the next. Even more basic than the influence of serial publication may have been Joyce's innate sense as an Irishman, writing as an exiled insider of that country where the storytelling tradition was so strong, that he could build a novel as a web of interwoven, developing, transformative stories. His bold and elaborate experiments with form enjoyed eclectic inspirations from European literature and art, but may also be properly appreciated within the tradition of the Irish novel itself. As I noted in the previous chapter, the turn toward Europe and beyond the English novel for inspiration was itself one of the chief directions among Irish novelists of this period, including those who published novels earlier than Joyce, such as Moore and Ó Conaire.

Like *Ulysses* and like many an Irish novel, *A Portrait of the Artist as a Young Man* (1916) was first begun as a short story. On 7 January 1904, Joyce "wrote off in one day, and with scarcely any hesitation, an autobiographical story that mixed admiration for himself with irony. At the suggestion of Stanislaus, he called it 'A Portrait of the Artist' " (Ellmann 1982, 144). What eventually emerged through demanding writing and rewriting over more than ten years was a novel whose five chapters (or books) each maintain the style and structure of a separate story. Each book ends with a sense of closure occasioned by the apparent climactic experience of the protagonist: at the end of book 1, Stephen is cheered by his schoolmates at Clongowes because he has gone to the rector to complain about his unjust pandybat punishment in class; book 2 culminates in his sexual experience with a Dublin prostitute; book 3, in a repenting Stephen's acceptance of Holy Communion; book 4, in his ecstatic, sensual, Dantesque vision of the beautiful girl wading in Dublin Bay; and book 5, in Stephen's first writings and the final diary entries about his dedication to art and necessary departure to Europe in the spirit of his mythical namesake, Daedalus, who taught his son Icarus to fly:

> Amen. So be it. Welcome, O life! I go to encounter for the millionth time the reality of experience and to forge in the smithy of my soul the uncreated conscience of my race.
> 27 *April:* Old father, old artificer, stand me now and ever in good stead. (253)

Significant here is Stephen's determination to discover the conscience of *"my race"*: he hopes to probe the depths of his heritage, remaining indomitably Irish, from the detached position of Europe. Joyce's *Portrait* is often seen as the least "Irish" of any of his novels, or even as anti-Irish. But these are misconceptions. The novel that ends with a pledge to forge an Irish conscience begins with oral Irish storytelling, in the voice of his father: "Once upon a time and a very good time it was there was a moocow coming down along the road and this moocow that was coming down along the road met a nicens little boy named baby tuckoo . . ." (7). Joyce thus introduces a protagonist whose first experience of narrative is the told tale taken from traditional materials; narrative begins for him by listening to the spoken words of an elder, as it did for William Carleton huddled by the fire in his family's cottage in Tyrone and as it would for Liam O'Flaherty soaking up the stories of old bold Irish heroes on Inis Mór. The opening of *Portrait* dramatically reenacts Dublin's oral Irish storytelling. Stephen's artistic life commences as he hears of "baby tuckoo." He remains supersensitive to spoken words and to sounds in general— whether listening to the bitter argument of his elders about Parnell over Christmas dinner, surviving the priest's horrific sermon about hell at the retreat, or meditating about the sounds of "kiss," "suck," and "the sound of the cricket bats: pick, pack, pock, puck: like drops of water in a fountain falling softly in the brimming bowl" (59). Joyce remains always interested, perhaps above all else, in the sound and the flow of language, as spoken and as heard, as thought in the inner recesses of the mind, and as twisted and transformed in the dream world.

No other writer wrote Irish dialogue, at least the special cadences of Dublin, more effectively than Joyce. Partly because *Portrait* is a novel seeking to universalize the experiences of a developing artist as a young man and to show his coming to grips with the wider world of philosophy and art, its narrator, who grows embryonically along with Stephen in a series of shifting, developing styles, is much less markedly "Irish" than those of *Ulysses* and *Finnegans Wake*. Yet in his dialogue, Joyce brilliantly captures both the Dublin talk of Stephen's many relatives and acquaintances, including Lynch, who swears in "yellow," and the very different western dialect of his friend Davin. He observes that Davin's speech contains both "quaintly turned versions of Irish idioms" and "rare phrases of Elizabethan English" (195), thereby precisely and accurately noting the two chief sources of English as spoken in Ireland: the Irish language itself and remnants of seventeenth-century English, preserved in isolated Irish linguistic pockets, from the chief period of English conquest and settlement. Having skipped his English lecture at university, Stephen tells the English dean of studies that the funnel with which the dean stokes the fire "is called a tundish in Lower Drumcondra . . . where they speak the best English" (188). Later he learns the particular truth of his retort: "That tundish has been on my mind for a long time. I looked it up and find it English and good old blunt English too. Damn the dean of studies and his funnel! What did he come here for to teach us his own language or to learn it from us?" (251). Again, Joyce cagily observes the linguistic phenomenon of archaic English preserved in Ireland while long since lost in standard English. And the English dean makes the supposedly "anti-Irish" Stephen feel more Irish:

—The language in which we are speaking is his before it is mine. How different are the words *home, Christ, ale, master,* on his lips and on mine! I cannot speak or write these words without unrest of spirit. His language, so familiar and so foreign, will always be for me an acquired speech. I have not made or accepted its words. My voice holds them at bay. My soul frets in the shadow of his language. (189)

Early in *Ulysses* Stephen is made to feel even more Irish by the English tourist, Haines, and the Ulster schoolmaster, Deasy, who calls Stephen a "fenian." Stephen is no self-pronounced Irish patriot; he recoils like Leopold Bloom and like Joyce himself from the blowhard brand of Irish nationalism. Yet defined against the contours of English speech and English values, he can only discover himself to be undeniably Irish. Joyce shaped his characters and his novels in a highly original but also peculiarly Irish fashion. Like his most talented contemporaries, he turned away from English models in favor of European ones—Flaubert, Ibsen, Homer—and in preference for his own Irish experience and the inspirations of the speech, the storytelling, the anecdotal narrative patterns, and the political and social obsessions and concerns of Ireland.

Reviewing criticism on *Portrait*, Thomas F. Staley notes that "the major topics of critical interest have been the character of Stephen Dedalus, especially his relationship to the author; Stephen's aesthetic theories as they are propounded in the novel and their comparison with Joyce's own art; structure; problems of irony and point of view; symbolic elements; mythic framework; psychological elements; the novel's influence; and the traditions from which the novel emerged" (1976b, 12). Yet it is ironic that critical attention to such "influence" and "traditions" has not often included the Irish novel—beyond the matter of Joyce's quiet rivalry with George Moore, the unresolved question of how much he may have been indebted to Moore's autobiography *Confessions of a Young Man* (1888), and the clearer influence of Moore's novel *The Lake* (1905). John Cronin (1969a) views the career of Gerald Griffin, who abandoned writing in exile in favor of retreat to an Irish monastery, as that of a Dedalus/Joyce in reverse. Among Joyceans of the previous generation, Harry Levin (1941) was the first to appreciate *Portrait* as a bildungsroman; Hugh Kenner (1956) rejected the view that it was a heroic, autobiographical novel and argued instead that it advanced an ironic critique; and William York Tindall (1959) led the way in symbolic and mythic interpretation. Beyond Levin's general appreciation, we should particularly recognize the central position of *Portrait* within the specific tradition of the Irish bildungsroman, an extremely popular and rich subgenre.[2] *Portrait* invites fruitful comparison and contrast with more conservative, cautious nineteenth-century novels such as Edgeworth's *Ormond* and John Banim's *The Nowlans* (which, like *Portrait*, examines a failed priest in Dublin), and with a number of novels that followed in the footsteps of Stephen Dedalus, such as John McGahern's *The Dark*. Partly because the *Portrait* examined such a quintessentially Irish experience of youth and partly due to the seeming predisposition of Irish novelists to use the bildungsroman form and focus on the transformations of youth, *Portrait* has left its stamp more indelibly on the Irish novel since Joyce than either *Ulysses* or *Finnegans Wake*—at least as measured by the number of subsequent Irish novels that contain striking affinities to it—such as Kate O'Brien's *The Land of Spices*, Edna O'Brien's *The Country Girls*, and McGahern's *The Dark*, among others. *Portrait* also can be seen as a kernel in the growth of the realistic Irish novel of this century, while *Ulysses* stands at the beginning (and *Finnegans Wake* in the midst) of a rich stream of more experimental, fantasy-filled novels. As we shall see in the next two chapters of this book, these two distinct strands of realism and fantasy—parallel fictional modes each showing the stamp of Joyce—dominated the period between 1920 and 1955.

Ulysses

Ulysses (1922) was begun in 1907 as a short story intended for *Dubliners*. It was rooted in one of Joyce's epiphanic experiences: a late-night binge in 1904 at the end of which Joyce had been rescued by Alfred Hunter, a kind Dublin Jew whom Joyce barely knew.[3] He began to imagine Hunter as a modern Irish Everyman, a notable nobody, a Ulysses. Quickly realizing that he could not fit the materials of his narrative into a single short story, Joyce abandoned the project for several years while he worked on *Dubliners* and *Portrait*. He then began redesigning it as a novel in 1914, wrote the first chapter, "Telemachus," in 1917, and published versions of parts of the novel serially in the *Little Review* before Sylvia

Beach courageously made possible its book publication in 1922. *Ulysses* relates a series of events unified in their realistic credibility; in fact, it can be said that the book nearly exhausts the possibilities of realistic fiction by examining eighteen hours of a single day and night in encyclopedic detail. However, it reads like a collection of stories—each of them with its own style, its own narrator, its own specific Homeric parallel, and its own symbolism. In *Portrait* Joyce had departed to an extent from the traditional novel's fabrication of a single narrative perspective and style; in *Ulysses* he exploded the old "unities" of the traditional novel altogether. Joyce may have wanted to explore the hypothesis that the "author" of the *Odyssey* was not a single poet, but rather a series of bards responding to the mythology and folklore surrounding the hero, whose somewhat different compositions over a period of time eventually resulted in what came to be compiled and preserved as the *Odyssey*. More likely, he wanted to subvert the traditional novel with its single narrator set up as a narrative dictator, showing us instead that reality consists of a series or set of interwoven, overlapping but distinct stories. In fulfilling this ambition Joyce had the rich tradition of Irish storytelling behind him. He could put the blather of the oral tradition into his novel, as he does for example in "Cyclops," which is set in a pub and narrated by an unnamed Dublin raconteur. He could also transform the fluid flow of the oral tradition by internalizing it, focusing on the inner stream of consciousness of his three chief "narrators," Stephen Dedalus, Leopold Bloom, and Molly Bloom.

In the course of his day Leopold cooks breakfast for Molly, visits the public baths, attends a funeral, goes about his work as a newspaper ad canvasser, eats lunch and dinner, visits a couple of pubs, continues a titillating correspondence with another woman, is sexually excited by a young woman at the beach, endures some anti-Semitism, worries about the affair Molly is having, meets the drunken Stephen at a party in a hospital, and finally rescues him from a whorehouse and a scrape in the street with an English soldier, taking him home to sober him up before he goes on his way. Before encountering Leopold, Stephen leaves the Martello tower in

Sandymount where he has been staying with his eccentric cohort Buck Mulligan, teaches his morning class at a school in Dalkey, walks along Sandymount Strand, delivers a letter by his schoolmaster to the editor of Leopold's newspaper, and then drinks and carouses the rest of the day. Molly stays home all day, makes love in the late afternoon to the manager of her singing tour, and eventually lies in bed thinking after Bloom comes home. The delicious Homeric parallels and parodies throughout *Ulysses* have been copiously traced: Leopold as Ulysses, Stephen as his unwittingly faithful "son" Telemachus, Molly as his certainly not conventionally faithful wife Penelope (as well as Calypso); Nestor transformed into Stephen's bigoted schoolmaster, Proteus into language beside the Irish sea, the Cyclops into a bad drunk, Nausicaa into a young woman who has read too many romances, Circe into a whorehouse madam, and so on.[4]

Ulysses continually reacts to and uses many features of the earlier Irish novel. Whether each of these instances was consciously intended by Joyce as a direct comment on one aspect or another of earlier Irish novels, or was instead an unconscious response that shows Joyce playing with conventions of the Irish novel even when he might not have been aware of it, we can in many cases not know, since Joyce was so reticent about most other Irish novels and novelists. Clearly, Joyce's references to George Moore in "Scylla and Charybdis" reveal his awareness of the Irish novel. Those uses of the conventions of the Irish novel that may have been unintentional are no less significant. Joyce, for all of his revolutionary practices and broad appeal, was more of an Irish novelist than he may have intended to be.

In the first chapter of *Ulysses*, "Telemachus," Joyce almost immediately introduces an English visitor to Ireland, Haines, who is concerned to understand the place: "We feel in England that we have treated you rather unfairly. It seems history is to blame" (*Ulysses* 1986, 17). Within the context of the history of the Irish novel as a whole, Haines recalls the heroes of Edgeworth's *Ennui* and *The Absentee,* John Banim's *The Boyne Water* and *The Anglo-Irish of the Nineteenth Century,* Hall's *The Whiteboy,* and many a nineteenth-century Irish fictional hero who came from England to make sense

of Ireland for a predominantly English readership. Stephen
calls a cracked mirror "a symbol of Irish art. The cracked
lookingglass of a servant" (6), therein closely echoing a
remark in a letter by Edgeworth noted in my first chapter.
Haines even wants to put together a collection of Stephen's
clever sayings, a kind of anthology of Joycean Bulls in the
spirit of the Edgeworths' *Essay on Irish Bulls* (1802). Mulligan
jokes that Haines's book might contain (in the manner of
the Edgeworths' book) "Five lines of text and ten pages of
notes about the folk and the fishgods of Dundrum" (11). In
immediate response to Haines's proposal, Stephen asks sar-
castically, "Would I make any money by it?" (14). He adds
that "I am a servant of two masters, an English and an
Italian," clarifying with "his colour rising" to the slow-witted
Haines that these are "the imperial British state . . . and
the holy Roman catholic and apostolic church" (17). Unlike
his stage-Irish countryman Buck Mulligan, who admits that
Haines is "dreadful" (4) and a "Sassenach" (8) but is nonetheless quite willing to let him stay in the tower and to play
the Irish fool in order to gain whatever money may be
forthcoming from him, Stephen insists to Mulligan, "If he
stays on here I am off" (4). He is at least as repulsed by
Mulligan's stage-Irish behavior in the company of Haines as
he is by Haines himself.

No stage-Irishman will either Stephen or Joyce be. The
rest of *Ulysses* makes clear that Joyce is as opposed to Haines
(whose very name is French for "hate") as Stephen is. Rather
than allow Haines to dominate the novel and become an
English hero who achieves a profound understanding of
Ireland, as in many nineteenth-century novels, Joyce keeps
his Englishman confined strictly to the margins of his novel.
He makes clear that Haines will remain only a naive fool
who can never approach the center of life in Dublin. Each
of Haines's infrequent reappearances after the first chapter
is significant. In "Scylla and Charybdis," having presumably
been duped into buying drinks for the crafty Mulligan, Haines
trots off to a bookstore in pursuit of a copy of Douglas
Hyde's *Love Songs of Connacht,* thereby missing Stephen's
disquisition on *Hamlet,* which he so much wanted to hear.
His cameo reappearance as the villain of a Gothic novel in

the "Oxen of the Sun" chapter makes even clearer his marginal, negative status: "The secret panel beside the chimney slid back and in the recess appeared—Haines! Which of us did not feel his flesh creep!" (336). Before moving back into concealment, Haines in this ludicrous manifestation orders Stephen, Mulligan, and the other drunken Irishman in the room to "Meet me at Westland Row station at ten past eleven" (337), but we have no indication that they will do so. Instead, we suspect that he will have to catch the last train out of Dublin by himself. Joyce subsequently abandons Haines entirely. Thus, Joyce totally inverts and subverts the Edgeworthian hero and the nineteenth-century English hero of the Irish novel in general, suggesting that no fictional Englishman can probe the depths of his pointedly Irish world and will only make a fool of himself in trying to do so. Instead, his hero is the sagacious Leopold Bloom, who as a Jew is an outsider in Ireland but takes pride in the fact that he was born there.

Joyce's portrait of the Anglo-Irish schoolmaster Deasy in the second chapter, "Nestor," reinforces his dismissal of Haines in the first. Stephen—and, we can be certain, Joyce too—is just as repulsed by Deasy as he is by Haines. When Deasy calls Stephen a "fenian," the supposedly anti-Irish Stephen can only respond like an Irish nationalist, immediately thinking of the title of the violent and reactionary old Unionist ballad (which was also the title of William Buckley's 1903 novel, published the year before Stephen has this thought), "Croppies lie down" (26). Like Haines, Deasy adds anti-Semitism to his repulsive brand of chauvinism. During his walk on Sandymount Strand in "Proteus," Stephen recalls several times (34, 36, 41) his meetings in Paris with the old exiled Fenian, Kevin Egan, thereby implicitly paralleling his artistic exile to Paris with Egan's political one; both needed to escape overweening English and Anglo-Irish dominance, among the other problems of life in Ireland.

Seeking to achieve a new kind of Irish European novel, Joyce injects into the pages of *Ulysses* several reactions, both implicit and explicit, to his perceived chief rival in this ambition, George Moore. At the end of "Telemachus," the heroic nude swim across the lake by Moore's Oliver Gogarty is transformed into a mock-heroic effort. The Joycean version of the real Oliver Gogarty, Mulligan, strips naked at the Forty-Foot swimming station; exclaims, "He who stealeth from the poor lendeth to the Lord. Thus spake Zarathustra" (19); and plunges comically into Dublin Bay. In "Scylla and Charybdis" Stephen has to endure listening to the stated opinion that *Moore* will write "our national epic" (158)— with the delicious irony of course that *Ulysses* instead now enjoys that status—as well as the mention of Moore's invitation of Mulligan (and not Stephen) to a gathering that night. Mulligan accepts while making fun of Moore in his absence, calling him with a prophylactic pun a "lecturer on French letters to the youth of Ireland" (176). "Scylla and Charybdis" is in general Joyce's swan song about the Irish Literary Revival, more tolerant than his early pamphlet "The Day of the Rabblement." Most of the Literary Revival's major figures either appear in this chapter or are mentioned, and the Revival movement is treated as a murky, tricky whirlpool of personalities. Vivian Mercier observes, "I resent those critics who perform a kind of caesarean section with Joyce, ripping him from the womb of Irish tradition generally and the Irish Literary Revival in particular. No passage in Joyce's work refutes them more effectively than 'Scylla and Charybdis' " (1982, 65). In it Joyce uniquely records his debt to the Revival poet and organizer George Russell ("A. E."), who lends Stephen money and had published some of Joyce's early stories: "A.E.I.O.U." (156).

Even though, as a Jew, Leopold Bloom perhaps has much more reason to be upset by Irish Catholicism than do the fictional protagonists of Moore and Gerald O'Donovan, Bloom is for the most part simply amused by it, remarking to himself in "Lotus Eaters" on the wonderful efficiency of the Church: "Good idea the Latin. Stupifies them first" (66). Moore had made an impact in *The Lake* by entering the mind of Father Gogarty and paying such close attention to him, but of course in *Ulysses* Joyce thoroughly outdoes him with Bloom, whom we follow into the outhouse in "Calypso." And in "Lotus Eaters" as well as "Sirens" Joyce injects an epistolary aspect (*The Lake* having been an epistolary novel): Bloom receives a flowered letter from a woman who interests him, and he writes back to her. Rather than express the lofty, noble moral sentiments of Moore's Rose Leicester, however, Joyce's "Martha" advances rather different notions to Bloom: "Are you not happy in your home you poor little naughty boy? I do wish I could do something for you" (63). In general, these examples of explicit and implicit uses of Moore's work in *Ulysses* show that Joyce was out simultaneously to deflate, burlesque, and outdo Moore at his own game.

The previously cited passage about Haines in the "Oxen of the Sun" is certainly not the only instance of Joyce's use of the Gothic novel. The entire "Hades" chapter is permeated with a Gothic atmosphere, complete with the infamous mystery about "Who is the man in the macintosh?" with which Joyce teases his reader in that chapter and occasionally later in the novel. The dark, dank world of "Hades" recalls Le Fanu's *The House by the Churchyard,* a novel that Joyce cited directly in *Finnegans Wake,* and other Gothic works such as Maturin's book with the Ulyssean theme, *Melmoth the Wanderer.* Similarly, the verbal bombast of the wordsmiths in the newspaper office in "Aeolus," especially Trinity Professor MacHugh's eccentric anecdotes, recall the early Trinity College chapters of Lever's *Charles O'Malley.*

Having rejected the Englishman Haines and the whole idea of the predominantly English readership—indeed, Tom Paulin remarks that *Ulysses* is still less liked in England than in Ireland and America (1984a, 143)—Joyce portrays within his thoroughly Irish fictional context Irishmen who at once are more villainous and disgusting yet more believable than any of the stock villains and dupes in the old stage-Irish fictions that were aimed at English prejudices. The Cyclopean "Citizen" is just one of many evil, ignorant Irishmen against whom the superior Leopold Bloom is measured. It is the Citizen who repeats to Leopold the question that the stage-Irishman Macmorris had been asked in *Henry V:* "What is your nation if I may ask?" (272). Leopold's reply, in contrast to the drunken, posing version of Shakespeare's stage-Irish Macmorris, is quiet, dignified, and clearly indicative of Joyce's own responses both to narrow nationalistic chauvinism and the fawning postures of the stage-Irish tradition: "Ireland. I was born here. Ireland" (272). Bloom goes on to speak quietly in favor of human love, the central value of the novel, in a scene in which this pacifist hero counters his opponent with calm, sensible words rather than with the violence employed by his less wily Homeric counterpart. Joyce deliberately selected as his protagonist a person as remote as possible from the traditional Irish hero of the knight in shining armor paraded through the Irish countryside—celebrating instead a self-effacing Dublin Jew. He thereby emphasizes that to be Irish and to be heroic is not necessarily to be Gaelic, rural, Catholic, or Ascendancy—the traditional, typical modes of fictional Irish heroism. At the same time he rejects the old stage Irishman—the like of Macmorris, Handy Andy, and their ilk. Bloom is often very funny, but he represents a pointed rejection of the stage Irishman. Indeed, he cautions Stephen against the stage-Irish Mulligan several times late in the novel. Bloom's brand of comedy is a much richer, deeper kind.

"Cyclops" may be the most obviously "Irish" chapter in the novel. It is told by a typical Dublin pub storyteller: "I was just passing the time of day with old Troy of the D.M.P. at the corner of Arbour hill there and be damned but a bloody sweep came along and he near drove his gear into my eye" (240). It is also filled with much mock-epic Irish material that looks ahead to the more extensive use of such material in *Finnegans Wake:* "of the tribe of Patrick and of the tribe of Hugh and of the tribe of Owen and of the tribe of Conn and of the tribe of Oscar and of the tribe of Fergus and of the tribe of Finn and of the tribe of Dermot and of the tribe of Cormac and of the tribe of Kevin and of the tribe of Caolte and of the tribe of Ossian, there being in all twelve good men and true" (265). The hilarious treatment of mock-epic Irish material in "Cyclops" also looks directly ahead to Flann O'Brien, creator of the mock-heroic Finn MacCool of *At Swim-Two-Birds,* who owed much to Joyce. Joyce's description of the Citizen must have been admired by O'Brien: "From shoulder to shoulder he measured several ells and his rocklike mountainous knees were covered, as was likewise the rest of his body wherever visible, with a strong growth of tawny prickly hair in hue and toughness similar to the mountain gorse (*Ulex Europeus*). The widewinged nostrils, from which bristles of the same tawny hue projected, were of such capaciousness that within their cavernous obscurity the fieldlark might easily have lodged her nest" (243). The scene in which the Citizen and the dog Garryowen speak Irish, with the dog subsequently composing a pseudo-Gaelic poem lamenting his lack of water, may have helped to inspire the chapter in O'Brien/na gCopaleen's *An Béal Bocht (The Poor Mouth)* in which a German philologist journeys to the Gaeltacht and tape-records the pure "Irish" discourse of a grunting pig. Joyce then explodes the mock-epic description of the dog and his "rann" with the voice of his Dublin raconteur: "So he told Terry to bring some water for the dog and, gob, you could hear him lapping it up a mile off" (256). The high humor of "Cyclops" depends on the continual contrast between its mock-epic material and the earth-bound, realistic voice of the pub hanger-on. In this respect "Cyclops" is a microcosm of the whole comic parallel between Homer's *Odyssey* and the world of Dublin in 1904. We move back and forth between the lofty, mock-epic narrative and the narrative in Dublin dialogue, with one often "translating" the other. Only at the very end of the chapter are these two sharply contrasting styles of narrative joined in a single sentence, which shows how the juxtapositional comedy of the whole chapter works: "And they beheld Him even Him, ben Bloom Elijah, amid clouds of angels ascend to the glory of the brightness at an angle of fortyfive degrees over Donohoe's in Little Green street like a shot off a shovel" (283).

Perhaps an even stronger case can be made for the tenth chapter of *Ulysses,* "Wandering Rocks," as a microcosm of the whole novel. Positioned precisely in the middle of the book, "Wandering Rocks" consists of nineteen short, separate, interwoven narratives each describing a different character or incident at the same midday hour. It is thus quite literally a microcosm of the eighteen chapters of the novel as a whole, plus one—the nineteenth episode in which the English viceroy, William Humble, parades by and is saluted by many of the characters of the other eighteen episodes. This "extra" nineteenth episode, this odd man out, may be taken as a postscript meant to portray the bowing and scraping, in the face of English dominance, by the Irish characters who populate Joyce's indigenous Irish world. Surely Joyce was aware of his English readership after all; so, he slyly flagellates rather than courts this readership here and elsewhere in the novel, as in his characterization of Haines. Certainly the viceroy is an emblem of power and control, one of the twin rocks of Church and State—along with Father Conmee, who in the first episode is obsessed with money and power— between which Bloom, Stephen, and the other pedestrians of Dublin have to steer a safe middle course. As hazardous first and last "bookends" of the chapter, as mirror represen- tatives of church and state, Father Conmee and the viceroy reflect Stephen's earlier statement to Haines that he is the "servant of two masters," the "imperial British state" and "the holy Roman catholic and apostolic church" (17).

Joyce must have especially wanted to emphasize these twin hazardous rocks and to shape a chapter out of so many separate episodes, because "Wandering Rocks" is the single Joycean episode not found in Homer. Homer's Ulysses is warned about the Wandering Rocks and steers completely clear of them, never encountering them. Joyce must have wanted to add this episode because it suited his narrative purposes particularly well. Here we witness Leopold buying the soft-pornographic novel *Sweets of Sin* for Molly and Stephen having a depressing encounter with his poor, un- schooled sister Dilly. But the other seventeen episodes of the chapter are focused on a variety of other characters ranging from Father Conmee and the viceroy to Corny Kelleher, Katey and Boody Dedalus, Blazes Boylan, Stephen's Italian teacher Almidano Artifoni, Ned Lambert, Tom Rochford, Simon Dedalus, Mulligan and Haines, and several others. Ellmann notes that in this chapter Joyce's "purpose was to bring the city of Dublin even more fully into the book by focusing upon it rather than upon Bloom or Stephen" (1982, 452). It is also truly a microcosm of how the whole book works, suggesting that life in general may be a collection of separate, interwoven stories told in different styles and based on different characters. However much Joyce may focus on Leopold, Stephen, and Molly throughout the novel, his is an impressively democractic book—reminding us continually that there are a lot of different people in a city like Dublin, and reality may simply depend on whose eyes we are looking through. In these ways "Wandering Rocks," like *Ulysses* as a whole, very much resembles both Joyce's collection of stories *Dubliners* and many another episodic, anecdotal, loosely structured Irish novel. Of course, even chapters that seem less obviously "Irish" than "Cyclops" and "Wandering Rocks," such as "Sirens"—which takes its inspiration from the musical fugue and from opera—are thoroughly Irish in their nearly fetishistic obsession with the *details* rather than some fictional whole. In many ways Joyce reminds us of the monks who decorated *The Book of Kells* so elaborately, apparently more caught up in their own highly ornamental designs than in the bare bones of the sacred text they were illustrating.

In "Wandering Rocks" Leopold Bloom briefly scans the potboiler *Sweets of Sin:* "All the dollarbills her husband gave her were spent in the stores on wondrous gowns and costliest frillies. For him! For Raoul! . . . Her mouth glued on his in a luscious voluptuous kiss while his hands felt for the opulent curves inside her deshabille" (194). Elsewhere in the novel Joyce plays with conventional styles of narrative more extensively, almost as if to show the reader that he has a command of those conventional forms and is perfectly capable of exploiting them for his own innovative ends. T. S. Eliot said of *Ulysses* that Joyce had "killed the nineteenth century" (quoted in Tanner 1984, 269), but it is also true that he made use of it in the novel. The entire first half of "Nausicaa," for example, is written in the style of a nineteenth-century romance, the kind of which Gerty McDowell has read too many. Joyce's most direct influence for the style of this chapter was the American Maria Cummins's *The Lamplighter* (1854), which also happened to have a protagonist named "Gerty" and which helped to mold the style of "Nausicaa" described by Joyce himself as a "namby-pamby jammy marmalady drawersy . . . style" (quoted in Ellmann 1982, 473). This limpid narrative might just have well have been found in many a nineteenth-century Irish romance:

The summer evening had begun to fold the world in its mysterious embrace. Far away in the west the sun was setting and the last glow of all too fleeting day lingered lovingly on sea and strand, on the proud promontory of dear old Howth guarding as ever the waters of the bay, on the weedgrown rocks along San- dymount shore and, last but not least, on the quiet church whence there streamed forth at times upon the stillness the voice of prayer to her who is in her pure radiance a beacon ever to the stormtossed heart of man, Mary, star of the sea. (284)

As loitering Leopold is drawn to the pale white wrists, the bosom, and the legs of Gerty McDowell, and as Gerty is attracted to Leopold as her knight in shining armor, Joyce allows them to achieve a climax proscribed by the decorum of nineteenth-century romances: Leopold masturbates in his pants as he watches Gerty bare her legs. Then, as in "Cy- clops," reality interrupts fantasy, this time from the per- spective of Bloom's consciousness: "Tight boots? No. She's lame. O! Mr. Bloom watched her as she limped away" (301).

Following the wild, huge, phantasmagoric "Circe" that has inspired so much Joycean criticism of the varieties discussed later in this chapter, "Eumaeus" is told in a traditional limited- omniscient narrative of falling action that Leopold himself might have penned. After all the amazing fantasy of the rest of the book, it is as if Joyce determined in this sixteenth chapter to show that he could once again write traditional narrative, albeit shaping it toward his own ends. Indeed, the very next chapter, "Ithaca," takes the journalistic realism of Defoe's *Robinson Crusoe* or Thoreau's *Walden* to exhaustive lengths, with Joyce recounting in catechetical, question-and- answer format almost every conceivable detail of experience, including an extensive and accurate budget of Leopold's financial transactions throughout the day.

Just as "Circe," with its constant, imaginative shifts of identity, looks ahead to *Finnegans Wake* where the moorings of identity are cast adrift, so does the final chapter, "Pe- nelope," with its uninterrupted, fluent flow of language. Its style was drawn partly from letters by Nora, her friends, and Joyce's mother—letters that often omitted punctuation and were described by Joyce's mother as "simply talking just as we would do at the fire here" (quoted in Scott 1984, 71). One step beyond Molly's stream of consciousness is the talk

of *Finnegans Wake,* and one step behind it is the oral storytelling and memoirs of a Peig Sayers or many a folk
seanchaí: "Yes because he never did a thing like that before
as ask to get his breakfast in bed with a couple of eggs since
the City Arms hotel when he used to be pretending to be
laid up with a sick voice doing his highness to make himself
interesting . . ." (608). It seems inconceivable that Molly's
narrative would have been crafted by a novelist of any other
country where the oral tradition is not as strong as it has
been in Ireland. This tradition has continually influenced not
only the style but the form of the Irish novel. As the foregoing
discussion has only begun to suggest, it seems unimaginable
that *Ulysses* could have emerged from any tradition other
than the Irish.

Finnegans Wake

Readers of *Finnegans Wake* have been searching for a
"center" in the book ever since it began to appear serially
as "Work in Progress" in the late 1920s. Joyce spent seventeen
years working on the book, then wryly noted that he expected
his "ideal reader suffering from an ideal insomnia" (*FW,*
120.14) to spend at least as long studying it. Indeed, a number
of Joyceans have persisted in doing just that for a good bit
more than seventeen years. This multilingual, continually
punning, cyclical book in four books without a definite beginning or end, structured to reflect both the Renaissance
Italian philosopher Vico's model of the four eternally recurring ages of humankind (as well as the circuitous course of
the Vico Road in Dalkey) and his countryman Bruno's binary
model of opposites, has eluded easy comprehension. It is
clear that as he continually revised the book over a number
of years, Joyce steadily made it more complex, more multilingual, more elusive. Indeed, the question of whether it
can properly be called a novel at all remains quite open.[5]
Subsequent Irish novelists, often influenced by *Portrait* and
Ulysses, have found in *Finnegans Wake* a point of no return.
So its influence on the Irish novel has remained hardly
discernible, making the book appear an aberration within
the tradition of the Irish novel. For Irish novelists as for

others, it has remained a much admired and little read book. As much as *Finnegans Wake* confounds the attempt, many Joyceans have persisted in trying to identify a narrative core or basic plot in the book. Michael Begnal, for example, typically tries to tie the whole book to the story of HCE, or "Earwicker," and his family:

The basic plot of *Finnegans Wake* is a level of narration which is interlaid, or sandwiched in, among several other levels. In brief, it unfolds like this: In Book II, chapter one—the children are outside, playing a game after school until their parents call them in at nightfall. Book II, chapter two—Shem and Shaun do their homework, while Issy sits on a couch, knitting and kibitzing. Book II, chapter three—Earwicker presides in the pub until closing time, finishes off the drinks left around, falls down drunk, and staggers up to bed later. Book III, chapter four—the Earwickers are awakened by the cries of Shem-Jerry; they soothe him, return to bed, make love, fall asleep as dawn is breaking. Book IV, chapter one—Anna Livia awakens, and her thoughts form the monologue which concludes the book. (1980, 45)

The problem is that even if he *is* a "protagonist" in the book, HCE is "Here Comes Everybody": within the dream world of the book, he is a Dublin publican, Finn MacCool, and scores of other people all mixed up together. So are all of the other characters in the book. Can we even meaningfully call them "characters," or refer to what these numerous creatures do in their various manifestations as a single "plot"? In his determination to ferret out the supposed "basic plot," Begnal is forced to ignore the entire first book of *Finnegans Wake* and several other chapters in it—not to mention the continual subversion of any clear, single identity in any of the characters. Just as easily did Anthony Burgess earlier "discover" *Finnegans Wake* to be all about the dream of a Dublin publican called Mr. Porter after a hard Saturday night's work, interrupted only by a period of wakefulness at the end of the book (Attridge and Ferrer 1984, 375–76). The debate about whether *Finnegans Wake* has any such narrative "center" continues to rage. One has the feeling that the book is better read like an encyclopedia or telephone book rather than a novel—in bits and pieces, with little regard for beginning, middle, or end, or for consistency in characterization and plot, or for any of the other traditional "unities."

As elusive as *Finnegans Wake* is as a narrative, and as complex as it is as language(s), it is nonetheless clear what the basic "style" of the book is. As William Irwin Thompson wrote perceptively years ago, "*Wake*-language . . . is spoken language; it is the storyteller's gab that is similar to the gab of the narrator in 'Cyclops' " (1964, 80). As much as it constantly borrows from many of the languages of the world in creating its own, the basic "language" of the book is an oral, *spoken* one. It is a kind of great blathering world folktale or myth whose most native language within its polyglot vision is the English of Joyce's native Ireland. At the beginning of his work on *Finnegans Wake*, "in 1923 . . . he kept a notebook of the commonplace Hiberno-English phrases used by his wife, Nora Barnacle, later published as *Scribbledehobble*" (McCrum, Cran, and MacNeil 1986, 187). Frank O'Connor often told the story of taking *Finnegans Wake* off the shelf at a party full of Dubliners who had never read the book, reading it aloud in a broad Dublin accent, and watching his audience double up in laughter. Sometimes Joyce's narrative sounds remarkably like many a character in many a popular nineteenth-century Irish novel:

Anam muck an dhoul! Did ye drink me doornail?
Now be aisy, good Mr. Finnimore, sir. And take your laysure like a god on pension and don't be walking abroad. Sure you'd only lose yourself in Healiopolis now the way your roads in Kapelavaster are that winding there after the calvary, the North Umbrian and Fivs Barrow and Waddlings Raid and the Bower Moore and wet your feet maybe with the foggy dew's abroad. Meeting some sick old bankrupt or the Cottericks' donkey with his shoe hanging, clankatachankata or a slut snoring with an impure infant on a bench. 'Twould turn you against life, so 'twould. (*FW*, 24.15–25)

More than a decade ago Petr Skrabanek complained, "It is a perverse situation that we have Basque and Bulgarian glossaries for *Finnegans Wake* but not Anglo-Irish. . . . Since

Joyce's English is Anglo-Irish, we should try to rectify our neglect and paradoxical omission of Anglo-Irish from Wakean studies" (1976, 79). Richard Wall added that "the most neglected major element of James Joyce's style is his use of the Anglo-Irish dialect of English" (1977, 121), and to fill this gap he has recently published *An Anglo-Irish Dialect Glossary for Joyce's Works* (1986). In his *Gaelic Lexicon for "Finnegans Wake,"* Brendan Ó Hehir had compiled Joyce's usages of the Irish language itself, rightly noting that Joyce had not quickly abandoned the study of Irish like the fictional Stephen but had attended Irish lessons over a two-year period. Ó Hehir further shows that Joyce had deliberately added the Irish during the revisions of *Finnegans Wake* (1967, vii and ix). Yet even Ó Hehir made the mistake of confusing the Irish language with Anglo-Irish or Irish-English, wondering how much Irish Joyce could have known since he spelled *siubhal* (which means simply "walking") as *shool*. "The difference between *siubhal* and *shool*," explained Skrabanek, "is not the difference between the 'right' and 'wrong' spelling, but the difference between Irish and Anglo-Irish. The spelling *shool* is well attested. There is also a difference in meaning as in the following excerpt from Samuel Lover, where "shooling" connotes "visiting" or "begging": 'Troth, you do me wrong, said the beggar, if you think I came shooling' " (79).

Lover, whose verse Joyce parodied in *Ulysses*, is just one of a number of earlier Irish novelists whom Joyce makes use of and even cites directly in *Finnegans Wake*. And as Richard Wall (1977) points out, whereas in the *Portrait* and *Ulysses* Joyce limits his use of Irish English to very specific, marked contexts that contrast with the rest of the narrative—in *Portrait*, Stephen's "tundish" and Davin's dialect; in *Ulysses*, Simon Dedalus's sarcastic reference to Stephen as "artist" (Anglo-Irish for "rogue"), the stage-Irish blarney of Mulligan, or the Irish chauvinism of the Citizen—in *Finnegans Wake* Joyce makes continual use of the dialect, adopting it as the home base of his narrative. John Garvin points out that "the Anglo-Irish idiom in *Ulysses* is reserved particularly for the vernacular of those characters who specialise in satire, censure, political controversy and comedy" (1977, 110). Even the title of the book contains an extra Anglo-Irish pun not usually noted by Joyceans: *Wake* suggests the Anglo-Irish pronunciation of "weak," as in the later sentence, "Tam Fanagan's weak yat" (*FW*, 276.21–22). Moreover, Joyce shows that he is well aware of the regional varieties of Irish-English. Part of HCE's status as an Irish Everyman, in more deliberately thoroughgoing fashion than Leopold Bloom, is the incorporation of the accents of all four Irish provinces in his speech—"his derry's own drawl and his corksown blather and his doubling stutter and his gullaway swank" (*FW*, 197.04–06). Interestingly, the most common Irish or Anglo-Irish phrase in *Finnegans Wake* is *sinn féin*—which means "ourselves alone" and was the slogan of irish independence and unity. This feature supports the impression that the creator of the seemingly anti-Irish Stephen Dedalus has in *Finnegans Wake* adopted the pose of a pro-Irish patriot, a nostalgic, exiled maker of the myth of Irish unity.

Among the many strange items that can be looked up in the huge encyclopedia that is *Finnegans Wake* are Joyce's parodies of or references to nineteenth-century Irish novelists, which are more obvious than any such uses of the tradition in *Ulysses*. For example, Joyce tags a footnote to his use of the word "hole," one which could just have well have appeared in *Castle Rackrent* or the *Essay on Irish Bulls:* "I have heard this word used by Martin Halpin, an old gardener from the Glens of Antrim who used to do odd jobs for my godfather, the Rev. B. B. Brophy of Swords" (*FW*, 266 n.2). At another point Joyce refers within a page and a half to works by William Carleton ("Rovy the Roder," *FW*, 228.24), Charles Kickham ("knocknacow," *FW*, 228.32), Gerald Griffin ("collegians," *FW*, 228.32; also "freightfullness whom he inhebited after his colline born janitor," *FW*, 224.10–11), Samuel Lover ("handy antics," *FW*, 229.02), and Michael Banim ("Croppy Crowhore," *FW*, 229.12).[6]

A connection that has been more often recognized in Joyce criticism is Joyce's use of Le Fanu's *The House by the Churchyard*, which like *Finnegans Wake* is a murky, mysterious tale set in Chapelizod, an outlying section of Dublin. Joyce had Le Fanu's novel in mind while working on *Finnegans Wake* and cited it directly in the book several times.[7] Marion W.

Cumpiano points to a speech in *Churchyard* by Devereux to
Lilias that has provided one source for Joyce's embodiment
in Anna Livia (whose name he spells at one point "Lylian")
as a feminine river of language:

Look at the river—is it not feminine? It's sad and merry, musical
and sparkling—and oh, so deep! Always changing, yet still the
same. I will show you the trees, or the clouds, or yourself, or the
stars; and it's so clear, and so dark, and so sunny—and so cold.
It tells everything, and yet nothing. It's so pure, and so playful,
and so tuneful, and so coy, yet so mysterious and fatal. I sometimes
think, Miss Lilias, I've seen the river spirit; and she's very much
like you! (quoted in Cumpiano 1979, 93)

Significantly, *Finnegans Wake* has always lent itself particularly well to an anthropological, mythical, or folkloric approach—to the tracing of particular myths and specific motifs
that run persistently through the book. In it Joyce compiled
his own extensive body of Irish oral tradition, extending and
integrating it outward toward the whole world, focusing all
the while on the talk of a number of shifting storytellers
who draw their stories from traditional materials and motifs.
As such the book reminds one of the Irish Folklore Commission's huge archive at University College, Dublin—packed
with transcriptions of a great many, very diffuse spoken
narratives difficult to reduce to any kind of simple "unity"
yet nevertheless sharing hundreds of common themes, characters, and motifs. Thus, though *Finnegans Wake* may not be
a novel at all, it probably returns more extensively to the
source of Irish fiction in the Irish oral tradition than does
any Irish novel. David Norris has suggested that in this book
"Joyce revenges himself for the taking away of the Irish
language by the English, for this linguistic exploitation. After
eight hundred years of occupation, he takes the English
language, and smashes it into smithereens, and hands it back
and says: This is our revenge. He makes the character Shem
boast that he will 'wipe alley english spooker, or multi-
phoniaksically spuking off the face of the erse' " (quoted in
McCrum, Cran, and MacNeil 1986, 188).

Joyce's Irish Context in Joyce Criticism

In spite of the many ways in which Joyce's books grew out of the distinctive Irish tradition, as soon as we turn to Joyce criticism we find that the questions of Joyce's place in this tradition and of his uses of the Irish tradition have still received relatively little attention. The pioneering work remains Vivian Mercier's *The Irish Comic Tradition* (1962), in which striking parallels are traced between Joyce and the Irish satirists and parodists of previous ages. Unfortunately, very few Joyceans have pursued the directions indicated by Mercier. I have noted Ó Hehir's *Gaelic Lexicon for "Finnegans Wake"* (1967). Also, an interesting article by Stanley Sultan shows that a native Irish source for *Ulysses* can be found in "The Voyage of Maeldun" *(Mael Dun),* a prose version in P. W. Joyce's *Old Celtic Romances* (1879) of the Old and Middle Irish type of "the 'Imram' or 'voluntary sea expedition' story" (1968, 104). Sultan points out that Joyce refers to "the solid man" Muldoon, and that "The Voyage of Maeldun" includes features that are found in *Ulysses* and *not* in the *Odyssey:* a horse race, a division into untitled sections, a similar name for the hero ("Maeldun" in Irish means "chief of the fort," "Leopold" in German "bold for the people"), and perhaps most interestingly of all, Maeldun's refusal (like Leopold's) to take revenge on his worst enemy (107). Sultan finds "Maeldun" to be "far more congenial to his pacific nature than just about any other heroic story, *The Odyssey* included" (108). He concludes that at the very least it is "a striking analogue" but more likely "an invisible contributor to his great novel" (105). The most extensive assessment of the relationship between Joyce's work and the older Irish tradition is found in James MacKillop's excellent recent book, *Fionn MacCumhaill: Celtic Myth in English Literature* (1986). MacKillop modestly calls Fionn, who was the most popular and persistent ancient Irish mythical hero, "one of the thousand faces in the monomyth" (180) of *Finnegans Wake,* rejecting the old received wisdom that the entire book is Fionn's massive dream. He then goes on to trace a great many significant uses of Fionn and transformations of him in the book. Furthermore, he cites art historian Paul Jacobsthal's emphasis that ancient Celtic art involves "ambiguity" and "the mechanism of dreams, where things have floating contours and pass into other things." MacKillop adds that these features are found "all through Irish tradition from before *The Book of Kells*, despite the presence of the occasional realist. For this reason, the reader of traditional Irish literature has prepared himself for some of the demands Joyce makes on the reader of *Finnegans Wake*" (164).

As I have already emphasized, attention to the relation between Joyce's other novels and the tradition of the Irish novel at large has been even rarer. Such attention has been confined almost entirely to notations of connections between Joyce and particular novelists—Griffin and Le Fanu before him, Beckett and Flann O'Brien after him, and the like. When Joyce's significance for the Irish novel as a whole is briefly mentioned, as in Seamus Deane's recent *Short History of Irish Literature* (1986), our appetite is only whetted for more: "In *Ulysses*, the modern Irish experimentation with language and form reaches a culmination. After it, the tremendous prestige of the English novel was never again so oppressive for Irish writers" (183). Deane adds the teasing, interesting thought that Joyce "universalized the plight in which the nineteenth-century Irish novelist had been trapped. Caught between two cultures, two languages and two audiences, English and Irish, they had been mired by history" (186). We need much more extensive consideration of the place of Joyce within the tradition of the Irish novel. My discussion above is intended to help provoke such consideration.

The Growth of Joyce Studies

For the most part, Joyce criticism has moved in very different directions. Recent surveys of the growth and current status of Joyce studies offer more detail than I will.[8] As Bernard Benstock writes, "Each generation redefines the set of Joycean problems, and every Joyce text . . . reactivates critical responses and approaches. For every critic who has attempted to nail shut a particular area of consideration, dozens immediately appear with crowbars to pull up the floorboards" (1985, 1). Joyce criticism mushroomed from the circle of advocates in the 1920s and 1930s (Pound, Eliot, Edmund Wilson, Stuart Gilbert, Frank Budgen, and a number of others) into the professional, academic, increasingly American Joyceans of the 1940s and 1950s (Harry Levin, Joseph Campbell, William York Tindall, Richard M. Kain, Hugh Kenner, and others). The 1960s and 1970s witnessed the full-blown Joyce Industry (with Joyceans too numerous to mention publishing in the newly founded *James Joyce Quarterly* and *A Wake Newslitter* and elsewhere, copiously examining the new editions of *Portrait* and *Ulysses* as well as Richard Ellmann's monumental 1959 biography). In our diverse and, I suppose, almost totally exhausted state in the late 1980s, we find "an arena in which sides line up for combat," as Benstock puts it (1985, 9).

A comparison of reviews of Joyce criticism published in the 1950s, 1960s, 1970s, and 1980s reflects how drastically matters have changed. Whereas Marshall McLuhan complained in 1951 of the "radically defective" state of the art, by 1965 Thomas F. Staley celebrated a boom in Joyce studies, citing over four hundred articles published during the period 1960 to 1965 alone. In 1976 Charles Rossman sensibly asked what new critical works could possibly offer to the ideal Joycean with the ideal insomnia, dividing Joyceans into those who see their subject as an enemy to be mastered and those who more pacifically seek understanding. By 1984 Stephen L. Tanner was focusing not merely on what sort of critical approaches Joyce's books were attracting but on how his work had in fact influenced and helped to shape those approaches, especially poststructuralism—calling Joyce a "proto-deconstructionist" (278). In light of this history of Joyce criticism, the most recent critical approaches seem in large part to be reactions against the male-dominated, American-dominated, New Critical, "know-it-all" approach of the Joyce Industry that reigned in the 1950s and 1960s. Psychoanalytic critics have probed below the surface of the affirmative novels championed by earlier critics in order to come to grips with the inner conflicts of Stephen Dedalus and Leopold Bloom. Turning away from America toward France for their inspiration, poststructuralists have denied the easy answers, clear facts, and stable fictional unity asserted earlier by the New Critics, stressing how each reader of Joyce rewrites the text in the free play of his mind. Feminists began by attacking gender-biased views of Stephen, Leopold, and Molly, and have tended to shift from an early critique of Joyce's male biases to an examination of some of the positive, androgynous aspects of his work. Critics with a political focus have rejected the received wisdom of an apolitical Joyce, devoting very recent attention to the understated but distinctive politics of his life and works.

Regardless of the critical approach, Joyce has clearly become the ultimate "teacher's pet," as one reviewer of the recent new edition of *Ulysses* entitled his review (Amis 1986). In a review of several recent guidebooks to Joyce, John Henry Raleigh (who admits that he is author of one himself) humorously paints the scenario of "an ideal student with an ideal desire to use all the resources he can muster to help him to comprehend the texts of the Master" (1985, 9). Pointing out that another Joycean seriously recommends reading *Ulysses* with his index book positioned constantly to one side of it and one of the books of allusions or annotations on the other, Raleigh proceeds to name title after critical title, picturing a student so overwhelmed by secondary Joyceana—dozens of reference and critical books and even the cassette and video tapes now available—that even an electronic page-turner could not get him through *Ulysses.* In their history of Joyce criticism, Sidney Feshback and William Herman examine how "Clive Hart designates three periods of *Wake* criticism" (1984, 762)—an example of how Joyce criticism itself has become canonical, with two Joyceans citing another Joycean about the periods of development of a great many *other* Joyceans (all as cited by *me*).

All of these flood tides of criticism exemplify Buck Mulligan's joke about how Haines's book would include "five lines of text and ten pages of notes about the folk and the fishgods of Dundrum." Joyce himself encouraged the growth of Joyce criticism, feeding Stuart Gilbert and Frank Budgen with information and helping to recruit the contributors to *An Exagmination Round His Factification for Incamination of Work in Progress* (1929). In it Samuel Beckett, William Carlos

Williams, and a host of other notables examined and celebrated *Finnegans Wake* fully a decade *before* it was completed or published, and Joyce himself contributed a cryptic letter under the name of "Vladimir Dixon." Of *Ulysses* Joyce is said to have remarked, "It will keep the professors busy for centuries arguing over what I meant, and that's the only way of insuring one's immortality" (quoted in Ellmann 1982, 521). Early drafts of Joyce's books—*Stephen Hero* (1944), for example, and David Hayman's *A First Draft Version of "Finnegans Wake"* (1963)—have not only been published but have in turn provoked numerous scholarly articles and books. Joyce fully intended to keep scholars busy, advising them in a footnote in *Finnegans Wake* to "wipe your glosses with what you know" (*FW*, 304 n.3). Like Joyce's work, the world of Joyce criticism is itself often comic. The student of Joyce should become familiar with this world of criticism but not let it become overwhelming. I wholeheartedly agree with Don Gifford, who writes that when he teaches *Ulysses* he tries to avoid an obsession with "Double-Crostic . . . elaborate exercise in clue teaching and puzzle solving" in favor of an appreciation of the novel's comedy and the fact "that it is a deeply felt and deeply moving book, ethical and prophetic. I try continually to spring the novel from the confines of the puzzle solver's laboratory and to reattach it to our lives that give it life" (1983, 45).

Psychoanalytic Approaches

Psychoanalytic approaches to Joyce have been encouraged by the clear connections between the works of Freud and Jung and Joyce's own life and works. He surely used their ideas in probing the deepest conflicts in the psyches of his characters, especially Stephen Dedalus and Leopold Bloom. These connections drew comment fairly early in Joyce criticism, but systematic psychoanalytic approaches to his work did not emerge until the 1960s and especially the 1970s. Joyce was probably first introduced to the ideas of the Viennese school through the talk of his fellow medical students. Stanislaus Joyce noted that as early as 1901–02 his brother "regarded psychology, which he was then studying, as the

basis of philosophy, and words in the hand of an artist as
the medium of paramount importance for the right understanding of the inmost life of the soul" (quoted in Brivic
1980, 10). Psychoanalytic approaches were further encouraged by the information in the appendix to Richard Ellmann's
The Consciousness of James Joyce (1977) that Joyce had bought
several works by Freud, Jung, and Ernest Jones in Trieste
perhaps during the period 1909–11 (Anderson 1982, 53).
The earliest such work purchased was Jung's *The Significance
of the Father in the Destiny of the Individual*, written when
Jung was still a faithful Freudian (Brivic 1982, 74), which
may have influenced Joyce's portrayal of a Stephen in rebellion against his own father and other "father figures,"
such as Father Dolan, the pandybatting priest in *Portrait*,
and Deasy in *Ulysses*. He read Freud's 1910 biography of
Leonardo da Vinci and used his notion of the "phallic mother"
threatening a young male's gender identity in both *Portrait*
and *Ulysses* (Kimball 1980). The oedipal view of *Hamlet* that
Stephen advances in the "Scylla and Charybdis" chapter of
Ulysses is very similar to Otto Rank's 1912 psychoanalytic
analysis of Shakespeare (Kimball 1976). Joyce bought Freud's
The Psychopathology of Everyday Life and subsequently included in *Ulysses* virtually every kind of parapraxis listed by
Freud (Anderson 1972).

Always delighting in such coincidences, Joyce remarked
that his surname was the English equivalent of "Freud" in
German (Ellmann 1982, 490). Jung treated Joyce's disturbed
daughter Lucia, wrote about *Ulysses* and *Finnegans Wake*, and
advanced the view that Joyce was actually a controlled schiz-
ophrenic who stayed sane by displacing his schizophrenia
onto his daughter and into his work, especially *Finnegans
Wake*—a theory since reiterated more than once in Joyce
criticism (as in Coleman 1963 and Andreasen 1973). One
Joycean assures us that he never fully appreciated *Portrait*
until he had a nervous breakdown and could understand
the Stephen who struggles to keep a grip on reality, muttering
to himself, "I am Stephen Dedalus. I am walking beside my
father whose name is Simon Dedalus. We are in Cork, in
Ireland. Cork is a city" (*Portrait*, 92; Klein 1976). Even though
Joyce was not a true believer in psychoanalysis, it is clear

from the mounting evidence that "he did more to transfuse this new perspective into the mainstream of Western literature than many a declared disciple" (Kimball 1980, 70).

At the same time, even Mark Shechner, the author of the first full-fledged, full-length psychoanalytic study of Joyce, has cautioned since the appearance of his book *Joyce in Nighttown: A Psychoanalytic Inquiry into "Ulysses"* (1974) that "properly used, psychoanalysis should be an aid to imagining, not a system of controls upon it" (1976, 271). Darcy O'Brien interjected "A Critique of Psychoanalytic Criticism, or What Joyce Did and Did Not Do," arguing that psychoanalytic criticism can better be applied to pre-Freudian authors who did not know about psychoanalytic ideas and thus were more like Freud's own patients. He added that Joyce himself was sharply aware of notions and motifs in his works purportedly "discovered" by many a psychoanalytic Joycean writing with "a puffed-up sense of his own importance" (1976a, 278). As Joyce noted in *Finnegans Wake*, "I can psoakoonaloose myself any time I want" (*FW*, 522.34–35). Furthermore, Joyce deliberately sought to dissociate himself and his novels from the Viennese school, constantly disparaging both Jung ("the Swiss Tweedledum") and Freud ("the Viennese Tweedledee") in his letters, fearing "the usurpation of the poet's power by the medicinemen" (Anderson 1982, 53). In *Finnegans Wake* he derided those who were "yung and easily freudened" (121). He preferred the systems of analysis of Aquinas and Vico to those of Freud and Jung. He disagreed with Jung's diagnosis of his daughter and himself, convinced that "a man who had so misconstrued *Ulysses* could scarcely be expected . . . to construe Lucia correctly" (Ellmann 1982, 680).

Yet disagreement and disdain seldom precluded influence and inclusion in Joyce's work—as in the cases of Oliver St. John Gogarty and George Moore as well as Freud and Jung. Regardless of Joyce's intention, classic Freudian criticism is useful in reading his novels. Jean Kimball's Freudian reading of the opening pages of *Portrait* is fairly convincing: Stephen may wet his bed as an infantile sexual substitute, he is drawn mostly to his mother who has "a nicer smell than his father" and plays the phallic "hornpipe" for Stephen to dance to, and he is frightened by Aunt Dante's threat about the eagles who will "pull out his eyes" if he pursues his fantasy of marrying the girl next door. These details point to "the image of the 'phallic mother,' which is also the source for the vulture-mother of Leonardo's fantasy" as analyzed by Freud (Kimball 1980, 62). Shechner calls *Ulysses* "both a psychoanalytic study of character and a documentary of Joyce's self-analysis. . . . In 'Scylla and Charybdis' this analysis takes the form of Stephen's parable of Shakespeare, while in 'Circe' Joyce discloses the contours of his most obsessive fantasies in the fantasy lives of Stephen and Bloom" (1974, 19). He points to the Joyce who implored Nora in his letters to "take me into the dark sanctuary of your womb" (quoted in Shechner 1974, 92) and "wanted both to revel in his wife's shit and to forge imperishable monuments to the Irish imagination. Might the two not have something to do with each other?" (1976, 273). The best answer is "sometimes." Joyce's use of psychoanalysis is clearest and most extensive in "Circe," where Stephen and Leopold both undergo dark nights of the soul and come to grips, respectively, with the specters of Stephen's mother and Leopold's father (who committed suicide) and son (who died shortly after birth). Shechner feels that Bella Cohen, the whorehouse madam who as "Bello" abuses a Leopold portrayed in the Circean fantasy as a transvestite and a "new womanly man," is simply "a particularly malign manifestation" of the "phallic mother" and "the bisexual manifestation in all of Joyce's women" (1974, 210).

At this point a psychoanalytic approach can aid a feminist one—the celebration of the androgynous Leopold, the "new womanly man." Turning to "Penelope," Shechner psychoanalyzes the critics, who traditionally tended to either sing Molly's praises as an "earth mother" or abuse her as a "thirty-shilling whore." He views the tactics of the old-school male critics of Molly as "the tactics of seduction—flattery and assault. The phenomenon of transference is not confined to the therapeutic couch; the dynamics of literary response depend on it" (1974, 296). Gabriele Schwab agrees that male criticism on Molly "has turned out to be more a documentation of male fears and wishes regarding women than an analysis of her character limited strictly to textual considerations" (1982, 81).

Sheldon Brivic finds Joyce moving in his career from a Freudian to a Jungian presentation of character—from Stephen Dedalus and the paralyzed characters of *Dubliners* to Leopold Bloom and the constantly changing characters of *Finnegans Wake.* "Like Freud," Brivic argues, the early Joyce took sex (or more often, the lack of it) as a "standard of truth," while both Jung and the later Joyce were more open to the unconscious. "This grant of authority to the unconscious is a crucial distinction between Freud's thought and Jung's; and also between Joyce's early works, where the prime issue is whether people can control their lives and the later ones in which they follow their destinies with growing dynamism" (1980, 11). In the last few years psychoanalytic reverberations in Joyce criticism have tended to move beyond Freud and Jung altogether and, within poststructuralist and feminist approaches to Joyce, into the ideas of "post-Freudians" like Jacques Lacan.

Structuralist, Poststructuralist, and Reader-Response Approaches

Structuralist, poststructuralist, and reader-response approaches have provided the most active and popular arena for revisionist Joyce studies in recent years. American Joyce scholars have been particularly influenced by Roland Barthes, Jacques Derrida, and other French structuralist, poststructuralist, or deconstructionist critics inspired in their turn by Joyce's work. As Derrida commented at the 1984 Joyce Symposium in Frankfurt, "Deconstruction could not have been possible without Joyce."[9] J. Hillis Miller adds, "There is little that deconstructive theory of narrative knows about the undecidability of words or of story lines which Joyce did not already know" (1982, 4). Likewise, Derek Attridge agrees that "deconstructive criticism of Joyce would have to be that which Joyce practices upon us as much as that which we practice upon Joyce."[10] This shift in rhetoric from the older generation of Joyceans is drastic. Jennifer Levine describes

the old Joyceans and the new Joyceans meeting at the Fifth
International Joyce Symposium in 1975: "They did not really
speak to each other, perhaps because they did not share the
same language" (1978, 17). Thomas F. Staley adds that among
those 1975 papers, "the French volume . . . seems remote
from the more traditional American concerns in the English
volume. But that was 1975. By 1979, at the Zurich Symposium
the critical approaches and theoretical concerns of the American and European participants had much more in common"
(1982, 255). The 1978–79 issue of the *James Joyce Quarterly*
was a "Structuralist/Reader Response Issue." Since that time
such concerns in Joyce criticism have become very much
"where it's at" (Benstock and Benstock 1982, 12). Here I can
only begin to suggest the directions and diversity among
these Joyceans. Charles Rossman (1982) offers a balanced,
concise overview of recent trends. Students should also consult a good introduction to current approaches in literary
criticism (such as Eagleton 1978).

In structuralist essays during the 1970s, Robert Scholes
and Eric Gould both stressed that in *Ulysses* the Homeric
parallels function as a kind of formal discipline helping to
structure the novel and at the same time allowing Joyce to
rewrite the myth and in turn be rewritten by it (Scholes
1974; Gould 1979). Their conclusions about this aspect of
Ulysses were very similar to Barbara Hardy's formalist reading
a decade earlier (1964), a critical development supporting the
sense that among Joyceans "phenomenological critics have
turned to a phenomenology of reading; psychological critics
have turned to a psychology of the reader's response; archetypal critics have become structuralists; and formalists
have been semioticians" (Sosnowski 1978, 53). One might
add that often structuralists have become poststructuralists.
In short, these Joyceans reflect shifts in literary criticism as
a whole. One suspects that such critical developments are
not so revolutionary as many of their proponents like to
claim and that a continuum of critical responses can be
discerned. In studying Joyce, one finds few new answers but
many new questions.

The first full-length attempt at a systematic structuralist or poststructuralist study of Joyce was Margot Norris's *The Decentered Universe of "Finnegans Wake"* (1974). Norris denied the existence of a "center," a single plot or "simple text," in *Finnegans Wake*, reminding us of Joyce's comment that "one great part of every human existence is passed in a state which cannot be rendered sensible by the use of wideawake language, cuttandry grammar, and goahead plot" (100). She insisted that "the greatest critical mistake in approaching *Finnegans Wake* has been the assumption that we can be certain of who, where, and when everything is in the *Wake*, if only we do enough research" (120). Rather than embellish a single story, Joyce constantly merges old themes and details as in a collage. He asked his aunt back in Dublin to send "any news you like, programmes, pawntickets, press cuttings, handbills. I like reading them" (130). He did not craft his book in the conventional, linear way, reminding us of his circular model by "beginning" on his first page with the second half of a sentence, the first half of which "ends" the book on its last page. Working on the *Wake*, he observed, "What the language will look like when I have finished I don't know. But having declared war I shall go on *jusqu'au bout*" (129–30). Within its pages we are reminded that "the unfacts, did we possess them, are too imprecisely few to warrant our certitude" (*FW*, 57.16–17) and that "every person, place and thing in the chaosmos . . . [is] changing every part of the time" (*FW*, 118.21–23).

Norris warns that "only by abandoning the novelistic approach to *Finnegans Wake* can readers free themselves from waking conventions and logic enough to enjoy the wholly imaginative reality of a dream-work . . . . By abandoning conventional frames of reference, readers can allow the work to disclose its own meanings, which are lodged in the differences and similarities of its multitudinous elements" (22). Like the structuralist scholar of myth and folklore, Norris analyzed the disparate strands of the book, its many variants, in order to discover common themes rather than a single plot. As in folklore, the point is not to find a single "authentic" story, but rather to look at all of the different versions of a story to see what they have in common:

In the decentered world of the *Wake,* this structure is not a single myth, as in *Ulysses,* but a series of major myths of creation, sin, and redemption . . . . The myths that contribute most to the thematic structure of *Finnegans Wake* include the Oedipus myth . . . Old Testament stories, the Gospels, the Irish legends of Finn MacCool, the Egyptian myths of Isis and Osiris, Greek and Roman myths, including Zeus and Leda, Romulus and Remus, and the modern biography of Charles Parnell. At the heart of each is a crime, a violation—specifically, an act of trespass over a forbidden boundary. (37)

At many points in her book Norris seems as much a budding poststructuralist as a structuralist, citing Derrida, talking about "deconstruction," and celebrating the indeterminancy of Joyce's book. This provoked Mary Robinson (1978) to complain that "the most serious problem with her book is her failure even to acknowledge that the structuralist view of myth and poststructuralist 'freeplay' tend to be theoretical antagonists that can be accommodated to each other only with difficulty, if at all" (169).

Joyceans who have pursued the directions suggested in Norris's book now write in a poststructuralist mode, turning away from a structuralist analysis of language and myth in favor of often playful "readings" of *Finnegans Wake* inspired by the writings of Jacques Derrida, Jean-Michel Rabaté, Stephen Heath, and the other poststructuralists of *Tel Quel.* This development reflects changes in literary criticism at large. *Finnegans Wake* has been at the center of the poststructuralists' endeavors. In a thirty-seven–page article entitled merely "Notes for Reading Joyce," Stephen Heath offers typical remarks: "Where criticism *ex*plicates, opening out the folds of the writing in order to arrive at the meaning, *Finnegans Wake* is offered as a permanent *inter*plication, a work of folding and unfolding in which every element becomes always the fold of another in a series that knows no point of rest . . . . The text is never closed and the 'ideal reader' will be the one who accedes to the play of this incompletion, placed in 'a situation of writing,' ready no longer to master the text but now to become its actor" (1984, 32). Jean-Michel Rabaté finds Joyce encouraging his readers in this playful, open-ended reading, pointing to the assertion that " 'I shall explex what you ought to means by this with its proper when and where and why and how in the subsequent sentence' (*FW*, 149.30–2): of course, the subsequent sentence brings no clarification. 'Hoping against hope all the while that, by the light of philosophy, (and may she never folsage us!) things will begin to clear up a bit' [*FW*, 119.04–06]: 'We shall perhaps not so soon see' [*FW*, 32.02]" (1984, 93). As Jennifer Levine emphasizes, Joycean poststructuralists "are as much interested in philosophers as in literary tradition. They relish in the difficulty of *Finnegans Wake* rather than seek to minimize it. They play with language themselves, casting into doubt the difference between literature and literary criticism. They're not so much interested in *genre*— say, 'novel'—as in *text*" (1978, 19). They are aware of being read in turn by Joyce—the author who anticipates in the *Wake* "carefully digesting the very wholesome criticism" (*FW*, 163.36). Joycean poststructuralists write mostly about *Finnegans Wake*, with the occasional exception of a Brook Thomas reading *Ulysses* as "the perfect example of Valéry's statement that 'a work of art is never finished, but only abandoned' " (1982, xiv). One reads the poststructuralists with the impression that they delight in Joyce as Woody Allen does in "The Irish Genius"—as "the most incomprehensible and hence the finest poet of his time" (1972, 117).

In Joycean circles some voices have been raised in protest against poststructuralist practice. In the preface to the most recent edition of *Ulysses*, Richard Ellmann contradicted Brook Thomas and Valéry: "Many writers stop writing at deadlines, and we do not say that their books are unfinished. Joyce finished his book in the sense of regarding his work as done and in another sense as well. Because Molly Bloom countersigns with the rhythm of finality what Stephen and Bloom have said about the word known to all men, *Ulysses* is one of the most concluded books ever written" (1986, xiv). Clive Hart, an early, leading pioneer in *Wake* criticism, feels that Derrida's and Norris's view of the *Wake* as (in Norris's words)

a "literary exemplar of deconstructive discourses of the twentieth century" would reduce the book to "a pathological
expression of the fear of authority" (1982, 162). Hart adds
the hope that "clear-sighted scrutiny" of the *Wake* "will show
more of its freely imaginative constructive power" (162) and
the conviction that "I do not yet know how to read *Finnegans
Wake*, but the more I can learn to read it simply, the happier
I believe I shall be" (158). Joyce himself advised one of the
professors to pay attention to the "linguistic phenomenon"
of reading the book rather than get lost among its allusions.
In his interesting book on reading Joyce as an act of translation, Fritz Senn remarks of currently fashionable theorists
that "I have read few of them and understood none" (1984,
x). He adds that "collectively, we have failed in a most
elementary way and that we are hardly qualified to discuss
Finnegans Wake with scholarly pretense. It is a pretense that
I, for one, can no longer keep up with a straight face" (xi).

Closely allied to the poststructuralist treatments of Joyce
sketched above is the impact of reader-response criticism on
Joyce studies, with increased attention to the effects of readers' assumptions and activities as distinct from authorial
intention. James J. Sosnoski uses the controversy about
whether Stephen in *Portrait* is heroic or ironic as a case
demonstrating his thesis that "hypotheses about the nature
of texts generate the facts of a given text . . . . Reading
warrants generate readings acts" (1978, 44). Sosnoski's point
could be broadened to the whole of Joyce criticism or, indeed,
to criticism of the Irish novel in general: psychoanalytic critics
are drawn to "Circe"; deconstructionists, to the *Wake*; historical critics, to the nineteenth-century novel; and so on.
Charles Rossman (1982) also focuses on *Portrait* in order to
affirm the validity of multiple interpretations of the text as
well as the importance of the author's intention. He cites
the case of Caroline Gordon, who argued in the 1950s that
Joyce spiritually damns Stephen at the end of the novel, as
an example of the definite possibility of *mis*reading the text.
Critics adopting a number of different approaches to Joyce
more and more have emphasized the central importance of
the reader. This is not to suggest, however, that all readings
of Joyce are valid or that "anything goes." One does best

to approach Joyce's books with great enthusiasm and Joyce criticism with great caution.

Feminist Criticism

As noted, in his reviews of Joyce criticism Thomas F. Staley (1982, 1983) pointed to the recent outburst of poststructuralist approaches to Joyce, contrasting the programs of the 1975 and 1979 International Joyce Symposia. In his own turn Staley's reviews can be cited as evidence of how recently feminist approaches to Joyce have blossomed and attracted attention in Joyce studies—for Staley, the grand old man of the *James Joyce Quarterly*, does not mention feminist approaches at all in those reviews (1982 and 1983).[11] Joyce attracted occasional feminist comment during the 1960s and 1970s, but Suzette Henke and Elaine Unkeless's collection of essays, *Women in Joyce* (1982), and Bonnie Kime Scott's *Joyce and Feminism* (1984) were the first books specifically devoted to this subject. Scott's book includes a useful overview of "Feminist Critics on Joyce" (117–32). She points out that the early phase tended toward negative criticism— with critics such as Florence Howe complaining that Joyce confined his female characters to limited roles that never included intellectual activity or art, and Carolyn Heilbrun in her afterword to *Women in Joyce* calling Joyce a misogynist and chauvinist, even though such a view was not the consensus of the other essays in that volume.

Scott emphasizes that feminist approaches to Joyce have now entered a positive phase exemplified by most of the other essays in *Women in Joyce* as well as Scott's own book with her notion of a "reintegrated feminism." She has recently added a second book (1987) assessing Joyce's work within the matrix of various feminist approaches. In their introduction to *Women in Joyce*, Unkeless and Henke emphasize that they and the other contributors to the volume are "contextual" critics who reject the "formalist or New Critical isolation of a work of art from its psychological, cultural, and economic environment," seeking to understand the work "within a larger frame of politics and history. Feminist analysis is, of course, a more specialized form of contextual interpretation. It attempts to examine the way in which a work of literature reflects, verifies, or criticizes prevalent beliefs about women, about gender identity and sex-role stereotyping, and about the relationships between the sexes in fiction" (xi). Feminist criticism of Joyce is thus a specific variety of political criticism; of course, Terry Eagleton (1978) has argued that *all* criticism is one form or another of political criticism, whether stated or unstated.

A number of scholars have in recent years celebrated the theme of androgyny in Joyce's works, especially in *Ulysses.* In 1975 Suzette Henke published in a psychoanalytic journal an article with the thesis that Leopold approaches Molly as "a surrogate son-husband," moving beyond "sexual possessiveness" to "the fertile terrain of *agape.*" She added that "Leopold is something special. He understands and feels what a woman is. And when all the Blazes have burned themselves out, Leopold will still be there to kindle the flame of love" (332, 334). The following year Elaine Unkeless, in an article entitled "Leopold Bloom as a Womanly Man," argued that "the Jungian notion that the female side of a man, his anima, lies in the unconscious is present in 'Circe.' . . . Bloom is an androgynous character; that is, he can balance the supposedly 'masculine' and 'feminine' aspects of himself and can transcend the stereotyped category of either" (1976, 40). In the fantasy world of "Circe," Leopold becomes a woman, is abused by the whorehouse madam Bella who becomes "Bello," and gives birth.[12] Unkeless does lament that while Joyce delighted in creating a womanly man, he seemed unwilling to posit seriously a manly woman, adding an article critiquing Molly as a "conventional" portrait of a woman (1982). Morris Beja complains that "to dismiss Molly Bloom as Joyce's male projection of a woman is, while accurate, beside the point—as it would be to dismiss Bloom as a gentile's Jew, or Joe Christmas as a white man's black, or Heathcliff, Lydgate, and Septimus Warren Smith as women's men" (1984, 121). And much as Leopold fantasizes about giving birth and assuming a passive "female" sexual role, Molly imagines herself in an aggressive "male" sexual role. Taking as his starting point Carolyn Heilbrun's notions about androgyny, the same Heilbrun who dismissed Joyce as a misogynist, Declan Kiberd champions Leopold as an "androgynous hero" (1985a, 171). Kiberd notes that Leopold's first act in the novel, his preparation of breakfast for Molly, is "a deed appropriate to the liberated contemporary husband, but in the Dublin of 1904 an act tantamount to perversion . . . . Already it is clear that Leopold has a strong element of the female in his personality, as he stays to straighten the bedspread or to flick an offending crumb off a bedsheet" (174). Leopold empathizes with the difficulties of women in childbirth or finding a toilet in the city center of Dublin (175). Kiberd adds that "Joyce himself, according to Maria Jolas, 'talked of fatherhood as if it were motherhood,' and his biographer remarks that 'he seems to have longed to establish in himself all aspects of the bond of mother and child'" (180). He also notes that Joyce preferred Ulysses to Jesus because Ulysses had lived with a woman and so was more truly an "all-round man" (168) and that "the Gaelic version of Joyce, 'Seoighe,' was a derivate of 'Sheehy' [or *sidhe*, the mythical female spirit of the wind], or so he claimed, since this confirmed his own self-image as a 'womanly man'" (171). Joyce wore "sparkling rings" in order to "advertise" the elegance of his sensitive hands (171). His memories of his mother were "fired by an almost feminist sense of outrage against her predicament: 'My mother was slowly killed, I think, by my father's ill-treatment, by years of trouble, and by my cynical frankness of conduct. When I looked on her face as she lay in her coffin—a face grey and wasted with cancer—I understood that I was looking on the face of a victim and I cursed the system which had made her a victim'" (173). Kiberd's book is a valuable instance of the "reintegrated feminism" advocated by Scott, according to which women can write not only about women but also about gender roles in male authors, and men can enter the critical dialogue too: Kiberd is a man who celebrates feminist impulses in the works of male authors. Other male critics who have responded to Joyce's androgynous vision include Richard Ellmann (1984), Robert Boyle (1984), and Richard Brown (1985).

Feminist appreciation of the androgynous Leopold has had to work itself past the sexism of Stephen, who in *Portrait* tends to view women merely as objects of fantasy (Eileen

Vance and "E. C.") or sources of sustenance (his mother). As Margaret Church notes, "told from Stephen's point of view, *Portrait* depicts women he uses, women he rejects, women he fears, and women he idealizes" (1981, 164). Earlier attacks on Joyce as "misogynist" simplistically identify Joyce with Stephen. But Suzette Henke (1975) explains Stephen's problems with women as part of his "adolescent priggish-ness," agreeing with Hugh Kenner's (1956) much earlier view of Stephen as an ironic, critical portrait of the artist as a *young* man. Leopold is mature; Stephen is immature. Joyce himself noted that he got tired of writing about Stephen because he "no longer interests me. He has a shape that can't be changed" (quoted in Ellmann 1982, 459). Scott (1984) extensively demonstrates that at least in the matters of his exposure to feminism and attitudes about women, Joyce himself is not to be confused with his portrait of Stephen. She focuses particularly on Joyce's contacts with the Irish women's movement through his friends Hannah and Francis Sheehy-Skeffington (the model for MacCann in *Portrait*). Strong young women such as Hannah Sheehy-Skeffington are reflected in Joyce's characterization of Miss Ivors in his story "The Dead" and Emma Clery in *Stephen Hero* and *Portrait*. Feminism attracted active young Irish women and became "just as essential a subject as nationalism for the brooding Joyce" (28). His youthful essay on Ibsen celebrated the "curious admixture of woman in his nature. His mar-vellous accuracy, his faint traces of femininity, his delicacy of swift touch"—with Joyce describing qualities that he cul-tivated himself—"are perhaps attributable to this admixture. But that he knows women is an uncontrovertible fact" (Scott 1984, 53).

Joyce was neither true believer in feminism and socialism nor opponent to either cause. Even a "priggish " Stephen says to McCann only that "You are right to go your way. Leave me to go mine" (*Portrait*, 198). Joyce was influenced by another Irish novelist deeply concerned with women's lives, George Moore. Further, during his years of struggle with *Ulysses* and *Finnegans Wake*, he was crucially aided and stimulated by a number of highly intelligent, courageous women, including Harriet Shaw Weaver, Sylvia Beach, and

Maria Jolas (Scott 1984, 115). To his wife, Nora, he wrote, "Guide me, my saint, my angel, lead me forward. *Everything* that is noble and exalted and deep and true and moving in what I write comes, I believe, from you. O take me into your soul of souls and then I will become indeed the poet of my race" (quoted in Henke 1983, 129). In male and mixed company Joyce sometimes made antifemale remarks as part of a pose that he abandoned in his serious work. Scott recounts the illustrative anecdote about his interaction with Mary Colum, who sought in conversation to get him to admit his debts to Freud and Jung: "Joyce squirmed and retorted, 'I hate women who know anything,' to which Colum replied, 'No, Joyce, you don't . . . . You like them,' and recalls: 'After a few seconds of silent annoyance, a whimsical smile came over his face, and the rest of the afternoon was pleasant for all three of us' " (117). The celebrated Joycean strategies of "silence, exile, and cunning" are, Kiberd reminds us, traditional feminine survival tactics (1985a, 173).

Feminist criticism of Joyce may be viewed as a particular variety of political criticism; it has also often drawn from psychoanalysis as well as poststructuralism. Scott calls Norris's book on *Finnegans Wake* "the most coherent feminist interpretation of that work to date, though this may not seem obvious from the title or declared method" (128). Norris's work has since taken a more clearly feminist slant. Scott notes that feminists are attracted to "post-structuralists like Jacques Derrida and Julia Kristeva who take woman as a central metaphor in their process of decoding language, and focus upon 'desire' as a force in language" (7). As we are beginning to see, there has been and should be considerable overlap and interaction among the major current critical approaches to Joyce. In "Circe," for example, the psychoanalytic critic finds Leopold and Stephen grappling with their family nightmares; the poststructuralist finds a loss of "center" that points ahead to *Finnegans Wake;* the feminist celebrates Leopold's androgyny; and the political critic (as we are about to see) may point to this chapter's setting among the underclass of Dublin or to evidence of Leopold's quietly socialist or progressive-nationalist ideals. No one of these emphases necessarily contradicts the others; indeed, they may all be viewed as complementary.[13]

Political Criticism

Terry Eagleton's point that *all* literary criticism can be seen as "political" in one way or another notwithstanding, political criticism on Joyce in the conventional sense—discussion of Joyce's own politics or application to his work of a specific political methodology such as Marxism—has been the rarest among the chief current approaches. This may be largely due to Joyce's own encouragement of the notion that he was apolitical, that he was an artist rising above politics, like Icarus soaring into the heavens. Yet we have to suspect that for the author whose earliest alleged composition was the poem "*Et Tu,* Healy" attacking Parnell's chief Irish opponent, the apolitical pose is a myth. Besides, Joyce did not deny his politics; he was simply quiet about his views. His story in *Dubliners* about the memory of Charles Stewart Parnell, "Ivy Day in the Committee Room," was his declared favorite. Tom Paulin (1984a) reads his letters supporting the Sinn Féin movement as evidence of a hope that Ireland would find its place among the nations and the fantasy that he himself would be welcomed back to an independent Ireland, much as Leopold Bloom emerges as "Lord Mayor of Dublin" in "Circe." At least since Herbert Howarth's *The Irish Writers, 1880–1940: Literature under Parnell's Star* (1958), Joyce's reverence for and anxiety about the martyred Parnell have been taken for granted. However, political criticism of Joyce was slow to move beyond Joyce's Parnellism into a consideration of his politics as a whole. This unusual critical quietism may be seen as a result not only of the common view that Joyce was apolitical but also as due to the early Marxist tendency to dismiss Joyce's work. *Ulysses* in particular "came to perform the unenviable role of whipping-boy for Marxist attacks of modernist literature—a rag to the red bull," Jeremy Hawthorn notes, adding that "nearly every Marxist account of *Ulysses* written in the 1930s commented upon the fact that its characters belonged to the petit-bourgeoisie, the class which, from a Marxist perspective, was most detached from decisive and influential social action, and was thus least able to understand social development" (1982, 112, 113). Even the great Marxist critic George Lukács dismissed Joyce in 1964 as subjectivist and escapist, "a decadent and solipsistic writer" (quoted in Naremore 1976, 113). Terry Eagleton suggested as late as 1976 that Joyce's work marked "a retreat from a history in crisis" (quoted in Hawthorn 1982, 115). Joyce himself was rather bemused by the early Marxist criticisms, remarking that "I don't know why they attack me—nobody in any of my books is worth more than a thousand pounds" (quoted in Hawthorn 1982, 112), and "I've never written about anything but common people" (quoted in Jameson 1982, 134). He even once described himself as a "socialistic artist" (quoted in Paulin 1984a, 144).

Fortunately, "of late there has been an increase," as Sidney Feshback and William Herman note, "in Marxian Joyce criticism with a new degree of sophistication and freedom" (1984, 757). Hawthorn explains that "since the 1930s Marxists have grown more interested in subjectivity as a result of a number of theoretical developments within Marxism. The work of Soviet psychologists such as Vygotsky represents one influential strand of work; the increasing concern with questions of ideology represents an even more persuasive theoretical development" (121). Like the feminist who separates Joyce from the "priggish, misogynist" Stephen, James Naremore distinguishes the Stephen of *Portrait* with his apolitical pose from Joyce, adding that "Joyce's protagonist lives in a world of abstractions, but the novel does not; in fact, one of Joyce's strengths as a writer is that he always shows us how consciousness is determined by a social position" (1976, 113). He views Stephen's involved theories and withdrawn behavior as elaborate defense mechanisms linked to the decline in his father's economic position and the resulting "disparity between his [own] real circumstances and the nobility he conceives for himself" (121). Fredric Jameson sees *Ulysses* as "the epic of the metropolis under imperialism, in which the development of bourgeoisie and proletariat alike is stunted to the benefit of a national petite-bourgeoisie," all "thanks to the domination of its foreign masters" (1982, 134, 135). He adds that the novel's last chapters expose "the

increasing social fragmentation and monadisation of late capitalist society, the intensifying privatisation and isolation of
its subjects" (139). Hawthorn agrees that "few novels show
their characters less as free, autonomous beings or more tied
to their society and its history" than *Ulysses* (116). He feels
that the book "affirms certain human values in their social
and historical specificity with such force that we cannot afford
to dismiss it or them" (124).

Similarly, the revisionist Irish nationalists of the Field Day
movement, advocating an inclusive notion of Irishness, have
recently stressed Joyce's quiet but insistent progressive nationalism as well as his socialism, Seamus Deane complains
that "the liberal and democratic impulse" in Joyce's novels
"has been considerably deflected by the takeover of them
by a class of experts," (1986, 186) with this "not so much
a tribute to Joyce's omnivorous knowledge as it is to the
strange epic and yet democratic form of his work" (1985b,
90). He counters the old view of an apolitical Joyce who
entertained nationalism and socialism but repudiated them
with the insistence that Joyce did not reject these ideologies
but rather incorporated them into his work: "The relationship
between literature and politics was not, for Joyce, mediated
through a movement, a party, a combination or a sect. For
him, the act of writing became an act of rebellion; rebellion
was the act of writing. Its aim was to bring into the world
a loveliness that still did not exist" (1985c, 99). Tom Paulin
insists that "*Ulysses* stands as an epic monument that faces
toward a united, independent Ireland. Joyce had nothing but
scorn for what is now termed 'the two nations theory' and
his wonderfully capacious imagination is the most inclusive
of any Irish writer's (in *Finnegans Wake*, everyone is invited
to the party)" (1984a, 143–44). He notes that Joyce exiled
himself to France like many an Irish rebel and identified
with Terence MacSwiney, the nationalist Lord Mayor of Cork
who died on hunger strike in 1920, after which Joyce wrote
angrily to his brother Stanislaus about the incident (1984a,
144). Paulin adds that while Joyce "sympathized with the
aims of Sinn Féin he criticised that movement for avoiding
social questions and 'educating the people of Ireland on the
old paps of racial hatred' " (1984a, 144). Joyce's politics are

reflected in the Stephen who thinks of Kevin Egan, the Fenian exiled to Paris, and even more in the Leopold, son of a Hungarian Jew, who counters the narrow racist chauvinism of the Citizen in "Cyclops" with calm words in favor of human freedom, progress, and love. In a lecture in Trieste, Joyce argued that "to exclude from the present nation all who are descended from foreign families would be impossible, and to deny the name of patriot to all who are not of Irish stock would be to deny it to almost all the heroes of the modern movement"—Fitzgerald, Emmet, Tone, Tandy, Davis, Mitchel, Butt, Biggar, and especially "Parnell, who was perhaps the most formidable man who ever led the Irish, but in whose veins there was not even a drop of Celtic blood" (1984a, 145).

Paulin believes that Leopold Bloom's progressive political views are "to be seen as a version of the Fabian socialism which Joyce took from Wells and the Webbs" (1984a, 146). He might well have added to that list of socialist influences Francis and Hanna Sheehy-Skeffington, Joyce's friends since university days in Dublin. Additionally, Dominic Manganiello, author of the pioneering book *Joyce's Politics* (1980), feels that Joyce's political code came closest to that of the American pacifist individualist, Benjamin Tucker, of whom Joyce is reported to have said, "Oh! he was the great political thinker!" (74). Manganiello also claims that Joyce's work incorporates the socialist and anarchist ideas of European thinkers such as Bakunin, Stirner, and Kropotkin. I must add that Leopold Bloom's political models are none of these people—rather Bloom cites Parnell and especially the Irish progressive nationalists enumerated in "Ithaca": "James Fintan Lalor, John Fisher Murray, John Mitchel, J. F. X. O'Brien" and "Michael Davitt" with his "agrarian policy" (*Ulysses*, 589). In "Eumaeus" we are told that Leopold was once "twitted with going a step farther than Michael Davitt in the striking views he at one time inculcated as a backtothelander" (*Ulysses*, 536). In "Penelope" Molly thinks about Leopold, "wasnt I the born fool to believe all his blather about home rule and the land league" (*Ulysses*, 634). Davitt, the founder of the Land League, is a particularly fitting model for Leopold in personality as well as politics, for in his later years he chose to be faithful to his socialist ideals even though it meant that he was scorned by Irish nationalists for doing so and thereafter faded into relative obscurity (Cahalan 1976). Leopold Bloom's understated, progressive political views; his sympathy for women; his endless linguistic playfulness; and his struggles with deep psychological conflicts have all attracted critics of every leading contemporary approach, who have taught us to look at Joyce in new, provocative ways. Bloom provides testimony to the epic, Ulyssean achievement of his creator. It may be true that Joyce criticism has become, as Joyce cautioned, a matter of "wipe your glosses with what you know." It is also true that one comes to know a good bit about virtually everything by reading Joyce.

5

Exposé of Ireland: Realists, 1920–55

On the Attack Against the Free State

The period between *Ulysses* (1922) and *Finnegans Wake* (1939) was marked by a great growth in the Irish novel as a whole, a flowering that has continued and increased up to the present day. Maurice Harmon writes that "modern Irish prose fiction may be said to have begun with George Moore and James Joyce and to have developed thereafter in two separate generations, that of the twenties and that of the fifties" (1976, 49). During the period between 1920 and 1955, Irish novels tended to follow two distinctly different modes: a conventional, often somewhat bitter realism exposing the constrictive difficulties of life in Ireland; and an experimental, fabulist mode seeking to escape such realities. Concerning the first, a pioneering critical work was Vivian Mercier's "Realism in Anglo-Irish Fiction" (1943), his unpublished doctoral dissertation. Both modes show the clear stamp of Joyce, with realist novelists following *Dubliners* and *A Portrait of the Artist as a Young Man,* and those novelists whom I shall call "fabulists" inspired by *Ulysses* and *Finnegans Wake*. The dean of the Irish realists of this period, Sean O'Faolain, asserted that "we have explored Irish life with an objectivity never hitherto applied to it, and in this Joyce rather than Yeats is our inspiration" (quoted in Lubbers 1985b, 101). Darcy O'Brien remarks that "to say that *A Portrait* has influenced subsequent Irish writing is like saying that *A Preface to Lyrical Ballads* influenced the English romantic movement" (1976b, 214). Robert Caswell found Irish novels during this period to be dominated by the themes of exile and resignation, with exile personified by Stephen Dedalus and resignation em-

179

bodied in Leopold Bloom (1967, 7). Of course, as I have
argued in chapter 3, both realism and fantasy had been
thoroughly injected into the Irish novel around the turn of
the century, before any of Joyce's novels appeared, and it
is clear that during the period 1920 to 1955 Irish novelists
were influenced by George Moore, James Stephens, and other
earlier Irish novelists, not just by Joyce.

Because Irish novels during this period are so numerous
and divergent, I shall examine them in two separate chapters—the realist novels in this chapter and the fabulist ones
in my next chapter. During the period from 1920 to 1955
all Irish novelists reacted to the frequently reactionary, puritanical tendencies of Irish society; the realists chose to
thoroughly expose those tendencies and the fabulists both
to escape and to lampoon them. To understand these tendencies one must have some sense of the political and cultural
history of the period.[1] On the surface, Irish history during
this period was dominated by the achievement of independence—which was spurred by the Easter Rising of 1916,
continued by the Sinn Féin movement and then the Anglo-
Irish War of 1919–21 (ended by a treaty that partitioned
Ireland between an independent, predominantly Catholic,
twenty-six southern counties and the Unionist, most Protestant, six northern counties), complicated by the bitter Civil
War of 1922–23 between supporters and "die-hard" opponents of the treaty, and more or less settled by the victory
of the treaty's supporters and their establishment of the Irish
Free State. The Free State subsequently employed in the
1930s, as its longest-serving head of state, its chief die-hard
opponent in the 1920s, Éamon de Valera; it promulgated a
constitution in 1937 and achieved complete independence in
1948, with the "six counties" kept in the United Kingdom
and generating unpleasant headlines ever since.

Despite the bitter difficulties of the period, Ireland did
move from political subjugation to independence, and one
might expect cultural and literary history to have been marked
by a heady celebration of liberation. Instead, the primary
literary theme was disappointment. Born around 1900, the
novelists of this period were raised in the midst of the
excitement of the Easter Rising and the Anglo-Irish War.

Indeed, several of them served as Irish nationalist soldiers. But by and large they were severely disillusioned by the failure to achieve complete Irish unity and even more by developments in Irish society in a "Free State" that must have seemed to them very ironically named. Instead of responding to the achievement of political home rule with increased liberalism, the Free State followed a different pattern evident in many new nation-states: the enforcement of a narrow, chauvinistic, self-protective brand of nationalism. For the ruling Free Staters and for Éamon de Valera, who soon became the dominant leader of the new state, to be Irish meant to be Catholic, Gaelic, and sexually "pure." De Valera's 1937 constitution "mirrored the bourgeois mind" and "was characterized not by bold affirmations of individual liberties, but by cautious qualifications of and restrictions upon just about every freedom it granted" (Harmon 1985, 34).

These conservative attitudes were reflected in the intellectual history of the period as well, especially in Daniel Corkery's books *The Hidden Ireland* (1925) and *Synge and Anglo-Irish Literature* (1931), in which he championed a romanticized Gaelic past at the expense of modern Irish writing in English. For writers the harshest result of the new puritanical ethos was the Censorship of Publications Act of 1929, under which many books that were felt to be not in line with the rigid new code, even the most innocent Irish books such as Eric Cross's delightful nonfictional portrait of *The Tailor and Ansty* (1942), were banned during the 1930s and 1940s. Censorship oppressed and alienated many of the novelists, to the point that O'Faolain responded to such treatment with the bitter but wry acknowledgment that "one likes to be in the tradition" (quoted in Doyle 1968, 38). Realist novelists were forced into attitudes of protest. As Frank O'Connor remarked, concerning Patrick Kavanagh's autobiography *The Green Fool* (1938): "It is O'Faolain's second novel *[Bird Alone]*; my own second novel *[Dutch Interior]*; it is Gerald O'Donovan's *Father Ralph*; it is *A Portrait of the Artist as a Young Man*; it is the novel every Irish writer who isn't a rogue or an imbecile is doomed to write when the emptiness and horror of Irish life begins to dawn on him" (quoted in Lubbers 1980, 70).

Considering what he characterized as "the difficulties of writing in a country where the policeman and the priest are in a perpetual glow of satisfaction," O'Faolain viewed the Irish novel of this period as an honorable failure that could never measure up to Joyce. He felt that in the face of "a broken world" (the title of one of his own short stories), the short story could succeed where the novel failed (1962, 103, 102). Indeed, the Irish short story as practiced by Liam O'Flaherty, Frank O'Connor, O'Faolain, and others enjoyed an unprecedented and rich brilliance during this period. As both writer and editor, O'Faolain played a central role, founding in 1940 the pioneering, liberal literary magazine *The Bell*—which, like the *Dublin University Magazine* a century earlier, was the most important such journal of the period, inspiring writers and readers as only George Russell's the *Irish Statesman* in the 1920s and the short-lived *Ireland Today* (1936–38) had done on a more minor scale during the preceding years.

But O'Faolain was a little too harsh on the novel. In this chapter I survey eighteen notable realist novelists before examining a number of the fabulists of the same period in my next chapter. Their works represent an impressive achievement. Several of these novelists—Liam O'Flaherty, Patrick Kavanagh, O'Faolain himself, Elizabeth Bowen, Kate O'Brien—are especially important figures; all of them are good novelists. A look at Diane Tolomeo's comprehensive survey of modern Irish fiction (1983) serves as a reminder of at least fifteen *other* realistic novelists during this period who merit attention, including Maurice Walsh and Patrick MacGill, but who must escape my attention here. Realist novelists of this period fall into three subgroups: novelists of the peasantry and lower middle class, who were primarily concerned to expose (in Irish as well as in English) the chief problems of Irish society; women novelists from the Ascendancy or the prosperous middle class who examined with particular effectiveness their own gender and caste; and, to look ahead to my next chapter, novelists who made use of both realism and fantasy.

Writing in Irish and the Novels of Séamus Ó Grianna

The puritanical, perversely counterproductive tendencies of the early Irish Free State are nowhere better exemplified than in the practices and policies regarding the Irish language and writing in Irish. The rigid requirement of Irish in the schools and the civil service squashed perhaps as much interest in the language as it encouraged. Today many more Irish people are able to speak Irish than was the case at the beginning of the century, yet significantly fewer *do* speak Irish on a continual, daily basis, with the solidly Irish-speaking *Gaeltacht* regions continuing to shrink. Irish air traffic controllers are required to show proficiency in Irish to obtain their civil service job, but once on the job they are prohibited from using Irish on the airwaves, since most pilots could not understand it and might well crash their planes if given directions in Irish. Equally ironically, publishing in Irish has continued to grow during decades when the spoken language has diminished. Significantly, "before 1926 Irish books were published by the Gaelic League and a few foolhardy publishers, after 1926 much more by the government An Gúm ("the Plan") established in that year" (MacEoin 1969, 62–63). Following the ethos of the young Free State, An Gúm was very conservative, publishing many more translations and imitations of the classics—seemingly aimed at "children or nuns," in the acerbic view of Máirtín Ó Cadhain (1971, 147)—than new writings of any quality. By the 1940s the situation had improved, with the creation of alternative-styled journals such as *Comhar* (Cooperation) and *Feasta* (Henceforth), the newspaper *Inniu* (Today), the publisher Sáirséal agus Dill, and An Club Leabhar ("The Book Club"). A propensity for the short story was even more evident in Irish than in English, especially since the available means of periodical publication encouraged brevity. The novel in Irish has remained a relatively rare entity. But some notable novels in Irish did appear between 1920 and 1955. Interestingly, a number of them used urban settings, especially Dublin, partly in an attempt to bridge the gap between the rural Irish-

speaking areas and the Gaelic League readership in Dublin:
Éamonn MacGiolla Iasachta's *Cúrsai Thomáis* (The story of
Tomás) (1927), Barra Ó Caochlaigh's *Lucht Ceoil* (Musicians)
(1932), Séamus MacConmara's *An Coimhthigheach* (The outsider) (1939), and Séamus Ó Néill's *Tonn Tuile* (Floodtide)
(1947). Another sizeable, albeit often reluctant readership
could be found among students in Irish secondary schools,
where some of these books made their way into Intermediate
and Leaving Certificate curricula.

The career of Séamus Ó Grianna is representative of a
number of novelists writing in Irish as well as English during
this period. Like several of the novels just mentioned,
Ó Grianna's first, *Mo Dhá Róisín* (My two Roseens) (1920),
a romantic tale of the Easter Rising, was set in Dublin. His
other nine novels all focus on his native place of Rann na
Feirste in the Donegal Gaeltacht. Like several of the other
novelists discussed in this chapter—Peadar O'Donnell, Michael McLaverty, Patrick Kavanagh—Ó Grianna was from
the North and of humble, rural origins. He wrote as a
disappointed rebel who was imprisoned for a year and a
half for his role on the nationalist side in the Civil War. Ó
Grianna focused in his novels on the loss of the traditional,
rural way of life that he had known in youth. Because An
Gúm paid a pound per thousand words for translations, like
many other writers he wasted a good deal of his talent
translating long classics for them. He was about as popular
as a writer in Irish can be and the most prolific novelist to
date in Irish, publishing ten novels between 1920 and 1968.
Yet because of his translations, his Civil Service position,
and a misperception that he was simply part of the "Father
O'Leary school" of writing, Ó Grianna was for a long time
compared unfavorably to his brother, Seosamh MacGrianna
(a specialist in the short story), and dismissed as a serious
writer, still often suffering that judgment. Only relatively
recently have scholars begun to appreciate Ó Grianna's novels. Just before Ó Grianna's death in 1969, Gearóid MacEoin
called him "at present the most underrated writer writing in
Irish" (1969, 61). More recently, Nollaig MacCongáil (1983)
has provided useful information about Ó Grianna's career,

and Philip O'Leary has published an excellent, appreciative
article (1986a) about his novels.

As O'Leary stresses, much of Ó Grianna's work laments
the loss of the Gaelic way of life in Donegal, developing in
its most pointedly cultural and linguistic form the theme of
disappointment that dominates the novels of this period in
both languages. Many of his central characters suffer from
poverty and delusions of grandeur, running off to Scotland
and America to make their fortunes and returning only too
late to Donegal to discover that they have irreparably lost
the life that they loved. When the protagonist of *Caisleáin
Óir* (Castles of gold) (1924), for example, returns home after
many years in America to look for the woman he loved, he
finds her but they fail to recognize each other. Learning her
identity, Séimi realizes that he can't go home again to de-
populated Gaelic Donegal, and so he leaves town on foot,
passing an old man who mutters, "Tá sé fuar" ("It is cold")
(155). Séimi can only agree, and face his permanent exile.
On the book jacket of the most recent edition of this novel,
Tomás Ó Fiaich points out that Ó Grianna laments the decline
of Rann na Feirste much as Charles Kickham memorialized
his beloved Mullinahone. I might add that *Caisleáin Óir* also
recalls Carleton's *The Emigrants of Ahadarra*. Ó Grianna was
also interested in the plight of women. The heroine of *Bean
Ruadh de Dhálach* (A red-haired O'Donnell woman) (1966)
helps lead her whole village out of poverty to Scotland and
then to America. This novel attracted a recent scholarly article
entitled "Saoirse na mBan i *Bean Ruadh de Dhálach*" (Women's
liberation in *Bean Ruadh de Dhálach*) (O'Leary 1986a, 81
n.57). Stylistically, Ó Grianna was influenced by both Peadar
Ó Laoghaire and Pádraic Ó Conaire, steering a middle course
between Ó Laoghaire's rigid imitation of the folktale and Ó
Conaire's bolder experiments. Always known by his pen-
name "Máire," Ó Grianna adopted as his usual narrator a
Donegal woman, Máire Ní Dhomhnaill. He made use of the
traditional story form as well as the increasingly popular
Gaelic genre of the autobiography (since Máire usually presents her narrative in *memoir* form), but within the context
of a modern novel rather than a literary folktale such as Ó

Laoghaire's *Séadna*. Ó Grianna's work calls for more serious critical attention.

Liam O'Flaherty

Like Ó Grianna, Liam O'Flaherty (1896–1984) was a native of the Gaeltacht (Inis Mór in the Aran Islands) who was forced to exile himself from it in order to survive, he was a disappointed Irish rebel, and subsequently he became a prolific novelist (in English). Unlike Ó Grianna, O'Flaherty remained an angry, rebellious personality; he would never have been caught dead translating books for An Gúm or working in the civil service, although he compromised his talent in other ways on more than one occasion. O'Flaherty is the most celebrated among the novelists considered in this chapter, and certainly the recipient of the most critical attention.[2] As I have explained in detail elsewhere (Cahalan 1983, 134–40), in many ways O'Flaherty's career reads like a somewhat more successful version of William Carleton's a century earlier. Like Carleton, O'Flaherty aimed for the priesthood as a young man but instead became a "spoiled priest" and remained bitterly anticlerical; he was unashamedly self-serving in the strategies he used to launch his literary career; his work shows the strong influence of the Irish language, storytelling tradition, and traditional culture in general, and is strengthened by an instinctual command of rural manners and speech; and he used his novels as polemical vehicles for his pronounced views of Irish society.

Most critics feel that O'Flaherty was at his best in his sharply focused short stories about human and animal life on Inis Mór, a number of which were first written in Irish. However, with the early encouragement of the London editor Edward Garnett, O'Flaherty clearly set out to make his name as a novelist, publishing some seventeen novels, fourteen of them appearing during his intensely productive years of 1923–37. These are powerful, compelling, uneven books. James Plunkett's comment about O'Flaherty's most enduring novel could be applied to several of his novels: "*Famine* page by page seems a badly written book but its totality is extraordinary" (quoted in Boland 1972, 42). He was no careful stylist: he believed in writing quickly and passionately, commenting to Garnett that slow attention to style would hamper his artistic statement. As the *other* most celebrated Irish novelist of the 1920s and 1930s, O'Flaherty wrote with a style, point of view, and literary vision diametrically opposed to Joyce, and much closer to Hemingway or Jack London: short, blunt, simple, active sentences and photographically visual descriptions as part of his distinctive literary naturalism. The description of Brian Kilmartin's death at the end of *Famine* (1937) exemplifies these features:

The old man lay still with his arms stretched out.
The dog became silent and lay down on his belly. Then he raised his snout and sniffed the air. He shuddered. Then he dragged himself along the ground until he came to the old man's naked foot. He smelt it. He rose slowly to his feet, raised his mane slightly, and advanced, an inch at a time, smelling along the old man's naked shins and thighs. He started and growled when he came to the shirt. Then he made a little circuit, lay down on his belly once more, and dragged himself, whining, to the head. He smelt the face. He whined. He smelt again. His mane dropped.
Suddenly he raised his snout, sat back on his haunches, and uttered a long howl. Then he lay down on his side and nestled against the old man's shoulder. (448)

This representative passage also reveals O'Flaherty's close identification of people with animals, a characteristic of his worldview. Like other literary naturalists, he regarded the behavior of animals as just as intricate and interesting as that of humans (especially as described in some of his short stories), and he sympathized most with people who are driven instinctually and are as in need of a place in nature as animals. O'Flaherty's novels explore this need. Sean O'Faolain called him an "inverted Romantic," a felicitous description: following naturalism, O'Flaherty emphasized the entrapped, tragic fate of his characters, but solace and beauty were always to be found in primitive nature, the unifying principle beyond innocence and despair.

O'Flaherty's naturalistic worldview had its inspiration both in life as he knew it growing up on Inis Mór and in his reading of European novelists, especially Zola and Dostoyevski. Added to his literary naturalism was an angry Irish brand of socialism shaped by James Connolly and his book *Labour in Irish History* (1910). Connolly was interested in Irish nationalism as a force that could complement the rise of the Irish working class, and as a result he fought and died in the Easter Rising of 1916. Connolly saw the Famine, the Land War, and the early twentieth-century nationalist struggle as the pivotal events in modern Irish history, and these were the very events that O'Flaherty examined in his three historical novels, *Famine* (1937), *Land* (1946), and *Insurrection* (1950) (Cahalan 1983, 140–53). O'Flaherty was involved in an abortive socialist attempt at revolution in Dublin in early 1922, and he criticized O'Casey's *The Plough and the Stars* (1926), even though it was written by the Irish writer whom he most admired, because the play scathingly portrayed the Easter Rising in which Connolly had given his life. However, O'Flaherty was never one to maintain orthodoxy of any kind, socialist or otherwise, with careful consistency. Instead, perhaps the most enduring, dominant theme in his novels is the same one that obsessed Ó Grianna and the next two novelists to be discussed, Peadar O'Donnell and Michael McLaverty, as it had Carleton a century earlier: the loss of the simple, traditional, rural Irish way of life. Like these other writers, O'Flaherty wrote out of his own experience—the necessity of leaving Inis Mór in order to make his way in the world and the inevitability of the alienation he experienced in Dublin. "You can't go home again," these writers lament, especially when home is an impoverished Gaeltacht district.

O'Flaherty's novels tend to divide fairly evenly between the two contrasting settings of Dublin and the rural west. Brian Donnelly's point about O'Flaherty's first and most famous Dublin novel can be applied to all of his Dublin novels: "If for Joyce the city of Dublin was the centre of Irish paralysis, for O'Flaherty in *The Informer* it has become the centre of dehumanization, the place in which man's break with nature is most obviously and forcefully apparent" (1974, 77). In *The Informer* (1925), Gypo Nolan is a poor, lumbering, animalistic man who informs on a rebel for a twenty-pound reward and is inevitably destroyed. Generally this novel's exploitation of the Irish political scene just after the Civil War, its use of the thriller formula, and its subsequent immortalization on the Hollywood screen by John Ford in his 1935 film come to mind when one thinks of *The Informer*. Seduced by the huge success of *The Informer*, O'Flaherty unfortunately spent years trying to repeat the feat: *Famine* was dedicated to John Ford, and a novel such as *Land* reads more like O'Flaherty's script for the popular film he hoped it would become rather than the novel it should have been. Yet unmistakably, Gypo Nolan is the first of a series of protagonists who are all, as Vivian Mercier put it, "warped by the city" (1966, 38)—and, one might add, destroyed by it. Gypo is continually treated by O'Flaherty, in the words of the novel, as "a wild animal stalking in a forest" (6), and he wants to escape back to the countryside whence he came, but he cannot. Larry Gilhooley of *Mr. Gilhooley* (1926) is another misplaced person, like Gypo a doomed creature of instinct rather than intellect: Gilhooley tries to care for, reform, and live with a young prostitute, but ends up strangling her after she cannot return his feelings for her. *The Assassin* (1928) and *The Puritan* (1931) add satiric attacks on Irish society to the portraits of (respectively) McDara and Ferriter. *The Puritan* is a full-fledged assault on the Free State puritanism that led to censorship, stretched by O'Flaherty to what he saw as its logical conclusion: murder. Like Gilhooley, Francis Ferriter kills a supposed prostitute—not as the result of a frustrated love affair but rather as the divine justice demanded by his fanatical puritanism, expressed in his manuscript "The Sacrifice of Blood." O'Flaherty turned naturally to a rural rodent, the incorrigible ferret, to capture the Dublin Free State mentality. Years later he returned to this image and added that of the weasel in describing Bartly Madden, the countryman protagonist of *Insurrection* (1950), who finds himself fighting and dying in the Easter Rising by accident, "like a rabbit" standing "hypnotized by a weasel's deadly stare" (39), "flushed from a warren by a ferret" (152), in this case the unstoppable British foe.

O'Flaherty's rural novels demonstrate that staying in or returning to the Gaeltacht is no easier than trying to survive in Dublin, although rural existence at least offers more tragic dignity. After wandering the globe in dissolute fashion for two years doing odd jobs, O'Flaherty had returned to Inis Mór in 1921 to try to heal himself, but found himself unable to stay for more than a few months. This experience was recounted in his second novel, *The Black Soul* (1924), in which "The Stranger" comes to "Inverara" to soothe his shellshocked "black soul," becomes involved with a frustrated and eventually widowed married woman, Little Mary, and leaves the island with her at the end. The Stranger is able to overcome his cynical distance from natural life but cannot live freely on the island.

The two novels that have been most highly praised by scholars, *Skerrett* (1932) and *Famine* (1937), both focus on the futility yet tragic dignity of trying to live naturally on the land. David Skerrett is O'Flaherty's idea of a hero—a defiant schoolteacher who comes to the island of "Nara" (Inis Mór thinly disguised) as an outsider, becomes a champion of its traditional culture and language in spite of his initial aversion to them, but is destroyed by the island's priest because his ideas and practices are too revolutionary. "Such men, though doomed to destruction by the timid herd, grow after death to the full proportion of their greatness" (287). *Famine* is more convincing, more compelling, and O'Flaherty's best novel because in it he achieves more detachment and a fuller perspective by exploring the social and historical fabric of the Great Hunger. Its heroes are an old man and his young daughter-in-law, Brian and Mary Kilmartin. Living in the same house in the "Black Valley," the two are at each others' throats in the early chapters of the novel, but Brian comes to admire Mary's dynamic strength, and the catastrophic events of 1845–46 draw the two together, culminating in the moment at the end of the novel when the dying Brian hands Mary a chunk of mortar from above the family fireplace to take with her to America as a symbol of the family's survival. Many elements of O'Flaherty's novels, such as the characterization of the grisly land agent Chadwick in *Famine*, recall nineteenth-century Gothicism in novels such as Maturin's *Melmoth the Wanderer*, Carleton's *The Black Prophet*, and Le Fanu's *The House by the Churchyard*, as A.

Norman Jeffares notes in regard to *Skerrett* (1985, 50). In
criticism to date, the courageous Mary Kilmartin has attracted
no feminist appreciation, and it is even more surprising that
while Marxist critics have written about the "apolitical" Joyce,
no Marxist critique of the life and works of the self-pro-
claimed Marxist O'Flaherty has appeared—perhaps reflecting
the critics' felt need to recapture the prestigious Joyce for a
Left to which O'Flaherty obviously already belonged.[3]

Peadar O'Donnell and Michael McLaverty

O'Flaherty's popularity helped inspire a whole new group
of "peasant novelists"—reminiscent of the generation of the
Banims, Griffin, and Carleton a hundred years previously,
among whom Carleton had been the only true peasant.
Among the novelists considered in this chapter, Ó Grianna,
O'Flaherty, Peadar O'Donnell, Michael McLaverty, and Patrick Kavanagh were all of "peasant" background (although
by this time the word was no longer fashionable), and many
of the others were lower-middle-class or middle-class townspeople, as were the Banims and Griffin. Like their nineteenth-
century predecessors, this generation of writers sought to
capture Irish life with a new realism—not primarily for the
edification of English readers, but first and foremost for the
reformation of a growing Irish readership. Among these
novelists, none was so successful as O'Flaherty, and none
more like him than Peadar O'Donnell (1893–1986). It is not
surprising that in 1946, when he succeeded Sean O'Faolain
as editor of *The Bell*, O'Donnell praised O'Flaherty in its
pages as "our greatest novelist" (quoted in Cahalan 1983,
217 n.16), since like O'Flaherty O'Donnell was originally
from a remote Gaeltacht area, was a committed socialist, and
explored very similar subjects and themes in his novels. But
more than O'Flaherty, O'Donnell acted on his socialist beliefs
throughout his life.[4] He remarked to Benedict Kiely that "the
writing of novels was of secondary importance to his revolutionary activities and his work for social reform. Despite
such a disclaimer from O'Donnell, it was Dr. Kiely's belief
that his other activities helped give more direct force and
conviction to his novels, which were also characterised by

a knowledge of the minute details of the Donegal countryside and of the islands off the coast" (Cooney 1985, 11). During his long life O'Donnell was a schoolteacher, an organizer for the Irish Transport and General Workers' Union, a participant on the Republican side in the Anglo-Irish and Civil wars, editor of the revolutionary newspapers *An tÓglach* (The volunteer) and *An Phoblacht* (The republic), a founder of the progressive IRA splinter-group the Republican Congress, organizer of support against Franco in Spain, editor of *The Bell,* campaigner for improved economic conditions in the west of Ireland, opponent of the atomic bomb and the war in Vietnam, and a delegate to the World Peace Congress. In the midst of all of these activities, O'Donnell was also a good novelist, especially during his busiest years in the 1920s and 1930s. Both as socialist activist and novelist he was more persistent than Francis Hackett, author of *The Green Lion* (1936), who left Ireland because of his disillusionment with the repressive Free State. Considering O'Donnell's impressive career, it is no surprise that a summer school was held in Donegal to examine and celebrate his career while he was still alive, in the summer of 1985—which O'Donnell attended, remarking humorously that it was like being at his own funeral.

In his novels O'Donnell drew from his own experiences and his knowledge about difficult northern social conditions. His first novel, *Storm* (1925), was an apprentice work with a protagonist suspiciously resembling himself—a schoolteacher who eventually leaves his island off the western coast to join the nationalist struggle. In *Islanders* (1928) O'Donnell concentrated on the ethnography of the island people and their attempts to resist the tide of emigration to the Lagan Valley in County Down, to Scotland, and to America, but he imposed on his material a romantic plot of only passing interest. *Adrigoole* (1929) is a more compelling novel based on a real incident concerning a mother and her children who were found dead of starvation after the mother was shunned by her Free State neighbors following the imprisonment of her Republican husband during the Civil War. Hughie Dalach, who returns home at the end of this novel to find most of his surviving family victimized by such a fate, goes mad.

All through the novel he thinks dark thoughts about the necessity for the Donegal native to go "out into the world sometime or deeper into the bog" (26), the bog which "sucks an' sucks at any strong life above it" (239). In his focus on the pattern of forced emigration to the Lagan, Scotland, and America, O'Donnell is very similar to Ó Grianna—and also to Patrick MacGill, who emigrated to Scotland at age fourteen and wrote novels about the struggles of Irish migrant laborers in Scotland.

O'Donnell's most interesting novels are *The Knife* (1930) and *The Big Windows* (1955). *The Knife* is set in the Lagan Valley, that midway zone for the Donegal native, and focuses on the difficulties encountered by the Godfrey Dhus, a Catholic family who have bought a farm in a Protestant region, and the role played by their Protestant neighbors, the Rowans. This novel is distinguished by a spare, dramatic narrative and a strikingly sympathetic portrait of the Rowans, especially Sam Rowan, who rescues Brian Godfrey Dhu ("the Knife") from jail at the end of the novel and falls in love with his sister, Nuala. O'Donnell often remarked that he admired the Protestant Orangemen, insisting that they were the only real fighters left in Ireland. In his romantic merger of Sam Rowan and Nuala Godfrey Dhu at the end of the novel, he returns to the wishful thinking of many a nineteenth-century Irish historical novelist who similarly joined Protestant hero and Catholic heroine. O'Donnell's added ideal is socialist: he believed that the Protestant and Catholic proletariat had far more in common than their rulers, just as did the working classes of Ulster and Scotland who found themselves in competition. However, Terence Brown claims that often in both O'Flaherty's and O'Donnell's novels "class politics and social analysis give way before an appreciation of the west as a place of fundamental natural forces, of human figures set passively or heroically against landscapes of stone, rock and sea in a way that makes their works less radical than they perhaps thought they were" (1985, 94). Grattan Freyer (1976) and Michael Higgins (1985) add the distinction that O'Donnell is less romantic about animals and more concerned with people not in isolation but in community. He demonstrated his sense of humor in *On the Edge of the Stream* (1934), a novel about the comic consequences of the "communist" red-baiting of a rural cooperative. In *The Big Windows* (1955) O'Donnell showed that he was not opposed to change in rural Donegal, as he also proved many times in his long life of political and social activism. In this novel Brigid Manus insists to her husband that their home will have big windows, not the traditional claustrophobic panes, and she also wins out in her insistence on having a doctor attend to the birth of their first child, to the secret relief of women who lost children in childbirth under the traditional taboo against the presence of a doctor. As Freyer writes, for O'Donnell "the big windows always open on a new world, different, but just as exciting, just as vital, as the disappearing old" (1976, 114).

Strikingly similar to O'Donnell's novels are those of Michael McLaverty (b. 1907), who lived part of his childhood on Rathlin Island off the northern coast of County Antrim. McLaverty added to O'Donnell's focus on the difficult but proud life of northern islanders and their forced emigration a well developed attention to what happens to his Rathlin Islanders after they move to Belfast. Like O'Donnell, Mc-Laverty began as a schoolteacher, but he remained in that career, working as a math teacher and headmaster in Belfast while also publishing novels and short stories. While always writing about poor Catholics in his novels, in them McLaverty seems neither strongly political nor "Catholic." He focuses instead on how the uprooting of the poor from the countryside to the working-class districts of industrial Belfast violated a traditional faithfulness to the land that seems almost pre-Christian (and thus pre-sectarian) in its values. By implication, the urban alienation experienced by Mc-Laverty's poor Catholics might as well have applied to many of the poor Protestants in Belfast, a point that O'Donnell would have appreciated, although McLaverty makes no such political point explicit. His characters do not "question the premises of the system that seems to oppress them, and their . . . social innocence," John Wilson Foster notes, "reminds one of Hardy's innocence" (1974, 37). Foster, the chief scholar of Ulster fiction, sees McLaverty as perhaps the most central twentieth-century novelist in exploring the theme of the "blighted land" that pervades Ulster novels beginning with Carleton, while McLaverty substitutes "the depletion of rural manpower and industrial oppression" for Carleton's evil landlords as the chief evil (1974, 23). Of course, as we have already seen in O'Flaherty, the themes of the "blighted land" and the urban alienation and oppression experienced by rural people in the big city are not limited to northern writers; much of Foster's very perceptive analysis could be extended to Irish fiction at large.

Among the several novelists in this period who explore the conflict between country and city life, McLaverty is unique because he focuses on Belfast, the most industrialized city in Ireland, and because he contrasts rural and urban settings within single novels rather than limit himself to either the countryside or the city in each novel like the other writers do. His approach is underscored by the basic structure of his first and perhaps best novel, *Call My Brother Back* (1939): it is separated into two books, "The Island" and "The City." The MacNeill family is forced to leave Rathlin Island for the Falls Road area of Belfast, and young Colm MacNeill loses his link to the land, his education, and his older brother Alec in the process. This is the only novel by McLaverty with any public politics in it: in the midst of the Anglo-Irish War, Alec joins the IRA and gets shot dead in the family's front hallway. Even here, though, political tragedy seems subsumed by the more basic theme of the lost land. As Foster notes, Alec's shooting can be viewed symbolically as "the price exacted by the land for his worldly knowledge (specifically the knowledge of injustice) and for his condemnation of the island" (1974, 45). At the end of the novel Colm rides a tram up out of Belfast and feels soothed by the countryside, but inevitably must take the return trip, tensing up as he reenters Belfast. *Lost Fields* (1941) begins with country people already living near the Falls Road, struggling to make ends meet. Young Peter Griffin briefly escapes to his grandmother's house in the countryside, but later she feels compelled to move in with the family in Belfast when times get worse for them and they need her pension. Peter's older brother Hugh wants to get married and move into her room, even demanding that she move into the workhouse (the ultimate emblem of degradation), and when the grandmother finally dies before suffering such a fate, Peter's mother is flooded with guilt, realizing that "it was like tearing up an old bush and trying to coax it to grow again" (170). Leaving an unrepentant Hugh to live in Belfast, the rest of the Griffins move into the grandmother's empty house, deciding that rural poverty is preferable to urban poverty.

McLaverty is no naive romantic idealist who believes simply that the countryside is good and the city is bad. In his next novel, *In This Thy Day* (1945), as if in deliberate counterpoint to *Lost Fields*, he showed how rural old people can oppress the young, preventing marriage by refusing to let go of their land. And in *Truth in the Night* (1951), Martin Gallagher moves back to Rathlin Island from Belfast only to encounter mounting tragedy: he falls in love with a widow from the mainland who feels rejected by her dead husband's island family, but after he marries her both she and her daughter die and Martin is left to eke out an existence all by himself. The schoolteacher protagonist of *The Brightening Day* (1965) retreats to Connemara but finds no lasting refuge there from the vicissitudes of the community. Examined as a whole, McLaverty's novels suggest that the conflict between country and city may be unresolvable, at least under the particular conditions of the North at mid-century.

Comic Relief: Patrick Kavanagh and Oliver Gogarty

Two writers who are better known in other contexts— Patrick Kavanagh (1904–67), perhaps the best Irish poet after Yeats, and Oliver St. John Gogarty (1878–1957), Dublin jack-of-many-trades and the Buck Mulligan of *Ulysses*—each contributed a picaresque novel offering some comic or at least ironic relief to the rural and urban difficulties under examination here: Kavanagh's *Tarry Flynn* (1948) and Gogarty's *Tumbling in the Hay* (1939). Both Kavanagh and Gogarty were renowned as comic "characters" in Dublin, a city with a well developed appreciation for eccentricity, quite remote from McLaverty's Belfast, "a stern iron town of aspect unendearing" as Kavanagh's friend Myles na Gopaleen (Flann O'Brien) called it in one of his *Irish Times* articles (1968, 152). Kavanagh was born within three years of McLaverty in the same northern county, Monaghan, but in *Tarry Flynn* his portrait of the lost rural past is as satiric as McLaverty's is earnest. This novel is a belated bildungsroman or *Künstlerroman* (artist-novel) about the thirtyish Tarry/Kavanagh's decision to leave his native farm and village for Dublin. Like Yeats's John Sherman, Tarry has to leave because his inner artistic vision is too much at odds with the grotesque social world of a place in which "hating one's next-door neighbour was an essential part of a small farmer's religion" (172): he must go or "he would be up against the Finnegans and the Carlins and the Bradys and the Cassidys and the magic of the fields would be disturbed in his imagination" (187). He is tired of women who all look the same and neighbors who all think the same and who all delight when he gets in trouble. His will be "lost fields" just as surely as McLaverty's; the novel's depictions of the arid socioeconomic backdrop to Tarry's personal universe make it surprising that Foster neglects it in his *Forces and Themes in Ulster Fiction*. Yet Tarry leaves not because of poverty but so that he can follow his Blakean vision in freedom. As his influential, wandering, picaresque uncle advises him just before Tarry agrees to leave with him, "The best way to love a country like this is from a range of not less than three hundred miles" (185). This recalls Stephen Dedalus's dictum that "the shortest way to Tara was *via* Holyhead" (*Portrait,* 250). Rather than leave the country, Tarry/Kavanagh will proceed to Dublin and become the "peasant poet," writing the alternately grim and joyous works about his native, rocky slopes of Monaghan that immortalized his name.

Gogarty's *Tumbling in the Hay* reads almost as if it recounts the adventures of Tarry/Kavanagh once inside the pubs of Dublin. It contains a series of loose, rambling, lighthearted experiences of a set of young vagabonds which very much recall some of the novels of Charles Lever, especially *Charles O'Malley*. Like Lever, Gogarty was a Trinity College graduate, a doctor, and an unforgettable character and wit. His edu-

cation was as formal as that of Kavanagh (who left school
at the age of twelve) was informal. Like Lever's Trinity
protagonists, Gogarty's Gideon Ouseley can afford to carry
on with his wild pubmates in the knowledge that he will
eventually pass his exams and enter prosperity. *Tumbling in
the Hay* is as anecdotal and loosely constructed as any of
Lever's early novels—a series of separately entitled tales. It
is also partly an episode in the notorious "lifelong battle"
between Gogarty and Joyce "in which Gogarty was severely
worsted" (Ellmann 1982, 207). Midway in the novel we meet
a "Kinch" (Mulligan's nickname for Dedalus in the first
chapter of *Ulysses*) who is revealed as derivative in his
knowledge and rude to boot. " 'If you understand drama,
or rather tragedy—' Kinch began. Good Lord! I thought. Am
I to have it all over again?" (282). *Tumbling in the Hay* is
full of laughs. Unfortunately, like Buck Mulligan in *Ulysses*,
the humor of this novel wears thinner as the novel rambles
along. The last word will always be Joyce's.

Life in the Provinces: Sean O'Faolain, Frank O'Connor, and Francis MacManus

Several notable novelists exposed life in the smaller cities
and larger towns of Ireland, showing them to be different
than either Dublin or the countryside, yet populated by
similarly oppressed and repressed but also persistent characters. Cork was examined by Sean O'Faolain and Frank
O'Connor, and Kilkenny (the Banims' town) by Francis
MacManus. A bit later in this chapter I shall consider Kate
O'Brien's Limerick and the smaller towns of Mary Lavin,
Brinsley MacNamara, and Mervyn Wall. These are quite
particular yet very similar places.

In many ways O'Faolain's career seems the most central
among all of the realistic novelists of this period, as he
evolved from a young rebel into the guiding literary and
cultural conscience of his generation. Born and christened as
John Whelan in 1900, O'Faolain (b. 1900) grew up with the
twentieth century and with the new Irish nation (Cahalan
1983, 114–15). As a young man he joined the Irish Vol-

unteers, studied Irish, adopted the Irish form of his name, fought on the Republican side in the Civil War, earned a bachelor's degree at University College, Cork and a master's at Harvard, and returned to Ireland in 1928, determined to be a writer. He fulfilled this ambition with admirable industry, artistry, and erudition, publishing a number of short stories, novels, and biographical and cultural studies during the 1930s, the peak period of his creativity. By the early 1940s he had replaced Yeats as the foremost man of Irish letters, tremendously influential not only in his fiction but also in his non-fictional writings and editorial role with *The Bell*. "O'Faolain and *The Bell*," as Vivian Mercier notes, "were one and the same" (Doyle 1968, 99). Eilís Dillon is just one among many who testify to O'Faolain's great influence: as a young writer she realized that "O'Faolain was a model from whom a great deal could be learned," especially about how to use the inspiration of Russian novelists such as Turgenev in a novel like O'Faolain's first, *A Nest of Simple Folk*, and soon after beginning to read *The Bell*, "his principles were fixed in my mind" (Dillon 1976, 37, 40). James Plunkett adds that in reply to his own apprentice submissions to *The Bell*, O'Faolain "would write back and say not to call a 'meal' a 'repast' and to cut it down and speak plainly and if you didn't have anything to say not to say it" (quoted in Boland 1972, 42). As a cultural critic O'Faolain contributed a level-headed liberalism that served as influential antidote to the earlier high-flown romanticism of Yeats and conservative nationalism of Daniel Corkery, and he courageously attacked the puritanism of the Free State. Benedict Kiely calls him "after Mr. Yeats himself . . . the most civilizing influence this country has ever had" (quoted in Clarke 1987, 12).

Like O'Faolain himself, the protagonists of O'Faolain's novels during this period are all frustrated but persistent rebels. The three of them form a progressive trilogy of sorts: Leo Donnel in *A Nest of Simple Folk* (1933) is a vagabond nineteenth-century Fenian who passes on his rebelliousness to young Denis Hussey in the early twentieth century; Corney Crone in *Bird Alone* (1936) is a young man resembling Denis who models himself on a grandfather much like Leo Donnel and experiences the loss of all that he loves; and Frankie

Hannafey in *Come Back to Erin* (1940) is an older man who
slowly comes to realize that his rebel stance has become
outdated in the Ireland of the 1930s. These novels also
underscore the movement in Irish society from the countryside to the city that I have been discussing: *A Nest of Simple
Folk* is divided into three parts entitled "1854–1888, The
Country," "1888–1898, The Town," and "1898–1916, The
City"—tracing Leo Donnel's moves from Foxehall to Rath-
keale to Cork as well as reflecting the more general social
shift. The other two novels are set in Cork (with an abortive
trip to London in *Bird Alone* and to New York in *Come Back
to Erin*), while rural Limerick contains the ancestral, beloved,
but elusive, lost fields for O'Faolain's protagonists as it did
in O'Faolain's own family heritage. Each protagonist botches
sexual relationships as much as political rebellions, with out-
of-wedlock pregnancy a recurring motif; each is an antihero
who seems emblematic of a Free State Ireland unable to
succeed as a moral free agent or to overcome the moral
scruples of late Victorian Ireland. Each "remains in basic
discord with Irish society" (Harmon 1966, 140), satisfied with
neither the romantic past nor the bourgeois present. In spite
of himself and Ireland, however, each survives, returning to
Ireland rather than leaving it like Dedalus/Joyce. Although
at times they break down as too diffuse and indicative of
his self-confessed preference for the short story, O'Faolain's
realist novels helped to shape Irish approaches to the sometimes overlapping fictional forms of the historical novel, the
bildungsroman, and the family chronicle (Cahalan 1983,
116–21). In my next chapter I shall consider O'Faolain's very
different later novel, *And Again?* (1979), a playful fantasy
that demonstrates his considerable artistic versatility and endurance. The seemingly immortal O'Faolain (still alive at this
writing) continues to loom as a major figure in need of much
more detailed exploration.

   The career of Frank O'Connor (1903–66), whose real name
was Michael O'Donovan, bears many resemblances to
O'Faolain's. This is not surprising, since both grew up in
Cork under the tutelage of Daniel Corkery, whose conserv-
ative influence both soon moved beyond. Like O'Faolain,
O'Connor fought with the Republicans in the Civil War and

purged his post-war depression by means of an impressively versatile career—as a librarian, member of the board of the Abbey Theatre, creative writing lecturer in the United States, and author of two novels, a play, Gaelic translations, several critical, biographical, historical, and travel books, and above all the short stories that represent his most enduring legacy. O'Connor was the most accomplished Irish story writer since Joyce, and the most prolific and persistent, bar none. He was a hot-blooded, brilliant personality who rose out of youthful poverty in Cork, and his career is one of the most fascinating in Irish literary history. Luckily, to help us trace it we have the best Irish literary biography since Ellmann's *James Joyce*, James H. Matthews's *Voices: A Life of Frank O'Connor* (1983).

O'Connor was also like O'Faolain in that he was a better short story writer than novelist. As Matthews notes, "he was a storyteller interested more in the flash points of human experience than in sustained artifice" (1980, 501). The "lonely voice" championed by O'Connor and the "broken world" lamented by O'Faolain lent themselves more naturally to the short story. Both writers virtually gave up on the novel after 1940. Of course, we have seen that this instinct for the shorter form, growing largely out of the oral tradition that influenced O'Connor and O'Faolain like many another Irish writer, is evident throughout the development of the Irish novel and certainly in the best Irish novel, the vast interwoven narrative tapestry that is *Ulysses*. Both of O'Connor's novels, *The Saint and Mary Kate* (1932) and *Dutch Interior* (1940), are centered on an innocent young protagonist who encounters the bizarre, difficult adult world in episodic narrative vignettes that read like they wanted to be short stories. Both novels contain marvellous depictions of working-class Cork eccentrics as well as depressingly domineering fathers and abusive husbands, and both are distinguished by a nearly perfect ear for Cork dialogue and a nostalgic evocation of innocent youth and youthful misinterpretation of adult realities. In the first novel, Mary Kate McCormick endures the cast of Irish comic grotesques who surround her—particularly "the saint," a young man whose religious mania prevents him from loving or understanding her. In the grimmer second novel, Stevie Dalton glimpses the lives of people with po-

tential and people who have failed, with O'Connor making
a kind of *Winesburg, Ohio* out of the working-class world of
Cork from which he emerged. Like O'Faolain's antiheroes,
O'Connor's protagonists remain frustrated but survive. These
novels reflect an authorial love/hate relationship with Ireland
that could not be permanently solved by exile in the Joycean
manner, because O'Connor and O'Faolain had committed
themselves to Ireland for better and for worse.

Francis MacManus (1909–65) stands apart from O'Connor,
O'Faolain, and the other novelists who attacked the most
bourgeois values of the Irish Free State. Unlike their works,
his never were banned under the Censorship Act. In the
quiet acceptance of the Irish people (even at their worst) that
is reflected in his novels, MacManus is closer to Ó Grianna
or McLaverty. Like McLaverty, he was for a long time a
schoolteacher, before joining Radio Éireann in 1948 as general
features editor. MacManus advanced his artistic credo in a
series of articles in the *Irish Monthly* during the 1930s (Cahalan 1983, 123–26). He saw himself as a Catholic novelist,
with realism and Catholicism as the core of his work, and
rejected the naturalism of Zola and O'Flaherty. He was no
simple Catholic propagandist, stressing in his article "The
Artist for Nobody's Sake" that artistic success or failure is
quite distinct from moral good and evil (1935, 178). As a
Kilkenny man transplanted to Dublin, he was geographically
further from Daniel Corkery but aesthetically closer to Corkery's views. Along with the Norwegian novelist Sigrid Undset's trilogy *Kristin Lavransdatter* (1920–22), Corkery's cultural
study *The Hidden Ireland* (1925) was a chief inspiration for
MacManus's trilogy of historical novels, *Stand and Give Challenge* (1934), *Candle for the Proud* (1936), and *Men Withering*
(1939). These three novels are unified by a focus on the
Gaelic poet and schoolmaster Donnacha Ruadh MacConmara,
one of the eighteenth-century figures celebrated by Corkery,
portrayed by MacManus as struggling through the Penal Age
and surviving to witness the 1798 rising in Wexford (Cahalan
1983, 126–30). *Men Withering* in particular is one of the best
Irish historical novels.

MacManus published a total of eleven novels, most of
them appearing during the 1930s and 1940s and set in

Kilkenny and its environs. Like many of the other realistic novelists of this period, he sought to expose the obscure, difficult conflicts found among the people of the towns and countryside—an otherwise "hidden Ireland" of the twentieth as well as the eighteenth and nineteenth centuries. His characters range from the benign to the bitter: examining the Irish people, Benedict Kiely notes, MacManus "takes them as he finds them. In his novel *The Greatest of These . . .* he finds them with peace blossoming in their souls. In *This House Was Mine* he finds them as mean as dirt, as mean as the dirt that the land-hungry and the worldly-wise can pride themselves on possessing" (1950, 26). Several of MacManus's novels deal with conflicts between the middle class and the peasantry in Kilkenny, entering a middle-class world bearing some resemblances to Kate O'Brien's Limerick, although O'Brien's characters are more definitely upper-middle-class and generally proud of it.

In *This House Was Mine* (1937), Martin Hickey is prevented by his prideful father, who approaches marriage like he does land purchase, from marrying their servant, and witnesses the eventual loss of the family home, which is regarded as divine retribution for the family hubris in which Martin himself participates. Alice Lennon in the rivetting *Watergate* (1942) returns from America to find her family home inhabited by her sister and husband but controlled by a grasping peasant, the tinker woman Ruby Butters, whom Alice eventually supplants, but only at the expense of her own freedom and dignity. Ruby Butters is one of a series of demented, almost Faulknerian characters in MacManus's novels. In *The Wild Garden* (1940), orphaned young Margaret Kane is abused by the demonic beau of her apathetic stepmother, the butcher Spigott, and rescued only through the intervention of her uncle and a kind priest. In *The Fire in the Dust* (1950), which Denis Cotter calls "MacManus' chief novel" (1980, 414), the sexually repressed but frenzied Miss Dreelin responds to the futility of her attempt to marry the widowed Mr. Golden by "playing the wicked stepmother to his children before she had the ring on her finger" (191), eventually indirectly causing the death of young Stevie Golden. MacManus's narrator is often a close witness to sinful deeds—

Stevie's friend Larry Hackett, Margaret's uncle in *The Wild Garden*. MacManus balances his portraits of pride and madness with images of charity. In *The Greatest of These* (1943), the Bishop of Dunmore befriends an ex-priest who was banished by the former bishop, with both of them rediscovering kindness and friendship in old age. Like Thomas Kilroy's later novel *The Big Chapel* (1971), this one is based on ecclesiastical conflicts in Callan, County Kilkenny, during the 1870s. In his sympathetic understanding of the Irish character, "MacManus is the diametric opposite of James Joyce," Cotter notes, "and is also estranged from his acerbic contemporaries—O'Flaherty, O'Faolain, and O'Connor. . . . His literary achievement, however, is often quite as high as theirs, and certainly needs reevaluation" (1980, 2–3).

Women Novelists: Elizabeth Bowen, Molly Keane, Kate O'Brien, Maura Laverty, and Mary Lavin

This period was marked by the emergence of a generation of women novelists—Elizabeth Bowen, Molly Keane, Kate O'Brien, Maura Laverty, Mary Lavin—who focused on Ascendancy and middle-class Irish life, continuing a devotion to realism that was earlier evident in novelists such as Maria Edgeworth, Emily Lawless, and Somerville and Ross. Edith Somerville was still active during the early part of this period; we have already seen in chapter 3 that her best individual effort, *The Big House of Inver*, was published in 1925. While the critical reputation of Elizabeth Bowen has always been secure, an appreciation for the works of the others has for the most part been forthcoming only within the last few years. The novels of Keane, O'Brien, and Laverty have been reprinted only since 1980 by feminist presses such as Arlen House and Virago. These writers are only now entering the canon—if there can be said to be a clearly established one for the Irish novel—and feminist or other current critical analysis of their novels is mostly still to come. Bowen's reputation was made mostly within the context of the modern *British* novel, not the Irish one, and an understanding of her as an Irish woman novelist is still in a largely undeveloped state.

Irish women novelists during this period explored many of the same conflicts within Irish society that their male counterparts did, such as the repressive nature of Irish society and the reverberations of Irish politics. Yet at the same time the five women whom I shall discuss here stand apart somewhat. While I have already surveyed a series of male novelists from the peasantry and the lower middle class who focused on those strata of Irish society, the women novelists came from the Ascendancy and middle class, as reflected in their novels. In my next chapter I shall examine a group of male novelists who retreated into fantasy, but Irish women novelists, from Maria Edgeworth in 1800 to Jennifer Johnston in the 1980s, have seemingly always remained devoted to the realist mode (even if adopting a romantic approach to it, as Sydney Owenson did). Similarly, Lady Gregory wrote realistic comedies while Yeats indulged in fantastic mythological plays, and O'Casey wrote plays depicting Irish women as courageous realists and Irish men as aimless daydreamers. An adequate understanding of such predilections among Irish women novelists will have to await a full study of the distinguished tradition they represent, but it is clear that sexism and oppression of women will be found central to a satisfactory explanation of the phenomenon. For now, one can only venture that Irish women attempted novels only when they could financially afford to, and that when they did so they were determined to make realistic sense of their own Ascendancy and middle-class traditions. Beyond that, one might hypothesize that they found the realist novel suitable to the selfless social role of women, since it can be perceived as a "selfless" form in which the author seems to disappear in the act of narrative reporting. A realistic domestic focus was a way of responding to the domestic sphere to which women were confined, whereas fantasy might have been perceived as dangerous in showing too much of the individual mind and fantasies of a female.

Elizabeth Bowen (1899–1973) exemplifies these patterns very clearly. Bowen spent most of her life in England and set eight of her ten novels there, but grew up in and later returned to a Big House in County Cork, always reflecting a thoroughly Anglo-Irish perspective. Just as Bowen insisted that her Ascendancy predecessor Sheridan Le Fanu's novel *Uncle Silas* was "an Irish story transposed to an English setting" (quoted in McCormack 1980, 141), Gary Davenport points out that a thoroughly Anglo-Irish consciousness permeates all of Bowen's "English" books as well (1974, 34). In her most celebrated Irish novel, *The Last September* (1929), the one she herself described in a later preface as "nearest to my heart" (1964), Bowen continued that subgenre which has always seemed to be dying off but never dies, and in which women have specialized from 1800 until the present day: the Big House novel. *The Last September* has competed with Somerville's *The Big House of Inver*, and more recently with Aidan Higgins's *Langrishe, Go Down* (1966), Jennifer Johnston's *The Captains and the Kings* (1972), and John Banville's *Birchwood* (1973) for the title of best twentieth-century Big House novel. Ever since Edgeworth's *Castle Rackrent* (1800), the Big House has continued to suffer a memorable demise within the plots of Irish novels yet survive as a powerful symbol. Frank Tuohy defines the Big House novel as dominated by the Big House itself as setting and symbol as well as by a social world full of snobbery and distance, deprivation versus passion for sport (especially hunting), and "inadequate men and masculine women" (1985, 201). The basic plot of *The Last September* is so typical as to appear allegorical. During the Anglo-Irish War, young Lois Naylor promises to marry an English soldier, Gerald Lesworth, but she is unable to love him and he is not accepted by her domineering mother. Finally Gerald is shot dead in an ambush, and the Naylors' Big House is burnt to the ground (in a fictional projection of Bowen's feelings about her own family estate in County Cork).

The complex psychology of this story is well underscored if one contrasts it with the plot of a novel such as Sydney Owenson's *The Wild Irish Girl*, which Bowen's novel reverses. Like many nineteenth-century Irish novelists, Owenson sent an Englishman to fall in love with a romantic Irish heroine just as she would have liked her English readership to do with Ireland. Writing after the establishment of the Irish Free

State, Bowen portrays the significantly named Lesworth as a romantic in pursuit of Lois, who wishes she could love him but finds herself caught amidst complicated loyalties. For the people of her caste, Bowen noted in her preface, "inherited loyalty to England—where their sons went to school, in whose wars their sons were killed, and to whom they owed in the first place their lands and power—pulled them one way; their own latent blood-and-bone 'Irishness,' the other" (ix–x). *The Last September* is "the perfect illustration of Elizabeth's tenet that life 'with the lid on' is both more frightening and more exciting than life 'with the lid off' " (Glendinning 1977, 73). Lois and Gerald seem allegorical emblems of Ireland and England. At one point Lois remarks: "Can you wonder this country gets irritated? It's as bad for it as being a woman" (66). Like a wife oppressed by a husband, Anglo-Irish characters experience a peculiar love/hate relationship with England. It is within this feminine Big House tradition that *The Last September* is to be understood (Davenport 1974, Laigle 1984, Tuohy 1985, Lassner 1986), not the torturous English psychology of Harriet Blodgett's insistence that Lois's "refusal to accept him as a male dramatizes her refusal to accept her own higher (latent, masculine) aspect, without which there cannot be selfhood" (1975, 18). Like *The Last September*, the less noted and less successful *A World of Love* (1955), Bowen's only other novel to be set wholly in Ireland, "develops the tension between the former glory of the Anglo-Irish tradition and the present-day decline of the estate which the novel takes as its setting" (Davenport 1974, 34).

Under the pen name of M. J. Farrell, Bowen's friend Molly Keane (b. 1904) published several novels during the 1930s and early 1940s, at least two of which, *Mad Puppetstown* (1931) and *Two Days in Aragon* (1941), appear modelled on *The Last September*. Then she faded into nearly total obscurity. Recently, though, Keane has staged a comeback in old age under the encouragement of feminist presses, publishing *Good Behaviour* (1981) and *Time After Time* (1983) and witnessing the republication of several of her earlier novels. At worst, her fiction seems a lighter rehash of the fading Ascendancy world explored by Bowen, described by herself as "my dearest friend in life" (quoted in Devlin 1984b, x), as presented in books containing (in Keane's own mocking description of the female Ascendancy novel) "seventy thousand words through which the cry of hounds reverberates continuously" (1934, 28). At her best, though, Keane explores the sexual conflicts of Ascendancy women with a boldness not found in Bowen. In *Devoted Ladies* (1934), a woman travels to Ireland—with Keane thereby adapting the nineteenth-century convention of the male hero who makes such a journey. She wants to marry a generous if dull Anglo-Irishman there, but is black-mailed and prevented from doing so by her cruel lesbian ex-lover. Writing about lesbians and homosexuals had been unheard of in Irish fiction. As Keane notes, "Before then no one thought anything of two elderly ladies setting up house together. . . . I was excited by finding out about lesbians and homosexuals. It was new. It made a subject" (quoted in Devlin 1984a, x). In *The Rising Tide* (1937), the assertive Cynthia survives marriage to a dashing young Anglo-Irishman, widowhood, and affairs with two men whom she eventually rejects, a married Englishman and a rich, alcoholic American. Cynthia emerges as an image of the decaying Ascendancy, as the giddy excitement of her young adult life is gradually replaced by the futility of her self-indulgence. At the end of the novel she sees a young man (with whom she thought she might attempt an affair) embracing another, younger woman, and she realizes that she is too old. So is the Ascendancy. Comments Keane, "People simply didn't visualize any change coming. They believed life would go on like that for all time . . ." (quoted in Devlin 1984b, xiv). Keane is an uneven writer, but her novels are important social studies of a neglected aspect of Irish life—the frustrations of Ascendancy women.

The best Irish woman novelist of the 1930s and 1940s, and one of the most important Irish novelists of any period, was Kate O'Brien (1897–1974). Unlike other novelists who focused on either the Ascendancy or the peasantry and the lower middle class, O'Brien devoted all of her Irish novels to a probing examination of the upper-middle-class Catholic people of "Mellick" (Limerick). They were representative of the new Catholic upper class cited by historian Joseph Lee:

"The movement up the scale of well being and respectability was evident both from their growing prominence in the economy and more visibly from spreading suburbs which they inhabited on the fringes of the cities and larger towns. Fewer in numbers, but superior in social status, and generally also in their style of living were the owners of the larger businesses and professional men" (quoted in Ryan 1984, 126). Eavan Boland adds that O'Brien's subject is the "Ireland between the mortgaged acres of Maria Edgeworth and the strong farms of Mary Lavin's short stories. It was an Ireland of increasing wealth and uneasy conscience, where the women wore stays and rouged their cheeks, had their clothes made by Dublin dressmakers and tried to forge the hauntings of their grandparents" (1980, xi). The families of Mellick live in *Catholic* Big Houses, with a new sense of proprietorship also approached in the slightly less affluent Catholic world of MacManus's *Watergate* or (later) John Broderick's *The Waking of Willie Ryan* (1965). O'Brien's focus on this prosperous Catholic upper middle class has been described as pioneering and unique, and in many ways it is, yet a very close nineteenth-century predecessor can be identified: Gerald Griffin, who, as we saw in chapter 1, gave similarly detailed attention to the middle-class Daly family of County Limerick in *The Collegians*, one of the best Irish novels of the nineteenth century. In the family saga *Without My Cloak* (1931), O'Brien's first novel and winner of the Hawthornden and James Tait Black prizes, Denis Considine experiences a conflict much like that of Hardress Cregan in *The Collegians:* he loves a young peasant woman but is unable to marry below his station. Others resolve the conflict for them: Danny Mann drowns Eily in *The Collegians* and Father Tom banishes Christina to America in *Without My Cloak.*

Like Molly Keane, O'Brien developed a fictional focus on women that included an understanding of the stresses of their sexuality and the psychology of their relationships with other women. She had "an unswerving faith in womankind, most of whom find themselves 'imprisoned in a code of response, a minuet of programmed answers and expectations.' Love is the pivot of their emotional lives" (Ryan 1982, 322). In *Without My Cloak*, Caroline Considine tries to escape her dull husband, but she is no more able to make a new life with the Protestant man whom she meets in London than Denis is able to marry Christina. In Mellick, one does not transgress the borders of religion and class in these matters. *The Ante-Room* (1933), O'Brien's second novel and her own favorite, tells the story of Agnes Mulqueen, who is plagued by a secret love for her sister's husband, eventually encouraged by him, but refuses to get more involved with him because her loyalty to her sister runs deeper than her feelings about him. O'Brien manipulates point of view adeptly, adding to her chief focus on Agnes the perspectives of several of the characters who surround her. Her best novels enjoy the balance and maturity of a Jane Austen, and appear much less loosely constructed than many Irish novels. One wonders about how much these qualities are linked to O'Brien's solid status in the middle class, the traditional province of the novel but a fairly unusual one for an Irish novelist. The detached objectivity of her writing may also be explained partly by the fact that she lived abroad for years, in Spain as a governess and then in England. Her career includes a European dimension found also in Joyce and subsequent novelists such as Francis Stuart, Samuel Beckett, and Aidan Higgins. Two of her most popular novels, *Mary Lavelle* (1936) and *That Lady* (1946), are set in Spain.

O'Brien's penetrating study of the interwoven lives of a mature woman and a young girl, *The Land of Spices* (1941), was banned under the Censorship Act "because a single sentence referred to a homosexual act between a young musician and the heroine's father. The absurdity was compounded by the fact that the heroine had embraced the religious life in reaction to her discovery of her father's predisposition" (Reynolds 1982, vi). Earlier *Mary Lavelle* had also been banned—an act for which O'Brien exacted literary revenge, like O'Flaherty in *The Puritan*, centering *Pray for the Wanderer* (1938) on a writer who is rejected by his native land and in turn rejects it. *The Land of Spices* is one of the best novels of this period, rivalled perhaps only by O'Flaherty's *Famine* and Bowen's *The Last September*. It is the story of Helen Archer, whose isolation as the English Superior of an Irish convent is overcome by her generous, platonic love for a young student, Anna Murphy. The two are drawn together because each has experienced a great loss—Helen's father, Anna's brother—and each has an unusually intelligent, sensitive personality. This novel becomes partly a bildungsroman in which Anna develops an artistic consciousness, maturing to the point when "her wings were grown and she was for the world" (280) like Stephen Dedalus in *Portrait*, which is echoed at several points. Like Leopold Bloom, Helen Archer is a surrogate parent figure, but intervenes much more directly and persistently in the life of Anna Murphy. Her most forceful moment comes when she forces Anna's thick-headed grandmother to allow Anna to accept a university scholarship. It is significant that Helen is an Englishwoman who has been sent to Ireland; like Keane in *Devoted Ladies*, O'Brien modifies the old nineteenth-century convention of the male English hero who journeys to Ireland. Similarly, Angèle Maury in *The Last of Summer* (1943) is a young actress raised abroad who visits her relatives near Mellick, falls in love with her cousin Tom, but finally realizes that she is too much of an outsider to successfully marry into an Irish family like his. You can't go home again, especially if you never grew up there to begin with. Angèle's departure at the end, like Helen's at the end of *The Land of Spices*, reflects O'Brien's own exiled posture (Reynolds 1987).

Maura Laverty (1907–66) also celebrated in her fiction the attachment between a young girl and a strong older woman. Like O'Brien, Laverty worked as a governess in Spain, before returning to live in Ireland. This experience was captured in her novel *No More Than Human* (1944), the sequel to her very popular first novel, *Never No More* (1942), which has recently been reprinted. *Never No More* was praised in its original preface by O'Faolain: "For me the book was a case of love at first sight, and I cannot imagine that it will not win the same immediate affection everywhere (v). O'Faolain pointed out the book's use of the oral tradition, with a narrative "as garrulous and as meandering as a village gossip so that any story is liable to be deflected by three intervening stories, or to begin in the best gossip style" (vi). *Never No More* tells the story of young Delia Scully growing up surrounded by the warm love of her grandmother; like O'Brien

in *The Land of Spices,* Laverty celebrates a nurturing relationship between two females, though her novel is much
lighter in tone and depth. It is filled with images of cooking,
just as her popular cookbooks contain stories. While *Never
No More* is set in a small town, her interesting novel *Lift Up
Your Gates* (1946) follows young Chrissie Doyle on her paper
route through the Dublin slums, providing insights into the
lives of a variety of characters. The common thread among
her novels is her focus on "the sensitive, innocent point of
view of girls and women" (Scott 1980, 363).

Benedict Kiely noted at the end of the 1940s that he would
have said that Kate O'Brien had written the only studies of
the "Irish provincial middleclass" if Mary Lavin (b. 1912)
had not recently emerged (1950, 56–57). Like O'Faolain and
O'Connor, Lavin is best known for her excellent short stories
but also wrote a pair of novels. She admits her preference
for the short story, reflected in the fact that both of her
novels proceed like a series of stories, separately entitled as
we move from one family member to the next. Like Denis
Considine in *Without My Cloak,* Gabriel Galloway in Lavin's
The House in Clewe Street (1945) pursues an eventually futile
relationship with a young peasant woman, Onny Soraghan.
Onny is a bolder, freer soul than O'Brien's Christina, and,
after Gabriel has run off to Dublin with Onny to escape the
rigid moral codes of his family and town, it is he who is
banished, when Onny begins an affair with a painter. In
this novel Lavin indicts narrow-minded, middle-class, small-
town life, much as Brinsley MacNamara and, later, John
Broderick did. Like Laverty in *Lift Up Your Gates,* Lavin
balanced her depiction of the small town with a sympathetic
portrait of life in working-class Dublin, *Mary O'Grady* (1950).
Its protagonist is introduced as a woman who has learned
to survive in Dublin but longs for her native countryside,
like McLaverty's Belfast characters. Mary O'Grady endures
the death of her husband and two of her daughters and
their fiancés. At the end of the novel she is left consoling
her surviving daughter, who has just left her cruel husband,
in a scene recalling the conclusion of Sean O'Casey's play
Juno and the Paycock. Like O'Casey, Lavin champions the
love and endurance of a mother. Once again, as in O'Brien

and Laverty, we return to an appreciation of how a young woman is nurtured by an older woman. These writers opened up new perspectives on the lives of women in the Big Houses and the small towns, influencing the next generation of realist novelists of the 1960s and thereafter, which also included an impressive series of women, such as Edna O'Brien, Jennifer Johnston, and Julia O'Faolain.

Realist Novels by Fabulist Writers: Forrest Reid, Brinsley MacNamara, Eimar O'Duffy, and Mervyn Wall

We have seen how most of the novelists discussed in this chapter exposed the confinement of life in the Irish Free State, expressing a disappointment that political independence had not led to increased social or intellectual freedom but rather to a pervasive narrow-mindedness. While the realist strategy was one of exposé, we shall see in the next chapter how another group of novelists in the same period chose to escape or parody the Free State in fabulist fictions. The realist and fabulist modes really represent two sides of a single literary coin. Faced with the realities of the Free State, the best novelists tended either to attack or to retreat. The satirist, of course, could escape and attack simultaneously. Most novelists felt drawn very strongly to one mode or the other, becoming either a realist or a fabulist, with little middle ground. A few, though, did publish both kinds of novels, and a few other novelists mixed realism and fantasy within single works. Here I shall first examine Forrest Reid's use of both realism and fantasy, and then mention the realistic novels of three fabulists who will be discussed more in my next chapter: Brinsley MacNamara, Eimar O'Duffy, and Mervyn Wall. These writers are all linked to each other and to the other novelists of the period by their attention to the dominant mid-century fictional theme of disappointment, which each explores in one way or another.

Forrest Reid (1875–1947) is difficult to categorize, not only because he blends realism and fantasy but also because his career demonstrated an endurance outlasting the confines of a single period, with sixteen novels published over a span of four decades. He published novels as early as the first decade of this century, but did his best work in the 1930s. He was educated at Cambridge and spent a quiet life in Belfast. In his fiction as well as his career Reid seemed far from the mainstream of Irish life and writing, and this helps to explain his slight critical reputation. In 1974 John Wilson Foster suggested that in light of the increase in popularity of myth and archetypal criticism as well as the recent study of children's literature—concerns appropriate to Reid's novels—that there might be a Reid revival, but then accurately predicted that the eccentric nature of Reid's work would probably prevent any such development (198–99). Denis Cotter writes:

> A distilled summary of the archetypal Reidian novel of the developing self runs somewhat as follows: A boy reaching adolescence in a lower-middle-class family in Protestant Ulster has had a particularly lonesome childhood. He feels estranged from his parents; he feels particularly estranged from their narrow evangelical religion. He delights in nature, especially in landscape and in animals. . . . Dreams assuage his loneliness most of all, for in them he meets his playmate, a boy of his own age. Sometimes the real world will nearly approximate to this dream world: the dream-companion will come to life. The idyll that then ensues is temporary, for the process of growing up is relentless. Inevitable maturity . . . means entering the dull world of work, the wretchedness of marriage, alienation from joy. The Reidian *Bildungsroman* is suffused with a terrified nostalgia, each page a record of youth's lovely moment and a step closer to the its final doom. (Cotter 1982, 116–17)

Cotter's précis of Reid's fictional world very effectively applies to his chief works during the 1930s and early 1940s: the Tom Barber trilogy and *Peter Waring*. Reid wrote his trilogy "backwards," beginning with Tom in late adolescence in *Uncle Stephen* (1931) and then examining him in early adolescence (*The Retreat*, 1936) and childhood (*Young Tom*, 1944). He was never able to write effectively about adulthood in his novels, confessing that "I could get on swimmingly until I reached . . . the point where a boy becomes a man.

Then something seemed to happen, my inspiration was cut off, my interest flagged" (quoted in Foster 1980, 566). Tom Barber escapes from the drab realities of his youth into an exotic dreamworld populated by ghosts, talking animals, and mythical Greek, Oriental, and Arabic entities. He eventually flees from his forbidding parents to the care of his mysterious Uncle Stephen, who is capable of making his body vanish and rematerialize. Tom's soulmates are always other young males or surrogate fathers like Uncle Stephen. Cotter argues that "Reid's novels of adolescence are the record of a frustrated, consciously sublimated homosexuality. Further, it is a fixated homosexuality, a sexuality which has not moved beyond adolescent desire" (1982, 117). In *Peter Waring* (a revision of *Following Darkness,* 1912), Reid adds to his adolescent world a surrogate mother, the wealthy Mrs. Carroll of Derryaghy House, in whose arms Peter finally tells his whole story at the end of the novel. Like Stephen Dedalus, Peter Waring struggles to develop an artistic consciousness, but it is striking that Peter never reaches adulthood and is left literally attached to his mother-figure at the conclusion rather than the beginning of the novel. Reid's novels invite Freudian analysis, such as the kind advanced by Foster when he calls Peter's overly strict father "anal-retentive" (1974, 145) and Peter's friendship with another boy, latent-homosexual.

As much as Reid's dreamy fictional world often obscures it, there exists a significant social and historical context for the struggles of his protagonists. Foster points out that "what really offended Reid was the notion of social descent from respectability into squalor. Product of a Presbyterian merchant family that had come down in the world, Reid was early imbued with both disdain and apprehension at the sight of seediness and frayed decency. This was transferred to his boy-heroes," and helps to explain why "realism and fantasy vie with each other in his work" (1974, 139, 141). Much like Stephen Dedalus, Tom Barber and Peter Waring retreat to an internal, imaginative world not only because they have active minds but also because they wish to escape the increasingly depressing real worlds that surround them. Like McLaverty's characters, Peter Waring is forced to live in diminished circumstances in Belfast while longing for the countryside. He misses the opulent Big House of Derryaghy in Newcastle, County Down, not McLaverty's impoverished Catholic cabins on Rathlin Island. It is striking, though, how McLaverty and Reid, writing about opposite ends of the Northern social spectrum, both focus on the individual psychologies of their characters in ways that lift them above the sectarian conflict that historically contributed to their problems.

Brinsley MacNamara, Eimar O'Duffy, and Mervyn Wall were all disappointed nationalists in one way or another, like a number of the other novelists, and all three were also known as playwrights and government or civil service officials. MacNamara and O'Duffy began as realists and then went on to do their best work in the fabulist mode, whereas Wall made his name as a fabulist and later demonstrated that he could write effective realistic novels, too. These three are thus also hard to categorize. Brinsley MacNamara (1890–1963), whose real name was John Weldon, might just as well have been discussed at the beginning of this chapter, especially since his realistic novels came earliest in the period. Frank O'Connor, echoing Yeats's words about Standish O'Grady and the Irish Renaissance, called MacNamara the writer who in his own way began modern Irish realism. Benedict Kiely added that "long before Sean O'Faolain wrote *Come Back to Erin* or before Frank O'Connor forgot his fighting enthusiasms and commenced a new, and often extravagant, battle against prudery, the revolution had for MacNamara turned as sour as a bad pint. He had the unique merit of being disillusioned when most of his contemporaries were enthusiastic" (1950, 15). His first novel, *The Valley of the Squinting Windows* (1918), remained his best-known or rather most infamous work: "the book was publicly burned in the best medieval fashion in Delvin" (McDonnell 1980, 418), his hometown in County Westmeath, whose natives knew that their town was the source of MacNamara's ridicule for his fictional Garradrimna. This novel recounts the townspeople's disdain for Nan Brennan, who had an affair with a wealthy townsman before entering a respectable if dull marriage with another man; for her son John, who abandons studies for the priesthood and develops an ineffectual love for Rebecca Kerr, the schoolteacher; and for Rebecca, who ends up getting pregnant by Nan's out-of-wedlock first son and removed from her job and from the town. More memorable than the story itself was MacNamara's unforgettable image, captured in his title and repeated throughout his text, of the stodgy, nosy, bourgeois townspeople as personified in their windows: "She saw many a head suddenly fill many a squinting window, and men and women they met on the road turn around with a sneer to gaze back at her" (25). Andrew E. Malone "described MacNamara as the originator of the 'squinting windows' school of Irish realistic fiction" (quoted in McDonnell 1980, 418), a label that stuck despite the varied nature of his later work.

MacNamara's second novel, *The Clanking of Chains* (1920), added a disillusioned political dimension to his attack on small-town life. Its protagonist, Michael Dempsey, is a Sinn Féin idealist trapped in the town of Ballycullen with its stultified social hierarchies. That same year, Eimar O'Duffy (1893–1935) published another early disillusioned nationalist critique, the long autobiographical novel *The Wasted Island* (1919), which presented (six years before O'Casey's play *The Plough and the Stars*) a critical view of the 1916 Easter Rising. Like O'Duffy himself, who served with the Irish Volunteers, his protagonist Bernard Lascelles joins Eoin MacNeill in opposing the Rising and trying to stop it. Part roman à clef, part bildungsroman, part political novel, and part romance, *The Wasted Island* is an interesting novel but is clogged with too many historical details. His second novel, *The Lion and the Fox* (1922a), is a historical novel in the mold of Standish O'Grady that gets bogged down in too much history and too little fiction. O'Duffy as realistic novelist is almost unrecognizable from the O'Duffy who went on to write an excellent, hilarious, satiric trilogy.

Mervyn Wall (b. 1908) is best known for fabulist fictions written in the 1940s that allowed his satiric mind to run riot. Yet *Leaves for the Burning* (1952) captured his own real, confined world living in yet another small town and working for the Irish Civil Service; *No Trophies Raise* (1956) attacked the Irish business scene in the 1950s; and *Hermitage* (1982) dealt with the survival of an Irish political prisoner. A story of petty bureaucrats and frustrated ambitions and desires, *Leaves for the Burning* is centered on three old college chums who go on a drinking spree: Lucien Burke, mired in the civil service, in trouble with his boss, and wishing he had proposed to a woman he had loved years ago, Theodora Conroy; Frank Peebles, an eccentric painter on his way to the Yeats burial in Sligo; and Bob McMunn, who has everything the other two thought they wanted (including the woman they had admired in school) but reveals that he is just as miserable as they are. Finally Lucien proposes to Theodora but she rejects him, telling him it is too late. Writing toward the end of the period that we have been considering, Wall leaves us feeling that it is the autumn of existence: Lucien "walked on, conscious of impending night. As he went up the avenue, he saw that the gardener had put flame to the heap of leaves, and smoke was creeping across the grass filling the evening with the ancient, pervasive scent. On the ground about his feet rustled the fallen leaves, the brown and silver coinage of autumn" (217).

John Wilson Foster's astute analysis (1974) of both the sociohistorical roots and the Freudian ramifications of Forrest Reid's fiction is suggestive of the kind of increased critical versatility needed in scholarship on the Irish novel during this period. Recent critical celebration of the work of novelists such as Kate O'Brien and Molly Keane is another example, all too rare, of how new critical understanding has had an impact. Were it not for the recent republication of several of the novels of O'Brien, Keane, and Laverty by feminist presses, these novelists might have remained lost in obscurity. Considering the political and historical nature of the novels that we have considered in this chapter, it comes as no surprise that most of the criticism of them has been political and historical in emphasis. With very few exceptions, critical articles and books have been limited to individual novelists and have concentrated on biographical, political, and historical aspects. Comparative studies of different novelists have been rare, even though Benedict Kiely's early book (1950) about the fiction of the period suggested many such comparisons. My own first book (1983) compares O'Faolain,

MacManus, and O'Flaherty as historical novelists. John Zneimer's book (1970) on O'Flaherty is existentialist in focus, and such a departure from the usual straightforward biographical approach is refreshing. We need more comparative studies and a greater variety of critical approaches to realist Irish novelists.

6

Fantasia: Irish Fabulists, 1920–55

The Forms of Fabulism

Like James Stephens before him, James Joyce had demonstrated for other Irish novelists the rich possibilities of imaginative fiction that departs from realist practice. That Stephens and Joyce had by no means exhausted these possibilities became quite clear from the work of the impressive group of fabulists who came after them, including three novelists commonly linked to Joyce and celebrated as his best successors or rivals: Flann O'Brien, Samuel Beckett, and Máirtín Ó Cadhain. The fabulist authors (a few of whom wrote realist as well as fabulist works) shared with the realists a revulsion with what they saw as the puritanical and oppressive tendencies and practices of the ironically named Free State during the period 1920–55. While the realist novels attack these features of Irish society by exposing them, the fabulist novels travel to freer, more remote realms, distant in time or space, which often suspiciously resemble modern Ireland. Thus, Irish fabulist fiction often becomes satire, taking its literary license not only from Stephens and Joyce but also (especially in the case of Eimar O'Duffy and Flann O'Brien) from the great Irish pioneer of satire, Jonathan Swift.

Modern Irish fabulist fiction tended to adopt two somewhat divergent if often overlapping modes: mythological or medieval romance (with Stephens's *The Crock of Gold* and *The Demigods* as central models) and experimental novel or anti novel (with Joyce's *Ulysses* and *Finnegans Wake* looming as the imposing masterpieces). For models of the mythological romance, one could look back even before Stephens to the fiction of Standish James O'Grady and Yeats. Indeed, as Augustine Martin notes, there lurked "at the margins" of many nineteenth-century Irish novels "a belief in a world of fairies, witches and ancient gods, a belief in the spiritual and the visionary, a sense of eternity surrounding and sometimes invading the world of time. . . . There is no doubt that the fairies and the ancient gods provided the Irish prose writer with a remarkable opportunity for experimental fiction, for breaking with the conventions of realism in pursuit of a purer sense of reality" (1985a, 110, 112). This fiction was experimental yet at the same time rooted in the Irish literary tradition going back to the ancient mythological cycles. Mythology, romance, and experimentalism interacted with each other. The influence of James Stephens, the best early twentieth-century writer in this mode, was a very accessible one for Irish writers from 1920 to 1955 partly because his work was consistent with the Irish tradition and partly because of his own very affable personality.

The case of Joyce's influence is different. Even more than Joyce's own relationship with earlier Irish novelists, the reaction of subsequent Irish writers to his work very much exemplifies (rather understandably) Harold Bloom's notions about "the anxiety of influence," with the later writers overshadowed by their great literary father but often seeking to "destroy" him. After *Ulysses* and *Finnegans Wake,* what was left for the experimental Irish novelist to do? Some Irish novelists, such as the realist Kate O'Brien, felt compelled to deny, rather unconvincingly, Joyce's influence altogether: "The Joyce influence, which is or has been everywhere in Europe, is not now very evident in Irish writing. It is as if there is a kind of revolt against this greatness" (1977, 312). More forthright is the boast of "The Novelist" in Brinsley MacNamara's *The Various Lives of Marcus Igoe:* "I'll beat Joyce at his own game!" (1929, 195). As we shall see, the entire career of Flann O'Brien was a pointed, frustrated, oedipal struggle with the specter of Joyce. Others, such as Máirtín Ó Cadhain and Francis Stuart, managed to go assuredly their own way while at the same time they were very much marked by Joyce's achievement. The Irish novelist who knew Joyce best, Samuel Beckett, responded most originally to Joyce's artistic vision and style by creating a body of work that is in many ways diametrically opposite to his.

Realists as Fabulists: MacNamara and O'Faolain

The appeal of the fabulist mode in modern Irish fiction—much more evident than in English and American novels during the same period—is perhaps best demonstrated by the fact that even some of the most celebrated Irish realists could not resist writing this kind of fiction: Liam O'Flaherty published an erotic, mythical, short tale, *The Ecstasy of Angus* (1931), about how the god of love, Angus, conceives Genius in the goddess Fand and dies, having lost his youth and immortality; the satiric bard of the "squinting windows," Brinsley MacNamara, took the hints of fantasy within his earlier realist novels several steps further, in *The Various Lives of Marcus Igoe* (1929); and the very dean of Irish prose realism, Sean O'Faolain, having given up on the realist novel in favor of the short story after 1940, more recently published his own highly entertaining fantasy novel, *And Again?* (1979). Even though separated by several decades, MacNamara's and O'Faolain's novels lend themselves to close comparison, not only because their authors had previously made their names as realists, but because they tell very similar stories. Both books probe and question the fateful directions of one's life, in fabulist transpositions of the traditional autobiographical novel: MacNamara's protagonist lives several different "lives" simultaneously, while O'Faolain's hero lives for 128 years forward in historical time but backwards in personal, developmental time, shrinking into infancy and finally evaporating in a matchbox. In their playful experiments with human life and death, these novels are similar to other Irish fabulist novels such as Joseph O'Neill's *Wind from the North* (1934), Flann O'Brien's *The Third Policeman* (1967), and Máirtín Ó Cadhain's *Cré na Cille* (1949).

MacNamara's Marcus Igoe experiences literally what most of us only fantasize about occasionally: What if our lives had taken a different course? What if we had moved elsewhere? What if we had married someone else and had different children, or never married or never had children? MacNamara's narrative shifts between contrasting scenarios.

Marcus marries Nancy the bookkeeper and has children, while lamenting that he had not married Mary Margaret Caherlane, who left for America. Yet we subsequently learn that Mary Margaret "had never gone away only remaining to become the plump and somewhat strong-tempered woman he had married" (56), living and dying with him, childless. Like James Thurber's later hero Walter Mitty, "a remarkable feature of the mind of Marcus Igoe was its mutability. It could suddenly stop moving in one direction to begin moving in quite a contrary way without, as it appeared, the least effort in the world" (110). A cobbler like the leprachauns, Marcus eventually journeys to Dublin, where he meets "The Novelist," apparently MacNamara himself, who earns the wrath of his friend "The Poet" for "bringing up your characters from Garradrimna and drinking with them" (194–95) and the resentment of Marcus for his own treatment: "That's a damn lie for him anyway!" (190). Marcus finally abandons the Novelist, willing his fortune to a young man who will return to Garradrimna, the town of the "squinting windows," and carry on his identity there. "He had a notion that the many 'lives' he had lived here were, in a sense, but a promise of the many future lives he would yet live in various stages which would eventually place Marcus Igoe amongst the stars" (257). This novel ends in a suggestion of eternal recurrence very similar to the conclusion of Flann O'Brien's *The Third Policeman*.

O'Faolain's *And Again?* is equally imaginative and even more entertaining. After almost getting hit by a truck that kills a young boy instead, James J. Younger receives an offer in the mail from the gods (signed "*Is mise le meas*, Secretary to the Department of External Affairs, Olympus") to relive his life backwards, an offer he cannot refuse, "to decide, once for all, whether what you humans call Experience teaches you a damned thing" (6). Beginning at retirement age in 1965, Younger lives with and loves in turn a woman, her daughter, and her granddaughter—each of whom, of course, grows older and further beyond his reach as he himself gets younger. In a hilariously literal Freudian twist, the granddaughter eventually serves as Younger's mother, taking care of him and complaining, when he becomes too small to mow the lawn, "Those effing Irish husbands!" This novel is not only a sheer comic romp but also a fascinating autobiographical retrospection. O'Faolain himself was born within a few days of Younger in 1900 and has enjoyed an unusually long, active, and diverse career that has taken him from the early days of Joyce to the latter days of his fellow near-immortal, Beckett. At the end of this novel the granddaughter takes up the narrative for the infant Younger, writing diary entries like Stephen at the end of *Portrait* and musing, "It could well be that if each of us lived much longer than normal with, like him, all our original faculties unabated we would become more diverse, and from frequent movement through our diversities not more wise about our selves but more uncertain of them. He and I often talked about Yeats's vain search for what he called a 'Unity of Being' and when we came down to actual cases had to agree that in history all that those men and women who seem to have been completely unified had was a concentration on one aspect of their selves to the exclusion of all the others" (275). *And Again?* offers impressive, entertaining testimony to O'Faolain's own endurance and diversity.

The Satiric Voice of Eimar O'Duffy

The earlier fabulist novelists of this period—Eimar O'Duffy, Lord Dunsany, Joseph O'Neill, Austin Clarke, Mervyn Wall—followed James Stephens in drawing heavily from mythological and medieval Irish materials to create their fantasies. Those whose reputations burgeoned later—Flann O'Brien, Samuel Beckett, Máirtín Ó Cadhain, Francis Stuart—wrote more radically experimental works, responding to what Richard Kearney has described as "the Joycean shift from the novel as quest to the novel as question," giving rise to "a new 'critical' tradition, which we might term a counter-tradition" (1979, 393). The writings of both groups of writers are extremely impressive and diverse: O'Duffy, Dunsany, Wall, O'Brien, and of course Beckett (along with Brinsley MacNamara) made their names as playwrights as well as novelists, and Austin Clarke was much more prolific and better known as a poet. At the same time, their road to literary success was neither straight nor narrow. O'Duffy, O'Neill, Wall, and O'Brien were all frustrated civil servants; Dunsany was often dismissed by the Irish as a wealthy British dilettante; O'Brien was best known in Ireland as a newspaper columnist, and Ó Cadhain and Stuart for their political activities; while Beckett appeared to be the ultimate exile, writing his best novels in French. Yet these writers' novels share evidence of a command of Irish and other literary traditions as well as a highly imaginative capacity to challenge literary conventions and make us both laugh and think.

Among all of these novelists, none has been more unjustly neglected and is more in need of reprinting and reexamination than Eimar O'Duffy (1893–1935). As Diane Tolomeo notes, O'Duffy "has only recently been rediscovered in literary circles" (1983, 279). His "Cuanduine trilogy"—*King Goshawk and the Birds* (1926), *The Spacious Adventures of the Man in the Street* (1928), and *Asses in Clover* (1933)—has been out of print for more than a half-century, yet is as insightful and certainly as funny as anything else written anywhere during this period. *King Goshawk* is in particular a comic and satiric masterpiece. As I noted in my previous chapter, O'Duffy had already published strident realist novels, the roman à clef and bildungsroman *The Wasted Island* (1919) and the historical novel *The Lion and the Fox* (1922a); his *Printer's Errors* (1922b) and *Miss Rudd and Some Lovers* (1923) were two somewhat more lighthearted minor realist novels. O'Duffy's wildly critical imagination blossomed when he departed from realism and entered the realm of satiric fantasy. He did so shortly after losing his job in the Irish Department of External Affairs in 1925; as with Joseph O'Neill, Mervyn Wall, and Flann O'Brien, one has to wonder to what extent O'Duffy's fantasies were provoked by the dingy, boring realities of a civil service job.

In *King Goshawk and the Birds* O'Duffy brings the ancient Irish hero Cúchulainn back to modern Dublin, just as Joyce had done with Ulysses and Stephens with Angus Óg and Pan a few years earlier. Concerning O'Duffy's comic reincarnation of Cúchulainn, Augustine Martin notes that "it is probably not a coincidence that O'Duffy situates his action

in the area of Barney Kiernan's pub where the comic transformations of Joyce's 'Cyclops' episode take place. And it is
certainly not a coincidence that O'Duffy's chief character is,
like Stephens's [in *The Crock of Gold*], a Philosopher with a
capital P" (1985a, 115). Recalling that *The Crock of Gold* ends
with Angus Óg's impending trip to Dublin to free the Philosopher and the "mind of man," one might read *King
Goshawk* as O'Duffy's sequel—a comic study of what happens
when the gods arrive in Dublin. Overall, though, in terms
of literary predecessors O'Duffy's trilogy is more Swiftian.
In *King Goshawk* the great Cúchulainn is like Gulliver among
the Lilliputians; in *The Spacious Adventures of the Man in the
Street*, Aloysius O'Kennedy is transported to the planet Rathé
as Gulliver is to Brobdingnag or Laputa; and *Asses in Clover*
is as full of political, social, economic, and religious satire
as anything in Swift. O'Duffy is funnier than Swift and is
surpassed as comic satirist only by Flann O'Brien/Myles na
gCopaleen (the period's other chief disciple of Swift). When,
for example, Cúchulainn is accosted by the employer of
Aloysius O'Kennedy (whose body he is borrowing) for being
late to work, he becomes angry and his consternation is
described in memorable fashion:

His whole body was contorted. His ribs parted asunder, so that
there was room for a man's foot between them; his calves and
his buttocks came round to the front of his body. . . . For such
was his appearance when his anger was upon him; as testify the
Yellow Book of Leccan and the other chronicles; which, if any
man doubt, let him search his conscience whether he have not
believed even stranger things printed in newspapers. For myself,
I think the chroniclers are the more trustworthy, as they are
certainly the more entertaining; for, if they lie, they lie for the
fun of it, whereas the journalists lie for pay, or through sheer
inability to observe or report correctly. (58–59)

Cúchulainn has been recruited by the Philosopher of Sto-
neybatter to do battle with King Goshawk, an evil industrial
baron who has "bought up all the song-birds, and proposes
to cage them, and charge a fee to those who would hear
them sing" (31). The Philosopher and Cúchulainn also have

to contend with Dublin's mirror-image political parties, the Yallogreens and Greenyallos, who recall similar adversaries in *Gulliver's Travels* and prefigure today's Irish political parties of Fine Gael and Fianna Fáil, which take turns mismanaging the country. Cúchulainn finds himself quite distracted from his appointed task by modern Dublin itself, a city that O'Duffy was as determined to immortalize as Joyce: "Come, O Muse, whoever you be, that stood by the elbow of immortal Zola, take this pen of mine and pump it full of such foul and fetid ink as shall describe it worthily" (52). Instead of taking on Goshawk, Cúchulainn joins the Bon Ton Suburban Tennis Club in order to attract young ladies, becomes a wildly impressive tennis player, finally gets married, and ascends to Tir na nÓg (the Land of Youth), shedding O'Kennedy's body and leaving behind a prodigious son, Cuanduine or Cú an Duine, "the Hound of Man" (116), who carries on the campaign against Goshawk.

Cuanduine reads Dublin newspaper articles that rival the later gems of Myles na gCopaleen and even contain hilarious accounts from "Dublin District Court" (one of Myles's funniest departments): a man is tried for killing three children while driving 100 miles per hour through a crowded street, but explains that he had never driven before and so is fined £5 and advised to "take lessons before again driving through crowded thoroughfares" (148). Again like O'Brien/na gCopaleen, O'Duffy spares not the academics, describing the dons of Trinity and University Colleges turning up for Cuanduine's speech armed with bad eggs and stink bombs but then fleeing in cowardice. "As to the actual sequence of events: whether the holy and undivided men of Trinity, who were in front, were first seized with panic and swept away the sea-divided Gaels in their flight; or whether the latter fled first and the men of Trinity, demoralised by finding themselves without supports, fled after them: on these points historians are divided according to the source from which they draw their salaries" (194). O'Duffy's books are episodic in the best Irish narrative tradition: once having established his basic comic conceit focused on the ludicrous juxtaposition of ancient heroism and petty modernism, he can (and does) spin his yarns indefinitely. He ends his hilarious first volume with Goshawk unconquered, promising to return to the struggle in a later volume.

First, however, O'Duffy proposed to escape dear dirty Dublin altogether. *The Spacious Adventures of the Man in the Street* sets out to answer the question of what happened to Aloysius O'Kennedy after he rented his body to Cúchulainn: he found himself on the planet of Rathé, hovering (like Gulliver over Laputa) above the city of Bulnid (an obvious anagram of Dublin). True to the Irish oral tradition, this whole book is delivered as a series of stories by O'Kennedy— to his employer, as an extended excuse for *why* he is so late to work and deserves to get his job back. As with *Gulliver's Travels*, much of the comedy of this book hinges on reversal, and in this case O'Duffy's target is the Irish approach to sex—as if O'Duffy wanted to guarantee his censorship by the Irish Free State whose employment he had left. TheRatheans, O'Kennedy soon learns, enjoy frequent, diverse, guiltless sex—but are extremely uptight about food and are "monophagous," eating just one fruit all their lives. O'Kennedy enjoys a blissful sexual encounter with a young Rathean woman who is shocked when he asks for a bite of food afterwards. Later he reads a brilliantly written Rathean novel about "a woman who has eaten a wild strawberry in her childhood, and whose whole life is made miserable by the fear of the iniquity becoming known. When finally she is betrayed she goes out into the night to die rather than endure the shame which would have followed" (131). Like Mervyn Wall in *The Unfortunate Fursey* (1946), O'Duffy thereby lampoons repressive Irish attitudes and practices regarding sex, in this very funny science-fiction novel.

In *Asses in Clover* O'Duffy returns to the planet Earth and lets fly satirically at a variety of economic and religious topics, as if seeking to cover whatever evils in the world remained; he was to suffer a premature death, at the age of forty-two, two years after this book appeared, and his later work was produced during years of failing health and financial difficulty and included three detective potboilers. In *Asses in Clover* he vents his spleen over the American capitalist causes of the Great Depression: now King Goshawk sits in council in

Manhattan, discussing the state of the economy in an American accent, pronouncing that "You can starve all of the people some of the time, and some of the people all of the time, but you can't starve all of the people all of the time" (23). In eerily prophetic fashion, O'Duffy describes a disarmament conference stalled over how many weapons each nation should use to slaughter the others, and his "Assinine" government spokesman's explanation of why Assinaria has attacked Faraway should make today's student of Central America sit up and take notice:

Critics of the Government have said that this action is a violation of the Treaty for the Renunciation of War; but let me tell them that it is nothing of the sort. By that treaty we promised "to renounce war as an instrument of national policy." Let our critics note the exact wording of this document on which they rely in their nefarious purpose of defaming their own country in the eyes of the world. In the first place, this action of ours is not war at all. We have never declared war on the Farawavian nation. We have merely despatched what might be called a force of armed guardians of the peace to protest our legitimate interest. It is true that these guardians of the peace have bombarded several towns and routed several Farawavian armies, but that was because their purely pacific intentions were met by violent resistance. (122–23)

At the end Cuanduine deposes King Goshawk, but O'Duffy leaves us with the strong impression that his kind remains always with us. His trilogy ends with one god explaining to another why the human experiment has failed: "During his last few hundred years, when he was already far gone in decay, he achieved a mastery of natural forces that was marvellous in a race so stupid, but his wickedness and folly were such that it did him more harm than good" (330). Writing before World War II and the advent of atomic and nuclear warfare, O'Duffy demonstrated that Irish storytelling strategies and mythological materials can be made not only entertaining and relevant but, as transformed by his imagination, also prophetic in contexts that extend well beyond Ireland.

The Romances of Lord Dunsany, Joseph O'Neill, and Austin Clarke

Compared to O'Duffy's trilogy, the fantasies of Lord Dunsany, Joseph O'Neill, and Austin Clarke are more conventional romances, yet they also draw from mythology and medieval history in order to make points about life in the twentieth century. Edward Plunkett, Lord Dunsany (1878–1957), was a loyal British peer from County Meath and a modern Renaissance man—sportsman, soldier, adventurer, and chess champion as well as novelist, storywriter, and playwright. Politically, he certainly did not fit the typical Irish mold. Having fought as a young man in the British Army in the Boer War in South Africa (where he met and befriended Rudyard Kipling), he later volunteered to serve on the British side during the Easter Rising, during which he was seriously wounded. Given such military and political credentials, "although he produced a few plays for Yeats and the Abbey Theatre over the course of years, and though these were popular successes in America as well as in England and Ireland, Dunsany could hardly have received great national accolades in a country in which he was so preeminently for the British Crown" (Bowen 1980, 219). Critics tended to belittle him as a dilettante—not a serious writer. Yet he published more than fifty-five books.

By 1920 Dunsany was one of the two best known Irish prose fantasists along with James Stephens. Early books such as *The Gods of Pegana* (1905) and *Time and the Gods* (1916) had celebrated "a mythology which was not Celtic but entirely of his own devising" (McHugh and Harmon 1982, 193). In this regard, Dunsany was a successor of William Blake and a predecessor of J. R. R. Tolkien. Most of his numerous fantasies are not focused on Ireland in either subject or setting. One exception is *The Curse of the Wise Woman* (1933), which combines a nostalgia for old Ireland and its folkways with an anti-industrial, environmentalist critique. Dunsany's old wise woman, who believes that Tir-na-nÓg is buried in the bog bordering her house, delivers her curse upon the Peat Development Syndicate that would destroy it, and is obliged by the arrival of storms that wreck the project. One suspects that Dunsany is simply fabricating a good story here as much as advancing a critique. He felt that the purpose of fiction was to entertain and tell a story for its own sake (Duperray 1984).

Joseph O'Neill and Austin Clarke were much more thoroughly Irish in their sensibilities and interests. Both of them abandoned promising careers as Gaelic scholars and subsequently wrote romances focused on the medieval Gaelic world. O'Neill (1878–1953) spent most of his career as a civil servant in the Irish Department of Secondary Education, which he headed from 1923 to 1944. His invitation to Yeats to visit one of the schools under his charge inspired Yeats's poem "Among School Children." Yet O'Neill "was never quite taken seriously by his literary friends who considered him an Irish educator who wrote novels to escape from the humdrum of his job" (Lynch 1983, 4). His narrator's opening words in his novel *Wind from the North* (1934) can certainly be read as underscoring his boredom with his job and his desire to escape dreary twentieth-century realities: "What I desire above everything is to go back again to Dyflin away from this twentieth-century world that has grown strange and lonely to me. . . . Of my life before my strange adventure there is little to tell. I was a clerk in one of the Government offices here in Dublin. . . . I will not therefore weary the reader with any further details about myself" (9). After being hit by a tram in Dame Street, O'Neill's unnamed clerk finds himself in the body of one Olaf Ulfson during the days just before Brian Boru defeated but was himself killed by the Norsemen at the Battle of Clontarf in 1014. This reminds one of the similar fictional conceits of O'Duffy's *King Goshawk* and *The Spacious Adventures of the Man in the Street* as well as Flann O'Brien's later *The Third Policeman*. O'Neill's anti-hero remains unfulfilled in both worlds, medieval and modern: he detests his clerkship and after he returns to it, he would like to escape back to the eleventh century, but the Norsemen among whom he lived never accepted him, suspecting that he was an evil troll inhabiting Ulfson's body. *Wind from the North* both seriously and comically portrays humanity as trapped between the past and the present.

Whereas Joyce transports Ulysses and Finn MacCool from the past to the present—as does O'Duffy with Cúchulainn and also Flann O'Brien with Finn—O'Neill reverses the time-jump, putting his homely clerk in the shoes of an ancient would-be Norse hero, but he is unable to attain heroism. *Wind from the North* is not merely an escapist book, but a serious as well as entertaining novel reacting to the influence (as in Francis MacManus's historical trilogy) of the Norwegian historical novelist Sigrid Undset, whom O'Neill thanks in a postscript (341) for reading the manuscript, and also responding to the psychological emphases of Freud, Jung, and Conrad (Lynch 1983, 13).

Austin Clarke (1896–1974) lost his teaching job in literature at University College, Dublin, in 1921, "apparently because he had not been married in a church" (Kinsella 1980, 156–57). A central theme throughout his works, as in Eimar O'Duffy's and Mervyn Wall's, is the conflict between Irish puritanism and erotic love. Clarke was one of the two or three best Irish poets since Yeats, and the most responsive of all of them to Yeats's charge in "Under Ben Bulben" to younger Irish poets to "Sing the lords and ladies gay / That were beaten into the clay / Through seven heroic centuries." Clarke's earliest volumes were epic Irish mythological poems in which he sought to employ Gaelic poetic techniques in English, especially assonance, which Clarke felt "takes the clapper from the bell of rhyme." His best poems were his later short, often satiric lyrics, such as "Penal Law" in *Night and Morning* (1938): "Burn Ovid with the rest. Lovers will find / A hedge-school for themselves and learn by heart / All that the clergy banish from the mind, / When hands are joined and heads bow in the dark."

Not surprisingly, since they combine erotic love stories with social criticism, Clarke's first two prose romances, *The Bright Temptation* (1932) and *The Singing-Men at Cashel* (1936), were both banned by the Free State censors. As Clarke remarked about his poetry, "I load myself with chains and try to get out of them." Such is the predicament of the protagonists of all three of his prose romances. In *The Bright Temptation*, a reprise of the Diarmuid and Grania story, young Aidan and Ethna find themselves in love with each other but plagued with guilt about "The Evil One" who, the clergy insist, motivates their desire for each other. Nor is love any easier to pursue in marriage: in *The Singing-Men at Cashel*, Clarke's unfortunate heroine Gorlai has to endure two bad husbands—one who wants no sex and one who wants only sex—before she can be charmed by Nial in a luckier third marriage. In Clarke's final medieval romance, *The Sun Dances at Easter* (1952), Orla is advised to make the pilgrimage to St. Naal's well to get the cure that will enable her to provide her husband Flann with a child. There she finds that the "cure," much to her surprise, is provided by a virile, other worldly lover. Behind Christian mysticism lurks pagan Eros. All three of Clarke's romances are shot through with an irony captured in the voice of a narrator who makes pronouncements about how "the Adversary" or "The Evil One" is always trying to lead us into Sin, while his plots illustrate how such a narrowly moralistic view prevents people from living natural, happy lives.

Mervyn Wall advanced a similar message in two even more biting, satiric, hilarious books, *The Unfortunate Fursey* (1946) and *The Return of Fursey* (1948), which have remained popular enough in Ireland that they have recently been reissued together as *The Complete Fursey* (1985). Slyly avoiding any descriptions of sex (viewed by the Irish, as we learn from the pungent conclusion to *The Unfortunate Fursey*, as the worst evil), Wall managed to escape censorship of these books, even though they contain a thoroughgoing attack on the mores of the Irish church and state. He even includes in *The Return of Fursey* a Censor with two independently moving eyes—one to focus on the "dirty" words and one to read everything else—who finds the Old Testament to be "in general tendency indecent." In both books "the real power lies with the local archbishop, a churchman who bears not a little resemblance to the late Dr. John Charles McQuaid. (Perhaps this is the reason why that worthy sent his emissary round the bookshops of Dublin when *The Unfortunate Fursey* was published, requesting booksellers not to carry it. Such a request was, in those days, equivalent to a command)" (Linehan 1986, 4). As in the case of Eimar O'Duffy, Joseph O'Neill, and Flann O'Brien, Wall's wild fantasies were in

part an attempt to escape "what he considered to be fourteen
extremely depressing years in the Irish civil service" (Hogan
1980b, 674). He did manage to escape literally as well as
imaginatively from the civil service, when he was hired by
Francis MacManus at Radio Éireann, and then in 1957, with
the help of Sean O'Faolain, he became secretary of the Irish
Arts Council, a job he held until his retirement in the mid-
1970s. During this later period, Wall published the realist
novels discussed in my last chapter, but his crowning achievement remained the wonderful world of Fursey, his picaresque
medieval monk.

True to the tradition of Swift and O'Duffy, Wall's brand
of satire depends on ironic reversals of morality. In *The
Unfortunate Fursey*, Fursey is forced to become a witch even
though he tries his pathetic best to be good. In *The Return
of Fursey*, he responds to his misfortunes by resolving to be
evil, but instead finds himself venerated as a heroic saint
and martyr. As the Abbot of Clonmacnoise observes in the
first book, "A lifetime's study and observance has convinced
me that in the land of Ireland anything may happen to
anyone anywhere and at any time, and that it usually does"
(224). Fursey's experiences convince him that "it seems a
perilous thing to be alive at all" (227). His misfortunes begin
with the invasion of his room at Clonmacnoise by all the
demons of hell, because his stammer prevents him from
pronouncing the incantations necessary to keep them out.
After getting tossed out of the monastery, he marries a woman
who immediately dies—after passing on to Fursey her powers
of witchcraft and transforming him against his will into a
wizard and sorcerer. He is eventually brought to trial, with
the Devil serving as his unsolicited defense attorney. The
point of Wall's satire comes in the marvellous dénouement
of *The Unfortunate Fursey*, when the Devil strikes a deal with
the Catholic clergy of Ireland: he will exempt Ireland from
temptation to sex in exchange for their abandonment of
preaching against "simony, nepotism, drunkenness, perjury
and murder" (233). This proposal their spokesman finds quite
persuasive:

"These sins which you mention," said the friar after a long,
cautious pause, "are but minor offences when compared with the

hideous sin of sex. What you somewhat exaggeratedly term drunkenness, perjury and murder are perhaps but the exuberance of a high-spirited and courageous people. Nepotism is, after all, merely an offshoot of the virtue of charity. As for simony, we know all about that. The cry of simony is usually raised by evil-minded persons who are unwilling to subscribe to the upkeep of their pastors." (233)

Satan promises each priest the biggest house in his town—an offer met by great applause. Privately, he boasts to Fursey that "I appear to have the souls of the Irish clergy in my bag for all time," yet complains that "It'll give Hell a considerable Irish ecclesiastical character. . . . Before long Hell will hardly know itself. It will bear an extraordinary resemblance to an annual General Meeting of the Catholic Truth Society" (234–35).

After Fursey runs off to England with his beautiful new wife, Maeve, in *The Return of Fursey* she is stolen from him by a delegation sent by Cormac Silkenbeard of Cashel (also the setting of Clarke's *The Singing-Men at Cashel*). In revenge Fursey resolves to embrace evil, return to Ireland, and wreak havoc. Instead, as luck would have it, he arrives back at Clonmacnoise just as the Vikings are sacking the place. Since the monks successfully escape just at that moment, they decide that Fursey was "a glorious apparition" bringing about their salvation. So he is revered and canonized—a scenario that Fursey happily plays along with—but after failing to win back his wife, he walks off into the sunset. "Fursey and the others are still there, trampled into the earth or road and field these thousand years" (234). This closing assurance is doubly believable since it is clear that Wall's subject all the way through has been the repressive Ireland of the 1940s at least as much as the shadowy world of medieval monasticism.

Flann O'Brien / Brian O'Nolan / Myles na gCopaleen

Flann O'Brien (1911–66) was one of the best and most versatile of Irish novelists, and his career illustrates many of the features of the Irish novel's development during this period. O'Brien's real name was Brian O'Nolan, and he was best known in Ireland as Myles na gCopaleen (a name borrowed from Dion Boucicault's nineteenth-century stage-Irish play *The Colleen Bawn* and meaning literally "Myles of the Little Horses"). "Myles" was his pen name when writing "Cruiskeen Lawn" ("the little full jug") for the *Irish Times,* the column that over a quarter-century "deservedly attained," as Anthony Cronin has noted, "a local celebrity far surpassing that of any individual piece of journalism that twentieth-century Ireland has known" (quoted in de Bréadún 1986, 8). His first novel was the wildly experimental *At Swim-Two-Birds* (1939), which Joyce admired—calling it "a really funny book" and O'Brien "a real writer, with the true comic spirit" (Clissman 1975, 79). Yet *At Swim-Two-Birds* got lost in the grim era of World War II, until its republication in 1960 was followed by a new appreciation for O'Brien as an early absurdist novelist. While he had completed his three best novels by 1941, his newfound popularity beginning in 1960 provoked O'Brien, who for years had been writing only his "Cruiskeen Lawn" column, to produce two more novels before his death in 1966: the lesser works *The Hard Life* (1961) and *The Dalkey Archive* (1964), a rewrite (but not improvement) of an earlier, but only posthumously published novel, *The Third Policeman* (1967). By that time he was also known as a member of the Irish equivalent of the "Beat Generation," which included such writers as Brendan Behan and Patrick Kavanagh, who plied themselves with alcohol and carried on in Dublin pubs such as McDaid's. Their story is memorably recounted in John Ryan's memoir, *Remembering How We Stood: Bohemian Dublin at Mid-Century* (1975). On the fiftieth anniversary of Bloomsday, 16 June 1954, O'Brien, Kavanagh, and Ryan set out trying to retrace all of Bloom's steps through Dublin, but the story has it that they failed to progress beyond the second pub; a three-minute film of the endeavor has been preserved. Behan died in 1964, O'Brien in 1966 (on April Fool's Day), and Kavanagh in 1967. It is said that O'Brien's last words, to a friend who was pouring a bit of water into O'Brien's glass of gin beside his hospital bed, were "Almighty God, are you trying to drown it entirely?" (Quoted in Ryan 1975, 43).

O'Brien now receives more critical attention than any other Irish novelist except for Joyce and Beckett, and has been the subject of a large comprehensive study (Clissman 1975). A lively conference in Dublin in 1986 marked the twentieth anniversary of his death and included not only scholarly presentations but also an appearance by someone claiming to be de Selby, O'Brien's most famous or infamous character, with the gathering capped by "sapient colloquy" in some of O'Brien's favorite pubs (de Bréadún 1986). O'Brien continues to live on in the Irish imagination, with people frequently recounting his stories in Dublin pubs; for several weeks during 1976, a number of individuals playfully continued the controversies surrounding de Selby in the letters column of the *Irish Times*. As far as academic scholarship goes, "most critical studies focus either on O'Brien's first novel or on his many-sided personality" (Tolomeo 1983, 289). As a corollary of these emphases, it should be added that a great many critics have written about Joyce's influence, with some viewing O'Brien as his disciple (Adams 1977; Kearney 1979), yet a few others (Powell 1971; Mays 1974; Benstock 1982; Browne 1984) recently stressing how he increasingly reacted *against* Joyce. Bernard Benstock writes that "two factors . . . stood solidly and discouragingly in the way of the good novelist circa 1939: the enormous accomplishment of Irish novelist James Joyce and the vociferous and often conflicting demands of Ireland itself on its writers" (1982, 22).

As Seamus Deane notes, "O'Brien's reaction to Joyce's work and, later, to Joyce's fame is one of the most astonishing examples of the 'anxiety of influence' to be found, even in Ireland where the closeness of the small literary community stimulates fiction and friction of varied quality and unvaried regularity." Deane adds that "the absorption of Joyce in the early novels, which led to their enrichment, declined into a running battle with his reputation in his later work, leading to its impoverishment" (1986, 195). Considering the declining productivity and quality of O'Brien as a novelist after 1941 (ironically, the year of Joyce's death), Harold Bloom's specific theory in *The Anxiety of Influence* (1973) about the great writer who overwhelms his "offspring" is persuasive, since O'Brien suffered the most in his oedipal struggle with Joyce's influence; we might say that the "father" "killed" the "son" rather than the other way around. Such a theory seems particularly applicable to a writer whose first novel describes (in a novel within a novel within the novel!) the revenge of Orlick Trellis, product of his novelist father Dermot's rape of one of his own characters: Orlick tortures Dermot to death in a novel of his own. O'Brien's last novel, *The Dalkey Archive* (1964) exacts literary revenge on Joyce himself, who is found to be still alive, working as a bartender, denying authorship of *Ulysses* and *Finnegans Wake*, writing pamphlets for the Catholic Truth Society, and trying to join the Jesuits. Declan Kiberd (1984a, 27) adds that Bloom's theory also applies to O'Brien's novel in Irish, *An Béal Bocht* (1941), a pointed parody of Tómas Ó Criomhthain's great Gaelic autobiography, *An tOileánach* (1929).

However, despite whatever "anxiety of influence" O'Brien may have struggled with, it is equally clear that he loved and admired both Joyce's and Ó Croimhthain's works, and that *At Swim-Two-Birds* (1939), *The Third Policeman* (which was completed in 1940 although not published until 1967), and *An Béal Bocht* (1941) are virtuoso performances that transcend their influences. The professional enthusiasts collected around Joyce (the Joyceans) and Ó Criomhthain (the *Gaeilgeoirí* or pious "True Gaels") were the ones O'Brien detested, not Joyce and Ó Criomhthain themselves. Although many people misunderstood *An Béal Bocht* as an attack on Irish speakers or Ó Criomhthain himself, O'Brien expressed the hope concerning *An Béal Bocht* "that all who read it . . . will be stimulated into stumbling upon the majestic book upon which it is based" (quoted in Ó Háinle 1984, 70). His remarks about Joyce over the years in "Cruiskeen Lawn" (which, collected as *The Best of Myles* [1968], is a comic masterpiece in its own right) reveals a complicated ambivalence, with admiration as well as scorn reflected even in an avowedly satiric column. As late as 1962 O'Brien complained that Faulkner had received a Nobel Prize for Literature and not Joyce, insisting that Joyce was "of more general world significance than either Yeats or Shaw" (Powell 1971, 61). Many of his references to Joyce are whimsical and even self-deprecating: in 1942 he registered supposed nostalgia for the days when "twenty years ago . . . poor Jimmy Joyce abolished the King's English, Paulsey Picasso started cutting out paper dolls and I . . . founded the Rathmines branch of the Gaelic League." Joyce "he praised on the one hand for his ingenious realistic dialogues and damned on the other for impenetrability" (Powell 1971, 51, 50). Confessing that he had unsuccessfully begun *Finnegans Wake* at least five times, O'Brien asked: "What would you think of a man who entered a restaurant, sat down, suddenly whipped up the tablecloth and blew his nose in it? You would not like it—not if you owned the restaurant. That is what Joyce did with our beloved tongue that Shakespeare and Milton spoke" (quoted in Powell 1971, 59). His own approach to punning, both in "Cruiskeen Lawn" and in his novels, was to explode and deflate puns and clichés by taking them literally, rather than mythologizing and universalizing them as did Joyce. Possessor of an M.A. in Irish from University College, Dublin, where like Joyce he was an outstanding student, O'Brien was proud of his precise command of languages. Mervyn Wall recounted that "the only time I ever saw him taken aback" and "crestfallen" was when he realized from Wall's clarification that he had failed to realize the significance of the Irish name for Anglesea Street on its street-sign in Dublin (Mays 1974, 254).

O'Brien's strongest scorn was reserved for Joyceans more than for Joyce himself. Echoing Patrick Kavanagh's poem "Who Killed James Joyce?," O'Brien complained in 1959: "Witness the shower of gawms who erupt from the prairie universities to do a 'thesis' on James Joyce" (quoted in Powell 1971, 60). He referred to Richard Ellmann as the "238th American to attempt the grim task of writing a book on Joyce," and publicly warned Ellmann that if he contacted him during his biographical research, "I guarantee that I will frighten the life out of him by the disclosure of the state of my mind" (54). Probably jealousy as much as disdain motivated such remarks, for "the publisher's refusal of *The Third Policeman* in 1940, the outbreak of war and the intense local Dublin-based cult of Myles na gCopaleen among the readers of *The Irish Times* seemed to enhance the contrast between O'Brien's fortunes and those of Joyce" (Deane 1986, 194).

Probably O'Brien could not have imagined the amount of scholarship that would grow up around his own novels during the years after his death.

O'Brien's first novel, *At Swim-Two-Birds*, is the book that staked out his innovative position in the company of Joyce and Beckett. Later O'Brien dismissed this novel as juvenalia, but it continues to entertain and challenge an increasing number of readers and to provoke more scholarship than any of his other novels. It is narrated by an unnamed, intellectual, slothful University College, Dublin, undergraduate who acts suspiciously like a parody of Stephen Dedalus and (since "one beginning and one ending for a book was a thing I did not agree with") begins by presenting us with three different beginnings—one about The Pooka, a second about Mr. John Furriskey who was born at the age of twenty-five, and a third about Finn MacCool whose thighs were "as thick as a horse's belly, narrowing to a calf as thick as the belly of a foal. Three fifties of fosterlings could engage with handball against the wideness of his backside, which was large enough to halt the march of men through a mountain-pass" (10). Certainly O'Brien was acquainted with Joyce's Cyclops, although he did not know that Finn MacCool would also turn up in *Finnegans Wake* in the same year that *At Swim-Two-Birds* appeared. O'Brien's title refers to a place associated with the mythical Sweeney, a mad poet suspended in the trees between heaven and earth who serves as a central emblem in the novel. His playful, artful use of Irish mythology shows the influence of James Stephens, whose work he admired. O'Brien's Finn MacCool sounds much like Stephens's comic Philosopher: "It is true that I will not, said Finn" (17). Sweeney's verses included actual translations from Middle Irish that O'Brien had done for his master's thesis.

These characters provide only part of O'Brien's bizarre stories-within-stories which, coming in 1939, represent what can only be described as a pre-postmodernist use of popular culture and Irish narrative tradition. The unnamed student narrator is writing a novel about Dermot Trellis, a pubkeeper who, like himself, divides his time between writing and lethargy. Trellis wants to warn people against sin, but knowing that he has to fill his moral tract with enough prurient interest to keep readers' attention, he borrows from his friend William Tracy, an author of cowboy romances, a method whereby characters magically appear already full-grown. He thereby creates the depraved Furriskey and the pure Sheila Lamont, whose beauty provokes him to make love to her himself, and he borrows Finn MacCool and the cowboy heroes Shorty Andrews and Slug Willard. Dermot's son Orlick begins a novel of his own in which the Pooka tortures Dermot, but Dermot is saved by the bell when the original narrator passes his exams and abandons the novel. *At Swim-Two-Birds* constantly deconstructs itself, even providing several quick synopses in lieu of full narration of action. As Anthony Cronin wrote on April Fool's Day, 1986, in an *Irish Times* article memorably entitled "Post-Structuralist, Post-Modernist, Post-Everything": "He deconstructed his own text long before deconstruction was ever heard of. . . . Here we have an author who pre-empts the methodology of contemporary criticism and confuses its established categories, misplacing himself in date to such an extent as to cast doubt on whether such a phenomenon as post-modernism can be said to exist, and deconstructing his own text before anybody else can get their hands on it. What, in such a case, is criticism to do?" (12).

Cronin is not exaggerating O'Brien's procedure in *At Swim-Two-Birds,* for not only does he continually subvert his own text fictively—even traditional critics have long agreed that it is an "anti-novel"—but he includes within his own novel a deconstructive (if somewhat tongue-in-cheek) theory of the novel: "A satisfactory novel should be a self-evident sham to which the reader could regulate at will the degree of his credulity. It was undemocratic to compel characters to be uniformly good or bad or poor or rich. Each should be allowed a private life, self-determination and a decent standard of living" (33). He adds that "the modern novel should be largely a work of reference" (33). He will allow no main plot and subplot, no fictional caste system: Jem Casey with his proletarian verses ("A Pint of Plain is Your Only Man!") is as important as Sweeney muttering among the trees or the unnamed narrator lying in bed for days at a time.

Even funnier and better novels are *The Third Policeman* and *An Béal Bocht*. It has been remarked that *At Swim-Two-Birds* was provoked by Aldous Huxley's *Point-Counterpoint* more than by anything Joyce wrote; by the same token, the closest predecessor to *The Third Policeman* is Ambrose Bierce's marvellous story "An Occurrence at Owl-Creek Bridge." Here as in Bierce "it was as if the daylight had changed with unnatural suddenness . . ." (21). The again unnamed narrator hatches a scheme with one John Divney to kill old Phillip Mathers for his money, in order to finance his research on the crackpot scientist and philosopher de Selby. He does so but is in turn killed by Divney. He is not aware of his own demise while he experiences the bizarre events and characters that dominate his twilight zone: his arrest by Sergeant Pluck and Policeman MacCruiskeen, for whom everything is "about a bicycle" and who assures him that he can be happily hanged since he has no name and therefore is nobody; his own soul, Joe, who constantly advises him; and, of course, de Selby. De Selby never actually appears in *The Third Policeman* as a character (as he does in *The Dalkey Archive*); instead, as in many a scholarly work (and also in *Castle Rackrent, Finnegans Wake,* and Beckett's *Watt*), much of the action takes place in the footnotes as well as in the narrator's lengthy digressions. One footnote about de Selby is six pages long (144–49). One of de Selby's many sayings explains the narrator's central problem: "A journey is a hallucination" (44). The narrator is dead, but does not know it, and is doomed to relive his life endlessly in ignorance. As O'Brien assures us at the end, "Hell goes round and round. In shape it is circular and by nature it is interminable, repetitive and very nearly unbearable" (173). Yet it is also, at least in this case, very funny—packed with details such as de Selby's theory about the interchange of molecules, which helps to explain why postmen who spend many hours on bicycles begin to stand like a bicycle and why in turn bicycles begin to take on human characteristics. The novel contains a long erotic scene involving a postman riding a female schoolteacher's bicycle. It is a tightly constructed, wildly imaginative and experimental world of interwoven tales.

An Béal Bocht (The Poor Mouth), published under the name of Myles na gCopaleen, is an even more highly condensed, equally if not more hilarious book—and, along with Padraic Ó Conaire's *Deoraíocht* and Máirtín Ó Cadhain's *Cré na Cille*, one of the three best novels in Irish.[1] In *An Béal Bocht* O'Brien/na gCopaleen demonstrates his mastery of the Irish language. The book is ostensibly a parody of Ó Criomhthain's *An tOileánach (The Islandman)* (1929), the first of the three great County Kerry Gaelic autobiographies along with Muiris Ó Súilleabháin's *Fiche Blian ag Fás (Twenty Years a-Growing)* (1933) and Peig Sayer's *Peig* (1936). To remove any doubt about the source of the parody, O'Brien's subtitle is *nó An Milleánach* ("or the Fault-Finder"), which rhymes with *An tOileánach*, and the narrator (who is finally given a name, but not his own name!) continually tells us (echoing Ó Criomhthain's famous saying) that "Ní bheidh ár léitheidí arís ann" or "Our likes will never be there again"—and that Ambrose the Pig's likes will not be there again, nor will the likes of the fireplace's bad smell be there again, *etcetera ad nauseum*. Another object of parody is Séamus Ó Grianna: O'Brien takes a scene from Ó Grianna's novel *Caisleáin Óir* in which the protagonist is given his official name "James Gallagher," and burlesques it, explaining how his protagonist at last has a name but that it is not his *own* name:

Bhí maide ramha fálta aige 'na ghlaic. Bhí rabhartha feirge ag gabháil de fá 'n am so, agus bhí greim chun gnótha aige ar an mhaide lean dhá láimh. Tharraing sé thar a ghualain é agus thug anuas orm go tréan le fead gaoithe, gur bhuail buille tubaisteach sa chloigean orm. Thuiteas i laige ón mbuille sin acht sular cailleach na céadfaithe ar fad orm chuala scread uaidh:
"Yer nam," ar seisean, "is Jams O'Donnell". (*An Béal Bocht*, 25)

He had an oar in his grasp. Anger had come over him in a floodtide at this stage and he had a businesslike grip of the oar in his two hands. He drew it over his shoulder and brought it down hard upon me with a swish of air, dealing me a destructive blow on the skull. I fainted from that blow but before I became totally unconscious I heard him scream:
—Yer nam, said he, is Jams O'Donnell! (*The Poor Mouth*, 1973, 30)

This scene is the ultimate inflation of the descriptions of cruel schoolmasters found in *A Portrait of the Artist as a Young Man* and in many other Irish fiction writers, just as O'Brien mercilessly lampoons stage-Irish conventions in English at other points. Entertaining us and also indicating that O'Brien/na gCopaleen's Corkadoragha is a fictional phantasmagoria merging all of the major, disparate Irish-speaking areas, "Jams O'Donnell" assures us about his fellow students that "cuid aca ag lapadánacht ar an mbóthar gan aon tsiúl aca. A lán as Daingean Uí Chúise, cuid as Gaoth Dobhair; dream eile aniar ar an tsnámh as Árainn" (*An Béal Bocht*, 24): "Some of them were crawling along the road, unable to walk. Many were from Dingle, some from Gweedore, another group floated in from Aran" (*The Poor Mouth*, 29). On the compass sketched at the beginning of *An Béal Bocht*, all four of its points are shown pointing west.

The Gaelic Leaguers from Dublin, the *Gaeilgeorí*, bear the brunt of the author's satiric attack on rural Irish poverty: "Daoine-uaisle a tháinic i mótors ó Bhaile Átha Cliath ag breánú na mbochtán, mholadar go h-árd é as ucht a bhochtanais Ghaelaí agus dúradar nach Ghaelach. Buidéal beag uisce abhí ag Ó Sánasa uair, bhris duine-uasal é de bhrí, mar dúirt sé, gur *spile* sé an *effect*" (*An Béal Bocht*, 77); "The gentlemen from Dublin who came in motors to inspect the paupers praised [Sitric O'Sanassa] for his Gaelic poverty and stated that they never saw anyone who appeared so truly Gaelic. One of the gentlemen broke a little bottle of water which Sitric had, because, said he, it spoiled the effect" (88). One of the *Gaeilgeorí* constantly cites "Father Peter" and (as the only Irish literature worth reading) *Séadna*, which Myles insisted in "Cruiskeen Lawn" was not literature at all. Another delivers a lengthy address, amidst driving rain at a *feis* (a festival), in which nearly every other word is "Gaelic"—for example:

"A Ghaeala," adúirt sé, "cuireann sé gliondar ar mo chroí Gaelach a bheith annso iniu ag caint Ghaeilge libh-se ar an gheis Ghaelaí seo i lár na Gaeltachta. Ní misdé dhom a rá gur Gaeal mise. Táim Gaelach óm bhathais go bonn no choise—Gaelach thoir, thiar, thuas agus thíos. Tá sibh-se go léir fíor-Ghaelach mar

an gcéana. Gaeil Ghaelacha de shliocht Ghaelach sea an t-iomlán
againn. An té atá Gaelach, beidh sé Gaelach feasta. Níor labhair
mise (ach oiread libh féin) aon fhocal acht Gaeilg ón lá rugadh
mé agus, rud eile, is fá'n nGaeilg amháin abhí gach abairt dár
ndúras riamh. (*An Béal Bocht*, 46–47)

—Gaels! he said, it delights my Gaelic heart to be here today
speaking Gaelic with you at this Gaelic feis in the centre of the
Gaeltacht. May I state that I am a Gael. I'm Gaelic front and
back, above and below. Likewise, you are all truly Gaelic. We are
all Gaelic Gaels of Gaelic lineage. He who is Gaelic, will be Gaelic
evermore. I myself have spoken not a word except Gaelic since
the day I was born—just like you—and every sentence I've ever
uttered has been on the subject of Gaelic. (*The Poor Mouth* 1973,
54)

Such passages mercilessly lampooned the reigning cultural
ethos of the Irish Free State—yet, like Mervyn Wall, O'Brien/
na gCopaleen cleverly escaped censorship by editing out
all sexual references himself (Ó Conaire 1973, 135). His satiric
indictment does not spare professional folklorists and lin-
guists: one of them is the butt of a long, hilarious chapter
describing how he delights in tape-recording the grunts of
a pig at a late-night gathering, convinced that it is the most
incomprehensible and hence the finest Irish that he has ever
heard. All of this is narrated by "Jams O'Donnell," the beauty
of whose naiveté surpasses even Gulliver's.

At their best the genius and hilarity of O'Brien's novels
are anecdotal in nature—the wild stories about de Selby, the
pathetic experiences of Jams O'Donnell—and seem rooted
more in the Irish storytelling tradition than in the tradition
of the novel. Of course, as we have seen more than once,
this pattern holds true for many Irish novelists for whom
the Irish storytelling heritage was often a more immediate
influence than the English and continental novel. Considering
O'Brien's huge anecdotal talents and judging from *The Best
of Myles*, it may be that he truly came into his own when
he began writing the short gems of the quarter-century-long
"Cruiskeen Lawn" column.

Samuel Beckett, Irish Novelist

Samuel Beckett (b. 1906) is at once the least obviously Irish novelist and the most important Irish novelist since Joyce. He began as more directly a Joycean disciple than Flann O'Brien or anybody else: like Joyce an honors graduate in modern languages, an admirer of Dante, and an emigré to Paris, Beckett met Joyce in 1928 and became his steadfast friend and follower. The connection was close enough that Beckett was invited to court Joyce's daughter, Lucia, whose schizophrenia deepened after he could not return her infatuation—and he remained a friend of the family, serving as best man at the wedding of Joyce's grandson Stephen in 1955 (Gluck 1979, 40). He helped Joyce overcome his failing eyesight by transcribing some of *Work in Progress* from dictation, even leaving his own stamp on a passage in *Finnegans Wake* (222) where "Sammy" is invited to "call on" (presumably Lucia). This is followed a page later (223) by the phrase "What is that," which inadvertently entered the transcription after Joyce apparently heard a noise in the background and then decided with amusement to "let it stand" when Beckett read back the dictation to him (Staples 1971, 422–23). Beckett contributed the lead essay to *Our Exagmination Round His Factification for Incamination of Work in Progress* (1929), defending the book that would become *Finnegans Wake* from the charge of obscurantism in "Dante . . . Bruno. Vico . . . Joyce," which contained a famous sentence that could be applied with equal validity to his own mature work: "His writing is not *about* something; *it is that something itself.*"

Like Joseph O'Neill, Austin Clarke (who appears in Beckett's *Murphy* as "Austin Ticklepenny"), and Joyce himself, Beckett passed up a promising academic career in order to devote himself to writing. Between 1928 and 1931, he served stints as lecturer at Campbell College in Belfast, at the École Normale Supérieure in Paris, and at Trinity College, Dublin (his alma mater), and he published his insightful and also self-revelatory critical book, *Proust* (1931). His early fiction— especially his unpublished novel "Dream of Fair to Middling Women" and his collection of stories *More Pricks than Kicks*

(1934)—shows the strong influence of Joyce. In his development as a novelist, however, Beckett took a very different direction almost opposite to both Joyce and his other chief supposed disciple, Flann O'Brien. Rather than evolve increasingly elaborate, ultimately affirmative fictions like Joyce, or finally retreat like O'Brien from the Joycean shadow back into realism, the mature Beckett devoted himself to an attempt to strip his fiction of plot, characters, and native idiom altogether, shifting to increasingly simpler and shorter fictions written in French. The brevity of his recent work leaves us with an ironic situation in which, as a *Times Literary Supplement* reviewer noted in 1970 (the year after Beckett won the Nobel Prize for Literature), in a comment that is even truer today, "as the author's writings diminish to a thin trickle the volume of criticism swells to a flood" (quoted in Friedman 1973, 383).

Unlike Flann O'Brien, Beckett obviously admired *Finnegans Wake*, was even more impressed by Joyce's later works than by his earlier ones, and has continued to express admiration for Joyce up until the present day. Reacting to the "anxiety of influence" more effectively than O'Brien did, Beckett's response to his literary "father" was the ultimately more productive, healthy one of setting out in his own original direction rather than either remaining in the Joycean shadows or going on the attack. The spirit of Beckett's response to Joyce is summed up by his typically humorous, self-deprecating, brilliant remark, "The more Joyce knew the more he could. He's tending toward omniscience and omnipotence as an artist. I'm working with impotence, ignorance" (quoted in Cohn 1971, 391). Beckett critics tend to divide into those who mention but do not add to an understanding of Joyce's influence, those who deny it altogether, and those who, like Adams (1977) and Gluck (1979), more reasonably view Beckett's writings as complementing Joyce's work rather than either blindly following it or rejecting it. Beckett's reputation is considerable enough that while still very much alive, he attracted an extensive if not definitive biography, published in 1978. That biographer, Deirdre Bair, notes that the young Beckett so idolized Joyce that even with his bigger feet he tried wearing shoes exactly like Joyce's, right down to the shoe size, but abandoned them after they nearly crippled him (1978, 71). Seamus Deane takes this as a parable of a writer who began as a Joycean disciple but then achieved greatness by deliberately walking in an opposite direction and in his own shoes (1985a, 134).

Such striking originality was not immediately achieved. Beckett's first published novel, *Murphy* (1938), is clearly a Joycean anti-novel bearing resemblances to O'Brien's *At Swim-Two-Birds*, published just a year later. Apparently Joyce himself noticed this similarity: in 1940 he asked an acquaintance in Paris to locate for him an article by the critic Maurice Denhof showing that these two novels were based on a single "théorie de composition," but it turned out that Denhof had died without publishing the article. Three decades later Sighle Kennedy acted on Denhof's intention, pointing out about the two novels that "both stray, widely and intentionally, from the path of the realistic novel; both indulge in witty, erudite, and often outrageous digressions; both are concerned in mysterious ways with the problem of madness; both weave uproarious chess games into their narratives. Most striking of all is that both portray as their central figures, young men who are primarily interested in retiring to the privacy of their own mental spheres" (1972, 251–52). Beckett's Murphy is assigned no first name and carries Ireland's most common surname, both suggesting his Irish Everyman qualities and allowing him to illustrate Murphy's Law ("Everything that can go wrong will!"). Like O'Brien's unnamed student narrator, he appears to be in part a ludicrous parody of Stephen Dedalus, another intellectual who cherishes his privacy. Beckett's Murphy does deny the unity of body and mind ultimately affirmed by Joyce, for he ties himself to a chair ("as described in section six," the narrator tells us on the second page of the novel) in an attempt to retreat completely into the recesses of his own mind. The putative plot of this novel involves an absurd comedy of manners in which Murphy is sought out in London by a whole crew of "puppets" ("All the puppets in this book whinge sooner or later," we are told, "except Murphy who is not a puppet" [122]): Miss Counihan, his Irish fiancée; Neary, the Corkman who was his teacher and now loves

Miss Counihan; Cooper, Neary's spy; Wylie, Neary's student and secretly Miss Counihan's lover; and Celia, the prostitute who lives with Murphy and tries to reform him. Beckett lampoons the traditional romantic plot, reducing it to a mad circle by reciting "Neary's love for Miss Dwyer, who loved a Flight-Lieutenant Elliman, who loved a Miss Farren of Ringsakiddy, who loved a Father Fitt of Ballinchashet, who in all sincerity was bound to acknowledge a certain vocation for a Mrs West of Passage, who loved Neary" (5). And Miss Counihan speaks ridiculously, exhaustingly, and finally a bit haltingly out of the old romances: "Do not leave me, oh do not walk out on me at this unspeakable juncture. . . . Oh hand in hand let us return to the dear land of our birth, the bays, the bogs, the moors, the glens, the lakes, the rivers, the streams, the brooks, the mists, the-er-fens, the-er-glens, by tonight's mail-train" (271, 272).

In his two novels in English, *Murphy* (1938) and *Watt* (1953), Beckett continually toys with the conventions of the novel, creating anti-novels. *Murphy* includes lengthy digressions by the narrator, direct addresses to a reader who is not treated kindly as a "dear reader" but rather with a certain amount of apologetic scorn: "It is most unfortunate, but the point of this story has been reached where a justification of the expression 'Murphy's mind' has to be attempted" (107)—and then, after a six-page discourse analyzing the dualistic separation of Murphy's mind from his body, the narrator assures us that "this painful duty having now been discharged, no further bulletins will be issued" (113). Celia is introduced to us on page ten through a chart listing age, wrist measurement, and numerous other tedious details, thereby making fun of traditional novelistic descriptions. The quest theme of the conventional novel is also exploded in *Murphy*. Even Joyce had affirmed Stephen's search for freedom and artistic beauty in *Portrait* and suggested that Stephen's and Leopold's meeting in *Ulysses* was meaningful in spite of (or because of) whatever comedy and pathos surrounded it. But Murphy escapes all those who seek him out, even Celia, by moving into a psychiatric hospital, choosing to work there because he admires the mental isolation of the patients, especially his chess-partner, Mr. Endon, whose ambition is to commit suicide by holding his breath. The other characters find Murphy in the hospital only after he has died of gas asphxiation. In a clear slap at the Irish Literary Revival, his will dictates that his ashes be flushed down the Abbey Theatre's toilet in Dublin, but instead Cooper ends up flinging them at someone in a London pub.

Beckett had found his own brief returns to Ireland to be humiliating and injurious to his health, especially when he was derided as a Parisian degenerate during cross-examination in the libel suit over Oliver Gogarty's *As I Was Going Down Sackville Street* in 1937. Thereafter he chose to remain in France during World War II, later insisting that "I preferred France in war to Ireland in peace" (Mays 1977, 198). *Watt* was published in 1953, though written a decade earlier while Beckett was a fugitive involved with the French Underground. Beckett's novels might mislead readers into thinking that he himself remained confined to his room, tied to his chair like Murphy. Yet the real Samuel Beckett is a kind, generous man who has shared many friendships, and after World War II the French government presented him with the Croix de Guerre in recognition of his work in the Resistance effort. True to his typical modest nature, his friends heard about this honor not from him but only from others. Beckett clearly had no interest in writing realistically about his war experiences like a Hemingway. Instead, his novels became increasingly freer of the trappings of realism—although undoubtedly stamped by the horror of Hitler's reign of terror, his own frequent illnesses, and other experiences.

Although deliberately vaguer about location and characterization than *Murphy*, *Watt* appears to be set in Ireland and is Beckett's most direct fictional response to the tradition of the Irish novel. Watt's quest is as unfulfilled as Murphy's: he journeys by train from central Dublin to suburban Leopardstown (described though never named), near Beckett's boyhood home, in order to work in the home of Mr Knott; he mysteriously sojourns (like Murphy, whom he resembles) in a mental institution where he tells his story to "Sam," a fellow inmate; and he finally leaves Knott's house, returns to the nearby train station, and waits for another train, taking him in we know not which direction. If Watt ("what?") is the question, the Knott ("naught" or "not") is the answer. Beckett's work has been analyzed in the light (or darkness) of philosophers ranging from Aquinas to Wittgenstein (Rabinovitz 1984, 124). Even more than Flann O'Brien in *At Swim-Two-Birds*, "when Beckett wrote *Watt*," as Hugh Kenner points out, "he was busy deconstructing the English novel, with Derrida a mere 14 years old" (1986, 3).

In a more immediate Irish fictional context, however, Watt is obviously Knott's servant in an Irish Big House, and *Watt* plays interesting tricks with the tradition of the Big House novel. Beckett's roots were in the Protestant Ascendancy, and as much as it appears disguised in his work he never lost "the Trinity College timbre of an Anglo-Irish academic whose world and skull are Irish first of all" (Rose 1971, 128). His works contain "ferocious assaults on the Protestant ethic" but follow "the Puritan ethic of relentless self-exploration" (Kiberd 1985b, 123, 130). As John Harrington points out, "*Watt* makes use of several staples of the 'Big House' novel: mistreated servants, including Watt; the questionable morals of a local fisherman's wife, Mrs Gorman; the shiftlessness of a pair of local workmen, 'the Galls, father and son'; and the physical misery of a diseased but prolific peasant family named Lynch, who devour scraps of food refused by Mr Knott's dogs" (1981, 5). This novel also contains a long, digressive, comic, and bizarre tale told by Arthur, the servant who eventually replaces Watt in Knott's Big House, recounting the adventures of Ernest Louit, a Trinity College academic who squandered a research grant and then invented an elaborate defense for the college grants committee. Such a story might have been expected in the pages of Charles Lever. *Watt* may be as one critic wrote "a devastating depiction of the cul-de-sac of modern Western rationalist philosophy," but closer to home it is in Harrington's words "a modern representative of [the] more familiar sort of divided sensibility" found in the Big House novel (5).

Written in French and deliberately stripped of setting and plot, Beckett's fiction after *Watt* appears to have little to do with the tradition of the Irish novel. His fictional masterpiece is the trilogy consisting of *Molloy* (1950), celebrated by most scholars as his best novel; *Malone Dies* (*Malone Meurt*, 1951);

and *The Unnamable* (*L'Innomable*, 1952) (see Fletcher 1964). He wrote in French in order to free himself from idiom and to simplify and universalize his work, and his "translations" of his work "back" into English were far more than simple translations (Kenner 1970). In *Molloy* the protagonist sets out looking for his mother, Moran later looks for Molloy, and neither one attains his objective. In *Malone Dies* Malone, who often recalls Molloy as well as Murphy and Watt, sits and writes, preparing to die. *The Unnamable* removes any pretence of protagonist or plot: the narrator (who now appears to be the author himself) disparages his own life and writings, deciding in his final words that "I don't know, I'll never know, in the silence you don't know, you must go on, I can't go on, I'll go on" (418). The trilogy is tedious, self-destructive, hilarious, brilliant, and uplifting. Facing the ineffable, it is a true deconstructionist text. With only a few exceptions (Bové 1982; Thiher 1983), the trilogy has attracted very few avowedly poststructuralist readings amidst the considerable literature surrounding it—as if to suggest that since Beckett (like O'Brien in *At Swim-Two-Birds*) had already deconstructed his own text, there was not too much left for a deconstructionist critic to say. Similarly, Seamus Deane suggests that a Marxist reading, as appealing as it is—with Beckett "read as an extreme instance of the alienation already registered in Joyce"—may be too easy: "Its serviceability makes it suspect. The very real differences between Joyce and Beckett are flattened when they are seen in this relatively facile way" (1985a, 124). Some years ago Barbara Shapiro (1969) advanced a "Psychoanalytic Reading of Beckett's *Molloy*," pointing out how Molloy asserts that "All my life, I think I had been going to my mother." Yet psychoanalytic interpretations of Beckett's work never became prevalent as they did with Joyce, and feminist readings of Beckett have not yet been forthcoming (though a character such as Celia in *Murphy* invites such an approach).

After *How It Is* (*Comment c'est*, 1961), a narrative that furt·er departs from conventional punctuation and syntax, Beckett abandoned the novel altogether (*Mercier et Camier* was published in 1970 but written decades earlier). In the last twenty years his works have become shorter and shorter, leading one to hypothesize that at the moment of his death he will utter just one word, the definitive word, and then cease. Despite his deliberate avoidance in his fiction of a realist examination of his own native place, it is striking how many clear references, echoes, and in fact descriptions of places in Ireland are contained in the trilogy. There are enough of these in Beckett's works that Eoin O'Brien has recently compiled a large, attractive collection of photographs of Irish Beckettian places (1986a, 1986b). Fintan O'Toole notes that "in *Molloy*, there are mentions of Three Rock Mountain, Killiney Strand, the Vale of Shanganagh, and Decco's Cave at Sallygap. In *Malone Dies*, there are Dun Laoghaire, Dalkey Island and the Muglins, and John O'God's Hospital at Stillorgan. *How It Is* and *Mercier and Camier* are set in the area between Leopardstown and Stepaside" (1986). Indeed, in the trilogy "the bleak Beckett landscape seems to be the Irish landscape after someone has dropped an H-bomb on it" (Hogan 1980a, 99). Beckett's narrators frequently refer to "the island," lamenting that they cannot escape their native place. And in his thorough dismantling of traditional narrative form, replacing it with the oral-styled monologues of a series of shifting but persistent versions of an artist as an old man, Beckett is more Irish than the Irish themselves. Vivian Mercier finds Beckett's macabre sense of humor to be true to the Gaelic comic tradition (even though he knows no Irish) and his puritanical presentation of sex to be similar to Swift's, concluding that "Beckett might be described as in the Gaelic tradition but not of it" (1962, 76). At least two articles *in Irish* celebrate his achievement as an Irish novelist (Ó Tuama 1978; Kiberd 1984b).

Máirtín Ó Cadhain's *Cré na Cille*

These same two articles compare Beckett's work to that of Máirtín Ó Cadhain (1907–70), generally recognized as the greatest novelist in Irish on the strength of his masterpiece, and sole published novel, *Cré na Cille* (Churchyard clay) (1949). One of them points out that Beckett wrote a poem that serves as an apt description of *Cré na Cille* (which presents the obsessive dialogues of the souls of the corpses in a Galway graveyard): "All the dead voices. / They make a sound like wings. / Like leaves. / Like sand. / Like leaves. / They all speak together. / Each one to itself. / What do they say? / They talk about their lives. / To have lived is not enough for them. / They have to talk about it" (Kiberd 1984b, 23). Ó Cadhain is even more commonly compared to Joyce, as by Caoilfhionn Nic Pháidín: "Rinne Ó Cadhain an rud céanna don Ghaeilge is a rinne Joyce don Bhéarla" ["Ó Cadhain did the same thing for Irish that Joyce did for English"] (1980, 48). Whereas Joyce sought to capture the language of sleep in *Finnegans Wake*, Ó Cadhain presented the language of the dead in *Cré na Cille;* both are characterized by a powerful orality and playfulness, and there is no question that Ó Cadhain much admired Joyce's work and was influenced by it. However, Ó Cadhain's characters are presented much more realistically than those of *Finnegans Wake*. His is the strategy of Swift in *Gulliver's Travels,* O'Duffy in *The Spacious Adventures of the Man in the Street,* and O'Brien in *The Third Policeman:* the reputed setting is in a remote, bizarre realm—the South Seas, another planet, the afterlife—but there we discover that people (even when they are inverted or exaggerated for comic and satiric purposes) are strikingly similar to those who inhabit the real world. O'Duffy's "Rathé," after all, is merely an anagram of "Earth." Much closer to *The Third Policeman,* which was unavailable when he was writing *Cré na Cille,* Ó Cadhain's conceit for the monologues and dialogues that make up his book appears to be that people continue their lifelong obsessions into death—that death is, in fact, much like life.

This hard-nosed and somewhat sardonic premise was rooted in Ó Cadhain's origins in Irish Ireland. Unlike the outsiders and professional *Gaeilgeoirí* lampooned by O'Brien, Ó Cadhain was born and raised in one of the most solidly Irish-speaking areas, Cois Fharraige, in County Galway, which "unlike some other Gaeltacht areas," for example West Kerry, "had not a strong literary tradition. His natural heritage was rather the magnificent Irish oral literature" (Ó Tuama 1972, 242). Ó Cadhain was an IRA activist, imprisoned during World War II, and often seen in Ireland as a political as much as a literary figure. After becoming well known as a writer and an authority on both Irish and European literature, he ended his career as a professor of Irish at Trinity College. He admitted that it was difficult to "give of one's best in a medium that is likely to be dead before the writer" (quoted in Cleeve and Brady 1985, 326), but nonetheless (unlike several other fiction writers whose first language was Irish, including Liam O'Flaherty) he insisted on writing exclusively in Irish, crafting excellent short stories as well as the influential critical work *Páipéir Bhána agus Páipéir Bhreaca* (Blank papers and written papers) (1969) and *Athnuachan* (Renewal), a second novel that was "highly praised by critics who read it in MS, but which he refused to be published, regarding it as unsatisfactory" (Cleeve and Brady, 326).

While some have hypothesized that he was inspired by the "Hades" chapter of *Ulysses*, by Edgar Lee Masters's *Spoon River Anthology*, or by Dostoyevski's story "Bobok," Ó Cadhain himself recounted the genesis of *Cré na Cille* in *Páipéir Bhána agus Páipéir Bhreaca* (33), remembering his experience helping to bury one of his neighbors in midwinter and having difficulty locating the right grave. Afterwards one neighbor imagined the old woman complaining that they may have buried her in the wrong place, and another remarked that she would do so endlessly and only in the best grammar (Ó hEithir 1977, 76). Thus begins *Cré na Cille*: "Ní mé an ar Áit an Phuint nó na Cúig Déag atá mé curtha?" ("I wonder am I buried in the pound plots or the fifteen-shilling plots?") (1949, 13). The speaker is Caitríona Pháidín, an old woman who is obsessed with a lifelong resentment against her sister Neil, who married the man she loved; Caitríona views her placement in a mere fifteen-shilling plot (about which she soon learns) as Neil's latest assault upon her dignity. One notes the Irish obsession with gravesites found also in Seumas O'Kelly's story "The Weaver's Grave."

The other dominant character in the book is An Máistir Mór (The Big Master), a linguistically learned though non-native schoolteacher who, when he learns that his young widow has remarried to the postman, delivers a series of curses upon him that would have made a Middle Irish satirist proud:

Luí fada gan faoilte air! Seacht n-aicíd déag agus fiche na hÁirce
air! Calcadh fiodáin agus stopainn air! Camroillig agus goile treasna
air! An ceas naon air! An Bhuí Chonaill air! Pláigh Lasaras air!
Éagnach Job air! Clar na muc air! (185)

[Long lying without relief on him! Thirty-seven diseases and twenty
needs on him! Hardening and obstruction of the arteries on him!
Clubfoot and a cross stomach on him! Nine sorrows on him!
Yellow Fever on him! The plague of Lazarus on him! The complaint
of Job on him! A pig's disease on him!]

An Máistir Mór's widow ends up burying the postman beside
him after *his* death, leaving them "like two dogs whose tails
have been knotted together" (Ó hEithir 1977, 79). The book
is presented as a series of "interludes" dominated almost
entirely by the stories and dialogue of the inhabitants of the
graveyard—resembling "in form . . . an expanded short
story" (MacEoin 1969, 65). *Cré na Cille* is thus the quintes-
sential Irish novel: a network of interwoven speaking voices,
true "to the inherited character of Irish storytelling, for this
penchant for vigorous and incisive dialogue has been one
of the outstanding features of the literature since its emergence in writing and doubtless before" (MacCana 1980, 59).
    Cré na Cille is marked by Ó Cadhain's imaginative use of
the Irish language and his uncanny insights into rural Gaelic
society. Ó Cadhain understood Gaelic idioms more profoundly than Father Peadar Ó Laoghaire but was much more
willing to experiment. Yet "the strangeness of the form, a
marked departure from the style of the realistic novel, worried
the reviewers. They recognized the novel as a major literary
achievement but deplored the biased description of the people—the absence of any kindness or softness in their nature—
and the lack of psychological realism in that the characters
remain static, as it were 'frozen.' However, recent criticism
has adverted to the comic dimensions of the work and stresses
the need to examine its structure in the light of the development of the novel form since Joyce" (Quinn 1983, 168–69).
Seán Ó Tuama praised Ó Cadhain's achievement but continued to criticize the characters of his novel as "static, typed,
underdeveloped"—a claim recently countered by the post-

modernist views of critics such as Caolfhionn Nic Pháidín (1980) and Charles Quinn (1983), who point out that such a criticism could also be levelled at writers like Beckett and O'Brien but that it misses the whole point: that today's world is one in which people are overwhelmed by the constraints of their existence and are unable to change. After all, the characters in the book are *dead*, not alive. Breandán Ó Doiblin (1974) views *Cré na Cille* as a comedy of manners. Declan Kiberd reminds us that a startled young William Butler Yeats was approached by an old countryman in Sligo who informed him that he was tired of Kickham and the other rural Romantics and wished for " 'a work in which the people would be shown up in all their naked hideousness.' Many decades were to pass before that wish was granted in the nineteenforties by O'Brien's *An Béal Bocht* and Ó Cadhain's *Cré na Cille"* (1980, 52). Ó Cadhain himself was proud that a stranger pointed to him in Dublin and said to the man beside him, "There goes *Cré na Cille."* Despite (or perhaps partly because of) the magnitude of Ó Cadhain's achievement, we still await both an English translation of *Cré na Cille* and a comprehensive critical study of his life and work.

Francis Stuart

Another novelist often compared to Beckett, yet in many ways the most difficult Irish novelist to categorize, is Francis Stuart (b. 1902). Stuart has published more than twenty novels since 1930, spanning the generations among Irish writers; W. J. McCormack has characterized him as "The Long-Distance Winner" (quoted in Moore 1971, 428). After the publication of his unusual autobiographical novel *Black List/Section H* in 1971, Stuart's reputation burgeoned in such a way as to suggest that he belongs among the novelists of the 1970s and 1980s—yet his first novel, *Women and God* (1931), appeared seven years before Beckett's first. Like Beckett, Stuart came from Protestant Ascendancy origins (although he converted to Catholicism) and exiled himself to Europe, viewing his native country deliberately from the perspective of an outsider even after he moved back there in 1957. In *Black List/Section H*, which constantly bridges the usual gaps

between fiction, autobiography, and criticism, he asserted
that "post-Joycean fiction had two paths to choose between
and it seemed to be taking the old, well-tried one, with its
practitioners producing novels and stories easily recognizable
as realistic portrayals of local character and situation. . . .
A few tricks had been learned from [Joyce], but his obsessive
kind of writing was not inspiring any of the H's contemporaries to delve deeper into themselves" (183). Except, of
course, for Beckett, who made self-scrutiny the sole subject
of his fiction. As Seumas Deane notes, "Stuart, imaginatively
obsessed with the figure of dishonour, and Beckett, equally
entranced by the figure of inertia, go further than their
contemporaries in thus ratifying their social delinquency,
making contact and even identification with a community of
outcasts the central preoccupation of their work" (1986, 216).
Roger Garfitt adds that Stuart "manages to be positive over
very much the same ground over which Beckett is negative"
(1975, 220).

Deane succinctly summarizes Stuart's persistent code: "From
the outset of his strange career in 1923 to the present, Stuart
has consistently adhered to an evangelical belief in the importance of a chosen few, for whom the possibility of a new
preternatural tenderness of feeling and awareness would be
nurtured to the point at which it would replace the existing
subnormal world. The necessary prelude to this new dis-
pensation was suffering and disgrace; the scapegoat figure,
who would assume the burden of pain, was the artist. In
Stuart, therefore, the religious sensibility is dominant and
peremptory to a degree not known before in Irish writing"
(1986, 214–15). His models in this regard are novelists like
Dostoyevski and Lawrence. Noting that Stuart persistently
examines violence, Deane claims that this is something "which,
remarkably, no other Irish writer has done" (216), but in
point of fact Liam O'Flaherty (who takes H under his wing
in *Black List/Section H*) similarly focused on victims of violence and on heroic outcast figures in a number of his novels.
Like O'Flaherty, Stuart pursued a rebellious path in his career:
taking the Republican side in the Irish Civil War, he was
captured and interned; after lecturing at Berlin University
during World War II, he was imprisoned by French occu-

pation troops; later still, he became involved with nationalist rebels in the north of Ireland. It appears that "whatever cause he joined he left it as soon as it became successful. . . . His search is for holiness through sin" (Deane 1986, 216). Stuart, who at the age of eighteen married Iseult Gonne and described his encounters with Yeats in *Black List/Section H*, pursued Yeats's youthful ideal of the outcast artist much more literally than did Yeats himself, who gladly courted worldly success.

Stuart's many novels are unusually well suited to brief summary since they tell essentially one recurrent story: an outcast artist type of man survives the violence of war and engages in exploitative sex, finally rejecting both in favor of a quiet, platonic life with a formerly victimized woman and often a small community of like-minded survivors. In Stuart's novels "Woman may hold intuitive wisdom, and be moulded by suffering; but she is very much the mute companion of the man's researches" (Garfitt 1975, 218). Ezra Arrigho declares at the end of *Redemption* (1949), "After the days of vengeance there comes a new breath. Here and there, among those who have survived, comes a new vision" (47), deciding that "there were other modes of communion beside the old and played-out ones, other cults beside the marriage-cult and the family cult" (209).

Stuart departs from realism in unusual ways. His fiction is either so literally real as to render the term "realism" inadequate, as in *Black List/Section H*, or it is shot through with fantasy and fable, as in most of his other novels. George Moore—who is another close predecessor to Stuart, both as Ascendancy-Protestant-turned-Catholic and as eccentric outsider—had earlier written an autobiography that uses many of the strategies of a novel, in his trilogy *Hail and Farewell* (1911–14); *Black List/Section H* is a novel whose materials are very directly those of Stuart's own life experiences. Virtually all of the characters are given their real names—except for the Kafkaesque protagonist "H" himself (Stuart's actual first name is Henry), perhaps indicating that Stuart was least confident of his own identity, which H constantly searches for in the book. The narrator of *A Hole in the Head* (1977) becomes, like Beckett and O'Brien, self-deconstructive: "For the first time since my private crisis (Christ, why the genteel phrase?) I was on my own in the normal, public world of erotic encounters (another euphemism; a sense of guilt makes me phony in thought and word)" (49). His novels borrow quite a bit from actual events—the Irish Civil War, World War II, the Northern troubles, and others—but these are commonly transposed into another realm, as if to suggest that Stuart realized that the ideal world he was looking for could be found only in the future or elsewhere. At the beginning of *Pigeon Irish* (1932), for example, we are told that "the time of the Prologue is in the future; and the rest of the novel, several months later" (6). *A Hole in the Head* obviously recounts some features of the Northern troubles— with Belfast thinly described as "Belbury," the IRA as the "B.A.M.," and the Protestant UVF as the "L.D.F."—but in it Stuart's protagonist Barnaby Shane has a relationship with Emily Brontë, whom Stuart adopts as an emblem of Celtic melancholy.

Stuart's most recent novel, *Faillandia* (1985), is a fable attacking the narrow puritanism of Irish church and state, particularly the anti-divorce referendum, but he does not find any humor in these matters like Eimar O'Duffy did. Stuart is the only nearly totally humorless Irish fabulist. While Beckett's brand of supposed existential despair is actually very often funny and uplifting, most readers will find Stuart's apocalyptic, ultimately at least nominally affirmative novels to be much more depressing. At the end of *Faillandia*, Gideon Spokane, having lost his lover to a bullet intended for him, and now in a platonic relationship with a woman, is described studying the erotic parts of *Ulysses* with her and then listening to her read the accounts of Jesus' crucifixion in the Bible. One prefers to read either *Ulysses* or the Bible itself—or the best of O'Duffy, Wall, O'Brien, Beckett, or Ó Cadhain.

7

New Voices: The Contemporary Novel

Improving Conditions

During the last thirty or so years, an impressive growth in the number of Irish novels and Irish novelists has occurred. In 1960 Stephen P. Ryan asked, "What has become of the Emerald Isle's once promising literary revival?" (1960, 149), but today one is hard-pressed to know where to best begin a discussion of the embarrassment of riches in contemporary Irish literature. In this period more than thirty worthy novelists must compete with each other for recognition.[1] Historically linked to the growth of the middle class in England and America, the novel has typically prospered when a nation comes of age—which is exactly what finally began happening in Ireland in the late 1950s. The contemporary novelist and critic Thomas Kilroy notes that "there is the widely accepted view nowadays among the historians that contemporary Ireland derives from the late fifties, that from that period one can trace the economic, social and cultural changes by which the country . . . moved from being an essentially rural-based, tradition-bound society to something resembling a modern, urbanized, technological state. . . . Something important appeared to happen in the arts, too, in that decade" (1982, 171). Censorship eased. People in Ireland became more interested in the rest of the world and in economic development. The conservative Éamon de Valera was replaced as head of state by the progressive Seán Lemass. Evaluating Lemass's administration between 1958 and 1963, Terence Brown asserts that "Irishmen and women believe now, as they believed then, that those five years represented a major turning point in Irish fortunes" (1985, 241). Ireland experienced an economic boom during the 1960s, it joined the European Economic Community in 1973, and even though recession arrived in the late 1970s, Ireland remains in many ways a much more modernized country than it had been before 1960. State patronage of the arts improved the situation and status of the writer, and Irish publishing grew to the point where today there is a monthly magazine, *Books-Ireland*, whose purpose is to keep readers abreast of developments in the Irish book industry. Dublin's bookstores today are well stocked with a striking variety of new Irish novels.

While upper-class Catholic and rural Catholic novelists continue to emerge, the middle class is much more prominent today in both the authorship and the readership of the Irish novel. In general, the Irish readership today resembles the English readership of a century ago much more than the Ascendancy-dominated Irish readership of the nineteenth century. Yet it is striking how many of the earlier subgenres have continued to be prominent in the contemporary Irish novel. Historical novels have been particularly popular, appealing to the growing number of contemporary middle-class readers with both the time and the sense of detachment necessary to cultivate an interest in history (Cahalan 1983, 155–56, 177). Love stories are similarly profitable. The Big House form has been borrowed by writers such as Aidan Higgins, John Banville, and Jennifer Johnston. The bildungsroman remained a common fictional testing ground. The countryside and small towns have remained common settings at the same time that the city has become increasingly popular. More novels in Irish are being published than ever before, and there has emerged a strong group of women novelists. As one might expect, the influence of Joyce has been discernible. Relatively traditional realist novels have been much more common than experimental ones in the Joycean mode, almost as if in backlash. The middle class hankers mostly for realism, and Irish novelists frequently stay home and enjoy a relative prosperity that seemed virtually impossible in previous periods. Interestingly, the best novelists of the period, the ones with the most staying power throughout this period—including Benedict Kiely, Brian Moore, and John McGahern—tended to start out as realists but then later to experiment with more fabulist approaches. This chapter will begin with an examination of these novelists and then consider in turn novelists in Irish, women novelists, traditional realists, and novelists emergent within the last few years.

A Durable Northern Voice: Benedict Kiely

More widely noticed than any of the positive developments in Ireland during the last thirty years, of course, has been the violent strife in Northern Ireland since 1969, with guerrilla warfare waged among the British army, the Irish Republican Army and all of its splinter groups, and their Protestant equivalents. Not surprisingly, "the Troubles" have provoked quite a number of popular novels—novels such as Eugene McCabe's *Victims* (1976) and lesser works, which have been examined in several critical articles (Cronin 1969b; Deutsch 1976; McMinn 1980; Titley 1980). Brian Moore has commented, "If there is anything more depressing than Ulster fact it must be Ulster fiction" (Deutsch 1976, 132)—a remark to which John Wilson Foster (1974) might well take exception. Ulster produced the two most prolific and persistent novelists under consideration in this chapter, Benedict Kiely and Moore himself. Kiely has produced ten novels and a great many short stories and critical writings dating from the mid-1940s to the present day, while Moore has published fifteen novels since 1955. Among contemporary Irish novelists, Kiely and Moore are surpassed in the scope of their work only by Francis Stuart, who (as noted in chapter 6) is also originally from the North and has responded to its violence in his fiction. Like Stuart, Kiely and Moore evolved from early realism into later strains of fantasy. Their works and those of a few of the other best novelists during this period suggest that an eclectic response to the divergent fictional models established by earlier Irish realists and fabulists—or by the early naturalistic Joyce and the later fantastist Joyce—has been the most fruitful one available to contemporary Irish novelists.

Eclectic is exactly the word to describe Benedict Kiely (b. 1919), described by his friend John Montague as "almost overcome by the variety of life" (quoted in Kennedy 1986, 7). Kiely published an insightful survey (1950) of the Irish novel between 1920 and 1950 in the midst of a ten-year period (1945–55) when he himself produced six novels and three other books. His first book (1945) was a Republican essay attacking the British partition of Northern Ireland, while his two most recent book-length fictions are direct attacks on the guerrilla movements in the North, both Catholic and Protestant. His early book on William Carleton, *Poor Scholar* (1948), is still the best single book on his fellow County Tyrone native. Kiely's career has followed Carleton's in several significant respects: both abandoned Tyrone and an early vocation for the priesthood in favor of Dublin and a literary career; both eschewed classical, controlled fictional forms, preferring the blustering style of the barroom balladeer; and both have been known as wide-ranging, contentious, impressive personalities.

Kiely's earliest novels were realist and autobiographical. Both *Land Without Stars* (1946) and *In a Harbour Green* (1949) are set in a Northern town in the days leading up to World War II and tell the story of a bookish man who wins a woman after his rival falls prey to violence (a policeman's bullet in the first novel and World War II in the second one). Like Kiely, Peter Quinn, protagonist of *Land Without Stars*, leaves the seminary and the North and sets off for a worldly life in Dublin. Like Brian Moore's *The Emperor of Ice-Cream* (1965) and James Plunkett's *Farewell Companions* (1977) later on, *In a Harbour Green* is a meditation upon life and death in Ireland during World War II, when the country was technically neutral but darkened by the shadows of wartime England.

The Cards of the Gambler (1953) was a new departure—a tour de force making more deliberate use of a folktale than any other Irish novel within a fictional tradition marked, as we have seen in previous chapters, by a pervasive oral influence. Kiely alternates brief "interludes" recounting segments of the gambler's story in its original fireside form with chapters transforming the story into a novel. He begins by describing an old man in his thatched cottage and tells us that he heard the folktale "from the man you're watching, and you, if you wait, will hear it from me. When I come to tell it, I will also add, subtract, divide, and multiply" (3).

Such are the makings of an Irish novel, Kiely suggests. In the folktale, the gambler gains from God the power to keep people from stealing his apples, stalls off Death but eventually goes to hell, from which he gets thrown out and, tossing aside his cards, finally enters heaven. In the novelistic chapters, the apples become a car, hell a mock-Gothic scene, heaven an airport, and both God and Death clerics. *The Captain with the Whiskers* (1960) also genuflects to the oral tradition: it is dedicated "to the memory of my father, Tom Kiely, who talked with the wizard Doran on the Cornavara Mountain in the County Tyrone" (5), and the wizard lurks as one of several emblematic figures haunting the boyhood of Owen Rodgers, who grows from innocence to experience. This novel continues its author's stylistic playfulness, with Kiely continually blending first-person and third-person narratives.

In *Dogs Enjoy the Morning* (1968), Kiely completely merges the world of fantasy and romance that always lurks around the edges of his earlier realist novels with the real world of twentieth-century Ireland. As with most of Kiely's earlier realist protagonists, Peter Lane has to undergo a sexual initiation as a crucial part of growing up—but this hero does so in the imaginary town of Cosmona, a strange place located somewhere in Ireland not too far from Dublin and populated by medieval pagans as well as by twentieth-century folk such as Peter. Always experimenting, and busy as a creative-writing teacher in the United States and as a Dublin journalist during this period, Kiely abandoned the form of the novel altogether for a time, as if finding it too confining for his garrulous narrative voice. Today he is as much or more celebrated for his short stories. *Proxopera* (1977) is a novella exposing and attacking an IRA bombing. *Nothing Happens in Carmincross* (1985) is a novel marked by Kiely's characteristic, ballad-like style: "Her hair it was the raven, her breath was honeydew. The words she whispered in my ear I will not tell to you" (86). This novel also reflects a return to the earliest roots of the Irish novel in its basic structure. Like Edgeworth and many another early Irish novelist, in *Carmincross* Kiely sends to Ireland an interested outsider, the Irish-American academic Mervyn Kavanagh, who traverses the countryside northward to witness both his mother's death and another brutal IRA bombing, flying back to New York at the end with a drink in his hand, a sadder if not wiser man. Kiely omits the suggested solutions of an Edgeworth or a Banim, for indeed in his view "Nothing Happens in Carmincross."

From the Old World to the New; From Realism to Fabulism: Brian Moore

Brian Moore (b. 1921) is the most talented and certainly the most prolific novelist to be considered in this chapter. Accordingly, he has received the most critical attention, with several studies (Foster 1974, 117–30 and 151–84; McSweeney 1976; Henry 1974) seeking to examine all of his novels. Moore left his native Belfast in 1948 for Canada, living in Montreal until 1959, when he moved to New York and subsequently to Malibu, California. The first of his fifteen novels to date appeared in 1955, and more of them are set in the New World than in Ireland. Here I shall limit myself to Moore's six Irish novels.[2] They divide evenly into two distinct groups: three early naturalistic Belfast novels and three more recent and nostalgic novels—two of them dabbling in fantasy and fable—set in Ireland both north and south. Like Kiely and some of the other best contemporary Irish novelists, Moore has tended to move from realism and naturalism into fabulism, but one finds hints of the latter interest in his early works and a continued attention to social realities among his later works. Like Kiely and others, he is an eclectic sort.

The Lonely Passion of Judith Hearne (1955) was immediately and widely hailed as an impressive first novel and remains Moore's most consistently praised work. Focused on her desperate consciousness, it tells the story of how a middle-aged piano teacher fails in her attempt to match herself with a returned Yank (the blowhard brother of her landlady), is discovered to be an alcoholic, dismissed by her landlady and dropped by her clients, treated with indifference by the local priest, and finally committed to a nursing home, having been virtually destroyed by societal forces. Moore has commented that "failure is a more interesting condition than success" (quoted in Prosky 1971, 109) and that "both Protestantism and Catholicism in Northern Ireland are the most desperate tragedies that can happen to people. . . . I feel there should be a pox on both their houses" (quoted in Foster 1974, 129). He called Joyce a "tremendous influence" and noted that "when I came to think about writing a novel, one thing I didn't want to do was an autobiographical novel because I thought 'Who can compete with *Portrait*? . . . Joyce and other people [had] written about loss of faith in intellectuals: no one [had] written about loss of faith in a very ordinary person" (quoted in McSweeney 1976, 55–56). In an act of what Keats had called "negative capability" or what Robert Green terms "authorial displacement" (1980, 29), Moore deliberately set out in *Judith Hearne* to write about a character in most ways opposite to himself. This novel artfully shifts its point of view among Judith, her intended beau Madden, the brother of her landlady, and the landlady's son Bernard, a rather Gothic lecher, *literatus,* and momma's boy. Responding to the "anxiety of influence," Moore avoided *Portrait* as a model, but nonetheless responded quite clearly to Joyce's influence in this novel. Not only does he adopt for his point of view a modified stream of consciousness and vividly describe a repressive Irish Catholic urban society, but Judith Hearne recalls no one so much as she does Maria, the protagonist of Joyce's story "Clay." Like Maria, Judith is ambivalently received as a weekly Sunday dinner guest of her more prosperous friends and their children in the suburbs, sitting home the rest of the time telling herself that all is well as she "moved her thin legs together and peered for comfort at her long, pointed shoes with the little buttons on them, winking up at her like wise little friendly eyes. Little shoe eyes, always there" (10). And like the other Moore, George, Brian Moore distinguished himself as a male novelist with a devotion to sympathetically understanding and focusing on female protagonists—in *Judith Hearne* as well as in several of his subsequent novels. His most recent Irish novel, *The Temptation of Eileen Hughes* (1981), presents three female narrators and a protagonist whose story offers a counterpoint to Judith Hearne's.

As Michael Toolan points out, the protagonists of all three of Moore's early Belfast novels depend heavily on psychological "fetishes" (1980, 100). Whenever she moves somewhere new, Judith Hearne immediately hangs her pictures of her aunt and the Sacred Heart near her bed. This is her last act in the nursing home at the end: "Funny about those two. When they're with me, watching over me, a new place becomes home" (223). Just before young Una Clarke tries unsuccessfully to seduce him in *The Feast of Lupercal* (1958), Diarmuid Devine—the male version of Judith Hearne—takes down the presumably disapproving picture of his father, but to no avail. In *The Emperor of Ice-Cream* (1965), the autobiographical bildungsroman that Moore had earlier sought to avoid writing, Gavin Burke depends upon the image of the Infant of Prague on his dresser. We learn from Moore's first three novels that such ikons do not provide enough help to allow one to satisfactorily survive; only leaving Belfast can do that, and that is what Moore did, seeking to rediscover Joyce's and Beckett's Paris in Montreal, New York, and Malibu.

The critical reception of *The Feast of Lupercal* has been more uneven than that of *Judith Hearne*, but it is also a compelling novel. Like Judith, Diarmuid Devine is defeated by the narrow-minded Catholic society that controls him. A thirty-seven-year-old Catholic schoolteacher and virgin who is nicknamed "Dev" (like the puritan head of state, de Valera) and who overhears another teacher refer to him as an "old woman" (9), Diarmuid attempts a new departure by taking an interest in Una Clarke, a nineteen-year-old Protestant from Dublin, but he has to endure both his failure to consummate any affair with her and the public humiliation of having her uncle, his superior, cane him like a schoolboy after he hears of Una's overnight stay in Diarmuid's flat. The story is specific to the world of Catholic Belfast in the 1950s, but the title and central conceit, as recounted by Diarmuid to his disloyal pupils, are ancient and look ahead to Moore's later fables: "The Feast of Lupercal was a feast of expiation celebrated on the fifteenth of February in honor of Lupercus, the god of fertility. . . . Barren women placed themselves in the path of the flogging priests, believing that by means of the strokes, the reproach of barrenness would be taken away from them" (209–10). However, Diarmuid's caning and its aftermath achieve neither expiation nor cure, but only confirm his isolation from life's feast. He must go on and do his job and keep his mouth shut.[3] Fantasy intrudes more frequently upon the world of Gavin Burke in *The Emperor of Ice-Cream*, for Gavin likes to read the poetry of Yeats, Eliot, MacNeice, and Stevens; like many readers, he fails to fully understand Stevens's poem "The Emperor of Ice-Cream," but he takes it as his motto. This novel, written after Moore had already published two novels set in America, recounts a variety of episodes united under the theme of Gavin's maturation during World War II. It is if "Moore, with two American-based novels behind him . . . were re-tracing his steps to pick up anything important he may have overlooked on his post-haste trek out of Northern Ireland en route to New York City" (Foster 1974, 123). Included are Moore's glimpses of 1930s socialists in Belfast, Gavin's un-resolved relationship with his girlfriend and his rebellion against his narrow-minded Catholic father, and his adven-tures with an army air-raid unit, culminating in his heroic and cathartic work among the victims of the German bombing of Belfast. Like a similar bildungsroman published in the same year, John McGahern's *The Dark*, this one ends with the protagonist's reconciliation with his father.

The conflict between Old and New World values has continued to provide Moore with his central allegory, often recast in fabulist form. Compared to his earlier Irish novels, Moore's later ones seem almost unrecognizable, but they do in fact represent a natural evolution out of the experimental American novels that he had been writing during the inter-vening years, in which characteristically an Irish-American protagonist contends with the freedom offered by the New World but increasingly looks back nostalgically to the tra-ditional values and sense of community left behind in Ireland. *Catholics* (1972), a short novel whose CBS television adap-tation did much to increase Moore's fame, is set on an island off the County Kerry coastline in the near future, at Muck

Abbey, where the Latin Mass and private confession are still practiced despite the contrary edicts of an increasingly secularized Church. Its abbot, Tómas O'Malley, is visited by an Irish-American priest, James Kinsella, a slick intellectual sent by Rome to bring reform to Muck Abbey. Clearly *Catholics* is an allegory enabling Moore to look longingly to Ireland from America, like many an Irish-American, and he makes the reader root for O'Malley, who finally rediscovers his own faith, rather than for the Americanized, secularized Kinsella. Raymond J. Porter (1975) and J. H. Dorenkamp (1978) celebrated Moore's supposed newfound Catholicism, whereas John Wilson Foster (1974) argues more persuasively that it is primitive community that Moore longs for rather than Catholic piety.

Similarly touched by nostalgia and fantasy, *The Mangan Inheritance* (1979) recounts an Irish-American's journey to the south of Ireland. Would-be poet and sometime journalist Jamie Mangan, having discovered a striking resemblance between himself and the nineteenth-century poet James Clarence Mangan, travels to his ancestral place. There, surrounded by other Mangans (one of whom he makes love to), he feels even more strongly that he is the poet and old Ireland reincarnated. Unable to stay, though, he returns to America: like Kiely in *Nothing Happens in Carmincross*, Moore borrows the old conceit of the foreign protagonist and visitor to Ireland, emphasizing that "You can't go home again," especially when you were not really from there to begin with.

The Temptation of Eileen Hughes (1981) is even more clearly an attempt to return full circle to his original place, almost as if to atone for *Judith Hearne*. Eileen, a Belfast shopgirl, is a younger version of Judith who succeeds where Judith failed: she escapes the clutches of Bernard McAuley, her wealthy employer who is insanely infatuated with her, and the machinations of Mona, Bernard's nymphomaniac, grasping wife, who tries to buy off Eileen. Significantly aided by an encounter with an American public relations man, Eileen finally declares her independence from the McAuleys, taking another job and going home to live with her kind-hearted mother. Here Moore continues his attention to Irishwomen of varying socioeconomic backgrounds: this novel is narrated through the contrasting streams of consciousness of Eileen, her mother, and Mona. It remains to be seen whether or not the impressively versatile Moore, having apparently reconciled himself with Ireland in these recent fictions, will write further Irish novels.

The Conscience of the Midlands: John McGahern

Like Moore, John McGahern (b. 1934) made an auspicious début with a penetrating portrait of an Irishwoman, *The Barracks* (1963), and has published an impressive series of novels marked by increasing experimentalism. Among critics he competes closely with Moore for first prize among contemporary Irish novelists; Coilin Owens is confident enough to pronounce that "McGahern's reputation as the leading Irish novelist is sure" (1980, 400). He has published only four novels to date as compared with Moore's fifteen, but each of them has won generally high praise. McGahern's artistic vision is rich enough to attract praise both from those who see him as a despairing existentialist (Garfitt 1975; Molloy 1977) and from those who view him as ultimately affirmative (Kennedy 1983; Fournier 1987). Like Moore—and perhaps inevitably like any Irish novelist who shows promise—McGahern has been compared frequently to Joyce. The parallels spring readily to mind, especially since McGahern's second novel, *The Dark* (1965), is like *Portrait* a graphic bildungsroman about a sensitive young Irish boy, and its banning cost its author his teaching job, causing him to go into exile. McGahern shares with Joyce and several of the best contemporary novelists—Kiely, Moore, Francis Stuart, Aidan Higgins—a frank determination to include a focus on sex as part of their characters' experiences and a willingness to continually experiment with style and form. Richard Kearney (1979) correctly places McGahern in the "critical tradition" of Joyce, Beckett, and Flann O'Brien.

Born in Dublin, raised in County Roscommon, a student and teacher in Dublin and then resident in England, Spain, and the United States before resettling in County Leitrim,

McGahern also reflects an increasing internationalism among Irish writers, although like Joyce he has chosen to set all of his novels in Ireland rather than shift his settings like Moore, Higgins, and John Banville or neutralize them like Beckett. His novels are linked by a set of common character types drawn from his own experience: a long-suffering mother (or aunt, in *The Pornographer*) who dies from cancer; a bull-headed, often violent, but nonetheless ultimately loving father; a sensitive, literary boy/man who tries to survive his parents and make his way in the world; and the female objects of his love or lust. Like Moore, McGahern first sought to avoid the self-centered bildungsroman in the mold of *Portrait* by focusing on a victimized, middle-aged woman, in *The Barracks*. Elizabeth Reegan lives with her policeman husband and his children by his first marriage. Life with a husband is not much easier than Judith Hearne's life without one, and cancer is even worse than alcoholism:

She was Elizabeth Reegan: a woman in her forties: sitting in a chair with a book from the council library in her hand that she hadn't opened: watching certain things like the sewing-machine and the vase of daffodils and a circle still white with frost under the shade of the sycamore tree between the house and the river: alive in this barrack kitchen . . . with a little time to herself before she'd have to get another meal ready: with a life on her hands that was losing the last vestiges of its purpose and meaning: with hard cysts within her breast she feared were cancer . . . Reegan was at court, the children were at school, she was in the kitchen, and did all these things mean anything? (42)

Her husband is at first simply "Reegan" to her, just as the father in *The Dark* is initially "Mahoney," but the isolation of each character's closest family member is eventually overcome. As Suzanne Fournier stresses, Elizabeth's "passage from restlessness and confusion to acceptance of mystery" is "a development within *The Barracks* too often overlooked by critics who focus exclusively upon the bleakness of tone and setting in McGahern's fiction" (1987, 140). The depth and complexity of McGahern's portrait of Elizabeth's marriage and her own consciousness can be measured in contrast to a truly negative, cynical presentation of an Irish marriage such as that found in an Irish novel published a few years later, Kevin Casey's *The Sinner's Bell* (1968). Casey echoes the empty inability to communicate that had been captured in Eliot's *The Wasteland*—"Ah I'm thinking. Can't you see that I'm thinking?" (100)—and describes a marriage so bleak as to be boring and flat in its misogyny. Elizabeth Reegan has her own thoughts, too, providing the narrative focus of *The Barracks,* and she must put up with an often self-centered husband, frequently indifferent stepchildren, and terminal cancer, but nonetheless she moves toward acceptance of her family and her condition. A former nurse, she had loved a doctor years ago in London but found him to be a self-destructive nihilist; at least Reegan is determined to build a world for himself. Illness and death are revealed as humanizing forces. Elizabeth gives Reegan her secret savings, they enjoy a Christmas at home, and Reegan shows some love for his wife before she dies. Elizabeth's death is consoled by love but existential—she is consoled by no belief in an afterlife, and her survivors simply go on, with Reegan's children asking him "is it time to light the lamp yet?" (191) at the end of the novel just as they had asked Elizabeth at the beginning.

Within the borders of a realistic novel, McGahern experimented with style and stream of consciousness in *The Dark* much as he had in *The Barracks* (as witnessed in the unusually punctuated sentence quoted above). The protagonist of *The Dark,* who is assigned no first name, is variously "I," "he," and even "you," with McGahern continually shifting among all available singular points of view and forcing the reader to examine his protagonist with as much objectivity and variety as possible. The book proceeds episodically, like a series of interwoven stories, true to the tradition of the Irish novel—which provoked one critic (Devine 1979) into an ill-advised attempt to impose from the outside a classical, four-part "structure" on the novel.

This novel's graphic descriptions of the boy's masturbatory fantasies and suggestions of homosexuality (latent in the boy's widowed father and perhaps active in his relative the priest), were plenty to invoke banning even by an Irish

Censorship Board somewhat less rigid than it had been in the 1930s. *The Dark* is more graphic than *Portrait,* with which the novel has been frequently compared, but in terms of the larger theme of the novel it seems truer that McGahern may have sought to undo rather than outdo Joyce at his own game. Like Stephen Dedalus, McGahern's rural protagonist is a bright student, initially attracted to the priesthood, struggling to escape the clutches of his father and make his way to the university. But the ending of *The Dark* could not more deliberately invert, subvert, and deflate the *dénouement* of *Portrait:* with the consent of his father, McGahern's young man opts to withdraw from University College, Dublin, and enter the civil service in Dublin, and the final words of the novel are "Good night so, Daddy" and "Good night, my son. God bless you" (142). This ending is probably more ironic than pious (of course, so may have been Joyce's); in any event, it has disappointed many readers. As Eileen Kennedy notes, "Stephen Dedalus is an urban hero who can leave Ireland boldly; but young Mahoney is a farmboy whose sights are set no higher than the city" (1983, 121).

The protagonist of *The Leavetaking* (1974) tries to reconcile himself with his mother much as his younger counterpart in *The Dark* had struggled with his father. He must do so, however, within the confines of memory and a single day, for *The Leavetaking,* which McGahern revised in a superior second edition (1975), concerns a teacher's last day at a Dublin school before leaving for England after being dismissed because his civil-law marriage to an American divorcée is not recognized by the Irish state or school system. Patrick's mind runs freely over his entire previous life—his earlier romances, his father, and especially his mother, who died of cancer. He finally resolves that his present love and his imagination can overcome past depressing reality: "The boat has slipped its moorings and is leaving harbour to trust to the open sea: and no boat needs so much trust to put to sea as it does for one body to go human and naked and vulnerable into the arms of another" (195). Because this ending obviously reflected McGahern's departure into exile after the banning of *The Dark* and his firing, many critics again linked this novel to Joyce and to Stephen's supposedly triumphant departure at the end of *Portrait.* But Elizabeth

Reegan had already rejected permanent life abroad in *The Barracks*, and so did McGahern.

Critics were startled by *The Pornographer* (1979), which tells the ribald, frequently comic tale of a Dublin writer of pornography who survives his beloved aunt's death and his guilt-ridden affair with a woman who moves to London and has his child there. The protagonist finally decides to move back home to the countryside and marry a nurse with whom he has fallen in love. In its intertextual blending of the protagonist's pornographic writings with his own story, *The Pornographer* recalls the American Nathaniel West's novel *Miss Lonelyhearts* or John Gardner's *October Light*. Autobiographically, *The Leavetaking* and *The Pornographer* can be viewed as alternate responses to McGahern's victimization after the publication of *The Dark*. It is as if in *The Leavetaking* McGahern was in part saying to the Irish censors and school officials, "Here's the real me whom you banned and fired"; and in *The Pornographer*, "Here's what *real* pornography looks like as opposed to what you confused with it in *The Dark*, and here's how even a real pornographer can be redeemed." In *The Pornographer*, the sexual encounters of the extratextual characters Colonel Grimshaw and Mavis Carmichael are held up for inspection, comic titillation, and finally rejection. Critics have been somewhat divided about how to read these parts of the novel, however. Michael Toolan (1981) views McGahern as wavering between the distinct roles of sympathetic historian and unsympathetic pornographer, while Kennedy (1983) and Fournier (1987) adopt a flatly affirmative view of the novel. The truth, as with so many things, may lie somewhere in the middle. McGahern is neither simply a positive, affirmative writer nor a negative, critical one, but both—a complex novelist with diverse and ambivalent responses to life.

Realism and Fabulism in Aidan Higgins, John Banville, William Trevor, and James Plunkett

It is striking that three of the most international-minded and experimental contemporary Irish novelists—Aidan Hig-

gins (b. 1927), John Banville (b. 1945), and William Trevor
(b. 1928)—turned to the venerable tradition of the Big House
novel as a frame within which to hang their fictions. In the
previous chapter we saw how a Big House novel was disguised within the fabulist contours of Beckett's *Watt*; in their
experiments Higgins, Banville, and Trevor make no attempt
to hide their status as Big House novelists, returning to the
roots of Irish fiction in the spirit of John Barth's Literature
of Exhaustion. Higgins's *Langrishe, Go Down* (1966), Banville's
Birchwood (1973), and Trevor's *Fools of Fortune* (1983) all
present a misbegotten male romantic quest. The best novel
among the three is Higgins's *Langrishe, Go Down*, which is
more clearly influenced by Faulkner *(Go Down, Moses)* than
by Beckett or Joyce, even though as a stream-of-consciousness
writer who attended Clongowes Wood College and wandered
Europe reading Joyce, Higgins more obviously invites the
Joycean link. Faulkner's vision of a decadent Southern aristocracy is clearly very accessible to Higgins and other Irish
Ascendancy novelists.

Langrishe, Go Down is a penetrating, brilliantly written
examination of the inhabitants of a decayed Anglo-Irish estate
in north Kildare during the 1930s—the sisters Imogen and
Helen Langrishe—and their intellectual and cynically ruthless
visitor, the German student Otto Beck. Like many an Irish
novel, this one grew out of a story—"Killachter Meadow"
in Higgins's collection of stories *Felo de Se* (1960). As Maurice
Harmon notes, Higgins's "sisters in the Big House are in
reality himself and his brothers" (1973, 15), who grew up
in a Georgian house on a seventy-two-acre farm in Celbridge,
County Kildare. The theme that dominates all of Higgins's
work, even more than the loss of the Irish Ascendancy world,
is the complex encounter of his Irish characters with the
wider world of Europe. Subsequently he published a travel
diary, *Images of Africa* (1971), a novel focused on an Irish
painter's life abroad, *Balcony of Europe* (1972), an uneven
autobiographical novel, *Scenes from a Receding Past* (1977),
and an epistolary novel about an Irish writer's affair with a
Danish poet, *Boenholm Night-Ferry* (1983).

Langrishe, Go Down remains the chief source of Higgins's
acclaim. It can be read as a political allegory concerning

Ireland's difficulty in lifting itself out of its past and successfully confronting a powerful Europe. Higgins follows the old convention of sending a foreigner to Ireland as narrative lens, but with a new variation: Otto Beck is a German rather than the usual Englishman or American, and he does not treat the natives kindly but ultimately cruelly, entering an affair with Imogen Langrishe with self-serving, cynical motives. Sam Baneham views their relationship as "a kind of extended metaphor for Anglo-German relations in the Era of Appeasement, when sections of the conservative establishment viewed the rise of a strong Fascist State as a possible ally against the spread of Communism and seemed to have lost the will to play a leading role in the European politics of the day" (1983, 172). In view of more recent incursions of German capitalists and their companies into Ireland, Otto's frank use of Imogen may function as a contemporary as well as historical allegory. Helen Langrishe, whose stream of consciousness begins the novel but then evaporates, eventually dies, unable to move beyond the past, but Imogen finally shoots a gun in the direction of the fleeing Otto, angry that her trust of him has been betrayed. Imogen is a survivor, both of the demise of the Ascendancy as reflected in her sister's death and the threat of Europe as embodied in Otto. As another version of the story of a victimized Irishwoman, *Langrishe, Go Down* is initially bleaker but finally and surprisingly more hopeful than Moore's *Judith Hearne* or McGahern's *The Barracks*.

John Banville, perhaps the most accomplished among younger Irish novelists at the moment, published in *Birchwood* the first fully fabulist Big House novel (unless *Watt* is admitted as such). He demonstrates an increased eclecticism and internationalism of influences and perspectives. Like Beckett, John Fowles, and Vladimir Nabokov—whom Seamus Deane (1976, 332) cites as an influence—Banville delights in reminding us in this novel of his artifice: "I began to write . . . and thought that at last I had discovered a form which would contain and order all my losses. I was wrong. There is no form, no order, only echoes and coincidences, sleight of hand, dark laughter" (174). His narrator, like Beckett's, regards narration as an act of necessary futility: "Forgetting all I know, I try to describe these things, and only then do I realize, yet again, that the past is incommunicable" (29). Banville's is "another version of that brand of self-consciousness which has been such a distinctive feature of one tradition (and that the major one) of Irish fiction which includes Joyce, Flann O'Brien, and Beckett" (Deane 1976, 334).

The Big House novels of Higgins, Banville, and Trevor also contain a strong Gothic strain that hearkens back to the nineteenth century; these are novelists "whose imaginations are closer to Sheridan Le Fanu than to Maria Edgeworth" (Donnelly 1975, 134). Banville combines Gothicism and fabulism. For example, we learn that the narrator's grandmother mysteriously exploded, providing an odd emblem for the demise of the Big House: "She may just . . . burst, but I cannot rid myself of the notion that the house itself had something to do with it" (80). *Birchwood* focuses on the narrator's attempt to sort out his family history, which is continually thwarted by Banville's deliberate subversion of chronology, on his search for his supposed twin sister, and on his picaresque adventures with the circus, directed by one Prospero. Finally it is admitted that the entire quest has been fabricated: "There is no girl. There never was . . . no Prospero either, there never is. . . . And so I became my own Prospero, and yours" (172). Interestingly, Banville's feeling that he had painted himself into a narrative corner by the end of *Birchwood* did not subsequently lead him, like Beckett, to increasingly shorter fictions, but rather to a retreat into more conventional work—a series of long novels of ideas focused on imaginative scientists, *Doctor Copernicus* (1976), *Kepler* (1980), *The Newton Letter* (1982), and *Mefisto* (1986). Like Flann O'Brien, Banville has responded to his own early experimentalism by becoming more conservative as a novelist. He "has indicated that his attitude towards fabulism 'has altered from at first a high enthusiasm, to, lately, a deep suspicion'," and he now "regards himself as an international writer looking to world fiction for ideas and inspiration rather than to Irish predecessors" (Molloy 1981, 29–30).

Somewhat in contrast to the increasingly international Banville, William Trevor is an Anglo-Irish novelist born in Cork but now living in Devon who, while setting most of his ten novels in England, has more recently reasserted his Irishness with his story collection *The News from Ireland* and his novel *Fools of Fortune* (1983). Like Higgins's *Langrishe, Go Down,* Trevor's early Irish novel *Mrs. Eckdorf in O'Neill's Hotel* (1969) focuses on a foreign character, a British woman who married a German, as an object of scorn. Mrs. Eckdorf is an idiotic, sentimental outsider whose misguided attempt to beautify a Dublin flophouse ultimately lands her in an insane asylum. In his Big House novel, *Fools of Fortune,* Trevor like Higgins shows the influence of Faulkner, specifically that of *The Sound and the Fury* and *Absalom, Absalom!.* Here the family surname is Quinton and one of the crucial stream-of-consciousness narrators is Imelda, the deranged young offspring of the ruined Ascendancy match of Willie Quinton and his English cousin Marianne. Like *Birchwood,* this novel is marked by neo-Gothicism and a frustrated romantic quest. Cutting through the shifting streams of consciousness, we learn that after one of the Quintons' workers was found hanging from a tree with his tongue cut out for informing to the British during the Anglo-Irish War, Willie's Ascendancy but nationalist father was shot by the British, and Willie has spent most of his life in exile after revenging this shooting and fathering Imelda. The players in this history are cast by Trevor in the image advanced by Willie's father and recounted by Marianne: "Fools of fortune, as his father would have said; ghosts we become" (234). As in Moore's *Judith Hearne,* McGahern's *The Barracks,* and Higgins's *Langrishe, Go Down,* it is the women who are most victimized, and as in the case of Mrs. Eckdorf's misbegotten journey to Dublin, the estrangement of Anglo-Irish Willie and English Marianne may reflect the situation of their Anglo-Irish creator resident in Devon.

Another novelist who published his first Irish novel in 1969 and whose work has shown an increasing interest in experiment is James Plunkett (b. 1920). Plunkett's development from working-class Dublin origins, a clerkship in the gas company, and a position as Jim Larkin's assistant in the Workers' Union of Ireland into a leading Irish novelist and television producer is a fascinating story (Cahalan 1980,

1986). Francis MacManus, Sean O'Faolain, and Frank O'Connor were important early mentors and helpers. Plunkett's first novel, *Strumpet City* (1969), is an impressive, panoramic historical novel drawing on the experiences of his father and other relatives and friends during the big Dublin transport labor lockout of 1913, on Plunkett's own later acquaintance with Larkin, its leader, and on his own earlier radio and stage plays about Larkin and the lockout (Cahalan 1978a). This novel is distinguished by an unforgettable cast of characters balanced among the Dublin working class, the wealthy employers, and the clergy in such a way as to invite the kind of dialectical, Marxist analysis of the variety advanced by George Lukács in his book *The Historical Novel* (Cahalan 1983, 179–90). It contains vivid descriptions and characterizations of working-class Dublin life rivalled among contemporary novels only by Christy Brown's *Down All the Days* (1971). *Strumpet City* was an immediate best-seller in Ireland and received further fame through its 1980 Irish television adaptation starring Peter O'Toole as Larkin, Peter Ustinov as King Edward VII, and Cyril Cusack as Father Giffley.

Plunkett's second novel, *Farewell Companions* (1977), was even more expansive historically, encompassing the world of its author's own youth from the 1920s until the 1950s, and reflects not only the contours of the Joycean bildungsroman but also an increasing narrative playfulness, especially in the character of O'Sheehan, who believes himself to be the mythical Oisín reincarnated and indulges himself in entertaining fantasies. In this novel Plunkett pushes public history into the background in order to focus on the private, complex development of his characters, especially that of his protagonist, Tim MacDonagh (Cahalan 1978b).

Along with Jennifer Johnston, the novelists surveyed thus far in this chapter—Kiely, Moore, McGahern, Higgins, Banville, Trevor, and Plunkett—are perhaps the most accomplished and promising in the contemporary period. It is striking that with the partial exception of Banville—and perhaps it is not at all fair to describe as conservative his imaginative meditations upon Copernicus, Kepler, and Newton—all of their careers have been marked by an increasing willingness to experiment, to move from early realist novels into works engaged to a greater or lesser extent in fabulism. Thus perhaps are best bridged the dominant earlier modes of the Irish novel in this century, as traced in my previous chapters.

Contemporary Novels in Irish: Eoghan Ó Tuairisc, Diarmaid Ó Súilleabháin, and Breandán Ó hEithir

Contemporary novels in Irish similarly reflect this kind of modulation between realism and fabulism. Irish-speaking areas have continued to shrink during the last thirty years, so that "the Gaelic novelist or short-story writer must create not only a new literary work but also an audience for it" (O'Leary 1986b, 18). It is therefore ironic that "as the language revival and the condition of the Gaeltacht entered a deep crisis during the past thirty years, modern Irish writing has experienced something of a renaissance, with a number of writers of the very first rank" (Ó Tuathaigh 1979, 117). This is not an entirely mysterious phenomenon, for support mechanisms for writers in Irish increased at the same time that the spoken language endured various threats: the language organization Gael-Linn was founded in 1953, the publisher Sáirséal agus Dill in 1945, and Raidió na Gaeltachta in 1972. In 1955 David Marcus was able to celebrate "an eager and widening awareness among the reading public and an atmosphere of excitement in the writing itself—two factors which, in supplementing each other, have generated continuous growth; and among the new writers which this activity has produced are many whose freshness and modernity might be said to have given Irish literature in Gaelic something it never had at any previous stage of its long development— an *avant garde* movement" (quoted in Brown 1985, 231).

These writers were motivated by political as well as literary concerns. During the 1966 observances of the fiftieth anniversary of the Easter Rising, for example, "a group of radical revivalists named 'Misneach' (Courage) . . . felt compelled to mount a week-long hunger strike in Belfast and Dublin to remind Irishmen and women of past idealism"; this group's founders included Máirtín Ó Cadhain and two of his best contemporary successors as novelists, Eoghan Ó Tuairisc and Diarmaid Ó Súilleabháin (Brown 1985, 270). Ó Cadhain linked Ó Tuairisc and Ó Súilleabháin as "evidently influenced by the modern French School of Malraux and Camus, and both deal with *la condition humaine,* with an awareness and a sophistication never before displayed in Irish writing" (1971, 149). A more obvious direct influence was Ó Cadhain himself, whose career as a fiction writer towers over subsequent writing in Irish much like Joyce's in English. As a native speaker from Inis Mór, the novelist and critic Breandán Ó hEithir is close to Ó Cadhain in background and published an article (1977) in homage of *Cré na Cille.* Ó Tuairisc published *The Road to Brightcity* (1981), a translation of nine stories by Ó Cadhain. Following Ó Cadhain's lead, these novelists were determined to write about Ireland, including the life of the city as well as the countryside, in a distinctly modern way. Their versatility is also impressive—Ó Tuairisc and Ó Súilleabháin (who were schoolteachers as well as writers) both wrote a number of plays and other works, and Ó hEithir is perhaps best known as a regular contributor to the *Irish Times.*

Ó Tuairisc and Ó Súilleabháin were both bilingual writers whose first language was English. Like several others of their generation, they reflect the increase of bilingualism in Ireland; we begin to see more writers publishing in both English and Irish. Richard Power, for example, whose chief achievement was a novel in English treated a bit later in this chapter, *The Hungry Grass,* also published a novel in Irish set in Galway and the Aran Islands, *Úll i mBárr an Ghéagáin (Apple on the Treetop)* (1958). Ó Tuairisc (1919–82), whose given name was Eugene Watters, published three novels in Irish— interestingly, they were his more serious works—and two rather more lightweight efforts in English. Like two novel- ists who had written novels about Northern Ireland, Tarlach Ó hUid (see O'Leary 1982) in *An Dá Thrá* (The two strands) (1952) and Séamas Ó Néill in *Máire Nic Artáin* (1959), Ó Tuairisc demonstrated an interest in politics and history. His first novel, *L'Attaque* (1962), was perhaps his best; tightly written and focused on the impact upon the Irish peasantry brought to bear by the French soldiers and Anglo-Irish republicans who joined them in the May rising of 1798, this novel rivals Plunkett's *Strumpet City* as the best historical novel of the period. Its chief focus is the consciousness of the reluctant peasant rebel Máirtín Caomhánach and it shows the influence of the ancient Irish epic the *Táin* and Tolstoy's *War and Peace* (Cahalan 1983, 169–75). Like several of the novelists in English already considered, Ó Tuairisc demonstrated an increasing interest in experiment. His second novel, *Dé Luain* (Monday) (1966), employs several interwoven streams of consciousness "designed to commemorate the 50th anniversary of 1916, and deals with the opening hours of the Revolution in Dublin, minute by minute, from midnight Easter Sunday to noon on Monday" (Ó Tuairisc 1981). Toward the end of his life Ó Tuairisc reflected that "though it won the Butler Prize, it has never been as popular with readers as *L'Attaque;* it is too complex, having dozens of perception centres in the weave of it" (1981). We have repeatedly noted such an interwoven quality to be typical of the Irish novel. Máirín Nic Eoin adds concerning the history in *Dé Luain* that "it is interesting in particular the emphasis Ó Tuairisc places on the role of the Citizen Army, a group whose part in the Rising, in contrast to that of the Volunteers, had been underestimated by historians and largely ignored" (1985). Ó Tuairisc's last novel, *An Lomnochtán* (The naked person) (1977), an autobiographical bildungsroman focused on his childhood in the 1920s, was originally begun in English around 1962 and then completed in Irish after 1974, in an experimental style influenced by both Ó Cadhain and Joyce (Nic Eoin 1985).

Ó Suilleabháin (1932–85) also moved from realism to experimentalism. Cathal Ó Háinle notes that "his first novel, *Dianmhuilte Dé* (The zealous mills of God) (1964), is traditional enough in diction and in subject matter. His second, *Caoin Tú Féin* (Keen for yourself) (1967), is a new beginning, for it and his third novel, *An Uain Bheo* (The moment of decision) (1968), rely heavily on the stream-of-consciousness technique and consequently make much use of a fragmented diction which is full of incomplete sentences and verbal

echoes" (1984, 75–76). Ó Súilleabháin's typical protagonist
is modern existential man, alone. Ian Ó Murchú in *Caoin Tú
Féin*, for example, is a hung-over schoolteacher who wonders
why his wife has just left and what his whole life means;
Louis Stein in *An Uain Bheo* is a Jew who experiences the
isolation of a Leopold Bloom and loses the woman he loves
in a car accident. Ó Súilleabháin's style, like his themes, is
bold but uneven, since "while the interior monologue technique enables him to portray admirably the fragmentariness
of life, his stylistic tricks—hyperbole, individualized syntax,
use of capitals and parentheses—tend to distract the reader"
(Quinn 1983, 170). Most prolific among novelists in Irish, Ó
Súilleabháin left behind five unpublished novels at the time
of his death in 1985 that his publishers, Coiscéim, are as of
this date in the process of bringing out. At this writing
Ciontach [Guilty] (1983a), *Aistear* [Journey] (1983b), and *Saighdiúir gan Chlaíomh* [Soldier without a sword] (1985) have
appeared. *Ciontach* was written in the form of a jail journal
and dedicated to its model, the author's republican uncle,
Diarmaid Ó Drisceoil. *Aistear* focuses on the experiences of
several ordinary people in the moments surrounding death.
Saighdiúir gan Chlaíomh is a fictionalized biography of the
Irish religious leader Edmund Ignatius Rice. Ó Súilleabháin's
reputation as a novelist is growing (O'Leary 1984), while
"for a more profound exploration of the questions that dominated Ó Súilleabháin's creative life we must await the publication of the other novels he left behind" (O'Leary 1986b,
18). His career illustrates both the challenges of trying to
write in Irish but also his steadfast determination to do so
(Ó Murchu 1984).

Ó hEithir (b. 1930), a nephew of Liam O'Flaherty, published in 1976 a novel that received perhaps more attention
than any other novel in Irish since Ó Cadhain: *Lig Sinn i
gCathú (Lead Us Into Temptation)*. A bildungsroman in the
tradition of *Portrait*, this novel deliberately confounds Irish
Catholic morality in a manner summed up by its title. The
protagonist, Martin Melody, a university student in "Bally-
castle" (Galway), has to steer a middle course between his
mother and his grasping, puritanical brother the priest, on
the one hand, and the forces of complete dissolution em-

bodied in his drinking companion Billy O'Grady, on the other hand. After making love to an uninhibited barmaid, Stella Walsh—*Lig Sinn i gCathú* is one of the few novels in Irish to treat sex so graphically and so positively—Martin flees Galway for Dublin and America in the company of Larry de Lacy, the rebel, following in the footsteps of George Moore's Oliver Gogarty and Joyce's Stephen Dedalus. The names of Ó hEithir's characters reflect his frank acceptance of bilingualism, involving the incursion of English into spoken and written Irish. Proinsias MacCana feels that "he has succeeded better than any other—including Máirtín Ó Cadhain—in adapting the idiom and rhythm of traditional Irish speech to the tempo of modern urban and industrial society" (1980, 61). Since 1976 Ó hEithir, like Flann O'Brien/Myles na Gopaleen earlier, has mostly devoted himself to his columns in the *Irish Times*.

While the production of novels in Irish runs far behind that of Irish novels in English—or, for that matter, behind that of poetry in Irish—the appearance in recent years of several other novels by other writers provides some indication that the novel in Irish may be experiencing a modest renaissance (Nic Eoin 1984). Like Ó hEithir an author of an article on *Cré na Cille,* Breandán Ó Doibhlin focused *An Branar Gan Cur* (The untilled field) (1979) on a train journey from Dublin to Derry by a young university lecturer whose despairing thoughts about Ireland provide us with "more a dissertation than a novel" (Quinn 1983, 170). Similarly, *Deoraithe* (Exiles) (1986) by Dónal MacAmhlaigh, already well known among Gaelic readers as the "Irish navvy in London" author of *Dialann Deorai* (Diary of an exile) (1960), examines the lives of three people waiting in a Galway pub for their train to Dublin. This basic conceit had been put forth many years earlier by Frank O'Connor in his play *In the Train* (1937). Fabulist, futurist novels in Irish have been published by Mícheál Ó Brolacháin in *Pax Dei* (1985), an Orwellian vision of a bleak postindustrial future, and by Annraoi de Paor in *Buan ar Buairt* (Forever vexed) (1985), a quirky study of an Irish academic. Indeed, "there has been a marked increase in the number and diversity of Gaelic novels over the past few years (O'Leary 1985).

Women Novelists: Edna O'Brien, Janet McNeill, Iris Murdoch, Eilís Dillon, Julia O'Faolain, and Jennifer Johnston

Also on the rise in recent years have been Irish novels by women, in part encouraged by the example of earlier women novelists, by feminist presses such as Arlen House in Dublin and Virago in London, and by the women's movement. The series of notable women novelists has expanded beyond the traditional Ascendancy background to include a writer like Edna O'Brien, a pioneer among contemporary women novelists, who comes from a small farm in County Clare. Irish women novelists continue to focus their work in realist modes, although O'Brien has attempted more experimental points of view in her more recent novels. They have sought to answer the question of what life is like in Ireland for women; indeed, the novels of O'Brien, Julia O'Faolain, Jennifer Johnston, and other contemporary women writers invite discussion together here because of their novels' common attention to the experiences of women. It should be noted that further critical comparison is needed between their novels and those of their female predecessors from Edgeworth to Lavin as well as those of male writers, from George Moore to John McGahern, who have devoted special attention to female protagonists.

Edna O'Brien (b. 1930) is the first and best known female novelist of the period—rivalled in the scope of her international fame perhaps only by Brian Moore, among Irish novelists of either gender. The appearance of her first novel, *The Country Girls* (1960), and its sequels, *The Lonely Girl* (1962) and *Girls in Their Married Bliss* (1964), created quite a stir because of their frank treatment of female sexual experience. The subject of these novels was located in previously uncharted fictional territory: the struggles, sexual and otherwise, of two typical young girls from County Clare, the earnest Kate and the racy Baba, who make their way together from a rural Catholic boarding school to jobs and flats in Dublin, and then, as young women, into unsuccessful marriages in London. O'Brien herself had followed the way of the James Joyces and the Brian Moores, beginning *The Country Girls* shortly after moving abroad in 1959.

Among Irish women novelists, O'Brien was preceded only by Molly Keane in her attention to the sexual experiences of young women, and only by Maura Laverty in her vivid portraits of a lower-middle-class girlhood in rural and small-town Ireland; O'Brien's graphic combination of these features met with a 1960s paperback readership in such a way as to guarantee that O'Brien would not suffer the obscurity that was the fate of Keane and Laverty, at least until very recently. O'Brien "survived not only the literary spite and backbiting of Dublin but an unhappy marriage, childbearing, mother-hood and uprootedness as well to become, by her thirty-fourth year, that rare thing, a writer earning a living by her craft," presenting us with "the paradox of the strong, in-dependent woman writing [about] women as victims" (Darcy O'Brien 1982, 183). As an Irish bildungsroman, *The Country Girls* reveals secrets found nowhere in *Portrait* or other such novels. In O'Brien's beloved elm grove "Baba and I sat there and shared secrets, and once we took off our knickers in there and tickled one another. The greatest secret of all" (10–11). At the same time, this novel cites Kate's love for Joyce's *Dubliners* and contains a passage modelled on the end of "The Dead" (Senn 1966, 222). Similarly, we learn in *The Lonely Girl* that Kate, now assailed by wolf-like older men in Dublin, appropriately enough reads James Stephens's *The Charwoman's Daughter* with sympathetic understanding.

O'Brien's character types—the cruel father, the victimized mother, lustful but ineffectual men—recur throughout her fiction. O'Brien herself has referred to Baba as her "alter-ego" (quoted in Popot 1976, 261):

Realizing that the earlier [ancient Irish] heroines were bawdy and the later [modern literary] ones lyrical I decided to have two, one who would conform to both my own and my country's view of what an Irish woman should be and one who would undermine every piece of protocol and religion and hypocrisy that there was. . . . Kate was looking for love. Baba was looking for money. Kate was timid, yearning and elegiac. Baba took up the cudgel against life and married an Irish builder who was as likely to clout her

as to do anything else. . . . Coming back to them I knew that
Baba's asperity had to prevail. Heroines don't have to be good
anymore, because more women are writing fiction and are eager
to express the more volatile part of themselves; equally they are
less beholden to men. (Edna O'Brien 1986, 13)

O'Brien wrote her "Country Girls Trilogy," recently repub-
lished (1986) as such, well before the rise of the contemporary
women's movement, "and the bravery of the accomplishment
ought not to be slighted (Darcy O'Brien 1982, 183).

O'Brien's departure in *Girls in Their Married Bliss* from the
autobiographical Kate as first-person narrator, replacing her
with the ribald voice of Baba, marked the beginning of a
stylistic experimentalism that has continued in her subsequent
novels and links the development of her work to that of
Kiely, Moore, McGahern, Trevor, Plunkett, Ó Tuairisc, and
Ó Súilleabháin. *Night* (1972), for example, is the Molly
Bloom–like monologue of Mary Hooligan, a middle-aged
woman who recalls her life. *A Pagan Place* (1970) returns to
the landscape and period of *The Country Girls*, but as described by a narrator who tells her own story in the second
person—the detached "you" also found in parts of Mc-
Gahern's *The Dark*, with which this novel and *The Country
Girls* could be compared on other scores as well. Several of
O'Brien's recent novels are set outside of Ireland, in London
or on the Riviera. Critics are divided as to the merits of
O'Brien's novels after "The Country Girls" trilogy, most of
which focus on a woman's inability to find happiness and
love either within marriage or outside of it; one of them is
married to a man actually named "Herod." For example,
one critic feels that O'Brien's books have become "a tedious
sojourn in decadence and despair" (Snow 1979, 83), whereas
another believes that "together with an evolving style, her
work shows an evolving vision of life" (Popot 1976, 257).
While *Night* has its good moments, when considering
O'Brien's more recent novels one has to agree that "none
of these has the surefootedness as when she is writing about
home" (McMahon 1985, 153). *A Pagan Place*, for example,
omits direct dialogue altogether—one of the chief strengths
of *The Country Girls* as contained in some of the unforgettable

exchanges of Kate and Baba. Recently other women such as Jennifer Johnston and Julia O'Faolain have been publishing better novels than O'Brien, but she remains a pioneer among them for her work in the early 1960s.

A writer who could not be much more remote in background from O'Brien is Janet McNeill (b. 1907), who grew up and lived in upper-class Protestant Belfast and nearby Lisburn, and wrote about that very different world. Yet McNeill's most notable Irish novel, *The Maiden Dinosaur* (1964), dealt around the same time with O'Brien's theme of sexual frustration, from the perspective of a woman who was sexually abused by her father and whose later interactions with men are marked by that experience. This protagonist is joined by other pained women characters, including one who thinks concerning her husband that "Justin hadn't had the baby, the long months, the fright of a tightening body, skin stretched and shiny and navel distended like a bubble, the pain or the drugging weakness, like a kitten washed up on the beach. He thought the baby was a parcel you could dump with a stranger until you were ready to collect it, not a piece of you torn away" (73). The economic world of genteel McNeill's women is very different from that of O'Brien's working-class women, but they also experience oppression by men.

Irish historical novels have in recent years been published by two women who provide female perspectives counterbalancing the traditionally male focus of that subgenre: Iris Murdoch (b. 1919) and Eilís Dillon (b. 1920). Like Elizabeth Bowen, Murdoch has lived most of her life in England and is much better known as an English novelist; Dillon made her name as an author of children's books. The two are very different in background—Murdoch from the Protestant Ascendancy, Dillon of Catholic, nationalist origins—but from Murdoch's *The Red and the Green* (1965) and Dillon's *Across the Bitter Sea* (1973) and *Blood Relations* (1977) we emerge with a very different view of modern Irish history than that found in Irish historical novels written by men. Murdoch's and Dillon's women wait at home, longing for a relationship that men, caught up in politics and rebellion, are unable or unwilling to give them (Cahalan 1983, 164–69, 190–95).

Murdoch goes so far as to portray her 1916 rebel, Pat Dumay, as a latent homosexual and misogynist, and in *Blood Relations* Dillon's Molly Gould is plagued by the knowledge that "she was expected to live through those days as if nothing special were happening, as if it were possible to bear them like a lady . . . as if she had no more to lose than anyone else, as if her whole life were not in the balance" (25). What good is romantic rebellion to the woman left behind?

Julia O'Faolain (b. 1932) has presented similarly pungent portraits of Irish history and politics from a woman's point of view in *No Country for Young Men* (1980). She is also author of an irreverent first novel set in Paris, *Godded and Codded* (1970), the nonfiction study *Not in God's Image: Women in History from the Greeks to the Victorians* (1973), and a novel about women living in a convent in ancient Gaul, *Women in the Wall* (1975). *No Country for Young Men* (whose title is obviously a biting comment on Yeats's already ironic line about Ireland being "no country for old men") marvellously merges a present-day story with its 1920s backgrounds. In the latter novel James Duffy, an Irish-American academic, comes to Ireland to make a propaganda film for the IRA front organization "Banned Aid" (Noraid). He falls in love with Grainne O'Malley, but Grainne is already burdened with an alcoholic, impotent husband and a lecherous, interfering cousin whose IRA lackey almost inevitably murders Duffy. As Ann Weeks points out, O'Faolain's plot is a retelling of the old Diarmuid and Gráinne myth—in which Fionn kills Diarmuid after he runs off with Gráinne, with Gráinne consenting to returning to live with the Fianna for the sake of her children—but "Grace O'Malley, however, does not capitulate in order to restore the 'order' derived from male principles; in this, O'Faolain's novel proves more optimistic than the controlling myth" (1986, 91). Weeks adds that O'Faolain's women characters are linked to the common people of Ireland, whom the male rebels view as "clay" to be molded to their purposes (92). The victimized Judith Clancy's memory is compared to a bog. O'Faolain thus provides a fresh feminist twist to the venerable tradition personifying the land of Ireland as a *sean bhean bhocht*, a poor old woman.

Also a daughter of a noted literary father (the playwright Denis Johnston), Jennifer Johnston (b. 1930) has published eight novels to date, establishing herself as the most impressive contemporary female Irish novelist. She specializes in short, lucid narratives marked by shifting points of view and a tendency toward continuous narration rather than sharply defined chapter divisions. More persistently than Aidan Higgins and John Banville, Johnston has adapted Big House settings and stories to her own ends, although she has also added to her range the working-class world of Derry in *Shadows on Our Skin* (1977) and small-town settings in *The Old Jest* (1979) and *The Railway Station Man* (1984). Her early novels reveal that surrounded by a violent and cruel society, unconventional male relationships are as doomed as those of women. In *The Captains and the Kings* (1972), the old Ascendancy widower Charles Prendergast, living alone in the significantly named Kill House, befriends a working-class Catholic boy, Diarmuid Toorish, but the boy's ignorant parents and Prendergast's own gardener conspire to destroy the friendship, and at the end of the novel Diarmuid is sent away to school and Charles dies. Here the Catholic working class appears villainous.

As if to balance this indictment, Johnston points her finger at evil upper-class characters in *How Many Miles to Babylon?* (1974) while telling an otherwise similar story. Despite the opposition of his hateful Ascendancy mother, Alexander Moore forms a fast friendship with Jerry Crowe, son of nearby peasants, and Alex and Jerry go off to World War I together. There, however, Alex is made an officer and prohibited from fraternizing with Jerry, a private. After Jerry goes AWOL in search of his father, who is missing in action, he is caught and condemned to death, and a maniacal English commanding officer orders Alex to direct Jerry's firing squad the following morning or face it himself. Alex elects a third option of his own—telling Jerry nothing of the choice he faces, Alex gets him pleasantly drunk, shoots him in the head at close range, and then awaits his own execution. Both of these novels are dominated by male characters, but as Shari Benstock points out, "this world is not masculine, not open, accessible, social, a world of action, but rather specifically feminine: closed, suffocated, lonely, and inward-looking." Benstock adds, "The 'woman's novel' predicates itself on the notion that social separateness is an *a priori* condition of the woman in contemporary society. Johnston's work seems to suggest that such exclusive status is not necessarily peculiar to women" (1982, 216).

Interestingly, all of Johnston's six other novels to date show how society as well as cultural and age differences render male-female love relationships difficult or impossible. In Johnston's second published but first written novel, *The Gates* (1973), Minnie McMahon lives amicably with her Uncle Prionnsias in their decaying ancestral home, but they get robbed by her boyfriend. Johnston is at her best when writing about an adolescent and an older surrogate father. In *The Old Jest*, eighteen-year-old Nancy Gulliver befriends a kind, mysterious older man whom she finds in the hut that she has fixed up near her home—and then witnesses his shooting at the end of the novel, the victim of British Black-and-Tan soldiers. In Johnston's most recent novel, *Fool's Sanctuary* (1987), Miranda Martin loses her IRA lover to IRA gunmen after he tips off Miranda's brother about an IRA plot to kill him. Having examined the older Irish Republican tradition in these two novels, in *Shadows on our Skins* and *The Railway Station Man* Johnston castigates the contemporary IRA. In the former novel young Joe Logan falls in love in Derry with Kathleen, an older schoolteacher, but she is engaged to a British soldier, gets beaten by some of the IRA cohorts of Joe's older brother, and leaves Derry for her home back in southern Ireland. Johnston, who was born in Dublin but now lives in Derry, clearly aimed to move beyond her typical southern Big House setting in this novel. In *The Railway Station Man*, middle-aged, widowed Helen Cuffe falls in love with Roger Hawthorne, a gentle Englishman devoted to restoring the town's railway station, but loses both Roger and her son in an IRA bombing. A painter, Helen is left only with the friendship of Damian, a young man whom she had painted on the beach who, like Roger and herself, rejects the IRA's violence. Less political and even bleaker is *The Christmas Tree* (1982), focused on the fading consciousness of Constance Keating, who is dying of cancer, thereby recalling both McGahern's *The Barracks* and O'Brien's *Night*. As Brian Donnelly notes, "Johnston portrays the sharp divisions that existed between the Ascendancy and the native Irish stock and, in doing so, she has succeeded in conveying a sense of poignant regret at the mutual loss which this failure of integration involved for the Irish nation as a whole" (1975, 137). She joins Maria Edgeworth, Sydney Owenson, Somerville and Ross, Elizabeth Bowen, and Molly Keane as the most impressive recent descendant of the impressive tradition of women Big House novelists—all of whom have found the Big House to be a particularly powerful and malleable symbol of alienation and isolation, merging the domestic and the psychological realms (see O'Toole 1985).

An interesting *Catholic* Big House novel has recently been published by Val Mulkerns (b. 1925). *The Summerhouse* (1984) blends five different narrators to expose the nasty interactions of a genteel family, suggesting that the family itself, not history, is to blame for the failure of this Big House. One of them builds a model summerhouse in their kitchen, and then, appropriately enough, finds that it will not fit through the door and must remain stuck indoors. Like Molly Keane, Mulkerns, who served as an assistant editor on *The Bell* in the early 1950s, published her first novel decades ago and has only recently reemerged after a long hiatus. Her novel *Very Like a Whale* (1986) is almost as despairing about middle-class Dublin life as *The Summerhouse* is about the life of the Catholic gentry, but more convincing and realistic about a world she knows better and tinged in the end by a gentle mood of acceptance.

The recent appearance of several other popular women novelists suggests that another Edna O'Brien or Jennifer Johnston may soon emerge. Clare Boylan's *Holy Pictures* (1983), a racy novel of Irish girlhood that recalls O'Brien's *The Country Girls*, was a success, as have been Maeve Binchy's *Light a Penny Candle* (1982) and *Echoes* (1985). The most celebrated recent first novel by an Irishwoman is Mary Leland's *The Killeen* (1985), focused on the lives of two women during the political turmoil of the 1930s, culminating in one of their children's horrible death and shameful burial in the *killeen,* a graveyard for unbaptized children. Like Éilis Dillon and Jennifer Johnston, Leland shows how women and children have suffered as victims of the romanticized male Irish political struggles of the past and present.

Conventional Realists: Michael Farrell, Walter Macken, Sam Hanna Bell, Anthony C. West, John Broderick, Richard Power, Thomas Kilroy, and Anthony Cronin

I have traced earlier in this chapter and in my previous chapter the recent fictional experimentalism of Francis Stuart, Sean O'Faolain, Benedict Kiely, Brian Moore, John McGahern, Aidan Higgins, John Banville, Diarmuid Ó Súilleabháin, Edna O'Brien, and a few others. It must be emphasized, though, that a much larger majority of contemporary Irish novelists have continued writing in a more traditional, realist vein— essentially the often socially and politically critical mode of 1920–55 as examined in chapter 5—almost as if the later Joyce and Beckett never existed. There is still much that Irish novelists want to say in a realist way about their country and its people, and since 1960 the publishers and readership for this kind of fiction have been more numerous and more encouraging for writers than ever before. Just as the romantic Irish Literary Revival led by Yeats came a century after the English one led by Wordsworth and Coleridge, it is as if realist Irish novelists are determined to enjoy a belated success denied to many of their predecessors in earlier periods. Most of the conventional contemporary realist novelists do not measure up in their fiction to Brian Moore, John McGahern, the other novelists surveyed in the first section of this chapter, or Jennifer Johnston. Nonetheless, the eight novelists surveyed in the next few pages—before I turn at the end of this chapter to four mostly more experimental novelists who have emerged only within the last few years—have published a variety of fine works over the past three decades. There are many other lesser contemporary realists who must be excluded from my survey. I should also remind the reader that with the exception of Edna O'Brien's *Night,* all of the novels of the women writers surveyed in my last section also fall within the realist mode.

Michael Farrell (1899–1962) well illustrates the persistence of realism. As one critic notes concerning his life's work, the long, posthumously published novel *Thy Tears Might Cease* (1963), "even though it is marvelously readable and accurate social history, the book owes nothing to modern fiction and could almost have been published not in 1963, but in 1863 by a second cousin of the Brontes" (Callaghan 1980, 234). As a bildungsroman and roman à clef examining the growth from boyhood to manhood of Martin Matthew Reilly during the placid, then turbulent 1910–20 decade, with particular attention to the Easter Rising as a turning point, this novel recalls Eimar O'Duffy's *The Wasted Island*. It is one of several notable bildungsromans that appeared during the 1960s— including McGahern's *The Dark*, Moore's *The Emperor of Ice-Cream*, O'Brien's trilogy, and Anthony C. West's *The Ferret Fancier*—all of which, Denis Cotter argues (1982), appear to have been involved in reinventing the fictional wheel rather than fully conscious of writing in a specific subgeneric tradition including O'Duffy, Joyce, and all the other earlier "Irish novels of the developing self." These novels were quite popular, *Thy Tears Might Cease* becoming something of a best-seller.

One of the most popular realists, one who published a long string of Macmillan/Pan best-sellers, was Walter Macken (1915–67). Also a playwright, actor, and leader of the Tai- bhdhearc (the Irish language theatre in Galway), Macken reached perhaps his widest audience with his trilogy of historical novels, *Seek the Fair Land* (1959), *The Silent People* (1962), and *The Scorching Wind* (1964), focused respectively on the adventures of romantic heroes during the Cromwellian reign of terror, the Great Hunger, and the Civil War. Macken knew Irish but chose to write his novels in a "cosmopolitan" English style. His ethos in his historical trilogy is Catholic and nationalist, ultimately championing his heroic protago- nists' discovery of peace beyond the violent events of history (Cahalan 1983, 157–64). Macken published a total of eleven novels between 1949 and 1971. Perhaps his best are the early *Rain on the Wind* (1950) and *The Bogman* (1952), both of which concern the struggles of a young Galwayman (a fisherman, a farmer) to establish an identity and find love despite the worst machinations of his relatives and the surrounding society. The typical Macken hero is initially dispossessed but ultimately redeemed. Readers found his vivid ethnographic details about life around Galway and his happy endings particularly appealing.

Sam Hanna Bell (b. 1909), Anthony C. West (b. 1910), and John Broderick (b. 1927) also focused on the enclosed societal worlds of rural and small-town places even more obscure than Macken's Galway, but have been less optimistic about the availability of clear solutions within those worlds. Difficult sexual relationships are portrayed very graphically by these writers. Sex is as tortured in Bell's Protestant County Down and West's Protestant County Cavan as it is in Broderick's Catholic Athlone, County Westmeath—suggesting that northern Protestant and southern Catholic attitudes towards sex may not be so far apart as public events and opinions in Ireland often suggest. Bell and West have both been critically neglected because they fall outside the "mainstream" of Catholic fiction from Joyce to Brian Moore, but their best novels are very fine indeed and contain many more similarities than differences with those of their Catholic contemporaries. At the same time, their clearest predecessors are northern Protestant novelists from earlier in the century; like Shan Bullock, Bell concerns himself in his best novel with the social and sexual life of the Protestant farmlands, and like Forrest Reid, West develops a bildungsroman focused on the consciousness of a young Protestant boy, one dominated by poetic and sexual fantasies.

Bell's *December Bride* (1951) tells the story of a ménage-à-trois between Sarah Gomartin and the brothers Hamilton and Frank Echlin. Initially a servant on their farm, Sarah lives with both brothers, has a child, and ends up marrying one of them only to legitimize her daughter's marriage. Such a story appears shocking and aberrant but was in fact modelled on an actual case (McMahon 1985, 148), "for in rural Irish areas such naive *ménages-à-trois* and *ad hoc* families, such scant regard for the sanctions of city law upon sexual and parental relations, are to be found" (Foster 1974, 54).

John Wilson Foster claims that Sarah "creates bad blood between the Echlins and their neighbours and . . . brings upon the Echlins something akin to a curse or blight" (1974, 54), but this seems an overly harsh verdict concerning her status in the novel and a misreading of Bell's intent. Rather, Sarah Gomartin emerges as a strong, courageous, and certainly persevering woman who lifts herself from servant to leader on the Echlin farm and flouts the will of the hypocritical minister and townspeople; Bell's presentation of the arrangement seems ironic and accepting rather than negative. He has published two other novels—*The Hollow Ball* (1961), about a Belfast footballer; and *A Man Flourishing* (1973), a historical novel about the 1798 northern Protestant rebels— but neither is as subtle and rewarding as *December Bride*.

West is similarly known for one novel, *The Ferret Fancier* (1963). It focuses on a boy's dual, overlapping pastimes: his husbanding of ferrets that are used to kill rabbits for sport and profit, and his fantasies about sex. He explicitly links the two: "The whole operation became in his mind like a steamy orgy as the hunters expressed their excited satisfaction by way of a running sexual commentary, every hole a female one and every tuft of moss a tuft of pubic hair, the ferret a kind of cock which they shoved into the holes to rape the waiting rabbits: a new kind of winey world, life short cruel and merry as possible" (38). To our relief, West's youthful protagonist finally withdraws from his dual quest, stumbling on toward some other, unknown destiny.

Sex is even seedier in the novels of John Broderick. His eleven novels are characterized by an ongoing attack on the mores of midland Ireland; they show talent but too often lapse into caricature at the service of overt didacticism. If Bell can be linked to Bullock and West to Reid, then Broderick's fictional father from earlier in the century is Brinsley MacNamara. Broderick is concerned with "the states of unfreedom in a society of squinting windows," seeing himself as a would-be Irish Balzac, admitting that his early novels are too negative and voicing "his own hope of being able to move from negativity to a novel 'written with love' " (Gallagher 1976, 235–36). In a no-holds-barred attempt to plunge beneath the quiet behavioral surface of his hometown of Athlone, Broderick's books are populated by ruthless, whore-like women, by weak, often homosexual men, and by hypocritical priests. *The Pilgrimage* (1961), for example, is a cynical, vacuous revision of Lawrence's *Lady Chatterley's Lover* in which Julia Glynn lives with her crippled husband but pursues affairs first with the family doctor and then with their bizarre young houseservant. Broderick is at his narrative worst when he informs us in its one-sentence final chapter that Julia's crippled, homosexual husband has been cured at Lourdes; here and too frequently elsewhere, his novels take on misogynist and gratuitous airs. As Michael Gallagher writes, whereas in Broderick's early novels "his plots point to a moment when his central character faces the essential emptiness of life with no illusions left, or when the reader is made to experience the ironic fragility of home-made shelters against truth," in several subsequent novels "these moments are not so marked" and "the pattern of disillusionment continues but not for the central characters" (1976, 238–39).

The protagonist of *The Waking of Willie Ryan* (1965) had a homosexual love affair and was committed to an institution by his sister-in-law and the parish priest, but returns to quietly vanquish his foes in his own way, the novel's title perhaps reflecting (in the manner of *Finnegans Wake*) his personal reawakening as well as his eventual death. This novel's only predecessor as a portrait of an Irish homosexual is Molly Keane's less sympathetic *Devoted Ladies* (1934). A fairly positive homosexual relationship is also described in *The Trial of Father Dillingham* (1982), which contains Broderick's perhaps most hopeful ending: Jim Dillingham learns that he was not expelled from the priesthood as he had thought, and resolves to embark on social service in South America with his friend the retiring bishop. Apparently attempting here the novel "written with love" that he earlier said he longed for, Broderick suggests that some kind of redemption might be available even in the absence of illusion and in the midst of dingy reality.

The Trial of Father Dillingham can be seen as a successor to several better novels about Irish priests that have appeared in recent years, following in their turn in the path of much earlier novels such as John Banim's *The Nowlans,* George Moore's *The Lake,* and Gerald O'Donovan's *Father Ralph.* These novels include James Plunkett's previously mentioned *Strumpet City*—two of whose best developed characters are the puritanical, troubled Father O'Connor and the visionary, despairing Father Giffley—Richard Power's *The Hungry Grass* (1969), published in the same year, and Thomas Kilroy's *The Big Chapel* (1971). Power (1928–70), whose death at the age of forty-two cut short a very promising career, published a novel in English (*The Land of Youth,* 1964) as well as the aforementioned one in Irish about life on the Aran Islands, but *The Hungry Grass* is the one by which he will be remembered. It begins by describing the death of Father Tom Conroy, who by all public accounts has led an uneventful, mediocre life—and shows via extended flashbacks that his life was difficult but anything but mediocre. "The 'hungry grass' of the title alludes to the *féar gortach* of oral tradition that causes extreme hunger in whoever treads on it" (MacKillop 1983, 86). We learn that in his last days Conroy sought to reconcile himself with his senile mother, who never really loved him, and with the rest of his family, and that he wished to do something for the suffering small farmers of his parish. He failed in both aims, but his final days, as brilliantly probed by Power's narrative, are filled with a nobility all their own. James MacKillop views *The Hungry Grass* as "a meditation on a devitalized rural society two generations after republican revolution" (1983, 57), while Terence Brown insists that Power's focus is "familial" rather than public, political, or social (1976, 246, 250). The depth of the novel is underscored by the fact that it can easily bear both of these contrasting readings. Similarly fusing the personal and public aspects of a priest's career is Kilroy's *The Big Chapel,* which examines the role of Father William Lannigan during the same ecclesiastic controversies of the 1870s in the town of Callan, County Kilkenny, that had also provided the subject of Francis MacManus's *The Greatest of These.* Like Power's priest, Kilroy's is troubled by the gap between what he intends to do and what he is actually able to do. In his sole published novel to date, Kilroy (b. 1934) examines "the relation between intention and act, the ironic contrast between man's private aspirations and the public gestures that result from those aspirations" (Cosgrove 1976, 299), suggesting that therefore "the past is a confused and confusing entity, unreliable as memory, as subject to variation as fiction" (Harmon 1973, 18).

Like Kilroy and Benedict Kiely, Anthony Cronin (b. 1926) is as well known in Ireland as a critic as he is as a novelist. A regular columnist for the *Irish Times,* Cronin has published a survey of Irish writers (1982) and a gritty memoir of his dissolute days of the 1950s in the company of Brendan Behan, Patrick Kavanagh, J. P. Donleavy, and John Ryan, *Dead as Doornails* (1976). Those days are also the subject of his best novel to date, *The Life of Riley* (1964), a picaresque, rather comic account of one Patrick Riley's downward progression from itinerant jobs in Dublin to total lethargy in England. While serving as associate editor on the *Trumpet,* Riley is ill advised by its Marxist editor, Prunshios Mc-Gonaghy (obviously modelled on Peadar O'Donnell), to visit a dosshouse in England in order to fully understand "the dialoctic [sic] process" (110). Riley follows this instruction all too literally. Cronin maintains his picaresque vision in *Identity Papers* (1979), in which the reputed grandson of the infamous nineteenth-century forger Richard Pigott sets about repeating Pigott's crimes, but then learns that he is not Pigott's descendant after all and resumes his own life more hopefully. Here Cronin appears to be close to the neo-Gothic mode of the recently emergent novelist Patrick McGinley.

Recent Novelists: Bernard MacClaverty, Neil Jordan, Desmond Hogan, and Patrick McGinley

The last few years have been marked by the appearance of a number of promising new novelists, including the novelists in Irish and the women novelists mentioned earlier. Finally here I wish to mention four others: Bernard Mac-Laverty (b. 1942), Neil Jordan (b. 1951), Desmond Hogan (b. 1951), and Patrick McGinley (b. 1937). So far MacLaverty is the best known internationally among them because of the popular success of his novel *Cal* (1983) in both its book and film versions. Born in Belfast and now living in Scotland, MacLaverty focuses in both of his very readable if uneven novels on complex personal responsibilities for a death. In *Lamb* (1980), the protagonist is a monk who flees a nasty northern Irish institution for wayward boys accompanied by an epileptic adolescent boy whom he wishes he could adopt. These two sacrificial lambs—the protagonist's name is Michael Lamb and the boy's name is Owen, which we are reminded (143) means "lamb" in Irish—enact a distorted version of the story of Abraham and Isaac, when Michael, named in the press as Owen's kidnapper, treats him to a few days of happiness and then, convinced that he cannot spare him many years of misery and epilepsy either by returning him to the institution or futilely attempting to adopt him, tragically kills him. In *Cal* (1983) the protagonist is a young northern Catholic who seeks to atone for his role as driver of the car in the IRA shooting of the husband of a beautiful young woman, with whom he ends up in an affair before she learns of his guilt and he is taken away, "grateful at last that someone was going to beat him within an inch of his life" (170).

MacLaverty's plots may strain our credulity, but they are still presented within the realist mode. The narratives of Jordan, Hogan, and McGinley are much more experimental. In their novels Jordan and Hogan inspect past realities through refracted mirrors. Jordan was a co-founder of the Irish Writers' Cooperative in 1974; since the publication of his second novel, *The Dream of a Beast*, in 1983, he has turned to film-making. His novels are themselves rather cinematic. *The Past* (1980) examines fairly traditional materials—the story of characters living through the days of the Abbey Theatre and the birth of the Irish Republic—but in a thoroughly nontraditional way. The narrator presents his fantasies about the lives of his ancestors, moving from confusion to hypothesis to doubt, finally implying that he can be sure of neither who his father is nor who he himself is. He can look at the photographs and other emblems of the past but never clearly solve them. Like Hogan and McGinley, Jordan constantly plays with style, point of view, identity, and sexual conven-

tion. In their novels sex is as likely as not to be homosexual
or incestuous. In Hogan's *The Ikon Maker* (1976), a mother
suspects that her son's school friend committed suicide because her son refused to have sex with him. She tracks her
son to London where she finds both his female and male
lovers, but she never sees him again. In *The Leaves on Grey*
(1980) Hogan's young characters experience everything from
a sexual threesome to monasticism. As in Jordan, a central
theme in Hogan's novels is the attraction but futility of trying
to piece together the fragments of the past. His most recent
novel, *A Curious Street* (1984), spins an interesting variation
on the conceit of the indefinitely receding mirror-images: here
the novelist presents a narrator who tells us about a novelist
writing a strangely romantic, Cromwellian historical novel
with a protagonist who tends to overlap with everybody
else. Faced with such a nightmare of history and narrative,
Hogan seems to suggest, neither novelist nor reader can
expect any solutions. The past merges into the present. Robert
Tracy suggests that this novel seeks to answer the question,
"What if [Joyce's] nightmare gave you a back kick?" and
reminds us that "the spirals of Newgrange and the interlaced
letters of the *Book of Kells* suggest this disdain for linearity
and chronology pictorially; HCE as Everyman, simultaneously
remembering and experiencing the entire human past, is its
most ambitious literary representation" (1986, 144, 147). Tracy
concludes that "*A Curious Street* represents a real, though
perhaps overambitious attempt by a young writer to measure
himself against the Joyce of *Finnegans Wake*, and to realize
that painful obsession with the past that is so characteristic
of Irish thought" (147).

Similarly, one strand in Patrick McGinley's *The Trick of
the Ga Bolga* (1985), which is dedicated "To Myles," is the
notion that characters can exchange identities. As Hugh Kenner writes in his review of this novel, "when writer and
reader are gathered together in the name of the fictional,
what gets ritually dismembered is all sense that character is
stable, causation reliable, all straight with the world. Not
even at Yale can they deconstruct Irish fictions. The authors
saw to it first" (1985, 20). McGinley is perhaps the most
entertaining and promising among recently emergent Irish

novelists. His novels are absurdist but not so remote from realism as Kenner's comment might suggest. *Bogmail* (1978) and *Foggage* (1984) are permeated with the local color, in setting and language, of McGinley's native County Donegal, and each novel includes within its often absurdist form an age-old narrative "hook": Who done it? Or, who is it? McGinley is an experimental mystery writer. Flann O'Brien's *The Third Policeman* is the clearest model for his kind of writing. Each of McGinley's novels has its central conceit, captured in its succinct title. In *Bogmail* it is the mysterious blackmailer rising from the bog to point an accusing finger at the murderous protagonist, in *Goosefoot* (1982) it is the nickname of a nasty plant and also the nickname of the novel's perverse villain, and in *Foggage* it is the incestuous protagonist's theory about the advantages of recycling farm grass and sexual partners. Like many another Irish novel, McGinley's most recent, *The Red Men* (1987), makes use of a motif from folklore—in this case, the Talents, the story of the old man who tests his four sons to determine which one will inherit his estate. Also, through Kenneth Potter in *Bogmail* and George Coote in *The Trick of the Ga Bolga*, McGinley incorporates the oldest of Irish novelistic conventions—the visiting Englishman who has a hard time understanding Ireland—while adding new twists all his own. A rather misogynist frame of mind mars some of McGinley's writing, but on the other hand *Goosefoot* celebrates Patricia Teeling's apparent eventual escape, via the Rosslare Ferry, from the generally evil, self-serving men who have threatened her throughout the novel.

In a promising way, McGinley's novels bridge the gap between realism and fabulism. Conventional realism may have exhausted itself at this point, while Joyce and Beckett have taken the fabulist mode to extremes that may represent a cul de sac for contemporary novelists. In light of the novels of Kiely, Moore, McGahern, and some of the other accomplished novelists examined in this chapter, it seems reasonable to conclude that eclectic experimentalism—freely borrowing from both realism and fabulism—may be the best way for the Irish novel to go in the future.

Conclusion

It is difficult to predict the future directions of the Irish novel, but not at all so to recommend new courses of action in scholarship on the subject. While one would think that Joyce scholarship at this point is practicing a critical version of the Literature of Exhaustion, it is clear that criticism on many other Irish novelists is still (as W. J. McCormack aptly put it about the study of Irish literature as a whole) in an "infantile stage" (1980, 266). Racing toward exhaustion, Joyce criticism has produced an embarrassment of riches, but scholarship on other novelists tends to limp along, merely introducing the lives and works of a few writers. Reading the existing criticism on the Irish novel might make one think that its history consists only of the works of James Joyce plus those of a handful of predecessors and successors, but we have seen that this is far from the true story. Studying contemporary Joyce criticism immerses one in a variety of approaches that might equally or more valuably be applied to other Irish novelists. One clear need in future scholarship on the Irish novel is much more detailed study—biographical, textual, and critical, from a variety of perspectives—of such writers as Emily Lawless, Gerald O'Donovan, Eimar O'Duffy, Brinsley MacNamara, Máirtín Ó Cadhain, Jennifer Johnston, and many other individual Irish novelists. Why is there no psychoanalytic reading of Maria Edgeworth's thoroughly psychological novel *Ennui*? No Marxist study of the Marxist Liam O'Flaherty? No feminist critique of Emily Lawless? No deconstructionist reading of many a "decentered" Irish novel other than *Ulysses* and *Finnegans Wake*? The list of possibilities could be made longer than the list of Irish novelists discussed in this book. As other starting points, Stephen Brown's *Ireland in Fiction* (1919) is available as a fairly exhaustive, annotated listing of many forgotten nineteenth-century novels, while the most extensive surveys of twentieth-century Irish novelists in English are Diane Tolomeo's essay (1983) and the belated second volume of *Ireland in Fiction* (Brown and Clarke 1985).

Criticism on the Irish novel has been largely predictable and is in need of greater variety. To a large extent, the criticism follows an imitative pattern according to which critics have served as the accomplices of their selected authors. Scholars writing about those nineteenth-century novelists who focused very directly on Irish history and society take a sociohistorical approach; Joyceans become poststructuralists when writing about *Finnegans Wake,* the book that continually deconstructs itself; and so on. If the novels themselves appear to dictate critical approaches, equally if not more prevalent is the reverse pattern, with a reader's warrant determining the choice of text. The deconstructionist chooses to write about *Finnegans Wake,* not *The Real Charlotte,* while sociohistorical critics focus on nineteenth-century novels rather than *Finnegans Wake.* Readers' warrants could be enforced much more consistently than they are in the case of the Irish novel. For example, in the future feminist critics, as I have indicated, could write much more about neglected Irish women authors than about Joyce.

This brings us to a second, still greater area of need in scholarship on the Irish novel, even more pressing than studies of individual authors: much fuller examination of particular periods, subgenres, and themes involving a number of novelists. We need books on such topics as Irish women novelists, novelists in Irish, Irish Victorian novelists, the Irish bildungsroman, the Big House novel, the Irish Gothic novel, and the fantasy. A Harold-Bloomian study of the recurrent "anxiety of influence" running through the Irish novel could certainly be written; it was Walter Benjamin's contention that every truly great work of art not only destroys a genre but helps to create another. There do exist several models for such books: Thomas Flanagan's *The Irish Novelists, 1800–1850* (1958), Maurice Harmon and Patrick Rafroidi's collection of essays on *The Irish Novel in our Time* (1976), John Cronin's essays on *The Anglo-Irish Novel: The Nineteenth Century* (1980), my own *Great Hatred, Little Room: The Irish Historical Novel* (1983), Augustine Martin's collection of essays on *The Genius of Irish Prose* (1985a), and John Wilson Foster's *Fictions of the Irish Literary Revival: A Changeling Art* (1987).[1] But this is an extremely short list of books for such a rich area of study. We also need full studies of several of the stylistic and formal aspects introduced in this book as distinctive features of the Irish novel: the strong influence of the oral tradition as seen in a preponderance of colloquial narrators and loose, episodic structures; the related pattern of the Irish novel as a web of interwoven stories; the developing use of Irish English and the whole interaction of writing in both English and Irish; and others.

I might have organized this book around any of these themes. This book's structure reflects my own critical commitment, which is fundamentally historical. Each novel is part of its historical moment, as reflected in its author's life, the history of the period, and its critical as well as popular reception. In turn we read these works in light of our own historical moment and our own individual experiences. Current critical approaches—poststructuralist, feminist, and all the others—must also be understood in light of the contemporary historical moment, as Terry Eagleton (1978) and others have shown. As Robert Scholes writes, "One does not have to be a Marxist to endorse Fredric Jameson's battle cry, 'Always historicize!' (the first words of *The Political Unconscious*)" (1985, 16). Similarly, William E. Cain concludes his overview of current critical approaches with the assertion that "we need to return the canon to history, making texts . . . into something other than objects for additional 'readings.' How have we come to perceive these texts as we do? What values do they embody? How did they serve the society within which they were written, and how is this history related to our own?" (1984, 262). These are the kinds of questions that I have been asking myself about the Irish novel in this book, and the kinds of questions that future scholarship will have to answer. In this regard, Malcolm Brown's *The Politics of Irish Literature: From Thomas Davis to W. B. Yeats* (1972) is in a general way exemplary. My own first book examines the politics of Irish historical novelists. We need books on the politics of other kinds of Irish novelists.

For one whose interest has always been historical, and after many years in which history was out of fashion in literary criticism due to longstanding anti-historical practices running all the way from the early New Critics to the structuralists and poststructuralists, it is exciting to witness the recent emergence of a determinedly new historical criticism. As Jerome McGann shows in his introduction to *Historical Studies and Literary Criticism* (1985), the best among even the old historicists, such as the great Homeric scholar Millman Parry, took anything but a simplistic, reductive view of history (as the New Critics claimed). In his 1936 essay on "The Historical Method in Literary Criticism," Parry stressed that when examining literature as part of history, "I make for myself a picture of great detail" (quoted in McGann, 11). We read literature and history in light of our own particular, contemporary history, resulting in an understanding that is as true as we can be both to history and to our own concerns about the present and the future. When we write about literature, we enter into a rhetorical collaboration between the historical text, our present critical concerns, and our future audience. In the second essay in McGann's collection, the Edgeworth biographer Marilyn Butler makes a case for "A Particularized Historical Method" that makes eclectic use of a variety of critical methods in order to "localize" a text in terms of all of the available cultural codes of its time (1985, 43–44). The Le Fanu biographer W. J. McCormack makes a similar point in an essay published during the same year: "It is true that, for a few years, it seemed the New Criticism had found immortality in Tir na nÓg. With the release of the text back once more into the dynamics of social form has come a renewed appreciation of the historical dimension inherent in all linguistic constructs" (1985, 48). The historical dimensions of the Irish novel have provided the chief concern of my brief survey— the central critical approach subsuming all the others.

The effects of critical tunnel vision in the study of the Irish novel can often be depressing. Critics so often see only familiar ground and ignore uncharted territories. Yet a healthy cultivation of peripheral vision can be liberating and exciting, especially for students and scholars with sharp eyes, energy, and independence of mind. So much about the Irish novel remains to be seen, understood, and explained.

Notes

1. DISCOVERING VOICES: THE IRISH NOVEL BEFORE 1830

1. My discussion of the eighteenth-century Irish novel depends on Ross's articles (1980, 1982, 1983) and Lubbers's survey of the Irish novel up to 1900 (1985a), contributions that are very important, but not yet well known. One hopes that Ross will extend and enlarge the directions of the work he has suggested in his articles, and that Lubbers will publish an English translation of his book in German, thus making his findings more widely accessible.

2. In a brief response in 1966 in the [London] *Times Literary Supplement* to Desmond Clarke's book *The Ingenious Mr. Edgeworth*, Christina Colvin, editor of Edgeworth's letters, criticized "Clarke's extreme theory that what Maria Edgeworth 'lacked was the gift of invention, but [that] was supplied by Edgeworth,' and his flip assertion that *Ormond* was "hastily constructed" (1966, 9). Replying to P. H. Newby's opinion that "Edgeworth's crime was not so much that he was a rather pompous and opinionated utilitarian but that he so conducted himself as to cause his daughter to love him uncritically and therefore adopt his opinions of literature and life unquestioningly," Edgeworth's biographer Marilyn Butler points out that "even this relatively mild account of 'Edgeworth's crime' puts the onus on him for the faults of the novels" (1972, 7).

3. In his 1976 review of research on Irish "Nineteenth-Century Writers," James Kilroy does not so much as mention the work of the Banims. In one way this was an oversight, since their novels were assessed in books by Krans (1903) and Flanagan (1958). In another way it reflects an increase in critical interest only within the last dozen years or so, reflected in a monograph on their work (Hawthorne 1975), reprints of no fewer than a dozen of their novels in the Garland series (1979–80), and a book chapter on their historical novels (Cahalan 1983). Flanagan had offered without evidence the view that in the collaboration of the two authors John was so much the stronger that "it seems sensible to depart from the usual practice of referring to 'the Banim brothers' " (1958, 175), but this view has been refuted with careful documentation by Robert Lee Wolff (1979a, vii–viii, xxi, xlix n.2) and others (Murray 1857, 191–92; Hawthorne 1975, 5, 136ff;

Cahalan 1983, 46). Of their fifteen novels, seven should be attributed to John Banim, five to Michael, and three to their joint collaboration; even the books that were written by one brother were sent to the other for suggestions and criticism. Among the three novels that I judge as the Banims' best—*Crohoore of the Bill-Hook* (1825), *The Boyne Water* (1826a), and *The Nowlans* (1826b)—the latter two are John's but the first is Michael's, indicating that he was not only an active novelist but at his best a very good one too.

4. Elsewhere I have explicated the Banims' historical novels in detail (Cahalan 1983, 43–66).

2. VARIATIONS ON IRISH THEMES, 1830–90

1. Complicating this impression is Carleton's 1838 letter to a London publisher, in which he asked for £ 70 for *Fardorougha* instead of the £ 50 Bentley had offered. "The truth is," Carleton wrote in chameleon fashion, "I would listen to no such terms at all were it not that I am anxious to get into the London Market" (Ray 1952, 186).

3. INVENTING MODERN FORMS, 1890–1920

1. Stephen J. Brown's annotated bibliography of *Ireland in Fiction* (1919) is a rich storehouse of many neglected novelists during this period in need of research. An example of the useful scholarship that can be done is William J. Feeney's recent article on "D. P. Moran's *Tom O'Kelly* and Irish Cultural Identity" (1986).

2. Thomas Flanagan, "Fact and Imagination in Ireland," a lecture presented in the Boston College Humanities Series, 9 October 1980, recorded with permission of Professor Flanagan.

3. Like many Irish novelists (such as James Joyce and Frank O'Connor), Moore was an inveterate reviser of his own writing, so much so that he rewrote and published distinct versions of both *A Drama in Muslin* (1886, rewritten as *Muslin*, 1915) and *The Lake* (1905 and 1921). The editions I cite are the later ones, although it is difficult to say which is preferable.

4. This and other translations from the Irish herein are mine unless otherwise cited.

4. JAMES JOYCE AND JOYCEAN SCHOLARSHIP: A HISTORICAL VIEW

1. Among the many introductions to Joyce that could be recommended to the beginner, two of the best remain Harry Levin's

(1941) and A. Walton Litz's (1966), which also serve as useful samples of traditional approaches to the subject.

2. In an excellent recent dissertation, Denis Cotter (1982) argues that *Portrait* bears striking resemblances to earlier Irish bildungsromans and their narrative patterns and themes, and that the history of the Irish bildungsroman is a story of Irish novelists continually "rediscovering" the form as if unaware of the tradition, yet at the same time copiously following it.

3. So much has been written about both *Ulysses* and *Finnegans Wake* that it is best if the reader is referred with judicious selectivity to some of the sources mentioned in my short survey, in the latter part of this chapter, of Joycean scholarship and especially the dominant current schools of Joycean criticism. Here I must limit myself quite strictly to a brief suggestion of the place of the Irish tradition within Joyce's work, and likewise, the place of these novels within the tradition of the Irish novel as a whole.

4. Among the best studies of Joyce's use of Homer are those by W. B. Stanford (1953, 1964), Hugh Kenner (1952, 1969), and Richard Ellmann (1957, 1962).

5. Joyceans as opposite as the conservative champion of the "classical" novel, S. L. Goldberg (1961), and the radical post-structuralist and feminist Margot Norris (1974) have denied that *Finnegans Wake* is a novel or that it can be treated as such.

6. Joyce's citation and use of these earlier Irish novelists have seldom been mentioned, except by Grace Eckley in a brief article (1977) about his use of Griffin.

7. As early as 1941 in an article in *Horizon*, Frank Budgen indicated that "commenting on a precis of Le Fanu's book I made for him in 1937, Joyce wrote, referring to that spot in Phoenix Park where the fierce Dangerfield struck down Sturk: 'The encounter between my father and a tramp (the basis of my book) actually took place at that part of the park' " (quoted in Budgen, 70).

8. Especially useful are Bernard Benstock's introduction to his collection of *Critical Essays on James Joyce* (1985); Sidney Feshback's and William Herman's "The History of Joyce Criticism and Scholarship" (1984); and Thomas F. Staley's survey of Joyce criticism in *Anglo-Irish Literature: A Review of Research* (1976a) as well as his 1983 update.

9. Quoted in Ellen Carol Jones, "Deconstructive Criticism of Joyce: Introduction," Proceedings of the Ninth International James Joyce Symposium, Frankfurt, June 1984; copyright 1985, text kindly supplied to me by both Ms. Jones and Bernard Benstock.

10. Attridge, "Criticism's Wake," 1984 "Deconstructive Criticism" proceedings, copyright 1985.

11. Similarly, Richard Brown's chapter on "Joyce and Feminism" (1985) opens with the mystifying sentence, "Joyce's writing has played little part in the upsurge of interest in feminism and feminist literary criticism that has taken place since the 1960s" (89), even though Suzette Henke and Elaine Unkeless's collection of essays on *Women in Joyce* (1982), Bonnie Kime Scott's *Joyce and Feminism* (1984), and several scholarly articles had already appeared.

12. A minority opinion is that of Cheryl Herr (1984), who argues that in "Circe" Leopold is not truly androgynous but merely an actor in a Victorian cross-dressing comedy.

13. This is not to advocate a critical hodgepodge of approaches such as can be found in Colin McCabe's *James Joyce and the Revolution of the Word* (1979), which tries all at once to be psychoanalytic, feminist, political, and above all poststructuralist. I have to agree with Tom Paulin that McCabe's book is "quite unreadable" (1984a, 143).

5. EXPOSÉ OF IRELAND: REALISTS, 1920–55

1. At least two excellent accessible studies have appeared in recent years (Murphy 1975; Brown 1985).

2. Four books on O'Flaherty's career as a novelist have appeared in recent years (Zneimer 1970; Doyle 1971; James H. O'Brien 1973; Sheeran 1976).

3. Ruth Sherry's useful article on "The Irish Working Class in Fiction" (1984) surveys Patrick MacGill, Michael McLaverty, James Stephens, and Frank O'Connor, but surprisingly fails to mention either O'Flaherty or O'Donnell.

4. See Freyer 1973; McInerney 1976; McHugh 1984.

6. FANTASIA: IRISH FABULISTS, 1920–55

1. O'Brien's career of writing in Irish has recently been examined by Brendán Ó Conaire (1986).

7. NEW VOICES: THE CONTEMPORARY NOVEL

1. Diane Tolomeo (1983) mentions as many *more* novelists (more than thirty others) during this period as I am able to discuss briefly in this chapter.

2. The reader interested in Moore's North American novels may consult John Wison Foster (1971).

3. While several critics view Moore as a contemporary existentialist, Foster (1968) insists that Moore's most abiding interest is in primitive communities and their ritual acts of exclusion.

CONCLUSION

1. There is also Barry Sloan's recent book on *The Pioneers of Anglo-Irish Fiction, 1800–1850* (1986), but it adds little to Flanagan's earlier (1958) book on the same subject and is rather inattentive to relevant recent scholarship.

Bibliography of Works Cited

Primary Sources: Irish Novels

Allingham, William. 1864. *Laurence Bloomfield in Ireland: A Modern Poem.* London and Cambridge: Macmillan.

Amory, Thomas. 1756, 1766. *The Life of John Buncle, Esq.: Containing Various Observations and Reflections, Made in Several Parts of the World, and Many Extraordinary Relations.* Reprint. London: T. Becket, P. A. Dehondt, T. Cadell, 1770.

Anonymous. 1781. *The Triumph of Prudence over Passion; or, The History of Miss Mortimer and Miss Fitzgerald.* 2 vols. Dublin: S. Colbert.

Anonymous. 1891. *Priests and People: A No-Rent Romance.* 3 vols. London: Eden, Remington.

Banim, John. 1825. *The Fetches.* In *Tales, by the O'Hara Family: Containing "Crohoore of the Bill-Hook," "The Fetches," and "John Doe."* Vol. 2. London: W. Simpkin and R. Marshall.

———. 1826a. *The Boyne Water; A Tale by the O'Hara Brothers.* Reprint. Lille, France: Université de Lille, 1976.

———. 1826b. *The Nowlans.* Reprint. 2 vols. London: Henry Colburn, 1827.

———. 1828a. *The Anglo-Irish of the Nineteenth Century.* 3 vols. Reprint. New York: Garland, 1978.

———. 1828b. *The Conformists.* In *The Denounced.* Vols. 2 and 3. Reprint. New York: Garland, 1979.

———. 1828c. *The Last Baron of Crana.* In *The Denounced.* Vols. 1 and 2. Reprint. New York: Garland, 1979.

Banim, John, and Michael Banim. 1825. *John Doe.* See John Banim 1825. Vol. 3.

———. 1842. *Father Connell.* 3 vols. London: Newby and Boone.

Banim, Michael. 1825. *Crohoore of the Bill-Hook.* See John Banim 1825. Vols. 1 and 2.

———. 1830. *The Croppy; A Tale of the Irish Rebellion of 1798.* Reprint. Dublin: James Duffy, 1865.

———. 1833. *The Ghost-Hunter and His Family*. London: Smith, Elder.

———. 1835. *The Mayor of Windgap*. 3 vols. London: Saunders and Otley.

———. 1842. *Father Connell*. 3 vols. London: Newby and Boone.

———. 1864. *The Town of the Cascades*. 2 vols. London: Chapman and Hall.

Banville, John. 1973. *Birchwood*. Reprint. London: Panther, 1984.

Beckett, Samuel. 1938. *Murphy*. Reprint. New York: Grove, 1957.

———. 1950. *Molloy*. Trans. by Beckett and Patrick Bowles. 1954. Reprint. London: Calder and Boyars, 1973.

———. 1951. *Malone meurt*. Trans. by Beckett as *Malone Dies*. 1956. Reprint. London: Calder and Boyars, 1973.

———. 1952. *L'Innommable*. Trans. by Beckett as *The Unnamable*. 1958. Reprint. London: Calder and Boyars, 1973.

———. 1953. *Watt*. New York: Grove; London: Evergreen.

———. 1961. *Comment c'est*. Trans. by Beckett as *How It Is*. 1966. New York: Grove.

———. 1970. *Mercier et Camier*. Paris: Editions de Minuit. Trans. by Beckett as *Mercier and Camier*. 1974. New York: Grove.

Bell, Sam Hanna. 1951. *December Bride*. Reprint. Belfast: Blackstaff, 1974.

———. 1961. *The Hollow Ball*. London: Cassell.

———. 1973. *A Man Flourishing*. Reprint. Belfast: Blackstaff, 1986.

Binchy, Maeve. 1982. *Light a Penny Candle*. London: Century.

———. 1985. *Echoes*. New York: Viking.

Birmingham, George A. 1907. *The Northern Iron*. Dublin: Maunsel.

———. 1912. *The Red Hand of Ulster*. London: Smith Elder.

Bowen, Elizabeth. 1929. *The Last September*. Reprint. New York: Alfred A. Knopf, 1964.

———. 1955. *A World of Love*. London: Jonathan Cape; New York: Alfred A. Knopf.

Boylan, Clare. 1983. *Holy Pictures*. Reprint. Middlesex: Penguin, 1984.

Brew, Margaret. 1880. *The Burtons of Dunroe*. 3 vols. London: Tinsley.

Broderick, John. 1961. *The Pilgrimage*. London: Weidenfeld and Nicolson.

———. 1965. *The Waking of Willie Ryan*. London: Weidenfeld and Nicolson.

———. 1982. *The Trial of Father Dillingham*. Reprint. London: Sphere, 1983.

Brooke, Henry. 1771. *The Fool of Quality: or, The History of the Earl of Moreland.* Dublin: Dillon Chamberlaine.

Brown, Christy. 1970. *Down All the Days.* Reprint. London: Pan, 1971.

Buckley, William. 1903. *Croppies Lie Down: A Tale of Ireland in '98.* London: Henry Colburn.

Bullock, Shan F. 1903. *The Squireen.* New York: McClure, Phillips.

———. 1924. *The Loughsiders.* London: George G. Harrap.

Carleton, William. 1839. *Fardorougha, the Miser; or, The Convicts of Lismona.* Reprint. Dublin: James Duffy, 1846.

———. 1845a. *Rody the Rover.* Dublin: James Duffy.

———. 1845b. *Valentine McClutchy, the Irish Agent; or, The Chronicles of Castle Cumber.* Reprint. Dublin: James Duffy, 1848.

———. 1847. *The Black Prophet: A Tale of Irish Famine.* London: Simms and McIntyre.

———. 1848a. *The Emigrants of Ahadarra: A Tale of Irish Life.* London: Simms and McIntyre.

———. 1848b. *The Tithe Proctor.* London: Simms and McIntyre.

———. 1852. *The Squanders of Castle Squander.* 2 vols. London: Illustrated London Library.

———. 1855. *Willy Reilly and His Dear Colleen Bawn.* 3 vols. London: Hope.

———. 1857. *The Black Baronet.* Dublin: James Duffy.

———. 1860. *The Evil Eye.* Dublin: James Duffy.

———. 1862. *Redmond, Count O'Hanlon, the Irish Rapparee.* Dublin: James Duffy.

Casey, Kevin. 1968. *The Sinner's Bell.* London: Faber.

Chaigneau, William. 1752. *The History of Jack Connor.* Dublin: Abraham Bradley.

Clarke, Austin. 1932. *The Bright Temptation: A Romance.* London: Allen and Unwin.

———. 1936. *The Singing-Men at Cashel.* London: Allen and Unwin.

———. 1952. *The Sun Dances at Easter.* London: Andrew Melrose.

Corkery, Daniel. 1917. *The Threshold of Quiet.* Reprint. Dublin: Talbot, 1946.

Cronin, Anthony. 1964. *The Life of Riley.* Reprint. Dingle, County Kerry: Brandon, 1983.

———. 1979. *Identity Papers.* Dublin: Co-op.

de Paor, Annraoi. 1985. *Baun ar Buairt* (Forever vexed). Dublin: Coiscéim.

Dillon, Eilís. 1973. *Across the Bitter Sea.* Reprint. London: Hodder Fawcett, 1975.

———. 1977. *Blood Relations.* New York: Fawcett Crest.

Dunsany, Lord [Edward Plunkett]. 1933. *The Curse of the Wise Woman*. London: Heinneman.

Edgeworth, Maria. 1800. *Castle Rackrent, an Hibernian Tale: Taken from Facts, and from the Manners of the Irish Squires, before the Year 1782*. Reprint. New York: Norton, 1965.

―――. 1809. *Ennui*. Reprint. London: J. M. Dent; New York: Dodd Mead, 1893.

―――. 1812. *The Absentee*. Reprint. London: J. M. Dent; New York: Dodd Mead, 1893.

―――. 1817. *Ormond*. Reprint. London: J. M. Dent; New York: Dodd Mead, 1893.

Farrell, M. J. See Molly Keane.

Farrell, Michael. 1963. *Thy Tears Might Cease*. London: Jonathan Cape.

Gogarty, Oliver St. John. 1939. *Tumbling in the Hay*. Reprint. London: Sphere, 1982.

Griffin, Gerald. 1829a. *The Collegians: A Tale of Garryowen*. Reprint. New York: D. Appleton, 1898.

―――. 1829b. *The Rivals*. Reprint. Lille, France: Université de Lille, n.d.

―――. 1829c. *Tracy's Ambition*. Reprint. Lille, France: Université de Lille, n.d.

―――. 1830. *The Christian Physiologist*. London: E. Bull.

―――. 1832. *The Invasion*. 4 vols. London: Saunders and Otley.

―――. 1836. *The Duke of Monmouth*. 3 vols. London: Bentley.

Hackett, Francis. 1936. *The Green Lion*. London: Nicholson and Watson.

Hall, Anna Fielding. 1845. *The Whiteboy*. London: Chapman and Hall.

Hartley, May Laffan. 1876. *Hogan, M.P.: A Novel*. 3 vols. London: Henry S. King.

Head, Richard. 1665. *The English Rogue: Described in the Life of Meriton Latroon, a Witty Extravagant: Comprehending the Most Eminent Cheats of Both Sexes*. London: Henry Marsh.

Higgins, Aidan. 1966. *Langrishe, Go Down*. New York: Grove.

―――. 1977. *Scenes from a Receding Past*. London: John Calder.

Hogan, Desmond. 1976. *The Ikon Maker*. Dublin: The Irish Writers' Co-Operative.

―――. 1980. *The Leaves on Grey*. Reprint. London: Pan, 1981.

―――. 1984. *A Curious Street*. Reprint. London: Pan, 1985.

Johnston, Jennifer. 1972. *The Captains and the Kings*. Reprint. London: Fontana, 1985.

―――. 1973. *The Gates*. Reprint. London: Fontana, 1985.

————. 1974. *How Many Miles to Babylon?*. Reprint. London: Fontana, 1984.

————. 1977. *Shadows on Our Skin*. London: Hamish Hamilton.

————. 1979. *The Old Jest*. Reprint. London: Fontana, 1984.

————. 1982. *The Christmas Tree*. New York: William Morrow.

————. 1984. *The Railway Station Man*. Reprint. London: Fontana, 1986.

————. 1987. *Fool's Sanctuary*. London: Hamish Hamilton.

Johnstone, Charles. 1774. *The History of Arsaces, Prince of Betlis*. 2 vols. London: T. Becket.

————. 1781. *The History of John Juniper, Alias Juniper Jack: Containing the Birth, Parentage, and Education, Life, Adventures, and Character of that Most Wonderful and Surprizing Gentleman*. 2 vols. Dublin: Price.

Jones, T. Mason. 1867. *Old Trinity: A Story of Real Life*. 3 vols. London: Bentley.

Jordan, Neil. 1980. *The Past*. Reprint. London: Sphere, 1982.

————. 1983. *The Dream of a Beast*. London: Chatto and Windus.

Joyce, James. 1916. *A Portrait of the Artist as a Young Man*. Corrected ed. New York: Penguin / Viking, 1964.

————. 1922. *Ulysses*. Corrected ed. New York: Vintage/ Random, 1986.

————. 1939. *Finnegans Wake*. Reprint. New York: Viking, 1959.

Kavanagh, Patrick. 1948. *Tarry Flynn*. Reprint. Harmondsworth, Middlesex: Penguin, 1978.

Keane, Molly. 1931. *Mad Puppetstown*. Reprint. London: Virago, 1985.

————. 1934. *Devoted Ladies*. Reprint. London: Virago, 1984.

————. 1937. *The Rising Tide*. Reprint. London: Virago, 1984.

————. 1941. *Two Days in Aragon*. Reprint. London: Virago, 1985.

————. 1981. *Good Behaviour*. Reprint. London: Sphere, 1982.

————. 1983. *Time After Time*. Reprint. London: Alfred A. Knopf, 1984.

Keary, Annie. 1875. *Castle Daly: The Story of an Irish House Thirty Years Ago*. 3 vols. London: Macmillan.

Kickham, Charles. 1869. *Sally Cavanagh; or, The Untenanted Graves*. Dublin: W. B. Kelly; London: Simpkin, Marshal.

————. 1879. *Knocknagow; or, The Homes of Tipperary*. Reprint. New York: Garland, 1979.

Kickham, Charles, and William O'Brien. 1886. *For the Old Land; A Tale of Twenty Years Ago*. Dublin: Gill.

Kiely, Benedict. 1946. *Land Without Stars*. London: Christopher Johnson.

————. 1949. *In a Harbour Green*. London: Jonathan Cape.

————. 1953. *The Cards of the Gambler*. London: Methuen.

————. 1960. *The Captain with the Whiskers*. London: Methuen.

————. 1968. *Dogs Enjoy the Morning*. London: Gollancz.

————. 1977. *Proxopera*. London: Gollancz.

————. 1985. *Nothing Happens in Carmincross*. Boston: David R. Godine.

Kilroy, Thomas. 1971. *The Big Chapel*. Reprint. Dublin: Poolbeg, 1982.

Laverty, Maura. 1942. *Never No More*. Reprint. London: Virago, 1985.

————. 1944. *No More Than Human*. London: Longmans.

————. 1946. *Lift Up Your Gates*. London: Longmans.

Lavin, Mary. 1945. *The House in Clewe Street*. London: Michael Joseph.

————. 1950. *Mary O'Grady*. Boston: Little, Brown.

Lawless, Emily. 1886. *Hurrish: A Study*. Edinburgh and London: William Blackwood.

————. 1890. *With Essex in Ireland*. London: Smith, Elder.

————. 1892. *Grania (The Story of an Island)*. New York: MacMillan.

————. 1894. *Maelcho*. 2 vols. London: Smith, Elder.

Lawless, Emily, and Shan F. Bullock. 1913. *The Race of Castlebar*. London: J. Murray.

Le Fanu, Joseph Sheridan. 1845. *The Cock and Anchor; A Chronicle of Old Dublin*. 3 vols. Reprint. New York: Garland, 1979.

————. 1847. *The Fortunes of Colonel Torlogh O'Brien: A Tale of the Wars of King James*. Dublin: James McGlashan.

————. 1863. *The House by the Churchyard*. 3 vols. London: Tinsley.

Leland, Mary. 1985. *The Killeen*. New York: Atheneum.

Lever, Charles. 1839. *The Confessions of Harry Lorrequer*. Dublin: W. Curry, June; Edinburgh: Fraser and Crawford.

————. 1841. *Charles O'Malley, the Irish Dragoon*. Reprint. Boston: Roberts, 1898.

————. 1845a. *The O'Donoghue*. Dublin: W. Curry.

————. 1845b. *St. Patrick's Eve*. London: Chapman and Hall.

————. 1856. *The Martins of Cro Martin*. Reprint. 2 vols. Boston: Little, Brown, 1900.

————. 1865. *Luttrell of Aran*. London: Chapman and Hall.

————. 1872. *Lord Kilgobbin*. London: George Routledge.

Lover, Samuel. 1837. *Rory O'More, a National Romance*. 3 vols. London: Bentley.

————. 1842. *Handy Andy*. London: F. Lover.

MacAmhlaigh, Dónal. *Deoraithe* (Exiles). 1986. Dublin: An Cló-chomar.

McCabe, Eugene. 1976. *Victims*. Reprint. Dublin: Mercier, 1979.

MacConmara, Séamus. 1939. *An Coimhthigheach* (The outsider). Dublin: Oifig an tSoláthair.

McGahern, John. 1963. *The Barracks*. Reprint. London: Panther, 1966.

———. 1965. *The Dark*. Reprint. London: Panther, 1967.

———. 1974. *The Leavetaking*. Rev. ed. Boston: Little, Brown, 1975.

———. 1979. *The Pornographer*. Reprint. London: Quartet, 1980.

McGinley, Patrick. 1978. *Bogmail*. Reprint. London: Fontana, 1986.

———. 1982. *Goosefoot*. Reprint. London: Fontana, 1984.

———. 1984. *Foggage*. Reprint. London: Fontana, 1985.

———. 1985. *The Trick of the Ga Bolga*. Reprint. London: Fontana, 1986.

———. 1987. *The Red Men*. London: Jonathan Cape.

MacGiolla Iasachta, Éamonn [Eamon MacLysaght]. 1927. *Cúrsai Thomáis* (The story of Tomás). Dublin: Hodges and Figgis.

Macken, Walter. 1950. *Rain on the Wind*. New York: Macmillan.

———. 1952. *The Bogman*. Reprint. London: Pan, 1972.

———. 1959. *Seek the Fair Land*. Reprint. London: Pan, 1962.

———. 1962. *The Silent People*. Reprint. London: Pan, 1965.

———. 1964. *The Scorching Wind*. Reprint. London: Pan, 1966.

MacLaverty, Bernard. 1980. *Lamb*. Reprint. Middlesex: Penguin, 1981.

———. 1983. *Cal*. New York: George Braziller.

McLaverty, Michael. 1939. *Call My Brother Back*. Reprint. Dublin: Poolbeg, 1979.

———. 1941. *Lost Fields*. Reprint. Dublin: Poolbeg, 1980.

———. 1945. *In This Thy Day*. London: Jonathan Cape.

———. 1951. *Truth in the Night*. Reprint. Dublin: Poolbeg, 1986.

———. 1965. *The Brightening Day*. Reprint. Dublin: Poolbeg, 1987.

MacManus, Francis. 1934. *Stand and Give Challenge*. Reprint. Cork: Mercier, 1964.

———. 1936. *Candle for the Proud*. Reprint. Cork: Mercier, 1964.

———. 1937. *This House Was Mine*. Reprint. Cork: Mercier, 1963.

———. 1939. *Men Withering*. Reprint. Cork: Mercier, 1972.

———. 1940. *The Wild Garden*. Dublin: Talbot.

———. 1942. *Watergate*. Reprint. Dublin: Poolbeg, 1980.

———. 1943. *The Greatest of These*. Reprint. Cork: Mercier, 1979.

———. 1950. *The Fire in the Dust*. London: Jonathan Cape; Dublin: Talbot.

MacNamara, Brinsley [John Weldon]. 1918. *The Valley of the Squinting Windows*. Reprint. Dublin: Anvil, 1984.

———. 1920. *The Clanking of Chains*. Dublin: Maunsel.

———. 1929. *The Various Lives of Marcus Igoe*. London: Marston.

McNeill, Janet. 1964. *The Maiden Dinosaur*. London: Geoffrey Bles.

Maturin, Charles. 1808. *The Wild Irish Boy*. 3 vols. London: Hurst, Rees, and Orme.

———. 1812. *The Milesian Chief: A Romance*. 4 vols. London: Henry Colburn.

———. 1818. *Women; or, Pour et Contre: A Tale*. 3 vols. Edinburgh: James Ballantyne.

———. 1820. *Melmoth the Wanderer: A Tale*. Reprint. London: Oxford University Press, 1968.

Moore, Brian. 1955. *The Lonely Passion of Judith Hearne*. Boston: Little, Brown.

———. 1958. *The Feast of Lupercal*. Reprint. London: Granada, 1983.

———. 1965. *The Emperor of Ice-Cream*. Reprint. London: Mayflower, 1967.

———. 1972. *Catholics*. Reprint. New York: Pocket, 1973.

———. 1979. *The Mangan Inheritance*. New York: Farrar, Straus and Giroux.

———. 1981. *The Temptation of Eileen Hughes*. Reprint. London: Triad / Panther, 1983.

Moore, George. 1886. *A Drama in Muslin*. Rewritten as *Muslin*. 1915. Reprint. New York: Boni and Liveright, 1922.

———. 1905. *The Lake*. Rev. ed. London: William Heinemann, 1921.

Morgan, Lady. See Owenson, Sydney.

Mulkerns, Val. 1984. *The Summerhouse*. Reprint. London: Futura / Macdonald, 1985.

———. 1986. *Very Like a Whale*. London: John Murray.

Murdoch, Iris. 1965. *The Red and the Green*. New York: Viking.

na gCopaleen, Myles. See Flann O'Brien.

O'Brien, Edna. 1960. *The Country Girls*. Reprint. Middlesex: Penguin, 1984.

———. 1962. *The Lonely Girl*. Reprint as *Girl with Green Eyes*. Middlesex: Penguin, 1964.

———. 1964. *Girls in Their Married Bliss*. Middlesex: Penguin, 1967.

———. 1970. *A Pagan Place*. Reprint. London: Penguin, 1971.

———. 1972. *Night*. London: Weidenfeld and Nicolson.

O'Brien, Flann [Brian O'Nolan]. 1939. *At Swim-Two-Birds.* Reprint. New York: New American Library, 1976.

———. 1941. *An Béal Bocht.* Reprint. Dublin: Cló Dolmen, 1975. Trans. by Patrick C. Power as *The Poor Mouth.* 1973. Reprint. London: Pan, 1975.

———. 1961. *The Hard Life.* Reprint. New York: Pantheon, 1962.

———. 1964. *The Dalkey Archive.* Reprint. London: Pan, 1976.

———. 1967. *The Third Policeman.* Reprint. London: Pan, 1974.

O'Brien, Kate. 1931. *Without My Cloak.* Reprint. Harmondsworth, Middlesex: Penguin, 1949.

———. 1933. *The Ante-Room.* Reprint. Dublin: Arlen House, 1980.

———. 1938. *Pray for the Wanderer.* London: Heinemann; Garden City, N.J.: Doubleday, Doran.

———. 1941. *The Land of Spices.* Reprint. Dublin: Arlen House, 1982.

———. 1943. *The Last of Summer.* Reprint. Dublin: Arlen House, 1982.

O'Brien, William. 1890. *When We Were Boys: A Novel.* London: Longmans, Green.

Ó Brolacháin, Mícheál. 1985. *Pax Dei.* Dublin: Taibhse.

Ó Cadhain, Máirtín. 1949. *Cré na Cille* (Churchyard clay). Reprint. Dublin: Sáirséal agus Dill, 1970.

Ó Caochlaigh, Barra. 1932. *Lucht Ceoil* (Musicians). Dublin: Oifig Díolta Foillseacháin Rialtais.

Ó Conaire, Pádraic. *Deoraíocht* (Exile). 1910. Reprint. Dublin: Cló Talbot.

———. 1926. *Brian Óg* (Young Brian). Reprint. Dublin: Comhlacht Oideachais na hÉireann, n.d.

O'Connor, Frank. 1932. *The Saint and Mary Kate.* London: Macmillan.

———. 1940. *Dutch Interior.* London: Macmillan.

Ó Doibhlin, Brendán. 1979. *An Branar Gan Chur* (The untilled field). Dublin: Gilbert Dalton.

O'Donnell, Peadar. 1925. *Storm.* Dublin: Talbot.

———. 1928. *Islanders.* Cork and Dublin: Mercier, 1963.

———. 1929. *Adrigoole.* London: Jonathan Cape.

———. 1930. *The Knife.* Reprint. Dublin: Irish Humanities Centre, 1980.

———. 1934. *On the Edge of the Stream.* London: Jonathan Cape.

———. 1955. *The Big Windows.* Reprint. Dublin: O'Brien, 1983.

O'Donovan, Gerald, 1913. *Father Ralph.* London: Macmillan.

———. 1914. *Waiting.* London: Macmillan.

O'Duffy, Eimar. 1919. *The Wasted Island*. Reprint. New York: Dodd, Mead.

———. 1922a. *The Lion and the Fox*. Dublin: Martin Lester.

———. 1922b. *Printer's Errors*. Dublin: Martin Lester.

———. 1923. *Miss Rudd and Some Lovers*. Dublin: Talbot.

———. 1926. *King Goshawk and the Birds*. London: Macmillan.

———. 1928. *The Spacious Adventures of the Man in the Street*. London: Macmillan.

———. 1933. *Asses in Clover*. London and New York: Putnam.

O'Faolain, Julia. 1980. *No Country for Young Men*. Middlesex: Penguin.

O'Faolain, Seán. 1933. *A Nest of Simple Folk*. London: Jonathan Cape.

———. 1936. *Bird Alone*. New York: Viking.

———. 1940. *Come Back to Erin*. Reprint. Westport, Conn.: Greenwood, 1972.

———. 1979. *And Again?*. Reprint. New York and Middlesex: Penguin, 1982.

O'Flaherty, Liam. 1924. *The Black Soul*. London: Jonathan Cape.

———. 1925. *The Informer*. Reprint. New York and London: Harcourt Brace Jovanovich, 1980.

———. 1926. *Mr. Gilhooley*. London: Jonathan Cape.

———. 1928. *The Assassin*. London: Jonathan Cape.

———. 1931. *The Puritan*. New York: Harcourt, Brace.

———. 1932. *Skerrett*. Reprint. Dublin: Wolfhound, 1982.

———. 1937. *Famine*. Reprint. Boston: David R. Godine, 1982.

———. 1946. *Land*. New York: Random House.

———. 1950. *Insurrection*. London: Gollancz.

O'Grady, Standish James. 1894. *The Coming of Cuculain*. London: Methuen.

———. 1896. *Ulrick the Ready; or, The Chieftains' Last Rally*. London: Downey.

———. 1897. *The Flight of the Eagle*. Reprint. Dublin: Talbot Press, 1945.

———. 1901. *In the Gates of the North*. Kilkenny: Standish O'Grady.

———. 1920. *The Triumph and Passing of Cuculain*. Dublin: Talbot; London: T. Fisher Unwin.

Ó Grianna, Séamus. 1920. *Mo Dhá Róisín* (My two Roseens). Dundalk: Preas Dhún Dealgan.

———. 1924. *Caisleáin Óir* (Castles of gold). Reprint. Cork and Dublin: Cló Mercier, 1976.

————. 1966. *Bean Ruadh de Dhálack* (A red-haired O'Donnell woman). Dublin: Oifig an tSoláthair.

Ó hEithir, Brendán. 1976. *Lig Sinn i gCathú (Lead Us Into Temptation)*. Dublin: Sáirséal agus Dill.

Ó hUid, Tarlach. 1952. *An Dá Thrá (The two strands)*. Dublin: Foilseacháin Náisiúnta.

O'Kelly, Seumas. 1917. *The Lady of Deerpark*. London: Methuen.

Ó Laoghaire, Peadar. 1898. Part Two of *Séadna*. With preface and translation. Dublin: Bernard Doyle.

————. 1904. *Séadna*. Dublin: The Irish Book Company.

————. 1907. *Niamh*. Dublin.

O'Neill, Joseph. 1934. *Wind from the North*. London: Jonathan Cape.

Ó Néill, Séamus. 1947. *Tonn Tuile* (Floodtide). Dublin: Sáirséal agus Dill.

————. 1959. *Máire Nic Artáin*. Dublin: Cló Morainn.

Ó Súilleabháin, Diarmaid. 1964. *Dianmhuilte Dé* (The zealous mills of God). Dublin: Sáirséal agus Dill.

————. 1967. *Caoin Tú Féin* (Keen for yourself). Dublin: Sáirséal agus Dill.

————. 1968. *An Uain Bheo* (The moment of decision). Dublin: Sáirséal agus Dill.

————. 1983a. *Ciontach* (Offender). Dublin: Coiscéim.

————. 1983b. *Aistear* (Journey). Dublin: Coiscéim.

————. 1985. *Saighdiúir gan Chlaíomh* (Soldier without a sword). Dublin: Coiscéim.

Ó Tuairisc, Eoghan. 1962. *L'Attaque*. Reprint. Mercier, 1980.

————. 1966. *Dé Luain* (Monday). Dublin: Figgis.

————. 1977. *An Lomnochtán* (The naked person). Cork: Mercier.

Owenson, Sydney. 1806. *The Wild Irish Girl, a National Tale*. Reprint. 2 vols. Hartford, Conn.: S. Andrus, 1850.

————. 1814. *O'Donnell, a National Tale*. 3 vols. London: Henry Colburn.

————. 1818. *Florence Macarthy, an Irish Tale*. 4 vols. London: Henry Colburn.

————. 1827. *The O'Briens and the O'Flahertys, a National Tale*. Reprint. 4 vols. New York: Garland, 1979.

Plunkett, James. 1969. *Strumpet City*. Reprint. Hertfordshire: Panther, 1971.

————. 1977. *Farewell Companions*. London: Hutchinson.

Power, Richard. 1958. *Úll i mBárr an Ghéagáin*. Dublin: Sáirséal agus Dill. Trans. by Victor Power as *Apple on the Treetop*. Dublin: Poolbeg, 1980.

————. 1964. *The Land of Youth*. New York: Dial.

————. 1969. *The Hungry Grass*. New York: Dial.

Reid, Forrest. 1931. *Uncle Stephen*. London: Faber.

————. 1936. *The Retreat; or, The Machinations of Henry*. London: Faber.

————. 1937. *Peter Waring*. Reprint. London: Readers' Union and Faber, 1939.

————. 1944. *Young Tom; or, Very Mixed Company*. London: Faber.

Riddell, Charlotte. 1865. *Maxwell Drewitt: A Novel*. 3 vols. London: Tinsley.

————. 1888. *The Nun's Curse: A Novel*. London: Ward and Downey.

Somerville, E. OE. and Martin Ross (Edith Somerville and Violet Martin). 1889. *An Irish Cousin*. 2 vols. London: Bentley.

————. 1891. *Naboth's Vineyard*. London: Spencer Blackett.

————. 1894. *The Real Charlotte*. Reprint. London: Quartet Books, 1982.

————. 1898. *The Silver Fox*. London: Lawrence and Bullen.

————. 1902. *A Patrick's Day Hunt*. Westminster: Archibald Constable.

Somerville, E. OE. and Martin Ross (Edith Somerville). 1919. *Mount Music*. London: Longmans, Green.

————. 1921. *An Enthusiast*. Reprint. London: Sphere, 1985.

————. 1925. *The Big House of Inver*. New York: Doubleday.

————. 1928. *French Leave*. London: William Heinemann.

Stephens, James. 1912a. *The Charwoman's Daughter*. Reprint. Dublin: Gill and Macmillan, 1972.

————. 1912b. *The Crock of Gold*. Reprint. New York: Collier, 1967.

————. 1914. *The Demi-Gods*. Reprint. Dublin: Butler Sims, 1982.

————. 1923. *Deirdre*. London and New York: Macmillan.

Sterne, Laurence. 1759–67. *Tristram Shandy*. Reprint. New York: Norton, 1980.

Stuart, Francis. 1932. *Pigeon Irish*. New York: Macmillan.

————. 1949. *Redemption*. Reprint. New York: Devin-Adair, 1950.

————. 1971. *Black List / Section H*. Carbondale and Edwardsville: Southern Illinois University Press.

————. 1977. *A Hole in the Head*. Nantucket, Mass.: Longship.

————. 1985. *Faillandia*. Dublin: Raven Arts.

Swift, Jonathan. 1726. *Gulliver's Travels*. Reprint. New York: Penguin, 1985.

Trevor, William. 1969. *Mrs. Eckdorf in O'Neill's Hotel*. Reprint. Middlesex: Penguin, 1982.

————. 1983. *Fools of Fortune*. Reprint. New York and Middlesex: Penguin, 1984.

Wall, Mervyn. 1946. *The Unfortunate Fursey*. London: Pilot.

————. 1948. *The Return of Fursey*. London: Pilot.

————. 1952. *Leaves for the Burning*. Reprint. Dublin and London: Millington, 1973.

————. 1956. *No Trophies Raise*. London: Methuen.

————. 1982. *Hermitage*. Dublin: Wolfhound.

————. 1985. *The Complete Fursey*. Reprint. Dublin: Wolfhound.

West, Anthony C. 1963. *The Ferret Fancier*. London: MacGibbon and Kee.

Yeats, William Butler. 1891. *John Sherman and Dhoya*. London: T. Fisher Unwin.

————. 1974. *The Speckled Bird*. Dublin: Cuala.

Secondary Sources: Criticism and History

Achilles, Jochen. 1981. "*The Charwoman's Daughter* and the Emergence of National Psychology." *Irish University Review* 11, no. 2 (Autumn):184–97.

Adams, Robert Martin. 1977. *Afterjoyce: Studies in Fiction after "Ulysses."* New York: Oxford University Press.

Allen, Walter. 1954. *The English Novel: A Short Critical History*. New York: Dutton.

Allen, Woody. 1972. "The Irish Genius." In *Without Feathers*. New York: Random House. 117–22.

Amis, Martin. 1986. "Teacher's Pet." Review of 1986 ed. of *Ulysses*. *Atlantic* 258, no. 3 (September):96, 98–99.

Anderson, Chester. 1972. "Leopold Bloom as Dr. Sigmund Freud." *Mosaic* 6:23–43.

————. 1982. "Introduction" (to section on "Joyce and Freud"). In *The Seventh of Joyce*. Ed. Bernard Benstock. Bloomington: Indiana University Press; Brighton, England: Harvester. 53–56.

Andreasen, N. J. C. 1973. "James Joyce: A Portrait of the Artist as a Schizoid." *Journal of the American Medical Association* 224, no. 1 (2 April):67–71.

Atkinson, Colin B., and **Jo Atkinson.** 1980. "Sydney Owenson, Lady Morgan: Irish Patriot and First Professional Woman Writer." *Éire—Ireland* 15, no. 2:60–90.

————. 1984. "Maria Edgeworth, *Belinda*, and Women's Rights." *Éire—Ireland* 19, no. 4:94–118.

Attridge, Derek and **Daniel Ferrer,** eds. 1984. *Post-Structuralist Joyce: Essays from the French.* Cambridge: Cambridge University Press.

Bair, Deirdre. 1978. *Samuel Beckett: A Biography.* New York: Harcourt Brace Jovanovich; London: Jonathan Cape.

Baker, Ernest A. 1924–39. *The History of the English Novel.* 10 vols. New York: Barnes and Noble.

Baneham, Sam. 1983. "Aidan Higgins: A Political Dimension." *Review of Contemporary Fiction* 3, no. 1 (Spring):168–74.

Becker, R. S. 1986. "George Moore: An Exile from the Nouvelle Athènes." *Éire—Ireland* 21, no. 1 (Summer):146–51.

Beckett, J. C. 1966. *The Making of Modern Ireland, 1603–1923.* New York: Alfred A. Knopf.

———. 1981. "The Irish Writer and His Public in the Nineteenth Century." *Yearbook of English Studies* 11:102–16.

Begnal, Michael. 1980. "*Finnegans Wake* and the Nature of Narrative." *Modern British Literature* 5:43–52.

Beja, Morris. 1984. "The Joyce of Sex: Sexual Relations in *Ulysses.*" In *Light Rays: James Joyce and Modernism.* Ed. Heyward Ehrlich. New York: New Horizon, 112–23.

Benstock, Bernard. 1982. "A Flann for All Seasons." *Irish Renaissance Annual.* 3:15–29.

———. 1985. "Introduction: Assimilating James Joyce." In *Critical Essays on James Joyce.* Boston: G.K. Hall. 1–18.

Benstock, Bernard, and **Shari Benstock.** 1982. "The Benstock Principle." In *The Seventh of Joyce.* Ed. Bernard Benstock. Bloomington: Indiana University Press; Brighton, England: Harvester. 10–21.

Benstock, Shari. 1982. "The Masculine World of James Joyce." In *Twentieth-Century Women Novelists.* Ed. Thomas F. Staley. Totowa, N.J.: Barnes and Noble. 191–217.

Blodgett, Harriet. 1975. *Patterns of Reality: Elizabeth Bowen's Novels.* The Hague: Mouton.

Bloom, Harold. 1973. *The Anxiety of Influence: A Theory of Poetry.* New York: Oxford University Press.

Boland, Eavan. 1972. "Dublin's Advocate" (interview with James Plunkett). *This Week,* 12 October:42.

———. 1980. Preface to Kate O'Brien's *The Ante-Room.* 1933. Reprint. Dublin: Arlen House, 1980. vii–xi.

Bostrom, Irene. 1963. "The Novel and Catholic Emancipation." *Studies in Romanticism* 2:155–76.

Bové, Paul. 1982. "Beckett's Dreadful Postmodern: The Deconstruction of Form in *Molloy.*" In *Deconstructing the Novel:*

Essays in Applied Postmodern Hermeneutics. Ed. Leonard Orr.
Troy, N.Y.: Whitston. 185–221.

Bowen, Zack. 1980. "Dunsany, Lord." In *Dictionary of Irish Literature.* Ed. Robert Hogan. Westport, Conn.: Greenwood. 217–20.

Boyd, Ernest. 1922. *Ireland's Literary Renaissance.* Reprint. New York: Barnes and Noble, 1968.

Boyle, Robert. 1984. "Joyce's Consubstantiality: Woman as Creator." In *Light Rays: James Joyce and Modernism.* Ed. Heyward Ehrlich. New York: New Horizon. 126–32.

Breatnach, Pádraig A. 1969. "*Séadna*: Saothar Ealaíne" (*Séadna*: A work of art). *Studia Hibernica* 9:109–24.

Brewer, Betty Webb. 1983. " 'She Was a Part of It': Emily Lawless (1845–1913)." *Éire—Ireland* 18, no. 4(Winter):119–31.

Brivic, Sheldon. 1980. *Joyce between Freud and Jung.* Port Washington, N.Y.: Kennikat.

———. 1982. "The Father in Joyce." In *The Seventh of Joyce.* Ed. Bernard Benstock. Bloomington: Indiana University Press; Brighton, England: Harvester. 74–80.

Brown, Malcolm. 1955. *George Moore: A Reconsideration.* Seattle: University of Washington Press.

———. 1972. *The Politics of Irish Literature: From Thomas Davis to W. B. Yeats.* London: George Allen and Unwin.

Brown, Richard. 1985. *James Joyce and Sexuality.* Cambridge: Cambridge University Press.

Brown, Stephen J. 1919. *Ireland in Fiction: A Guide to Irish Novels, Tales, Romances, and Folklore.* Vol. 1. Reprint. Shannon: Irish University Press, 1969.

Brown, Stephen J. and **Desmond Clarke.** 1985. *Ireland in Fiction: A Guide to Irish Novels, Tales, Romances, and Folklore.* Vol. 2. Cork: Royal Carbery Books.

Brown, Terence. 1976. "Family Lives: The Fiction of Richard Power." *Cahiers Irlandaises* 4–5:245–53.

———. 1985. *Ireland: A Social and Cultural History, 1922–85.* Revised edition of 1981 original book. London: Fontana.

Browne, Joseph. 1984. "Flann O'Brien: *Post* Joyce or *Propter* Joyce?". *Éire—Ireland* 19, no. 4 (Winter):148–57.

Buckley, Mary. 1974. "Attitudes to Nationality in Four Nineteenth-Century Novelists: Charles Lever." *Journal of the Cork Historical and Archaeological Society* 80, no. 230 (July–December):129–36.

Budgen, Frank. 1941. "Joyce's Chapters of Going Forth by Day." Rpt. in *Critical Essays on James Joyce.* Ed. Bernard Benstock. Boston: G.K. Hall, 1985. 64–79.

Bushrui, Suheil Badi, and **Bernard Benstock,** eds. *James Joyce: An International Perspective.* Totowa, N.Y.: Barnes and Noble, 1982.

Butler, Marilyn. 1972. *Maria Edgeworth: A Literary Biography.* Oxford: Clarendon.

———. 1985. "A Particularized Historical Method." In *Historical Studies and Literary Criticism.* Ed. Jerome J. McGann. Madison: University of Wisconsin Press. 25–47.

Cahalan, James M. 1976. "The 'Preacher of Ideas': Michael Davitt, 1881–1906." *Éire—Ireland* 11, no. 1 (Spring):13–33.

———. 1978a. "The Making of *Strumpet City:* James Plunkett's Historical Vision." *Éire—Ireland* 13, no. 4 (Winter):81–100.

———. 1978b. Review of *Farewell Companions,* by James Plunkett. *Éire—Ireland* 13, no. 2 (Summer):127–30.

———. 1980. "Plunkett, James." In *Dictionary of Irish Literature.* Ed. Robert Hogan. Westport, Conn.: Greenwood. 554–60.

———. 1983. *Great Hatred, Little Room: The Irish Historical Novel.* Syracuse: Syracuse University Press. Reprint. Dublin: Gill and Macmillan, 1984.

———. 1986. "James Plunkett: An Interview." *Irish Literary Supplement* 5, no. 1 (Spring):9–11.

Cain, William. 1984. *The Crisis in Criticism: Theory, Literature, and Reform in English Studies.* Baltimore and London: Johns Hopkins University Press.

Callaghan, Mary Rose. 1980. "Farrell, Michael." In *Dictionary of Irish Literature.* Ed. Robert Hogan. Westport, Conn.: Greenwood. 233–34.

Caswell, Robert. 1967. "The Irish Novel: Exile, Resignation or Acceptance." *Wascana Review* 2, no. 1:5–17.

Cave, Richard Allen. 1978. *A Study of the Novels of George Moore.* New York: Barnes and Noble.

Church, Margaret. 1981. "The Adolescent Point of View toward Women in Joyce's *Portrait of the Artist as a Young Man.*" *Irish Renaissance Annual* 2:158–65.

Clarke, Jennifer. 1987. "Q. and A. with Benedict Kiely." *Irish Literary Supplement* 6, no. 1 (Spring):10–12.

Cleeve, Brian. 1967. *Dictionary of Irish Writers: Fiction.* Cork: Mercier.

Cleeve, Brian, and **Anne M. Brady.** 1985. *Biographical Dictionary of Irish Writers.* New York: St. Martin's.

Clissman, Anne. 1975. *Flann O'Brien: A Critical Introduction to His Writings.* Dublin: Gill and Macmillan.

Cohn, Ruby. 1971. "Joyce and Beckett, Irish Cosmopolitans." *James Joyce Quarterly* 8, no. 4 (Summer):385–91.

Coleman, Elliott. 1963. "A Note on Joyce and Jung." *James Joyce Quarterly* 1, no. 1 (Fall):11–16.

Colvin, Christina Edgeworth. 1966. "Maria's Father." *Times Literary Supplement*, 6 January:9–10.

Connolly, James. 1910. *Labour in Irish History*. Reprint. New York: Donnely, 1919.

Cooney, John. 1985. "Kiely Praises Novel's Insight into Donegal." *Irish Times*, 26 August:11.

Corkery, Daniel. 1925. *The Hidden Ireland: A Study of Gaelic Munster in the Eighteenth Century*. Dublin: Gill.

———. 1931. *Synge and Anglo-Irish Literature*. London and New York: Longmans, Green.

Cosgrove, Brian. 1976. "Ego Contra Mundum: Thomas Kilroy's *The Big Chapel*." *Cahiers Irlandaises* 4/5:297–309.

Costello, Peter. 1977. *The Heart Grown Brutal: The Irish Revolution in Literature from Parnell to the Death of Yeats, 1891–1939*. Dublin: Gill and Macmillan.

Cotter, Denis. 1980. "MacManus, Francis." In *Dictionary of Irish Literature*. Ed. Robert Hogan. Westport, Conn.: Greenwood. 413–15.

———. 1982. *Irish Novels of the Developing Self, 1760–1960*. Ph.D. diss. University College, Dublin.

Cronin, Anthony. 1976. *Dead as Doornails: A Chronicle of Life*. Dublin: Dolmen.

———. 1982. *Heritage Now: Irish Literature in the English Language*. Dingle, County Kerry: Brandon.

———. 1986. "Post-Structuralist, Post-Modernist, Post-Everything." *Irish Times*, 1 April:12.

Cronin, John. 1969a. "Gerald Griffin, Dedalus *Manqué*." *Studies: An Irish Quarterly* 58:267–78.

———. 1969b. "Ulster's Alarming Novels." *Éire—Ireland* 4, no. 4 (Winter):27–34.

———. 1971. "George Moore's *The Lake*: A Possible Source." *Éire—Ireland* 6, no. 3 (Fall):12–15. Rpt. in *The Way Back: George Moore's "The Untilled Field" and "The Lake."* Ed. Robert Welch. Dublin: Wolfhound, 1982. 79–82.

———. 1978. *Gerald Griffin (1803–1840): A Critical Biography*. Cambridge: Cambridge University Press.

———. 1980. *The Anglo-Irish Novel. Vol. 1. The Nineteenth Century*. Belfast: Appletree; New York: Barnes and Noble.

Cumpiano, Marion W. 1979. "Hyacinth O'Flaherty and Other References to *The House by the Churchyard* in *Finnegans Wake.*" *A Wake Newslitter* 16, no. 6:91–94.

Davenport, Gary T. 1974. "Elizabeth Bowen and the Big House." *Southern Humanities Review* 8:27–34.

Dawe, Gerald, and **Edna Longley.** 1985. Introduction to *Across a Roaring Hill: The Protestant Imagination in Modern Ireland.* Belfast; Blackstaff. i–xiii.

de Bhaldraithe, Tomás, ed. 1982. *Pádraic Ó Conaire: Clocha ar a Charn* (Pádraic Ó Conaire: Stones in a heap). Dublin: Clóchomar.

de Bréadún, Deaglán. 1986. "Mylestone in the Year Suggested." *Irish Times,* 3 April:8.

Deane, Seamus. 1976. " 'Be Assured I Am Inventing': The Fiction of John Banville." *Cahiers Irlandaises* 4/5:329–39.

———. 1985a. "Joyce and Beckett." In *Celtic Revivals. Essays in Modern Irish Literature, 1880–1980.* London and Boston; Faber. 123–34.

———. 1985b. "Joyce and Stephen: The Provincial Intellectual." In *Celtic Revivals.* 75–91.

———. 1985c. "Joyce and Nationalism." In *Celtic Revivals.* 92–107.

———. 1986. *Short History of Irish Literature.* Notre Dame, Ind.: University of Notre Dame Press.

Denvir, Gearóid, ed. 1983. *Pádraic Ó Conaire: Léachtaí Cuimhneacháin* (Pádraic Ó Conaire: Memorial lectures). Indreabhán, Galway: Cló Chonamara.

Deutsch, Richard. 1976. " 'Within Two Shadows': The Troubles in Northern Ireland." *Cahiers Irlandaises* 4/5:131–54.

Devine, Paul. 1979. "Style and Structure in John McGahern's *The Dark.*" *Critique* 21, no. 1:49–58.

Devlin, Polly. 1984a. Introduction to Molly Keane's *Devoted Ladies.* London: Virago. v–xiv.

———. 1984b. Introduction to Molly Keane's *The Rising Tide.* London: Virago. v–xvi.

Dillon, Eilís. 1976. "Sean O'Faolain and the Young Writer." *Irish University Review* 6:37–44.

Donnelly, Brian. 1974. "A Nation Gone Wrong: Liam O'Flaherty's Vision of Modern Ireland." *Studies* (Dublin) 63:71–81.

———. 1975. "The Big House in the Recent Novel." *Studies* (Dublin) 64:133–42.

Dorenkamp, J. H. 1978. "Finishing the Day: Nature and Grace in Two Novels by Brian Moore." *Éire—Ireland* 13, no. 1 (Spring):103–12.

Doyle, Paul A. 1968. *Sean O'Faolain.* New York: Twayne.
————. 1971. *Liam O'Flaherty.* New York: Twayne.
Duperray, Max. 1984. "Lord Dunsany: sa place dans une éventuelle littérature fantastique irlandaise" (Lord Dunsany: His role in Irish fantastic literature). *Études Irlandaises* 9:81–89.
Eagleton, Terry. 1978. *Literary Theory: An Introduction.* Minneapolis: University of Minnesota Press.
Eckley, Grace. 1977. "The Werewolf Revisited, and Other Ghosts of Gerald Griffin." *A Wake Newslitter* 14:39–43.
Edwards, Duane. 1972. "The Narrator of *Castle Rackrent.*" *South Atlantic Quarterly* 71, no. 1 (Winter):124–29.
Ehrlich, Heyward, ed. *Light Rays: James Joyce and Modernism.* New York: New Horizon, 1984.
Ellmann, Richard. 1957. "The Divine Nobody." *Yale Review* 47:56–71.
————. 1962. "*Ulysses* and the *Odyssey.*" *English Studies* 43:423–26.
————. 1982. *James Joyce.* Revised edition of 1959 original book. New York: Oxford University Press.
————. 1984. "Prologue: Two Perspectives on Joyce." In *Light Rays: James Joyce and Modernism.* Ed. Heyward Ehrlich. New York: New Horizon. 1–10.
————. 1986. "Preface" to *Ulysses.* New York: Random. ix–xiv.
Epstein, E. L. ed. *A Starchamber Quiry: A James Joyce Centennial Volume, 1882–1982.* New York and London: Methuen, 1982.
Fallis, Richard. 1977. *The Irish Renaissance.* Syracuse: Syracuse University Press.
Feeney, William J. 1986. "D. P. Moran's *Tom O'Kelly* and Irish Cultural Identity." *Éire—Ireland* 21, no. 3 (Fall):17–26.
Feshback, Sidney, and **William Herman.** 1984. "The History of Joyce Criticism and Scholarship." In *A Companion to Joyce Studies.* Ed. Zack Bowen and James F. Carens. Westport, Conn.: Greenwood. 727–80.
Field Day Theatre Company. 1985. *Ireland's Field Day.* London: Hutchinson.
Finneran, Richard J. 1974. "James Joyce and James Stephens: The Record of a Friendship with Unpublished Letters from Joyce to Stephens." *James Joyce Quarterly* 11:279–92.
————. 1975. "Literature and Nationality in the Work of James Stephens." *South Atlantic Bulletin* 40, no. 4:18–25.
Flanagan, Thomas. 1958. *The Irish Novelists, 1800–1850.* New York: Columbia University Press.
————. 1966. "The Big House of Ross-Drishane." *Kenyon Review* 28:54–78.

Fletcher, John. 1964. *The Novels of Samuel Beckett*. Rev. ed. New York: Barnes and Noble, 1970.

Foster, John Wilson. 1968. "Crisis and Ritual in Brian Moore's Belfast Novels." *Éire—Ireland* 3, no. 3 (Autumn):66–74.

———. 1971. "Passage through Limbo: Brian Moore's North American Novels." *Critique* 13, no. 1:5–18.

———. 1974. *Forces and Themes in Ulster Fiction*. Dublin: Gill and Macmillan.

———. 1980. "Reid, Forrest." In *Dictionary of Irish Literature*. Ed. Robert Hogan. Westport, Conn.: Greenwood. 566–67.

———. 1987. *Fictions of the Irish Literary Revival: A Changeling Art*. Syracuse: Syracuse University Press.

Fournier, Suzanne J. 1987. "Structure and Theme in John McGahern's *The Pornographer*." *Éire—Ireland* 22, no. 1 (Spring):130–50.

Frayne, John, ed. 1970. *Uncollected Prose by W. B. Yeats. Vol. 1: First Reviews and Articles 1886–1896*. New York: Columbia University Press.

Freyer, Grattan. 1973. *Peadar O'Donnell*. Lewisburg, Penn.: Bucknell University Press.

———. 1976. " 'Big Windows': The Writings of Peadar O'Donnell." *Éire—Ireland* 11, no. 1 (Spring):106–14.

Friedman, Melvin. 1973. "Samuel Beckett and His Critics Enter the 1970s." *Studies in the Novel* 5:383–99.

Gallagher, Michael Paul. 1976. "The Novels of John Broderick." *Cahiers Irlandaises* 4/5:287–95.

Garfitt, Roger. 1975. "Constants in Contemporary Irish Fiction." In *Two Decades of Irish Writing*. Ed. Douglas Dunn. Chester Springs, Penn.: Dufour. 207–41.

Garvin, John. 1977. "The Anglo-Irish Idiom in the Works of Major Irish Writers." In *The English Language in Ireland*. Ed. Diarmaid Ó Muirithe. Cork and Dublin: Mercier. 100–14.

Gates, David. 1984. " 'A Dish of Village Chat': Narrative Technique in Sheridan Le Fanu's *The House by the Churchyard*." *Canadian Journal of Irish Studies* 10, no. 1 (June):63–69.

Gifford, Don. 1983. "A Memory at the Elbow: The Teaching of James Joyce's *Ulysses*." *Bulletin of the Association of Departments of English* 76 (Winter):43–45.

Glendinning, Victoria. 1977. *Elizabeth Bowen: A Biography*. Reprint. New York: Avon, 1979.

Gluck, Barbara Reich. 1979. *Beckett and Joyce: Friendship and Fiction*. Lewisburg, Penn.: Bucknell University Press.

Goldberg, S. L. 1961. *The Classical Temper: A Study of James Joyce's "Ulysses."* London: Chatto and Windus.

Gonzalez, Alexander G. 1984. "Paralysis and Exile in George Moore's *A Drama in Muslin.*" *Colby Library Quarterly* 20, no. 3 (September):152–63.

———. 1986. "Seumas O'Kelly and James Joyce." *Éire—Ireland* 21, no. 1 (Summer):85–94.

Gould, Eric. 1979. "Condemned to Speak Excessively: Mythic Form and James Joyce's *Ulysses.*" *Sub-stance* 22:67–83.

Green, Robert. 1980. "Brian Moore's *Judith Hearne:* Celebrating the Commonplace." *International Fiction Review* 7:29–33.

Gwynn, Stephen. 1936. *Irish Literature and Drama in the English Language.* London and New York: Nelson.

Hall, Wayne E. 1980. *Shadowy Heroes: Irish Literature in the 1890s.* Syracuse: Syracuse University Press.

———. 1982. "*Esther Waters:* An Irish Story." *Irish Renaissance Annual* 1, no. 1:137–56.

———. 1986. "Le Fanu's House by the Marketplace." *Éire—Ireland* 21, no. 1 (Spring):55–72.

Harden, Elizabeth. 1984. *Maria Edgeworth.* Boston: Twayne.

Hardy, Barbara. 1964. "Form as End and Means in *Ulysses.*" *Orbis Litterarum* 19:194–200.

Harmon, Maurice. 1966. *Sean O'Faolain: A Critical Introduction.* South Bend, Ind.: Notre Dame University Press.

———. 1973. "By Memory Inspired: Themes and Forces in Recent Irish Writing." *Éire—Ireland* 8, no. 2 (Summer):3–19.

———. 1985. "The Era of Inhibitions: Irish Literature 1920–60." In *Irish Writers and Society at Large.* Ed. Masaru Sekine. Gerrards Cross, England: Colin Smythe; New York: Barnes and Noble. 31–41.

Harmon, Maurice, and **Patrick Rafroidi,** eds. 1976. *The Irish Novel in Our Time.* Lille: Lille University Press.

Harrington, John P. 1979. "Swift through Le Fanu and Joyce." *Mosaic* 12, no. 3:49–58.

———. 1981. "The Irish Landscape in Samuel Beckett's *Watt.*" *College Literature* 11, no. 1 (Winter):1–11.

Hart, Clive. 1982. "Afterword: Reading *Finnegans Wake.*" *A Star-chamber Quiry: A James Joyce Centennial Volume, 1882–1982.* Ed. E. L. Epstein. New York and London: Methuen. 155–64.

Hawthorn, Jeremy. 1982. "*Ulysses,* Modernism, and Marxist Criticism." In *James Joyce and Modern Literature.* Ed. W. J. McCormack and Alistair Stead. Boston and London: Routledge and Kegan Paul. 112–25.

Hawthorne, Mark D. 1975. *John and Michael Banim (The "O'Hara Brothers"): A Study in the Early Development of the Anglo-Irish Novel.* Salzburg: Institut für Englische Sprache und Literatur.
————. 1980. "Banim, John, and Banim, Michael." In *Dictionary of Irish Literature.* Ed. Robert Hogan. Westport, Conn.: Greenwood. 91–93.

Hayman, David. 1963. *A First Draft Version of "Finnegans Wake."* Austin: University of Texas Press.

Heath, Stephen. 1984. "Ambiviolences. Notes for Reading Joyce." In *Post-Structuralist Joyce: Essays from the French.* Ed. Derek Attridge and Daniel Ferrer. Cambridge: Cambridge University Press. 31–68.

Henke, Suzette. 1975. "Joyce's Bloom: Beyond Sexual Possessiveness." *American Imago* 32, no. 4 (Winter):329–34.
————. 1983. "James Joyce and Women: The Matriarchal Muse." In *Work in Progress: Joyce Centenary Essays.* Ed. Richard F. Peterson. Carbondale and Edwardsville, Ill.: Southern Illinois University Press. 117–31.

Henke, Suzette, and **Elaine Unkeless,** eds. 1982. *Women in Joyce.* Urbana and Chicago: University of Illinois Press.

Henry, DeWitt. 1974. "The Novels of Brian Moore: A Retrospective." *Ploughshares* 2, no. 2:7–27.

Herr, Cheryl. 1984. " 'One Good Turn Deserves Another': Theatrical Cross-Dressing in Joyce's 'Circle' Episode." *Journal of Modern Literature* 11, no. 2:263–76.

Higgins, Michael D. 1985. "Liam O'Flaherty and Peadar O'Donnell: Images of Rural Community." *Crane Bag* 9, no. 1:41–48.

Hirsch, Edward. 1983. "A War between the Orders: Yeats's Fiction and the Transcendental Moment." *Novel* 17, no. 1 (Fall):52–66.

Hogan, Robert. 1980a. "Beckett, Samuel." In *Dictionary of Irish Literature.* Westport, Conn.: Greenwood. 97–102.
————. 1980b. "Wall, Mervyn." In *Dictionary of Irish Literature.* Westport, Conn.: Greenwood. 674–75.

Howard, William. 1979. "Regional Perspective in Early Nineteenth-Century Fiction: The Case of *Ormond.*" *Wordsworth Circle* 10, no. 4 (Autumn):331–38.

Howarth, Herbert. 1958. *The Irish Writers, 1880–1940: Literature under Parnell's Star.* London: Rockliff.

Jameson, Fredric. 1982. "*Ulysses* in History." In *James Joyce and Modern Literature.* Ed. W. J. McCormack and Alistair Stead. Boston and London: Routledge and Kegan Paul. 126–41.

Jeffares, A. Norman. 1980. "Yeats and the Wrong Lever." *Yeats, Sligo and Ireland: Essays to Mark the 21st Yeats International Summer School.* Totowa, N.J.: Barnes and Noble. 98–111.

———. 1982. *Anglo-Irish Literature.* London: Macmillan.

———. 1985. "The Realist Novel: 1900–1945." In *The Genius of Irish Prose.* Ed. Augustine Martin. Dublin: Mercier. 145–54.

Kearney, Richard. 1979. "A Crisis of Imagination (An Analysis of a Counter-Tradition in the Irish Novel)." *Crane Bag:*390–402.

Kennedy, Eileen. 1983. "The Novels of John McGahern: The Road Away Becomes the Road Back." In *Contemporary Irish Writing.* Ed. James D. Brophy and Raymond J. Porter. Boston: Iona College; Twayne. 115–26.

Kennedy, Sighle. 1972. " 'The Devil and Holy Water': Samuel Beckett's *Murphy* and Flann O'Brien's *At Swim-Two-Birds.*" In *Modern Irish Literature: Essays in Honor of William York Tindall.* Ed. Raymond J. Porter and James D. Brophy. New York: Iona College; Twayne. 251–60.

Kennedy, William. 1986. Review of Benedict Kiely's *Nothing Happens in Carmincross. New York Times Book Review.* 27 October:7.

Kenner, Hugh. 1952. "Joyce's *Ulysses:* Homer and Hamlet." *Essays in Criticism* 2:85–104.

———. 1956. *Dublin's Joyce.* Bloomington: Indiana University Press; London: Chatto and Windus.

———. 1969. "Homer's Sticks and Stones." *James Joyce Quarterly* 6:285–98.

———. 1970. "Beckett Translating Beckett: Comment c'est." *Delos* 5:194–211.

———. 1985. "A Deep and Lasting Mayonnaise." Review of *The Trick of the Ga Bolga* by Patrick McGinley. *New York Times Book Review* 21 July:20.

———. 1986. "Samuel Beckett: Putting Language in Its Place." *New York Times Book Review,* 13 April:3, 35.

Kiberd, Declan. 1980. "The Fall of the Stage Irishman." In *The Genres of the Irish Literary Revival.* Ed. Ronald Schleifer. Norman, Oklahoma: Pilgrim; Dublin: Wolfhound. 39–60.

———. 1982. "George Moore's Gaelic Lawn Party." In *The Way Back: George Moore's "The Untilled Field" and "The Lake."* Ed. Robert Welch. Dublin: Wolfhound. 13–27.

———. 1983. "Pádraic Ó Conaire agus Cearta an Duine" [Pádraic Ó Conaire and the rights of man]. In *Pádraic Ó Conaire: Léachtaí Cuimhneacháin* (Pádraic Ó Conaire: Memorial lectures). Ed. Gearóid Denvir. Indreabhán, Galway: Cló Chonamara. 46–57.

———. 1984a. "*An Béal Bocht* agus an Béarla" (*The Poor Mouth* and the English language). *Comhar* 43, no. 4:20–27.

————. 1984b. "*Cré na Cille:* Ó Cadhain agus Beckett." *Nua Aois* (*New Age,* the Annual Literary Journal of Cumann Gaelach [the Irish Society] at University College, Dublin). 9–23.

————. 1985a. "Joyce's *Ulysses:* Past Eve and Adam." In *Men and Feminism in Modern Literature.* New York: St. Martin's. 168–203.

————. 1985b. "Samuel Beckett and the Protestant Ethic." In *The Genius of Irish Prose.* Ed. Augustine Martin. Dublin: Mercier. 121–30.

Kiely, Benedict. 1948. *Poor Scholar: A Study of the Works and Days of William Carleton.* New York; Sheed and Ward.

————. 1950. *Modern Irish Fiction–A Critique.* Dublin: Golden Eagle.

Kilroy, James, ed. 1976. *Anglo-Irish Literature: A Review of Research.* New York: Modern Language Association.

————. 1983. *Recent Research on Anglo-Irish Writers.* New York: Modern Language Association.

Kilroy, Thomas. 1972. "Teller of Tales." *Times Literary Supplement,* 17 March:301–02.

————. 1982. "The Irish Writer: Self and Society." In *Literature and the Changing Ireland.* Ed. Peter Connolly. Gerrards Cross, England: Colin Smythe; Totowa, N.J.: Barnes and Noble. 175–87.

Kimball, Jean. 1976. "James Joyce and Otto Rank: The Incest Motif in *Ulysses." James Joyce Quarterly* 13, no. 3 (Spring):366–82.

————. 1980. "Freud, Leonardo, and Joyce: The Dimensions of a Childhood Memory." Rpt. in *The Seventh of Joyce.* Ed. Bernard Benstock. Bloomington: Indiana University Press; Brighton, England: Harvester. 57–73.

Kinsella, Thomas. 1980. "Clarke, Austin." In *Dictionary of Irish Literature.* Ed. Robert Hogan. Westport, Conn.: Greenwood. 156–61.

Klein, James. 1976. "Out of Mere Words: Self-Composition and *A Portrait of the Artist." James Joyce Quarterly* 13, no. 3 (Spring):293–301.

Kramer, Dale. 1973. *Charles Robert Maturin.* New York: Twayne.

Krans, Horatio Sheafe. 1903. *Irish Life in Irish Fiction.* New York: Columbia University Press.

Laigle, Deirdre. 1984. "Images of the Big House in Elizabeth Bowen's *The Last September." Cahiers Irlandaises* 9:61–79.

Lassner, Phyllis. 1986. "The past is a Burning Pattern: Elizabeth Bowen's *The Last September." Éire—Ireland* 21, no. 1 (Spring):40–54.

Levin, Harry. 1941. *James Joyce: A Critical Introduction.* New York: New Directions.

Levine, Jennifer. 1978. "Rejoicings in *Tel Quel.*" *James Joyce Quarterly* 16, nos. 1/2:17–26.

Lewis, Gifford. 1985. *Somerville and Ross: The World of the Irish R.M.* New York and Middlesex: Viking/Penguin.

Linehan, Fergus. 1986. "The Monk's Progress." Review of Mervyn Wall's *The Complete Fursey. Irish Times,* 22 February:Weekend 4.

Litz, A. Walton. 1966. *James Joyce.* New York: Twayne.

Lubbers, Klaus. 1980. "Die Erzählprosa des modernen Irland" (The fiction of modern Ireland). *Einführung in die Zeitgenös-sische Irische Literatur* (Introduction to contemporary Irish literature). Ed. J. Kornelius, E. Otto, and G. Stratmann. Heidelberg: Carl Winter/Universitätverlag. 63–78.

———. 1985a. *Geschichte der irischchen Erzählprosa von den anfängen bis zum ausgehenden 19. Jahrhundert* (A history of Irish fiction from the beginnings to the end of the 19th century). Munich: Wilhelm Fink.

———. 1985b. "Irish Fiction: A Mirror for Specifics." *Éire—Ireland* 20, no. 2 (Summer):90–104.

———. 1986. "Emancipatory Women in Late Nineteenth-Century Anglo-Irish Fiction: A Note on the Emergence of a Motif." *Canadian Journal of Irish Studies* 12, no. 1 (June):53–58.

Lynch, M. Kelly. 1983. "The Smiling Public Man: Joseph O'Neill and His Works." *The Journal of Irish Literature* 12, no. 2:3–72.

Lyons, F. S. L. 1971. *Ireland Since the Famine.* Reprint. Glasgow, Scotland; Fontana / Collins, 1975.

McCabe, Colin. 1979. *James Joyce and the Revolution of the Word.* London: Macmillan.

McCaffrey, Lawrence J. 1979. *Ireland: From Colony to Nation State.* New York: Prentice-Hall.

MacCana, Proinsias. 1980. *Literature in Irish.* Dublin: Department of Foreign Affairs.

McCarthy, Patrick A. 1983. "The Moore-Joyce Nexus: An Irish Literary Comedy." In *George Moore in Perspective.* Ed. Janet E. Dunleavy. Totowa, N.J.: Barnes and Noble; Naas, Co. Kildare: Malton; Gerrards Cross, England: Colin Smythe. 99–116.

MacCongáil, Nollaig. 1983. *Scribhneoirí Thir Chonaill* (Writers of Tirconnel). Dublin: Foilseacháin Náisiúnta.

McCormack, W. J. 1980. *Sheridan Le Fanu and Victorian Ireland.* Oxford: Clarendon.

————. 1985. " 'The Protestant Strain': Or, a Short History of Anglo-Irish Literature from S. T. Coleridge to Thomas Mann." In *Across a Roaring Hill: The Protestant Imagination in Modern Ireland*. Ed. Gerald Dawe and Edna Longley. Belfast: Blackstaff. 48–78.

McCrum, Robert, William Cran, and **Robert MacNeil.** 1986. "The Irish Question." *The Story of English*. New York: Elisabeth Sifton / Viking. 163–93.

MacDonagh, Thomas. 1916. *Literature in Ireland*. Dublin: Talbot Press.

McDonnell, Michael. 1980. "MacNamara, Brinsley." In *Dictionary of Irish Literature*. Ed. Robert Hogan. Westport, Conn.: Greenwood. 418–21.

MacEoin, Gearóid. 1969. "Twentieth-Century Irish Literature." In *A View of the Irish Language*. Ed. Brian Ó Cuiv. Dublin: Stationery Office. 57–69.

McFate, Patricia. 1979. *The Writings of James Stephens*. New York: St. Martin's.

McGann, Jerome J. 1985. "Introduction: A Point of Reference." In *Historical Studies and Literary Criticism*. Madison: University of Wisconsin Press. 3–21.

McHugh, James P. 1984. *Voices of the Rear Guard. A Study of "An Phoblacht,"* 1925–37: *Irish Republican Ideology in the Post-Revolutionary Era*. M.A. thesis. University College, Dublin.

McHugh, Roger, and **Maurice Harmon.** 1982. *Short History of Anglo-Irish Literature, from Its Origins to the Present Day*. Totowa, N.J.: Barnes and Noble.

McInerney, Michael. 1976. *Peadar O'Donnell: Irish Social Rebel*. Dublin: O'Brien.

MacKillop, James. 1983. *"The Hungry Grass:* Richard Power's Pastoral Elegy." *Éire—Ireland* 18, no. 3 (Autumn):86–99.

————. 1986. *Fionn MacCumhaill: Celtic Myth in English Literature*. Syracuse, New York: Syracuse University Press.

McLuhan, Herbert Marshall. 1951. "A Survey of Joyce Criticism." *Renascence* 4:12–18.

McMahon, Seán. 1985. "The Realist Novel After the Second World War." In *The Genius of Irish Prose*. Ed. Augustine Martin. Dublin: Mercier. 145–54.

MacManus, Francis. 1935. "The Artist for Nobody's Sake." *Irish Monthly* 63:175–80.

McMinn, Joseph. 1980. "Contemporary Novels on the Troubles." *Études Irlandaises* 5:113–21.

McSweeney, Kerry. 1976. "Brian Moore: Past and Present." *Critical Quarterly* 18, no. 2:53–66.

Madden-Simpson, Janet. 1984. "Anglo-Irish Literature: The Received Tradition." Introduction to *Women's Part: An Anthology of Short Fiction by and about Irishwomen 1890–1920.* Dublin: Arlen House. 1–19.

Manganiello, Dominic. 1980. *Joyce's Politics.* London: Macmillan.

Marcus, Phillip. 1970a. *Standish O'Grady.* Lewisburg, Penn.: Bucknell University Press.

——. 1970b. *Yeats and the Beginning of the Irish Renaissance.* Ithaca: Cornell University Press.

Martin, Augustine. 1977. *James Stephens: A Critical Study.* Totowa, N.J.: Barnes and Noble.

——. 1985a. "Fable and Fantasy." In *The Genius of Irish Prose.* Dublin: Mercier. 110–20.

——. 1985b. "Prose Fiction in the Irish Literary Renaissance." In *Irish Writers and Society at Large.* Ed. Masaru Sekine. Gerrards Cross, England: Colin Smythe; Totowa, N.J.: Barnes and Noble. 139–62.

Matthews, James H. 1980. "O'Connor, Frank." In *Dictionary of Irish Literature.* Ed. Robert Hogan. Westport, Conn.: Greenwood. 500–05.

——. 1983. *Voices: A Life of Frank O'Connor.* New York: Atheneum.

Mays, J. C. C. 1974. "Brian O'Nolan and Joyce on Art and on Life." *James Joyce Quarterly* 11, no. 3 (Spring):238–56.

——. 1977. "Mythologized Presences: *Murphy* in Its Time." In *Myth and Reality in Irish Literature.* Ed. Joseph Ronsley. Waterloo, Ontario: Wilfrid Laurier University Press. 197–210.

Mercier, Vivian. 1943. *Realism in Anglo-Irish Fiction.* Ph.D. diss. Trinity College, Dublin.

——. 1962. *The Irish Comic Tradition.* New York: Oxford University Press.

——. 1966. "Man Against Nature: The Novels of Liam O'Flaherty." *Wascana Review* 1, no. 2:37–46.

——. 1982. "John Eglinton as Socrates. A Study of 'Scylla and Charybdis.' " In *James Joyce: An International Perspective.* Ed. Suheil Badi Bushrui and Bernard Benstock. Totowa, N.J.: Barnes and Noble; Gerrards Cross, England: Colin Smythe. 65–81.

Meredith, Robert L. 1972. "William Carleton and Charles Lever." *Carleton Newsletter* 3, no. 2:11–14.

Miller, J. Hillis. 1982. "From Narrative Theory to Joyce, from Joyce to Narrative Theory." In *The Seventh of Joyce.* Ed. Bernard

Benstock. Bloomington: Indiana University Press; Brighton, England: Harvester. 3–4.

Molloy, Francis C. 1977. "The Novels of John McGahern." *Critique* 19, no. 1:5–27.

———. 1981. "The Search for Truth: The Fiction of John Banville." *Irish University Review* 11, no. 1 (Spring):29–51.

Molyneux, William. 1698. *Case of Ireland's Being Bound by Acts of Parliament in England, Stated.* Reprint. Dublin: Cadenus Press, 1977.

Moody, T. W., and F. X. Martin. 1984. *The Course of Irish History.* Rev. ed. Cork: Mercier.

Moore, Harry T. 1971. Postscript to Francis Stuart's *Black List / Section H.* Carbondale: Southern Illinois University Press. 427–42.

Morrison, Richard. 1965. "A Note on William Carleton." *University Review* (Missouri) 3 (Spring):219–26.

Mortimer, Anthony. 1984. "*Castle Rackrent* and Its Historical Contexts." *Études Irlandais* 9 (December):107–23.

Moynahan, Julian. 1984. "The Image of the City in Nineteenth-Century Irish Fiction." In *The Irish Writer and the City.* Ed. Maurice Harmon. Gerrards Cross, England: Colin Smythe; Totowa, N.J.: Barnes and Noble. 1–17.

Murphy, John A. 1975. *Ireland in the Twentieth Century.* Dublin: Gill and Macmillan.

Murray, Patrick. 1971. "Maria Edgeworth and Her Father: The Literary Partnership." *Éire—Ireland* 6, no. 3:39–50.

Murray, Patrick Joseph. 1857. *The Life of John Banim.* Reprint. New York: Garland, 1978.

Naremore, James. 1976. "Consciousness and Society in *A Portrait of the Artist*." In *Approaches to Joyce's "Portrait": Ten Essays.* Ed. Thomas F. Staley and Bernard Benstock. Pittsburgh: University of Pittsburgh Press. 113–34.

Newcomer, James. 1966. "*Castle Rackrent*: Its Structure and Its Irony." *Criticism* 8, no. 2 (Spring):170–79.

———. 1983. "Mrs. Samuel Carter Hall and *The Whiteboy*." *Études Irlandais* 8 (December):113–19.

Ní Chuílleanáin, Eiléan. 1985. "Woman as Writer: Dánta Grá to Maria Edgeworth." In *Irish Women: Image and Achievement.* Dublin: Arlen House. 111–26.

Nic Eoin, Máirín. 1984. "Urscéalaíocht na Gaeilge, 1974–1984" (The novel in Irish, 1974–1984). *Comhar* 43, no. 8:15–21.

———. 1985. Letter to author of 3 October.

Nic Pháidín, Caoilfhionn. 1980. "*Cré na Cille*: Ealaín na Mairechtála" (*Cré na Cille*: The art of living). *Comhar* 39, no. 10:43–48.

Norris, Margot. 1974. *The Decentered Universe of "Finnegans Wake": A Structuralist Analysis*. Baltimore: Johns Hopkins University Press.

O'Brien, Darcy. 1976a. "A Critique of Psychoanalytic Criticism, or What Joyce Did and Did Not Do." *James Joyce Quarterly* 13, no. 3 (Spring):275–92.

————. 1976b. "In Ireland After *A Portrait*." In *Approaches to Joyce's "Portrait": Ten Essays*. Ed. Thomas F. Staley and Bernard Benstock. Pittsburgh: University of Pittsburgh Press. 213–37.

————. 1982. "Edna O'Brien: A Kind of Irish Childhood." In *Twentieth-Century Women Novelists*. Ed. Thomas F. Staley. Totowa, N.J.: Barnes and Noble. 179–90.

O'Brien, Edna. 1986. "Why Irish Heroines Don't Have to Be Good Anymore." *New York Times Book Review*, 11 May:13.

O'Brien, Eoin. 1986a. *The Beckett Country: Samuel Beckett's Ireland*. Dublin: Black Cat.

————. 1986b. "Beckett Is of the World . . . But Irish." *Irish Times*, 12 April:1, 5.

O'Brien, Flann ["Myles na gCopaleen" / Brian O'Nolan]. 1968. *The Best of Myles*. Reprint. London: Pan, 1977.

O'Brien, James H. 1973. *Liam O'Flaherty*. Lewisburg, Penn.: Bucknell University Press.

————. 1974. "Carleton in a New Format." *Carleton Newsletter* 5, no. 1:6.

O'Brien, Kate. 1977. "Imaginative Prose by the Irish, 1820–1970." In *Myth and Reality in Irish Literature*. Ed. Joseph Ronsley. Waterloo, Ontario: Wilfrid Laurier. 305–15.

Ó Broin, Tomás. 1979. "*Deoraíocht*: Saothar Eispresiúnach" (*Deoraíocht*: An expressionistic work). *Feasta* 32, no. 6:13–19.

————. 1984. *Saoirse Anama Uí Chonaire: Compánach d'Urscéal Fiontrach 'Deoraíocht'* (The freedom of the soul of Ó Conaire: A companion to the innovative novel *Deoraíocht*). Galway: Officina Typographica.

Ó Cadhain, Máirtín. 1971. "Irish Prose in the Twentieth Century." In *Literature in Celtic Countries*. Ed. J. E. Caerwyn Williams. Cardiff: University of Wales Press. 139–51.

Ó Conaire, Breandán. 1973. "Flann O'Brien, *An Béal Bocht*, and Other Irish Matters." *Irish University Review* 3, no. 2:121–40.

————. 1986. *Myles na Gaeilge: Lámhleabhar ar Shaothar Gaeilge Bhrian Ó Nualláin* [Myles of the Irish: A Guide to the Gaelic Work of Brian O'Nolan]. Dublin: An Clóchomhar.

O'Connor, Frank. 1956. *The Mirror in the Roadway: A Study of the Modern Novel.* New York: Alfred A. Knopf.

————. 1962. *The Lonely Voice: A Study of the Short Story.* Cleveland: World.

————. 1967. *A Short History of Irish Literature: A Backward Look.* New York: Putnam.

Ó Doibhlin, Breandán. 1974. "Athléamh ar *Chré na Cille* (A reconsideration of *Cré na Cille*). *Léachtaí Cholm Chille* (Colmkille lectures) 5:40–59.

O'Faolain, Sean. 1942. Preface to Maura Laverty's *Never No More.* Reprint. London: Virago, 1985. v–ix.

————. 1962. "Fifty Years of Irish Writing." *Studies* (Dublin) 51:93–105.

Ó Háinle, Cathal. 1978. *Promhadh Pinn* (The proof of the pen). Maynooth, Ireland: An Sagart.

————. 1984. " 'The Inalienable Right of Trifles': Tradition and Modernity in Gaelic Writing Since the Revival." *Éire—Ireland* 19, no. 4 (Winter):59–77.

Ó Hehir, Brendan. 1967. *A Gaelic Lexicon for "Finnegans Wake," and Glossary for Joyce's Other Works.* Berkeley: University of California Press.

Ó hEithir, Breandán. 1977. "On *Cré na Cille* by Mártín Ó Cadhain." In *The Pleasures of Gaelic Literature.* Ed. John Jordan. Dublin and Cork: Mercier. 72–84.

O'Leary, Philip. 1982. "The Two Strands: Cultural Identity and Alienation in the Novels of Tarlack Ó hUid." *Proceedings of the Harvard Celtic Colloquium* 2:39–59.

————. 1984. "Sea Stories and Soul Searching: Vocation in the Novels of Diarmaid Ó Súilleabháin." *Proceedings of the Harvard Celtic Colloquium* 4:9–38.

————. 1985. "Light Reading in Irish." *Irish Literary Supplement* 4, no. 2 (Fall):48.

————. 1986a. "Castles of Gold: America and Americans in the Fiction of Séamus Ó Grianna." *Éire—Ireland* 21, no. 2 (Summer):70–84.

————. 1986b. "Gaelic Literature." *Irish Literary Supplement* 5, no. 2 (Fall):18–19.

Ó Muirithe, Diarmaid, ed. 1977. *The English Language in Ireland.* Cork and Dublin: Mercier.

344 THE IRISH NOVEL

Ó Murchú, Seosamh. 1984. "Diarmaid Ó Súilleabháin: Nóta Beathaisnéise" (Diarmaid Ó Súilleabháin: Biographical notes). *Irisleabhar Mhá Nuad* (Maynooth Journal). 7–20.

O'Neill, Patrick. 1980. "Image and Reception: The German Fortunes of Maria Edgeworth, Lady Morgan, Thomas Moore, and Charles Maturin." *Canadian Journal of Irish Studies* 6, no. 1:36–49.

Orr, Leonard. 1986. "Yeats's Theories of Fiction." *Éire—Ireland* 21, no. 2 (Summer):152–58.

O'Toole, Bridget. 1985. "Three Writers of the Big House: Elizabeth Bowen, Molly Keane, and Jennifer Johnston." In *Across a Roaring Hill: The Protestant Imagination in Modern Ireland.* Ed. Gerald Dawe and Edna Longley. Belfast: Blackstaff. 124–38.

O'Toole, Fintan. 1986. "A Stain upon the Silence." *Magill* (Dublin), April:48–54.

Ó Tuairisc, Eoghan. 1981. Letter to Author of 27 March.

Ó Tuama, Seán. 1972. "A Writer's Testament." *Ériu* 23:242–48.

———. 1976. "The Other Tradition: Some Highlights of Modern Fiction in Irish." *Cahiers Irlandaises* 4/5:31–47.

———. 1978. "Samuel Beckett, Éireannach" (Samuel Beckett, Irishman). *Scríobh* 3:37–41.

Ó Tuathaigh, Gearóid. 1979. "Language, Literature, and Culture in Ireland Since the War." *Ireland 1945–70.* Ed. J. J. Lee. Dublin: Gill and Macmillan; New York: Barnes and Noble. 111–23.

Owens, Coilín. 1980. "McGahern, John." In *Dictionary of Irish Literature.* Ed. Robert Hogan. Westport, Conn.: Greenwood. 399–401.

Paulin, Tom. 1984a. "James Joyce: A Centenary Celebration." In *Ireland and the English Crisis.* Newcastle upon Tyne, England: Bloodaxe. 143–47.

———. 1984b. "Nineteen Twelve." In *Ireland and the English Crisis.* 120–27.

Plunkett, James. 1972. *The Gems She Wore: A Book of Irish Places.* London: Hutchinson.

Popot, Raymonde. 1976. "Edna O'Brien's Paradise Lost." *Cahiers Irlandaises* 4/5:255–85.

Porter, Raymond J. 1975. "Miracle, Mystery, and Faith in Brian Moore's *Catholics.*" *Éire—Ireland* 10, no. 3 (Autumn):79–88.

Powell, David. 1971. "An Annotated Bibliography of Myles na Gopaleen's (Flann O'Brien's) 'Cruiskeen Lawn' Commentaries on James Joyce." *James Joyce Quarterly* 9, no. 1 (Fall):50–62.

Prosky, Murray. 1971. "The Crisis of Identity in the Novels of Brian Moore." *Éire—Ireland* 6, no. 3 (Autumn):106–18.

Quinn, Charles B. 1983. "Some Aspects of Contemporary Prose in Irish." In *Contemporary Irish Writing*. Ed. James D. Brophy and Raymond J. Porter. Boston: Iona College; Twayne. 157–72.

Rabaté, Jean-Michel. 1984. "Lapsus ex Machina." Trans. Elizabeth Guild. In *Post-Structuralist Joyce: Essays from the French*. Ed. Derek Attridge and Daniel Ferrer. Cambridge: Cambridge University Press. 152–72.

Rabinovitz, Rubin. 1984. *The Development of Samuel Beckett's Fiction*. Urbana and Chicago: University of Illinois Press.

Rafroidi, Patrick. 1972. *L'Irlande et le romanticisme: La littérature Irlandaise-Anglaise de 1789 à 1850 et sa place dans le mouvement occidental* (Ireland and romanticism: Anglo-Irish literature from 1789 to 1850 and its place in the European movement). Paris: Éditions Universataires.

———. 1973. "The Uses of Irish Myth in the Nineteenth Century." *Studies* (Dublin) 62:256–61.

Raleigh, John Henry. 1985. "Many Scholars, Many Roads: Joyce in America." *University Publishing* 14 (Spring):9–11.

Ray, Gordon N. 1952. "The Bentley Papers." *Library* (5th series) 7, no. 3 (September):178–200.

Reynolds, Lorna. 1982. Preface to Kate O'Brien's *The Land of Spices*. Dublin: Arlen House. vi–x.

———. 1987. *Kate O'Brien: A Literary Portrait*. Gerrards Cross, England: Colin Smythe; Totowa, N.J.: Barnes and Noble.

Robinson, Hilary. 1980. *Somerville and Ross: A Critical Appreciation*. Dublin: Gill and Macmillan; New York: St. Martin's.

Robinson, Mary F. 1978. "Does the River Liffey Freeze Well? A Critique of Margot Norris' *The Decentered Universe of "Finnegans Wake"* as Applied Structuralism." *Semiotic Scene* 2, no. 4:169–79.

Rose, Marilyn. 1971. "The Irish Memories of Beckett's Voice." *Journal of Modern Literature* 2, no. 1:127–32.

Ross, Ian Campbell. 1980. "The Triumph of Prudence over Passion: Nationalism and Feminism in an Eighteenth-Century Irish Novel." *Irish University Review* 10:232–40.

———. 1982. "An Irish Picaresque Novel: William Chaigneau's *The History of Jack Connor*." *Studies: An Irish Quarterly Review* 71:270–79.

———. 1983. "Thomas Amory, *John Buncle*, and the Origins of Irish Fiction." *Éire—Ireland* 18, no. 3 (Fall):71–86.

Rossman, Charles. 1976. "On Doing Unto Joyce Before He Does Unto You: Modes of Critical Engagement in Some Recent Joyce Studies." *Studies in the Novel* 8:351–66.

————. 1982. "The Reader's Role in *A Portrait of the Artist as a Young Man*." In *James Joyce: An International Perspective*. Ed. Suheil Badi Bushrui and Bernard Benstock. Gerrards Cross, England: Colin Smythe; Totowa, N.J.: Barnes and Noble. 19–37.

Ryan, Joan. 1982. "Women in the Novels of Kate O'Brien." In *Studies in Anglo-Irish Literature*. Ed. Heinz Kosok. Bonn: Bouvier. 322–32.

————. 1984. "Class and Creed in Kate O'Brien." In *The Irish Writer and the City*. Ed. Maurice Harmon. Gerrards Cross, England: Colin Smythe; Totowa, N.J.: Barnes and Noble. 125–35.

Ryan, John. 1975. *Remembering How We Stood: Bohemian Dublin at Mid-Century*. Dublin: Gill and Macmillan.

Ryan, Stephen P. 1960. "Ireland and Its Writers." *Catholic World* 192:149–55.

Scholes, Robert. 1974. "*Ulysses*: A Structuralist Perspective." In *Structuralism in Literature: An Introduction*. New Haven and London: Yale University Press. 180–90.

——. 1985. *Textual Power: Literary Theory and the Teaching of English*. New Haven and London: Yale University Press.

Schwab, Gabriele. 1982. "Mollyloquy." In *The Seventh of Joyce*. Ed. Bernard Benstock. Bloomington: Indiana University Press; Brighton, England: Harvester. 81–85.

Scott, Bonnie Kime. 1980. "Laverty, Maura." In *Dictionary of Irish Literature*. Ed. Robert Hogan. Westport, Conn.: Greenwood. 362–63.

————. 1984. *Joyce and Feminism*. Bloomington: Indiana University Press.

————. 1987. *James Joyce*. Brighton, England: Harvester.

Senn, Fritz. 1966. "Reverberations." *James Joyce Quarterly* 3, no. 3 (Spring):222.

————. 1984. *Joyce's Dislocutions: Essays on Reading as Translation*. Ed. John Paul Riquelme. Baltimore and London: Johns Hopkins University Press.

Shapiro, Barbara. 1969. "Toward a Psychoanalytic Reading of Beckett's *Molloy*." *Literature and Psychology* 19, no. 2:71–86; 19, nos. 3/4:15–30.

Shechner, Mark. 1974. *Joyce in Nighttown: A Psychoanalytic Inquiry into "Ulysses."* Berkeley: University of California Press.

————. 1976. "Exposing Joyce." *James Joyce Quarterly* 13, no. 3 (Spring): 266–74.

Sheeran, Patrick F. 1976. *The Novels of Liam O'Flaherty: A Study in Romantic Realism*. Atlantic Highlands, N.J.: Humanities.

Sherry, Ruth. 1984. "The Irish Working Class in Fiction." In *The British Working-Class Novel in the Twentieth Century.* Ed. Jeremy Hawthorn. London: Edward Arnold. 111–23.

Skrabanek, Petr. 1976. "Anglo-Irish in *Finnegans Wake.*" *A Wake Newslitter* 13, no. 5:79–85.

Sloan, Barry. 1982. "Samuel Lover's Irish Novels." *Études Irlandaises* 7:31–42.

———. 1984. "Mrs. Hall's Ireland." *Éire—Ireland* 19, no. 3 (Fall):18–30.

———. 1986. *The Pioneers of Anglo-Irish Fiction, 1800–1850.* Gerrards Cross, England: Colin Smythe.

Snow, Lotus. 1979. " 'That Trenchant Childhood Route?' Quest in Edna O'Brien's Novels." *Éire—Ireland* 14, no. 1 (Spring):74–83.

Solomon, Albert J. 1973. "A Moore in *Ulysses.*" *James Joyce Quarterly* 10:215–27.

Sosnoski, James. 1978. "Reading Acts and Reading Warrants: Some Implications for Readers Responding to Joyce's Portrait of Stephen." *James Joyce Quarterly* 16, nos. 1/2:43–63.

Staley, Thomas F. 1965. "Joyce Scholarship in the 1960s." *Papers on English Language and Literature* 1, no. 3 (Summer):279–86.

———. 1976a. "James Joyce." In *Anglo-Irish Literature: A Review of Research.* Ed. James Kilroy. New York: Modern Language Association. 366–435.

———. 1976b. "Strings in the Labyrinth: Sixty Years with Joyce's *Portrait.*" In *Approaches to Joyce's "Portrait": Ten Essays.* Ed. Staley and Bernard Benstock. Pittsburgh: University of Pittsburgh Press. 3–24.

———. 1982. "Following Ariadne's String: Tracing Joyce Scholarship into the Eighties." In *James Joyce: An International Perspective.* Ed. Suheil Badi Bushrui and Bernard Benstock. Gerrards Cross, England: Colin Smythe; Totowa, N.J.: Barnes and Noble. 250–77.

———. 1983. "James Joyce." In *Recent Research on Anglo-Irish Writers.* Ed. James F. Kilroy. New York: Modern Language Association. 181–202.

Stanford, W. B. 1953. "Ulyssean Qualities in Joyce's Leopold Bloom." *Comparative Literature* 5:125–36.

———. 1964. "The Reintegrated Hero." In *The Ulysses Theme.* New York: Barnes and Noble. 211–40.

Staples, Hugh B. 1971. "Beckett in the *Wake.*" *James Joyce Quarterly* 8, no. 4 (Summer):421–24.

348   THE IRISH NOVEL

Stevenson, Lionel. 1936. *The Wild Irish Girl: The Life of Sydney Owenson, Lady Morgan.* Reprint. New York: Russell and Russell, 1969.
Sullivan [Ibarra], Eileen. 1970. "William Carleton: An Introduction." *Éire—Ireland* 5, no. 1:81–86.
Sultan, Stanley. 1968. "An Old-Irish Model for *Ulysses*." *James Joyce Quarterly* 5:103–09.
Swift, Jonathan. 1729. *A Modest Proposal for Preventing the Children of Poor People in Ireland from Being a Burden to Their Parents or Country, and for Making Them Beneficial to the Public.* Reprint. In *The Norton Anthology of English Literature.* 4th ed. New York: 1979. 2144–151.
Tanner, Stephen L. 1984. "Joyce and Modern Critical Theory." *Arizona Quarterly* 40, no. 3 (Autumn):269–79.
Thiher, Allen. 1983. "Wittgenstein, Heidegger, The Unnamable, and Some Thoughts on the Status of Voice in Fiction." In *Samuel Beckett: Humanistic Perspectives.* Ed. Morris Beja, S. E. Gontarski, and Pierre Astier. Columbus: Ohio State University Press. 80–90.
Thomas, Brook. 1982. "Formal Recreation, and Re-Joycing the Re-Rightings of *Ulysses*." In *The Seventh of Joyce.* Ed. Bernard Benstock. Bloomington: Indiana University Press; Brighton, England: Harvester. 5–9.
Thompson, William Irwin. 1964. "The Language of *Finnegans Wake*." *Sewanee Review* 72, no. 1:78–90.
———. 1967. *The Imagination of an Insurrection: Dublin, Easter 1916: A Study of an Ideological Movement.* New York: Oxford University Press.
Thuente, Mary Helen. 1985. "Violence in Pre-Famine Ireland: The Testimony of Irish Folklore and Fiction." *Irish University Review* 15, no. 2 (Autumn):129–47.
Tindall, William York. 1959. *A Reader's Guide to James Joyce.* New York: Farrar, Straus, and Giroux.
Titley, Alan. 1980. "Rough Rug-Headed Kerns: The Irish Gunman in the Popular Novel." *Éire—Ireland* 15, no. 4 (Winter):15–38.
———. 1981. "Litríocht na Gaeilge, Litríocht an Bhéarla, agus *Irish Literature*" (The literature of Irish, the literature of English, and "Irish Literature"). *Scríobh* 5:116–39.
Tolomeo, Diane. 1983. "Modern Fiction." In *Recent Research on Anglo-Irish Writers.* Ed. James F. Kilroy. New York: Modern Language Association. 268–98.
Toolan, Michael. 1980. "Psyche and Belief: Brian Moore's Contending Angels." *Éire—Ireland* 15, no. 3 (Autumn):97–111.

———. 1981. "John McGahern: The Historian and the Pornographer." *Canadian Journal of Irish Studies* 7, no. 2:39–55.

Tracy, Robert. 1986. Review of Desmond Hogan's *A Curious Street*. *Éire—Ireland* 21, no. 1 (Spring): 143–47.

Tuohy, Frank. 1985. "Five Fierce Ladies." In *Irish Writers and Society at Large*. Ed. Masaru Sekine. Gerrards Cross, England: Colin Smythe; Totowa, N.J.: Barnes and Noble. 199–206.

Unkeless, Elaine. 1976. "Leopold Bloom as a Womanly Man." *Modernist Studies: Literature and Culture, 1920–1940* 2, no. 1:35–44.

———. 1982. "The Conventional Molly Bloom." In *Women in Joyce*. Ed. Suzette Henke and Unkeless. Bloomington: Indiana University Press. 150–68.

Wall, Richard. 1977. "Joyce's Use of the Anglo-Irish Dialect of English." In *Place, Personality and the Irish Writer*. Ed. Andrew Carpenter. New York: Barnes and Noble; Gerrards Cross, England: Colin Smythe. 121–35.

———. 1986. *An Anglo-Irish Dialect Glossary for Joyce's Works*. Gerrards Cross, England: Colin Smythe.

Watt, Ian. 1957. *The Rise of the Novel: Studies in Defoe, Richardson, and Fielding*. Reprint. Harmondsworth, England: Penguin, 1972.

Weeks, Ann. 1986. "Diarmuid and Gráinne Again: Julia O'Faolain's *No Country for Young Men*." *Éire—Ireland* 21, no. 1 (Spring):89–102.

Welch, Robert. 1985. "Some Thoughts on Writing a Companion to Irish Literature." *Irish Writers and Society at Large*. Ed. Masaru Sekine. Gerrards Cross, England: Colin Smythe; Totowa, N.J.: Barnes and Noble. 225–36.

Wolff, Robert Lee. 1979a. "The Fiction of the 'O'Hara Family'." Introduction to *The Denounced*. New York: Garland. v–lii.

———. 1979b. "The Irish Novels of Sydney Owenson, Lady Morgan." Introduction to *The O'Briens and the O'Flahertys*. New York: Garland. v–xxix.

———. 1979c. "*Knocknagow*, by Charles Joseph Kickham." Introduction to *Knocknagow*. New York: Garland. v–xi.

———. 1980. *William Carleton, Irish Peasant Novelist: A Preface to His Fiction*. New York: Garland.

———. n.d. *Nineteenth-Century Fiction, Series Two: Ireland from the Act of Union (1800) to the Death of Parnell (1891)*. Book catalog. New York: Garland.

Wright, Arnold. 1914. *Disturbed Dublin: The Story of the Great Strike of 1913–14, with a Description of the Industries of the Irish Capital*. London: Longmans, Green.

Yeats, William Butler. 1891. Introduction to *Representative Irish Tales*. Reprint. Gerrards Cross, England: Colin Smythe, 1979. Ed. Mary Helen Thuente. 25–32.

Young, Arthur. 1780. *A Tour in Ireland 1776–1779*. Reprint. Ed. A. W. Hutton. 2 vols. Shannon: Irish University Press, 1970.

Zneimer, John. 1970. *The Literary Vision of Liam O'Flaherty*. Syracuse: Syracuse University Press.

Index

Abbey Theatre, 128, 201, 230, 301
Act of Union of 1800, 1, 11, 25
A. E. (George Russell), 86, 100, 108–9, 119, 120, 142, 182
Allingham, William: *Laurence Bloomfield in Ireland*, 76
Amory, Thomas: *Life of John Buncle, The*, 12
Anglo-Irish War of 1919–1921, 89, 180, 192, 195, 206
Anti-Union Weekly Magazine, 25
Archdeacon, Matthew, 26

Banim, John: 4–5, 14, 26, 34–40, 42, 47–48, 49, 52, 59, 66, 71, 84, 101, 191, 198, 266, 309–10n3; *Anglo-Irish of the Nineteenth Century, The*, 39, 139; *Boyne Water, The*, 35, 37–38, 39, 40, 42, 45, 71, 139, 310; *Conformists, The*, 39; *Father Connell*, 40; *Fetches, The*, 36; *John Doe*, 36, 59; *Last Baron of Crana, The*, 39; *Nowlans, The*, 37–38, 40, 92, 106, 137, 299, 310; *Smuggler, The*, 40
Banim, Michael: 4–5, 26, 34–40, 47–48, 49, 59, 66, 84, 101, 153, 191, 198, 309–10n3; *Crohoore of the Bill-Hook*, 36–37, 40, 80, 310; *Croppy, The*, 39; *Father Connell*, 40; *Ghost-Hunter and His Family, The*, 40; *Mayor of Windgap, The*, 40; *Town of the Cascades, The*, 40
Banville, John: 206, 262, 272, 276, 278, 280, 291, 294; *Birchwood*,

206, 276, 279; *Doctor Copernicus*, 278; *Kepler*, 278; *Mefisto*, 278; *Newton Letter, The*, 278
Barnacle, Nora, 132, 173
Battle of the Boyne of 1690, 7, 71
Battle of Clontarf of 1014, 231
Beach, Sylvia, 137–38, 172
Beckett, Samuel: xx-xxi, 4, 6, 32, 66, 118, 126, 156, 158, 210, 221, 224, 225, 237, 240, 246–54, 257, 258, 260, 271, 272, 276, 277–78, 294; "Dream of Fair to Middling Women," 246; *How It Is*, 252, 253; *Malone Dies*, 251–52, 253; *Mercier and Camier*, 252, 253; *Molloy*, 251–52, 253; *More Pricks than Kicks*, 246; *Murphy*, 246, 248–50; *Proust*, 246; *Unnamable, The*, 252; *Watt*, 242, 249, 250–51, 276
Behan, Brendan, 236, 300
Bell, Sam Hanna: 296–97; *December Bride*, 296–97; *Hollow Ball, The*, 297; *Man Flourishing, A*, 297
Bell, The, 182, 191, 192, 199, 293
Bennett, Louie, 86
Big House Novels, xxii, 14, 16, 21, 32, 56, 69, 73, 76–77, 85, 90, 96, 107, 125, 206–7, 251, 262, 276–79, 291, 293, 305
Biggar, Joseph, 177
Bildungsromans, xxiii, 11, 12, 13, 24, 107, 121, 136, 137, 197, 200, 211, 217, 225, 262, 268,

About the Author

James M. Cahalan teaches in the English Department at Indiana University of Pennsylvania where he also directs the graduate program in Literature and Criticism and the Dublin Program of the University's Center for International Studies. Cahalan previously was director of the Irish Studies Program at the University of Massachusetts, Boston. He earned his B.A. at New College in Sarasota, Florida; his M.A. (on a Fulbright Fellowship) at University College, Dublin, with first-class honors; and his Ph.D. at the University of Cincinnati. Author of *Great Hatred, Little Room: The Irish Historical Novel*, Cahalan has also published numerous articles and reviews in journals such as *Éire—Ireland*, the *Irish Literary Supplement*, *University Publishing*, and the *Journal of Teaching Writing*.